RACE AN

IN CONTINENTAL PHILOSOPHY

Studies in Continental Thought

Race and Racism in Continental Philosophy

Edited by Robert Bernasconi
with Sybol Cook

6/05

INDIANA
University Press

Bloomington & Indianapolis

Publication of this book is made possible in part with the
assistance of a Challenge Grant from the National Endowment
for the Humanities, a federal agency that supports research,
education, and public programming in the humanities.

This book is a publication of

Indiana University Press
601 North Morton Street
Bloomington, IN 47404-3797 USA

http://iupress.indiana.edu

Telephone orders   800-842-6796
Fax orders   812-855-7931
Orders by e-mail   iuporder@indiana.edu

The paper used in this publication meets the minimum requirements of American National
Standard for Information Sciences—Permanence of Paper for Printed Library Materials, ANSI
Z39.48-1984.

Manufactured in the United States of America

Library of Congress Cataloging-in-Publication Data

Race and racism in continental philosophy / edited by Robert Bernasconi ; with Sybol Cook.
p. cm. — (Studies in Continental thought)
Includes bibliographical references and index.
ISBN 0-253-34223-6 (cloth : alk. paper) — ISBN 0-253-21590-0 (pbk. : alk. paper)
1. Racism. 2. Race. 3. Philosophy, European. 4. Philosophers—Europe—Attitudes. I. Bernasconi,
Robert. II. Cook, Sybol. III. Series.
HT1523 .R2514 2003
305.8—dc21
2002151519

1 2 3 4 5   08 07 06 05 04 03

Contents

Contents

vi

Acknowledgments

The editors would like to thank Kathryn Gines, Anika Simpson, and, above all, Mary Beth Mader, all of the University of Memphis, for their translations of the essays by Alain David and Léopold Senghor. Special thanks are due to Alain David for securing permission to publish an English translation of "Les Nègres," which appears as an appendix to *Racisme et Antisémitisme* (Paris: Ellipses, 2001). We also acknowledge Éditions du Seuil for permission to translate "Ce que l'homme noir apporte" from *Liberté 1: Humanisme et négritude* by Léopold Sédar Senghor (Paris: Seuil, 1964).

We would like to thank Janet Rabinowitch and Dee Mortensen of Indiana University Press for their encouragement and help at every stage in the preparation of this volume. Finally, we would like to acknowledge the contributions of Christine Harris, Jennifer Palumbo, Bethany Dunn, and Kristie Dotson, who completed the team that put this volume together.

RACE AND RACISM
IN CONTINENTAL PHILOSOPHY

Introduction

Robert Bernasconi

There is a long and strong tradition of African-American philosophers writing about race, but the recent explosion of interest in race theory among philosophers in English-speaking countries has so far been largely dominated by philosophers whose training and frame of reference is that of analytic philosophy. That marks a certain limitation not only in the resources available to them, but also in the questions discussed. The focus falls on the reality of the concept of race, its relation to biology, and such questions as whether racism implies a belief in race. Other questions, such as the relation of race to culture, to history, and to one's sense of self, which have long been discussed by Black philosophers throughout the world, have not been at the forefront of recent research in race theory. They appear as an afterthought. There is no better indication of this than the fact that for a while W. E. B. Du Bois's 1897 classic text "The Conservation of Races" came, as a result of Anthony Appiah's analysis of it, to be read as if it were an essay about the definition of race, and it was a while before Lucius Outlaw, Tommy Lott, Robert Gooding-Williams, and others managed to restore its broader significance. However, these same issues of the relation of race to culture, history, and lived experience were, throughout the twentieth century, pursued by representatives of what has come to be known in the English-speaking world under the somewhat unsatisfactory title of Continental philosophy. To be sure, the aim of this volume is not to contribute to the formation of an alternative field of study, "Continental race theory," that would be removed from—or, worse still, opposed to—"analytic race theory." Although I believe that there are questions in race theory that someone educated in Continental philosophy is in a better position to address than someone who is not, I also believe that this is a field of study whose urgency is such that sectarian differences have no place. The main aim of the present volume is, therefore, to draw attention to some of the

1

resources for race theory within Continental philosophy and make them accessible to all practitioners in the field.

A second aim of this volume is to encourage Continental philosophers who have not already done so to explore the wealth of thinking on race within their own tradition. But this also means to investigate its racism. An indispensable moment of any attempt to employ the resources of Continental philosophy within race theory must be a critical examination of Continental philosophy's own racism. The very term "Continental philosophy," although it is still virtually indispensable, is marked by a certain myopia: the failure to see more than one continent. The restriction of Continental philosophy to Europe is challenged here by the inclusion of studies on Du Bois, Suzanne Césaire, and Frantz Fanon, among others, but that does not mean that one can simply claim these thinkers for "Continental philosophy," as I shall explain in a moment. Continental philosophy's racism is addressed directly in the essays on Nietzsche, Heidegger, Voegelin, and Arendt, and particularly in the essay "Negroes" by Alain David.

I believe that among the places where the specific contribution of Continental philosophy to race theory is especially apparent is in its approach to racism within past philosophies. Analytic philosophers are conventionally oc cupied with the task of judging positions on the basis of arguments: what cannot be sustained on that basis is revised, improved upon, or discarded. The result is a streamlined version of the history of philosophy, somewhat removed from its context, in which the name of a philosopher is shorthand not for what he or she actually said but for the best arguments that can be constructed for the position. However, this means that the racism of a philosopher is easily put to one side. Kant's racism does not raise a question for his cosmopolitanism because cosmopolitanism can be defined in such a way as to exclude racism. Thus, the fact that Kant was a racist has no implications for contemporary Kantians. However, things are somewhat different for Continental philosophers. For example, a dialectical thinker, such as the later Sartre, would suspect that the invention of cosmopolitanism not only necessarily brings about a change in the nature of racism, but also calls for a certain racism to sustain it, a racism that will be directed against those peoples who resist cosmopolitanism. Alain David's critical approach is different and equally insightful. He investigates the question that was an obsession among natural historians in Europe, and of Kant in particular, and exposes its philosophical connections. He also celebrates the memory of Anton Wilhelm Amo, an African who studied philosophy in eighteenth-century Germany.

Du Bois also studied in Germany, and inevitably that has fueled speculation about the role of German philosophy in his thought. Kevin Miles reads Du Bois's implicit references to Hegel's world history in "The Conservation of Races" as an attempt to rewrite the historiography of the day as part of a political project primarily directed not to an understanding of the past but to a view of the future. Kevin Miles's essay, like Ronald Sundstrom's, is in part directed against Appiah's ultimately biological interpretation of Du Bois, and they both identify resources in Du Bois for maintaining a conception of race. However, although Sundstrom documents the influence of Hegel on Du Bois, he argues strongly against seeing Du Bois "as merely the darker reflection of some European or American pragmatist philosophy." Instead, he places Du Bois in the context of African-American strategies for racial justice at the end of the nineteenth century. By the same token, any attempt by Continental philosophers to appropriate, for example, Senghor or Fanon for Continental philosophy would be making the mistake of ignoring their specificity and their debts to their own traditions, which are not undone simply by their acknowledged debts to twentieth-century European philosophers.

Given the importance of the notion of race for any understanding of the history of the nineteenth and twentieth centuries, it would be surprising, even shocking, if the major European philosophers had not addressed it. And yet, in recent years their discussions of race were largely ignored by commentators. This was not the case with Nietzsche. Until the end World War II, he was a central figure, for both his critics and his followers, in debates on eugenics, or what the German called *Rassenhygiene*. In her essay on Nietzsche, Jacqueline Scott focuses particularly on Nietzsche's conception of Jews. Her important contribution to the growing literature on this subject is distinguished by her attempt to locate this theme in relation to the importance that Nietzsche attached to selective racial breeding, referring it to his concern with decadence, which was a highly charged term in the late nineteenth century.

It has been possible until relatively recently to believe that Heidegger, by contrast with Nietzsche, had relatively little to say about race as such. It was as if he had deliberately displaced race by focusing on the *Volk*. However, Sonia Sikka shows just how much Heidegger had to say specifically about race, and she carefully locates those discussions in their context. It is astonishing how often the "case of Heidegger" has been examined by philosophers who seem to have made little or no effort to examine what other German philosophers were saying at the same time. Sikka not only avoids making this mistake, but she also draws this scholarly project into a longstanding philosophical debate. By asking how Heidegger's anti-biologism might be reconciled with his appeal to a concept of the German *Volk* defined by descent, and by insisting that certain of his ideas need to be taken seriously in spite of the fact that they can—but need not necessarily—be put to a dangerous use, she sets the stage for her argument that there is nothing necessarily harmful about the fact that many people identify themselves, at least in part, with a biological line of descent.

David Levy champions Eric Voegelin's extensive writings on race, which, although they are now readily available in English translations, remain largely neglected. In his essay for this volume, Levy not only provides a helpful introduction to Voegelin's two important books, *Race and State* and *The History of the Race Idea: From Ray to Carus*, but he also locates them in the broader philosophical context. It is increasingly a feature of writing in the history of philosophy that more attention is given to context than hitherto, and Sikka and Levy both show why this is especially important in the case of race theory.

Both the Negritude movement in general and Léopold Sédar Senghor in particular are today, more often than not, discussed in philosophical circles only to serve as objects of criticism. Nevertheless, the judgments often seem to be based on limited knowledge of Senghor's work. His philosophical writing is still largely untranslated. In the appendix to this volume, Senghor's historic text in the 1939 volume *L'homme de couleur* appears in English translation for the first time. In this essay, which Fanon made the centerpiece of his critique of Senghor in *Black Skin, White Masks*, Senghor gave his answer to the question of what Blacks can contribute. It is a question that today would not be asked in the way he does, if it is asked at all, and Senghor's manner of answering it was to concede reason to Whites, so that Africans could lay claim to emotion. Or, more precisely, "emotion is Negro, as reason is Hellenic." However, Senghor said this not in the context of today's world, but in that of a volume that is sometimes so patronizing and, indeed, racist in tone that his famous formulation begins to be heard differently.[1] He was writing for an audience that apparently did not suspect that Blacks had any contribution of their own to make. To be sure, one should beware of claiming too much for Senghor. As he himself subsequently conceded, his thinking in this period owed much to Gobineau's *Essay on the Inequality of the Human Races*, and not only by way of opposition to it. Gobineau already saw civilization as the result of race mixing, and in his view, artistic genius in particular arose only after the intermixing of white and black. This perhaps was one source of Senghor's theory of cultural *métissage* that would continue to prove so important to his understanding of the Negritude movement, even if commentators often underplay it. However, because Senghor's idea of *métissage* came to present a radical alternative to the idea of assimilation to a dominant tradition, it remains important today.[2]

The idea of *métissage* provides the focus for T. Denean Sharpley-Whiting's essay on Suzanne Roussy Césaire. In Sharpley-Whiting's interpretation, Césaire "theorized a Negritude that recognized the racial and cultural *métissage*" of Martinique. If there is going to be a renewed appreciation for the Negritude movement in the near future, it is likely to be the result of foregrounding the hitherto largely forgotten role that women played in it, and nobody has done more than Sharpley-Whiting to give them the recognition that is their due.

Three essays on Fanon follow. Nigel Gibson investigates Fanon's critique, in the fourth chapter of *Black Skin, White Masks*, of Octave Mannoni's *Psychologie de la colonisation*, which is known in English as *Prospero and Caliban*.[3] Gibson criticizes what he calls the "overly psychoanalytic readings of Fanon by literary critics" and emphasizes the importance for Fanon of Jean-Paul Sartre and, particularly, Maurice Merleau-Ponty. Lou Turner's essay also puts the spotlight on Fanon's critique of Mannoni, but its major contribution lies in documenting the wealth of connections, many unsuspected, that tie Fanon and Richard Wright together. Richard Wright's credentials for being included, for example, in philosophy classes on existentialism have long struck me as impeccable, but he did not find his way into *The Dictionary of Existentialism* in spite of efforts to have him included.[4] Turner's essay is an important step in having Wright more highly valued in philosophical circles. Kelly Oliver's essay is a significant elaboration of the reading of Fanon that she presented in the first chapter of *Witnessing*.[5] Her essay elucidates both the place of the body image in race thinking and Fanon's discussion of Lacan. Taken together, the essays by Gibson, Turner, and Oliver deepen our appreciation of the philosophical significance of Fanon's *Black Skin, White Masks* and offer strong confirmation that we are entering a new era of Fanon research.

Fanon said that certain pages of Sartre's *Anti-Semite and Jew* were the best he had read,[6] and perhaps only Sartre has had a role comparable to Fanon's in the formation of Continental race theory. Erik Vogt offers a rich contemporary analysis of *Anti-Semite and Jew,* which shows why, in spite of certain defects that Sartre himself subsequently acknowledged, it has held its own at the center of discussions of racism for over fifty years. On the basis of a certain reading of *Anti-Semite and Jew,* Sartre has come to be seen by some as a proponent of the view that race is a social construction. However, Donna Marcano argues persuasively that the dogma that race is a social construction is simplistic insofar as it fails to explore the process that molds social construction. She skillfully contrasts the social constructionist position set out in *Anti-Semite and Jew* with the more complex account Sartre provided in his *Critique of Dialectical Reason.* Marcano favors the explanatory richness of the latter work. No essay in this volume states more clearly what Continental philosophy can bring to analytic race theory.

Sartre's *Critique of Dialectical Reason* found a vociferous opponent in Claude Lévi-Strauss, so it is appropriate to follow Marcano's argument for Sartre's *Critique* with Kamala Visweswaran's analysis of Lévi-Strauss's two major essays on race. Visweswaran places these essays in the context both of previous anthropological thinking on race, especially that of Franz Boas, and of Lévi-Strauss's own works. Her conclusion, that Lévi-Strauss left all the difficult questions about racism not just unanswered but unasked, contrasts sharply with Marcano's positive conclusion about Sartre's later thought precisely on this same issue.

Whereas Fanon and Sartre are enjoying increased attention and appreciation as a result of the growing interest in race theory, Hannah Arendt is someone whose reputation has begun to suffer because of her apparent failure to extend and modify her analyses of anti-Semitism in *The Origin of Totalitarianism* so as to accommodate anti-Black racism. At the same time as she exposes the shortcomings of Arendt's analyses of racism, Joy James skillfully shows what is still so powerful in Arendt. Moreover, James provides powerful insights into the kind of political analyses we need in order to come to terms with the contemporary world.

Racism is not confined to thoughts, utterances, and deeds, but finds its most important embodiment in institutions. Within the institution of philosophy, the treatment of African philosophy, its exclusion or marginalization to the point that it seems in constant need of self-justification, is particularly painful. Jason Wirth looks at this seemingly never-ending debate over the existence and identity of African philosophy. He closes his essay by admiring the way that Paulin Hountondji succeeds in establishing an approach that does not circumscribe it too narrowly: African philosophy is the critical activity of Africans. But what, then, is Continental philosophy? It, too, should not be circumscribed too narrowly, but it will surely never come to be understood simply as the philosophizing of those of European descent, which again underlines the asymmetry between the two labels.

This volume does not offer an answer to the question of the identity of Continental race theory. Indeed, this volume does not pretend to represent the full range of what currently goes under that name and is clearly vulnerable to criticisms along those lines. To be sure, this is a serious limitation, particularly if it is approached with the wrong expectations. But what is attempted in this volume is not a sampling of Continental race theory, but clusters of essays that will serve to foster research and teaching in some of the more central areas.

All of the essays in this volume engage in the work of text interpretation to one degree or another, and they acknowledge the need to approach the texts to be interpreted contextually. This is not by any means an exclusively "Continental" feature, but it is fair to say that analytic philosophers, by focusing on reconstructing arguments, are more inclined to sacrifice this dimension of the study of the history of philosophy than are members of other schools of thought. However, the essential point here is that attention to context is of particular importance when discussing race: for example, what is innocent in one context is racist in another, which is why one can never approach a racially charged situation with anything other than caution, sensitivity, and a commitment to listen. It is not enough, therefore, to recognize that the essays in this volume draw attention to the contextuality of racial discourse. They must themselves each be understood as arising from and reflecting specific times and places. This is not a limitation; it is, quite simply, inevitable. Indeed, it can become something positive when it is recognized as an invitation for others to reflect on the racial concepts in play within their own environment not just with a view to clarifying their specificity, but in order to identify their own racism and that of the dominant institutions with a view to doing something about it.

Notes

1. See Lilyan Kesteloot, *Black Writers in French*, trans. Ellen Conroy Kennedy (Washington, D.C.: Howard University Press, 1991), pp. 230–231.

2. See Léopold Sédar Senghor, "What Is 'Negritude'?" in Robert Bernasconi and Tommy Lott, eds., *The Idea of Race* (Indianapolis: Hackett, 2000), pp. 136–138.

3. O. Mannoni, *Psychologie de la colonisation* (Paris: Seuil, 1950); trans. Paula Powlesland, *Prospero and Caliban: The Psychology of Colonization* (London: Methuen, 1956).

4. H. Gordon, ed., *The Dictionary of Existentialism* (Westport, Conn.: Greenwood, 1999).

5. Kelly Oliver, *Witnessing: Beyond Recognition* (Minneapolis: University of Minnesota Press, 2001), pp. 23–49.

6. Frantz Fanon, *Peau noire, masques blancs* (Paris: Seuil, 1952), p. 146; trans. Charles Lam Markmann, *Black Skin, White Masks* (New York: Grove Weidenfeld, 1967), p. 181.

One

Negroes

Alain David

TRANSLATED BY KATHRYN GINES
AND MARY BETH MADER

I am going to speak—I am going to try to speak—about "Negroes." About "Negroes," therefore, not about "Blacks" or "Africans," or about the geopolitical or social or cultural reality of Africa, about which I don't know more than what everyone in Europe and France knows—that is, that Africa is far away and complicated—scarcely anything. Which is, all the same, a bit more serious than a simple not knowing—something that is not mine to describe, but that makes it such that I do not feel very proud before you. Something, therefore, that, barring further commentary, I can only confide to you. At least, with this half-confession (it is from the start my hope and the condition of possibility of the account that I will offer), I will have indicated the register in which philosophical discourse—the philosophical discourse of culpability, of the recognition of debt—must be inscribed today, with all the difficulty of specifying what "today" means. Likewise, recognition of debt can mean many things, but in any case it does not mean the attempt to assess this debt and settle accounts.

So, I will speak about Negroes, in accordance with the harshness of this word, as they figure without figuring in philosophical discourse, an absent presence and the absence of a presence, returning therefore, following this same emphasis, to philosophical discourse so as to point out the impact of a crisis there. The effects of this crisis are doubtless more immediately noticeable in the African reality, which is forced to take on Western rationality (there is perhaps no other), and thus traces out, but in terms inscribed in lieu of rationality—which does not mean in the "irrational" either—the contours or the promise, in the immanence of cultures, of a common human condition. All this could also be summed up in a phrase in the form of a joke, doubtless therefore more decisive than what my account proposes—"I am going to speak about Negroes." The phrase is in fact a title in a cartoon by Claire Bretecher, which is on the mark in its great irreverence—"Heidegger in the Congo."[1] I would like this "Heidegger in the Congo," which I did not dare write as a title, to be understood in the manner that I will now try to make heard: as meaning a humanism, another humanism, the humanism of the other man, as meaning, therefore—I say it still with a smile, but much more seriously— "Lévinas in Africa."

The Negroes, then. The most immediate observation is their absence from philosophical discourse. Not that they aren't mentioned in it, but they appear only in virtue of an "accidental" difference, which does not attain to essence, in Aristotle's language; it is a difference belonging to matter. Callias is white, but it is only by accident that he is white. "White" is said of Callias because as a man Callias is susceptible to receiving this quality.[2] Color is situated, sensibly, inside the form, which alone makes it appear. For the philosophy that adheres to forms, metaphysics, there are no white men and black men (any more than there were Jews and Greeks for St. Paul), but man in general, measured by the standard of the universal, of rationality: the man of the Rights of Man. And yet—as Burke objected regarding the French Revolution —the man of the Rights of Man is already *this* man, a Frenchman or an Englishman, as Callias, a man, nevertheless had to be called white. And as Bucephalus, a horse, was skittish. The philosopher, the metaphysician and humanist, cannot avoid having to transform himself into an anthropologist. So, what is the man of the Rights of Man?

Indeed, imagine a bit. Just imagine this picture: you are now at the University of Halle around 1740, and you are taking courses. The masters are prestigious, all is tinged with the memory of the famous Wolff—*clarissimus Wolff*, as Kant said—who disseminated Leibniz's thought, and whose works occupy several library shelves. And there is Martin Knutzen, Kant's teacher, and there are all the names that will contribute to forging German philosophy, and with it contemporary Western identity. And you, at the back of the amphitheater, you are marveling. You are straining your ears to better understand the Latin, forbidding for a twentieth-century man. And you stare wide-eyed to try to make out the faces. And then you can't believe it, and you ask your neighbor, who as it happens likewise can't believe his eyes and who feverishly consults the issue of the *Halle Review*—an old issue from 1736—that he holds in his hand: a man over there—a Negro!—is giving a presentation, a difficult presentation. You understood the title: "*De humanae mentis apatheia*" (On the insensibility of the human mind). And all of a sudden you hear, as in a dream, but very clearly now, the lecturer's voice: "To live and to feel are two inseparable predicates. The proof is in the convertibility of these two propositions: everything that lives necessarily feels and everything that feels necessarily lives, so that the presence of one necessarily implies that of the other."[3] You recognize in these words, which Michel Henry could have authored, the whole problematic of sensibility, as Kant will work it out with difficulty, and as phenomenology will think it out, and once again you are amazed. But already your neighbor has grabbed you by the arm: "Yes, that's it, Sir, look!" And then you read in the journal that he hands you, "The master Amo, hailing from Africa and more precisely from Guinea; an authentic Negro, but a humble and honorable philosopher."[4] But what is he doing there, you ask yourself, this Negro, at a time when his fellows are participating, under the whip, in the commercial development of the Antilles and the American continent? Superiority of metaphysics that sovereignly attests, in an exception that proves the rule, to what a whole slave society—for a long time, for centuries, right up to the threshold of our century!—abundantly and atrociously disputes: that black and white do not determine identity, that men are equal. The right of Men versus the Black Code.[5] So, then, Anton Wilhelm Amo (Amo, what a name!) "taught philosophy in Germany until 1753, then returned to his country."

But the metaphysician, let's say the one who grabbed you by the sleeve earlier, let's say even you yourself, at the moment of the discovery of the sensible —when, as Husserl has it, your right hand seizing your left hand, you exclaim to yourself (*es wird Leib, es empfindet*),[6] which, understood properly and translated as it should be, means "Did you see the Negro over there!"—this metaphysician, then, makes himself an anthropologist. This time, he speaks of the real Callias who is white, and of those who are not. He discovers "the Negroes." Metaphysically, white or black made no difference. Anthropologically, it is an entirely different matter. The anthropologist—Montesquieu, Buffon, and Rousseau all insist upon this—must take into account the particular conditions of life, the climate, nature, and everything that causes "white to seem to be the primitive color of nature, which climate, food, and custom corrupt and blacken."

Thus the Negroes, resulting from the degeneracy due to natural habitat, far from being men like you and I, men for whom color would not be an essential difference, are revealed for what they are: intermediaries between animal and man. The gap, therefore, between the metaphysician and the anthropologist, who is nonetheless one and the same man. The gap, for example, between the Kant of *Groundwork of the Metaphysics of Morals* refusing to make the human form coincide with the form of a particular world—

> *Es ist überall nichts in der Welt, ja überhaupt auch außer derselben zu denken möglich, was ohne Einschränkung für gut gehalten werden, als ein guter Wille.*

> There is nothing absolutely good in the world, or even, in general, out of this world, except a good will.[7]

—and the Kant who is the philosopher of history, discussing the races. I must quote a text here:

> The extreme humid heat of the warm climate must, on the other hand show quite opposite effects [. . .] from the preceding ones [the Mongols, discussed

just before]. [. . .] The growth of the spongy parts of the body had to increase in a hot and humid climate. This growth produced a thick, turned up nose and thick, fatty lips. The skin had to be oily, not only to lessen the too heavy perspiration, but also to ward off the harmful absorption of foul, humid air. The profusion of iron particles, which are otherwise found in the blood of every human being, and, in this case, are precipitated in the net-shaped substance through the evaporation of the phosphoric acid (which explains why all Negroes stink), is the cause of the blackness that shines through the epidermis. [. . .] Besides all this, humid warmth generally promotes the strong growth of animals. In short, all of these factors account for the origin of the Negro, who is well-suited to his climate namely, strong, fleshy, and agile. However, because he is so amply supplied by his motherland, he is also lazy, indolent, and dawdling.[8]

An oppressive text, as oppressive as the African heat, from the pen of he who the West claims was the thinker of human dignity. Isn't it necessary to abandon a metaphysics that permits such anthropological extensions, to find another discourse of dignity, where Blacks have their place beside Whites? Isn't this sufficient to reverse the signs of anthropologizing metaphysics? Doesn't modern ethnology arrive at such a reversal—let's say, to refer to modern ethnology by its most prestigious and impressive patronym—with Lévi-Strauss? Without claiming here to address the monumental work of Lévi-Strauss (which would require a great deal of time and talent), I would like to try to pose a question of principle to ethnology in general. The reversal of signs that it effects, the rupture with metaphysics, consists in no longer inscribing humanity in a form developed as absolute knowledge. Structure puts an end to the ontological argument. And yet it is not certain that ethnology avoids the trap in which metaphysics was locked. One can quickly characterize this trap in a word: race. *Race is that hyperbole of form affirming itself over against that which would prevent form. Race is like a transcendental condition of the ontological argument.* The multiplication of forms, in spite of the perhaps dubious enthusiasm of leftist thinking, does not trouble the racist, who accepts all of its terms, as Pierre-André Taguieff shows. To the racist, it is enough that the culture that he invokes, a culture that moreover is globalized, should be protected against the others. This is why—because of the principle of separation with which it constitutes and maintains cultures—ethnology comforts all those who would be tempted by apartheid. Thus, Lévi-Strauss is one of the authors most read and cited by the New Right in France. An unexpected return of the paradox upon which metaphysics had failed.

It is thus to metaphysics, to its status, to its possible end, that one must return. The crisis that affects metaphysics is certainly as old as metaphysics itself. And one could easily find its elements in Plato. It nevertheless belongs to modernity, since Kant, which thematized it as such and explicitly made of philosophy a reflection on the crisis. This reflection consists in an inquiry on visibility that metaphysics always presupposes—with the opening of the question "What is?"—at the risk of balancing its accounts by means of the ontological argument. Putting this course of reasoning into question, the reflection on the crisis—critical reflection—passes from enlightened reality (*veritas as adæquatio*) to the light that enlightens it; it becomes phenomenology. But phenomenology questions light in a sense that is not the sense in which metaphysics questions the being placed in the light. Because to recognize that light is not a being is to interrupt the continuity of the being disposed within a totality. It is to inscribe therein the Dark. Hegel, for whom manifestation had to be said in the same sense both of the being and of light (a superposition in his work, then, of metaphysics and of phenomenology), mentioned this so as to reject it: light is in itself identical to darkness. Thus:

> But one pictures being to oneself, perhaps in the image of pure light as the clarity of undimmed seeing, and then nothing as pure night—and their distinction is linked with this very familiar sensuous difference. But, as a matter of fact, if this very seeing is more exactly imagined, one can readily perceive that in absolute clearness there is seen just as much, and as little, as in absolute darkness, that the one seeing is as good as the other, that pure seeing is a seeing of nothing. Pure light and pure darkness are two voids which are the same thing.[9]

Therefore, for Hegel pure light and pure darkness are two instances of nothingness both of which, pure *nihil privativum*, have meaning only in their reciprocal negation—that is, only as engaged in a dialectical process. Thus, one speaks of disappearance only if it is the disappearance *of something*. Interruption will be, in this regard, the very condition of the continuity of the Whole as form—that is, as visibility, which is developed in the terms of the interruption. With Hegel, phenomenology returns once more to metaphysics, because the language of the being must not differ from the language of light: the ultimate modality of the ontological argument, the counterpart of which is the void of a language of pure interruption, the romantic and empty identity of light and darkness. The black sun of Melancholy[10]—even if one wanted to understand this as *Sehnsucht*, romantic nostalgia—has no being; it is nothing. Yet, isn't this the wager of poetry, a wager always reiterated, as bold as Pascal's wager (and in a sense identical to it): to speak without saying something, to say nothing, or to say pure light:

Nothing, not old gardens mirrored in eyes. (Mallarmé)[11]

My glass glows with a wine that flickers like a flame. (Apollinaire)[12]

Not developing in the form of a being to which it would be adequate to the point of being identifiable as a being, light "as such," light in poetry, shows nothing and is nothing. In its positivity, it is that which, surrounding and giving over the being, divides it and prevents it from totalizing. It thus inscribes in each instance of the being—in each instant—the suspension of the question, the Interruption, which indefinitely expresses itself: "Why is there something rather than nothing?" A sentence that metaphysics interprets at base thus: "Why isn't there all rather than nothing?"—still and always making the positivity of the nothing rest on the Whole so as to interpret it as *nihil privativum*, as *the nothing of the Whole* [*le rien du Tout*].[13] On the contrary, but enigmatically, poetry exposes the nothing as nothing—in the same sense (indeed!) in which a roll of film can be overexposed: a blinding light, a dazzlement where there is nothing to see, and where nothing is seen. But what is being said with this? What is the content of this meaning exposed in this manner? What do "nothing" and "something" mean in the question that has been posed: "Why is there something rather than nothing?"

I will restrict myself to a few remarks. First of all, in Husserl, interruption results from the horizontal structure. Being oriented toward the presentation of forms, phenomenological description is thus an infinite and interminable task and, as even Husserl avows, it is programmatic. In an article in which he acts as spokesman for Husserl, his assistant Eugen Fink recognizes the difficulty: "The mundane meaning of the words available to him cannot be entirely removed, for their meaning can be limited only by the use of other mundane words. For this reason no phenomenological analysis, above all the analysis of the deeper constituting levels of transcendental subjectivity, is capable of being presented adequately."[14] In other words, Husserlian phenomenology, for which everything depends on the sighting of the thing itself, does not overcome the level of ideality. He says that he says, and says that he says that he says—without perhaps ever arriving at singularity—which then would be the moment of the reduction. This equivocation is found again, perhaps with the greatest acuity, when Husserl questions the modes of givenness of the very idea of evidence—for him the principle of principles—that is to say, philosophy. Philosophy is *telos*, and this *telos* can *be* or *not be*. Its upspringing on this ground is *Greece*, the particular name of the universal; its possible incompletion is *Europe*, the name of a humanity oriented to and motivated by Greek destiny, a humanity written in history. The ethnocentrism and Eurocentrism of phenomenology, to be sure. But phenomenology easily puts aside the objection, for the requirements of dignity, and of respect, in the names of which one would reject this Eurocentrism, are those very requirements that, for the Husserlian phenomenologist, tearing humanity away from its myths, constitute humanity in its historic particularity as being oriented toward the universal—constitute it as European. So, many of the debates on Eurocentrism could come back to this reasoning: Does Negritude, beyond all the suspicions that reduce it to the complex of the colonized, perhaps partake of a formula that Derrida once issued regarding Lévinas: "In Greek in our language"?

But the real objection is not there; it is, rather, that of the recurrent feeling of not having finished with metaphysics. Isn't Europe, reliant as it is on the teleological perspective of the overcoming of the crisis, and in its very singularity, also a form? Namely, the intention, in the ordinary sense of the word, of phenomenology, but the intention whose ever-postponed realization constitutes, through this procrastination, form as metaphysics. At least, such are the stakes of the critique that Heidegger addresses to Husserl: Husserlian phenomenology would not yet have broken with metaphysics. The relation to the thing would not have to take on the appearance of an infinite task—an eidetic reduction that perhaps will never attain the transcendental; as the opening of the nothing, it would be idiom, singularity, and poetry right from the start. For Heidegger, then (I probably say it too quickly), the question of the meaning and understanding of the idiom remains. How does the nothing that destroys form achieve manifestation itself? Without returning to the range of Heidegger's complex responses, I simply ask whether there is indeed an interruption of metaphysics through these responses. Or, to say it another way, and perhaps more radically, insofar as myth is the narration in which temporal flow becomes space and achieves manifestation, as Lévi-Strauss holds, then metaphysics and, following it, phenomenology, with all their demythologizing motifs—nationality and Europe, or ontological difference and Germany—are still myth. Myth offered as such to an ethnological curiosity. Beyond Husserl or Heidegger, and perhaps in their own terms, the project of phenomenology —to question light—remains to be completed.

Let me restate the question: *Why is there something rather than nothing?* But poetry (for example, "black sun of Melancholy") suggests that, understood in its positivity, nothing (or light) is the black. What does black mean?

First of all, here, black is not the color black. It is the black of "All I can see here is black," the black of which one is afraid when one is afraid of the dark/black.[15] Black means nothing, nothing means black. Or, rather, nothing does not exactly mean black, since in nothing positivity is erased. Why is there something rather than black? According to this formulation, "black" is something, and yet, as I've said, it is nothing. Nothing other than dazzlement. Light itself. And this black that is nothing, without this nothing being nothing, is the something that prevents any something from belonging to the whole. One must, then, wonder what this positivity is that, inscribed in the nothing—an inscription of the nothing—converts the nothing into its enigmatic nuance of black. Or, as was said in children's riddles—and perhaps all this cannot truly be understood except in relation to childhood—*what is black without being a color and what is nothing while being something?*

One will have recognized, posed anew, the question of the transcendental reduction. Posed, let's say, from Michel Henry's perspective, or, as we noted earlier, from that of Anton Wilhelm Amo, whose text it is now time to take up again: "To live and to feel are two inseparable predicates. The proof is in the convertibility of these two propositions: everything that lives necessarily feels and everything that feels necessarily lives, so that the presence of one neces-sarily implies that of the other." But here is Michel Henry:

> Life [. . .] is what everybody knows, being that which we are. But how can "everybody," that is, each one insofar as it is a living being, know what life is, except insofar as life knows itself and where this original knowledge of oneself constitutes its proper essence? Because life feels and is felt in such a way that there is not anything in it that it doesn't feel or sense. And this is because the fact of feeling oneself is exactly what makes life life. Thus, all that bears within itself this marvelous property of feeling oneself is living, while all that lacks this is but dead.[16]

Thus are the terms of the reduction defined by Anton Wilhelm Amo and Michel Henry. Anterior to the world, that is, not ecstatically unfolded within it, subjectivity is life, transcendental life. Nothing of the world, since it is not inscribed there in its forms, and prior to any form, life is that of which Victor Hugo says,

> Then in Besançon, the ancient Spanish town,
> Tossed to air's flowing fancy like a grain,
> A child was born of blood both Breton and Lorraine
> An infant without sight, without color, without voice . . .
> It was I.[17]

It was I, in fact, without color, this black. But that's exactly the question for Michel Henry, as well: How can the black, as the obscuring of the world, pure immanence, auto-affection, affect itself to the point of making itself self and, giving itself to itself, to being an *ipse*? Or, further, what makes it the case that immanent subjectivity—that is, life, for Michel Henry or Anton Wilhelm Amo—is not quite simply the presence, as in any metaphysics, of the Whole, the soul of the world? And what makes it the case that the black, without belonging to the world from which it/he is stolen away, is nevertheless this black here, a singularity? More simply, let me repeat the question in its earlier expression: *what is black without being a color and nothing while being something?* Remaining with the terms that I just recalled, we would have sketched a mon-ster. Subjectivity, transcendental life, insofar as it is not of the world, looks like nothing. It is a monster. It remains to be said in virtue of what it appears, that is, how its singularity is given, how the monster is shown—how the black is revealed. In other words—a variant of the Heideggerian question "Why is there the being rather than nothing?"—one now wonders (here, again, a child's question), *Why are Negroes black?*

One could reformulate this last question as, In what form does what pro-ceeds from the interruption of forms appear? A contradictory and clumsy question? Without doubt! It is, nevertheless, Kantian, and it seeks, beyond the interruption signified by the antinomies, the solidarity of a ground—*Grundlegung,* the establishing of a ground—the firmness of a universal form, which nevertheless and paradoxically does not make a world.

16

It would be fitting at this point to extend Kant with Lévinas. The rupture, the distance introduced by the *als ob,* the as if, the special universality of the commandment that commands without regard to circumstances—commanding in this very way the impossible, assigning in this manner each self to itself according to the caesura of culpability ("We are all guilty, and I more than all the others": Lévinas constantly quotes this phrase from Dostoevsky)[18]—all this stems from a humanism that metaphysical forms interrupt, the humanism of the other man. In Lévinas's terms, at the moment when "I" begins, the other has already disappeared. A diachrony constitutive of the self: time is not the time of the world but the trace of the Other. The anteriority of a "before" when the effectiveness of form finds itself affected by a recurrent incompletion. "Before": the imperfection of the imperfect (tense) that expresses this opens onto an extraordinary predicate that qualifies nothing, or qualifies the nothing—Kant's or Husserl's transcendental, myself as other, this wholly other that makes me myself. Before: the child that I was—that now I was, having never been it—the child that now and ceaselessly disappears so that "I" might be. The disappearance reveals a deictic: this, this without form, this, the black that does not look like anything and who is me, this child who looks at me, only, to the point of drawing tears from me. But this, black, *because it has become this*—nothing as something—is indeed now the color black, more colored still than what the name of the color says of it. (A name that itself is not colored at all, and, like all names, is metaphysical.) It is this which shimmers in all the colors of the world and makes all of them explode, no longer consenting, except in fun, to stay within the forms that claimed to reveal them. The transcendental aesthetic, the moment of the sensible. It emerged earlier, in Halle, when someone said, "I saw a Negro over there."

Of course, the conclusion first of all would be this: *black is beautiful.* But these words cannot be said in the first-person. The first-person is the *cogito,* that of the *Discourse on Method.* The first-person posits the world, in its forms, in its structures, and ignores color. This means, first of all, that I have spoken only of imaginary Negroes. Nevertheless, let us understand imaginary in the Kantian sense, *Eibildungskraft,* and not *Phantasie:* transcendental receptivity. However, are there other Negroes than imaginary ones? There are, moreover, only men, as Aristotle said. Men and their suffering. Yet, how could the worst sufferings have come about without the imaginary? It is in the language of the imaginary that the Negroes are there (*Dasein*), looking at us, witnesses, as in Faulkner, to the sin that interrupts the continuity of the white world. Not as persons, but as what Quentin recognizes in *The Sound and the Fury* as "the obverse of the Whites with whom they live." Indistinct silhouettes that stand out in the dusty light of the South, pre-sensed in every blank/white,[19] as is the case for Joe Christmas in *Light in August.*

17

The imaginary Negro! One will doubtless agree that he is such: Faulkner is good support for this. But Africa? I said it at the start: As for Africa, I don't know. With shame and guilt, I am ignorant of the African reality. There is even less question of saying, in the place of Africans, what should become of Africa. Yet this concern already says a little bit too much. In a Husserlian mode it would translate as, "You, like us." And, therefore, you and us. Europeans, all we Europeans. The ineluctability of Eurocentrism, and perhaps thus the recurrence of the myth: about which it is still and always fitting to return to the necessity of the interruption. Here, I select from Apollinaire these baroque, colored, luminous—Negro—words of interruption, which, interrupting myself, I would like to appose to my lecture, abandoning the lecture to its capacity to deviate, hoping to make it resound on contact:

Sun neck cut

Notes

Translated with the permission of the author and the publisher, from *Racisme et Anti-sémitisme* (Paris: Ellipses, 2001), pp. 279–293. For the most part, this is the text of a lecture delivered at the University of Dakar in March 1989, presented again at a conference in Dijon, and first published in *Lignes*, no. 12 (Dec. 1990): 120–138.

1. This is a reference to a cartoon by French cartoonist Claire Bretecher. The cartoon depicts a woman reading a book entitled *Heidegger au Congo*. For an image of the cartoon, see http://www.figaroetudiant.com/loisirs/bd_livre/interviews/bretecher.php. Trans.

2. Aristotle, *De Interpretatione*, chapter 7, ll. 17a40–17b13. Aristotle differentiates universals from particulars. He explains that "man" is universal while "Callias" is particular. He also gives examples: "Every man is pale" and "No man is pale." Trans.

3. Antonius Guilielmus Amo, *De humanae mentis apatheia* (Wittenberg, 1734), p. 16. Trans.

4. Cf. Paulin Hountondji, "Un Philosophe africain dans l'Allemagne du XVIIIe siècle: Antoine-Guillaume Amo," *Les Etudes philosophiques*, I, 1970; trans. Henri Evans, "An African Philosopher in Germany in the Eighteenth Century: Anton-Wilhelm Amo," in *African Philosophy. Myth and Reality*, 2d ed. (Bloomington: Indiana University Press, 1996), pp. 111–30. Trans.

5. The Black Code refers to slave laws under French colonialism. Trans.

6. It becomes body, it has sensation. Trans.

7. Translation adapted from the French. Trans.

8. Immanuel Kant, "Von der verschiedenen Racen der Menschen," in *Der Philosoph für die Welt*, Part 2, ed. J. J. Engel (Leipzig, 1777), pp. 150–152; trans. Jon Mark Mikkelsen, "Of the Different Human Races," in Robert Bernasconi and Tommy L. Lott, eds., *The Idea of Race* (Indianapolis: Hackett Publishing Company, 1999), pp. 8–22. This quotation is from p. 17. According to the editors, this is the

first complete English translation of the 1777 version of Kant's essay. The only previous translation omitted a number of pages. Translation modified to conform with the French. Trans.

9. G. W. F. Hegel, *Wissenschaft der Logik*, Werke 5 (Frankfurt: Suhrkamp, 1969), p. 96; trans. A. V. Miller, *Hegel's Science of Logic* (London: George Allen and Unwin Ltd., 1969), p. 93. Trans.

10. "Black sun of Melancholy" is a line from a work by the French symbolist poet Gérard de Nerval (1808–55). It occurs in the poem "El Desdichado," one of the best known of the twelve sonnets that comprise *Les chimères*, published as an appendix to the 1854 volume *Les filles du feu*. Trans.

11. Stéphane Mallarmé, "Brise Marine," in *Poésies* (Paris: Gallimard, 1965), p. 40; trans. Keith Bosley, "Sea Breeze," in *The Poems* (New York: Penguin Books, 1977), pp. 90–91. Translation modified. Trans.

12. Guillaume Apollinaire, "Nuit Rhénane," in *Alcools*, ed. Garnet Rees (London: The Athlone Press, 1975), p. 94; trans. Anne Hyde Greet, "Rhenish Night," in *Alcools* (Berkeley: University of California Press, 1965), pp. 142–143. Translation adapted from the English. Trans.

13. *"Rien du tout"* means "nothing at all" in colloquial French speech. Trans.

14. Eugen Fink, "Die phänomenologische Philosophie Edmund Husserls in der gegenwärtigen Kritik," in *Studien zur Phänomenologie (1930–1939)* (The Hague: Martinus Nijhoff, 1966), p. 154; trans. and ed. R. O. Elveton, *The Phenomenology of Husserl* (Chicago: Quadrangle Books, 1970), pp. 143–144. Trans.

15. Besides meaning black, "le noir" also means the dark, as in "fear of the dark." Trans.

16. Michel Henry, *La Barbarie* (Paris: Grasset, 1987), p. 15.

17. Victor Hugo, "Ce siècle avait deux ans!" in *Feuilles d'automne* (1831). For the text with a translation of the complete poem, see *Selected Poems of Victor Hugo: A Bilingual Edition*, trans. E. H. Blackmore and A. M. Blackmore (Chicago: University of Chicago Press, 2001), pp. 32–35. The translation here is by Mary Beth Mader. Trans.

18. F. Dostoevsky, *The Brothers Karamazov*, trans. D. Magarshack (Harmondsworth: Penguin, 1984), vol. 1, p. 339. Quoted by E. Lévinas, for example, in his *Basic Philosophical Writings*, ed. Adriaan Peperzak, Simon Critchley, and Robert Bernasconi (Bloomington: Indiana University Press, 1996), pp. 102–144. Trans.

19. Among other senses, the French noun "blanc" means a "blank" or "emptiness," as well as "the color white" and "a white man or person." Trans.

Two

"One Far Off Divine Event"
"Race" and a Future History in Du Bois

Kevin Thomas Miles

It is to Hegel, perhaps, that we should apply what Alain has said of the subtler merchants of sleep who "offer us a sleep in which the dreams are precisely the world in which we live." The universal history of Hegel is the dream of history.

—Maurice Merleau-Ponty[1]

The mobilization of the Masses, when it arises out of the war of liberation, introduces into each man's consciousness the ideas of a common cause, of a national destiny, and of collective history.

—Frantz Fanon[2]

White man, hear me! History, as nearly no one seems to know, is not merely something to be read. And it does not refer merely, or even principally, to the past. On the contrary, the great force of history comes from the fact that we carry it within us, are unconsciously controlled by it in many ways, and history is literally *present* in all that we do. It could scarcely be otherwise, since it is to history that we owe our frames of reference, our identities, and our aspirations.

James Baldwin[3]

As early as 1897, W. E. B. Du Bois expressed his commitment to the theory of history with which he intended to mobilize Black Americans in a bid to have them recognized as fully enfranchised citizens in the United States.[4] In his well-known address delivered to the American Negro Academy, "The Conservation of Races," Du Bois claims that the people of the world can be divided into recognizable groups called races and that the most basic principle around which these races are organized and identified is that they are "always of common history, traditions and impulses, who are both voluntarily and involuntarily striving together for the accomplishment of certain more or less

19

vividly conceived ideals of life."[5] Some critics are troubled by this reference to history because it seems to suggest an unavoidable attachment to a linear genealogy that can be worked out only in terms of a biological conception of race. Now that such conceptions have rightfully fallen into disrepute, there is some danger that contemporary readers of Du Bois will mistake his notion of history as being grounded upon a metaphysics that must ultimately construe his discourse as preoccupied with a logic of nature that results in the production of "kinds" of people who belong to "races."

In this essay, I argue that Du Bois's primary concern is not an interest in rethinking biology; rather, he is interested in rewriting the historiography of his day. This distinction might initially sound like nothing more than a quibble when one thinks in terms of how Kant and Hegel understood history in relation to nature. It is arguably the case that Du Bois, like Kant and Hegel before him, believed that nature played some part in shaping history. It was not an altogether uncommon conviction to suppose that the history of creatures as a whole was in some way bound up in the story of the creation. My efforts are primarily concerned with drawing attention to what in "The Conservation of Races" signals Du Bois's emphasis on the historical rather than the biological. Ultimately, my contention is that we can hear in Du Bois's thinking something akin to an assertion that Arendt makes regarding Kant's understanding of history: "What matters in history . . . [is] . . . the secret ruse of nature that causes the [human] species to progress and develop all of its potentialities in the succession of generations. . . . Kant is never interested in the past; what interests him is the future of the species."[6]

It is also worth noting that in her study "Willing," in the second volume of *The Life of the Mind*, Arendt discusses Hegel's *Vorlesungen über die Philosophie der Geschichte* in a context that is useful in reading a philosophy of history in Du Bois. Arendt observes that the "world-historical significance" of the French Revolution for Hegel resides in his belief that this event discloses how "for the first time, man dared to turn himself upside down, 'to stand on his head and on thought, and to build reality according to it.'"[7] Hegel writes, "Never since the sun stood in the firmament and the planets revolved around him had it been perceived that man's existence has its center in his head, that is, in thought [*Gedanken*] by which he builds up the world of reality [*Wirklichkeit*]. . . . A spiritual enthusiasm thrilled through the world, as if reconciliation between the Divine and the world was now first accomplished [*als sei es zur wirklichen Versöhnung des Göttlichen mit der Welt nun erst gekommen*]."[8] David Levering Lewis comes close to making a related connection between Hegel and Du Bois in his discussion of what influence "the modernizing exponents of the *Vernunfstaat*" had on Du Bois during his *Lehrjahre*.[9] The whole of Du Bois's adult life seems to have been directed at raising up a people who would exemplify what Hegel confessed was the lesson he would never forget from the French Revolution: "Making public the ideas of how something ought to be [will cause] the lethargy of smugly sedate people [*die gesetzten*

Leute], who always accept everything as it is, to disappear."[10] The idea that Du Bois makes public is nothing short of the idea of a heroic people whose time to give to the world their peculiar gift approaches (*Zukunft*).

The notion of history in "The Conservation of Races" is teleological and is best understood in terms of an economy akin to the notion of "world history" that one finds in Hegel. The notion of history that Du Bois contemplates within the intellectual economy of "The Conservation of Races" is ultimately worked out on a spiritual plane where the purposive course of history is organized not with a view toward the past, but rather with a view toward the future. What is evident in Du Bois, as it is in Hegel, is a teleological conception of "world history" acknowledging the way that physical nature plays *a part* in the history of the world without making that role its primary interest. Hegel's articulation of the substance of history in this regard is unambiguous:

> To begin with, we must note that world history goes on within the realm of Spirit. The term 'world' includes both physical and psychical nature. Physical nature does play a part in world history, and from the very beginning we shall draw attention to the fundamental natural relations thus involved. But Spirit, and the course of its development, is the substance of history. We must not contemplate nature as a rational system in itself, in its own particular domain, but only in its relation to Spirit. (VPG 29; PH 16. Trans. modified)

Because Du Bois seems to have a project like Hegel's in mind[11]—namely, the course of history's progressive development—it is reasonably argued that some notion of Spirit is at the heart of his conception of history and that he contemplates biological nature as a rational system only in the sense that he understands it as somehow related to the objective of Spirit.[12]

Rereading "The Conservation of Races" as operating within an economy of a universal history is not intended as an attempt to deflect important criticisms of universal history from Du Bois's project. However, even if "The Conservation of Races" cannot be defended against critiques of universal history, it is still better read along lines laid out by Lucius Outlaw, who writes, "Du Bois' reconsideration of 'race,' then, is not simply an effort in taxonomy. Rather, it is part of a decidedly *political* project that involves prescribing norms for the social construction of reality and identity, for self-appropriation and world making."[13] If Du Bois is guilty of offering up a universal history it is not one that is naive, but one that is self-consciously aware of the pressing need for an intellectual enterprise that can do battle with convictions like Hegel's, which summarily dismissed all of Africa from even having entered upon the stage of world history.

The reason why Merleau-Ponty is at odds with Hegel's universal history illuminates the path intentionally taken by Du Bois. Merleau-Ponty asserts that "there is no universal history" (PP 51)[14] because the "ordinary" historian whom Hegel describes is wholly incapable of passivity in the project of gathering the raw materials of history into a coherent account. Historical inquiries do not, in Hegel's view, allow the historian to act simply as an uninvolved receptacle who receives data from the world in some purely objective fashion; the historian, as Hegel puts it, "brings his categories with him" (VPG 23; PH 11). Thus, for Hegel, the vision that a historian has of the world is by analogy as affected by these categories as anyone's sight must necessarily be when viewing the world through a pair of tinted glasses. Hegel thus insists that philosophers undertake the enterprise of understanding world history wearing the a priori spectacles of Reason. The historian will, then, view the world through the spectacles of rationality, and world history will, not surprisingly, appear rational. Reason is, for Hegel, the lens or category through which the philosophical eye gazes upon the world and understands its history: "Reason has ruled, and still is ruling in the world, and consequently in the world's history" (VPG 23; PH 11).

Merleau-Ponty argues that Hegel's universal history is questionable precisely because the gaze of rationality *is* capable of constructing a vision of the world made in its own image. This is, according to Merleau-Ponty, nothing less than an equivocation benefiting the philosopher of universal history: "Since history has been staged by him he finds in it only the sense he has already placed there, and in accepting it he merely accepts himself" (PP 49).

As far as "The Conservation of Races" is concerned, Du Bois can indeed be indicted under this charge because the idea of history at work in this piece is staged by him for reasons that should be obvious to anyone even remotely familiar with the status of black people at the time Du Bois is writing. The idea of history in "The Conservation of Races" is by necessity a reconstruction performed by one searching for himself by way of searching for his people. It is impossible to overemphasize the force of Du Bois's intentional appropriation of the written words of others in general and, in this case, of Hegel in particular, as his way both to establish himself as an intellectual leader and to reconfigure historical discourse so that a space is cleared for the political rise to power of people of color. Henry Louis Gates Jr. comments on "how curious this route to power was" taken by Du Bois, by citing an observation made by one of Du Bois's contemporaries, William H. Ferris: "Du Bois is one of the few men in history who was hurled on the throne of leadership by the dynamic force of the written word. He is one of the few writers who leaped to the front as a leader and became the head of a popular movement through impressing his personality upon men by means of a book."[15] In his own words Du Bois thought of himself "as a Negro and as an American" who was "swept on by the current of the nineteenth while yet struggling in the eddies of the fifteenth century" (SoBF 127). It is, then, with "The Conservation of Races" that Du Bois issues an initial call to arms announcing his intention to commandeer the word of history and press it into service on behalf of the Negro people in the name of his *Academy Creed* (WDW 825). It is because black people had been so willfully written out of world history that

Du Bois was compelled to counter with an equally willful reconstruction of what was already a reconstructed history. Du Bois assessed the prevailing discourse attacking African Americans as having produced "a world which yields [the African American] no true self-consciousness, but only lets him see himself through the revelation of the other world."[16] What has been noted in conjunction with some of the later work of Du Bois is already underway in this early essay, specifically, that Du Bois is using "history as a *strategy* to confront and overcome traditional, often white supremacist versions of American history." Du Bois would eventually look back on his own efforts and write, "History and the other social sciences were to be my weapons, to be sharpened and applied by research and writing."[17]

Priscilla Wald has additionally argued that it was Woodrow Wilson himself who "typified exactly the kind of visionary that inspired Du Bois to be revisionary."[18] When Wilson initiated his construction of an American identity, it was a monument unsurprisingly erected to include white Americans while excluding black ones.

> Du Bois knew that an equal place for African Americans in the nation, equal access to the rights and privileges of personhood, required a different story of the past. To be most effective and convincing, Du Bois's alternative story had not only to refute current stories but to analyze prevailing assumptions about the form of those stories as well as their content and language. He adopted the role of visionary historian that Wilson advocated, but with a markedly different outcome in form as well as content. . . . The history of African Americans in the United States could not, for him, be told as "one continuous story"; rather, it was a story that, having been repeatedly suppressed and repressed, must struggle against Wilson's continuous story. (CA 206)

This assessment by Wald needs to be pushed further than she takes it. She still has Du Bois as primarily concerned with a notion of history preoccupied with rewriting the past. However, as I have already suggested, the idea of history encountered in "The Conservation of Races" is revisionist not simply because Du Bois is trying to say something about the empirical past of African Americans that has not yet been said, but because he is operating according to a notion of history that he had no doubt learned by way of a mélange of venues exposing him at various levels to the historico-philosophic writings of Hegel and other German thinkers.[19] Du Bois does not content himself with simply revising certain "facts" because he is not interested in the exercises of the "ordinary historian"; he is primarily interested in the story of a people that has not yet come into view except for those possessed by the vision of Spirit's goal.[20] Du Bois is interested in "making public" a set of ideas that not only will be the uplift of a people, but will silence those fabricating a narrative in which black people have no role in history's past or future.

We can say of the notion of history in Du Bois what Houlgate has said of universal history in Hegel:

History . . . is the working out of the conflicts, clashes and interactions between and within states. It is clear, therefore, that history, as Hegel conceives it—history as the progressive development of humanity towards greater self-understanding—is inseparable from the *political* history of human development towards greater self-consciousness and freedom in states.[21]

Du Bois devoted his adult life to working out the conflict, the clash, and the problematic interaction that was in his day named "the Negro Problem" (WDW 825). What is plainly evident in "The Conservation of Races" is this idea of history as a progressive development of African Americans into a people who gain a "greater self-understanding" as they become increasingly conscious of who they are as a people actualizing their freedom through self-determination. In "The Conservation of Races," and later in *Dusk of Dawn,* Du Bois uses a notion of history that is clearly uninterested in looking backward in time at the empirical data or investigating "mere outward facts";[22] rather, he is interested in a notion of progressive history that will reveal what he believes is the teleological thought of Spirit fabricating itself into itself as the product of its own work. Spirit will in Du Bois, as it does in Hegel, construct itself into an objective world. The pertinent passage in Hegel is well worth citing at length since all of its principal parts reappear in Du Bois's conception of history in one form or another.

The very essence of spirit is *action.* It makes itself what it essentially is; it is its own product, its own work. Thus it becomes object of itself, thus it is presented to itself as an external existence. Likewise the spirit of a people: it is a definite spirit which builds itself up to an objective world. This world, then, stands and continues in its religion, its cult, its customs, its constitution and political laws, the whole scope of its institutions, its events and deeds. This is its work: this *one* people! Peoples are what their deeds are. . . . The function of the individual is to appropriate to himself this substantial being, make it part of his character and capacity, and thus to become something in the world. For he finds the existence of the people as a ready-made, stable world, into which he must fit himself. The spirit of the people, then, enjoys and satisfies itself in its work, in its world.[23]

This idealistic conception of historical progress in Hegel, as Houlgate notes, is not properly understood if it is imagined that Hegel has some particular conception of what the human condition will be in the future. Hegel's universal history is concerned with the future in the sense that "the plot of this story is the development of freedom" (IH 114). It is, according to Houlgate, in this sense that Hegel's universal history participates in idealism:

Hegel is a certain kind of "idealist" because he does not understand human character or identity to be some fixed, immutable "reality," but rather conceives of human beings as actively producing their character and identity in history. . . . The goal of historical activity, for Hegel, is thus for human beings to become conscious of themselves as freely and historically self-productive and

self-determining—not something fixed by nature—and for them to build their
world in accordance with that recognition. (FTH 33)

The universal history in Hegel's thought certainly has a teleology, but in
Hegel it is not predetermined: "It does not mean for him simply becoming
conscious of a given, fixed reality, or simply gaining a more accurate picture
of what we were like at the beginning of history. Rather, it means becoming
conscious of what we are by becoming conscious of the whole process whereby
we produce ourselves" (FTH 34). This is the task that Du Bois sets for himself, the uplift of a people to where they would become themselves. "I therefore take the world," Du Bois wrote in his diary while studying in Germany,
"that the Unknown lay in my hands and work for the rise of the Negro people,
taking for granted that their best development means the best development of
the world. . . . "[24]

Conceiving of "the rise of the Negro people" in terms of a *Volk* who *will*
become who they *are* illuminates Du Bois's gesture toward the Old Testament
promise made to Abraham before the birth of Isaac (P 57).[25] There are significant biblical underpinnings throughout this early essay by Du Bois, just
as there are theological underpinnings throughout Hegel's *Philosophy of History*. With the closing lines of his texts Hegel plainly expresses the teleological movement of Spirit with history in theological terms: "The History of the
World . . . is this process of development and the realization of Spirit—this is
the true *Theodicea*, the justification of God in History. Only *this* insight can
reconcile Spirit with the History of the World—*viz.* that what has happened,
and is happening every day, is not only not 'without God,' but is essentially
His Work" (VPG 540; PH 457). This theological dimension connects the notion of history at work in these two projects at yet one more level.

The argument that Appiah employs in his critique of Du Bois is so familiar
that it need not be reiterated at length here. The gist of Appiah's concern is
summarized in one of the questions that he raises and succinctly answers:
"Does adding a notion of common history allow us to make the distinctions between Slav and Teuton, or between English and Negro? The answer
is no."[26]

The indictment that Appiah issues, then, is that the claim in "The Conservation of Races" does not give us a formulation of race escaping the nineteenth-
century conception grounded in biological science. "We must establish,"
writes Appiah, "that what Du Bois attempts, despite his claims to the contrary, is not the transcendence of the nineteenth-century scientific conception
of race—as we shall see, he relies on it—but rather, as the dialectic requires,
a revaluation of the Negro race in the face of the sciences of racial inferiority"
(FH 30).

Appiah does well to point out the ways in which Du Bois has erred so long
as the remarks in "The Conservation of Races" and in *Dusk of Dawn* remain
inextricably bound to an attempt to connect the present to some point empiri-

cally fixed in the past. Appiah is also correct in identifying the elements in Du Bois's language that appear to depend upon the biological as such. Appiah's criticisms do, however, fail in at least one important respect: they fail to take seriously Du Bois's effort to think beyond the boundaries of the biological as it operates within the limits of an ordinary conception of history. The point at which Du Bois begins to express himself in terms of what he can feel better than he can explain more readily suggests an excess in his thought that outstrips his ability to give a master name to that about which he is speaking. Du Bois takes up a precarious position, and that is part of his greatness. What remains for readers of Du Bois today is not simply to discover flaws in his thinking, but perhaps to read him with the kind of generosity that Kant brings to his reading of Plato when he remarks in his *Critique of Pure Reason* that "it is by no means unusual, upon comparing the thoughts which an author has expressed in regard to his subject, whether in ordinary conversation or in writing, to find that we understand him better than he has understood himself. As he has not sufficiently determined his concept, he has sometimes spoken, or even thought, in opposition to his own intention."[27]

Hegel's notion of history, and, as I have been arguing, Du Bois's notion as well, is an understanding of history that thinks both the past and the future at the same time. In order to construe Du Bois's formulation as being utterly grounded in a biological conception, one has to ignore every indication that Du Bois has plainly engaged a notion of universal history, and ignore the transcendent "spiritual" criteria informing his identification and recognition of a certain folk as a race. One has to blatantly ignore the fact that Du Bois explicitly states, "No mere physical distinction would really define or explain the deeper differences—the cohesiveness and continuity of" the groups he identifies as races. Du Bois writes, "The deeper differences are spiritual, psychical, differences—undoubtedly based on the physical, but infinitely transcending them" (WDW 818). Du Bois's use of the expression "based on the physical" need not suggest anything more than the fact that the subject of his investigation concerns existential bodies that are shaped by the world that they occupy even while they give shape to it.

If Du Bois's use of such language as "striving," if his references to a "message" that has not yet been delivered, and if his invocation of "that perfection of human life for which we all long, that 'one far off Divine event'" do not indicate that his criterion for recognizing a race cannot be understood apart from its teleological realization, then Appiah should at least be able to engage Du Bois at the level of the theological elements in his thinking, elements that are obviously operating eschatologically. On the contrary, Appiah summarily dismisses these features in Du Bois's thinking by flatly stating, "We do not need the theological underpinnings of this argument" (FH 30).

These theological underpinnings are as relevant to Du Bois's project as they are to Hegel's. Not only is Du Bois's writing replete with allusions to New Testament theology, but this theology has as one of its most distinctive features an eschatology that holds the end in view from the very beginning, an end that shapes history from the start. That is, New Testament eschatology is encountered not only as a moment of justification, but as confirmation as well. Believers are confirmed at the *eschaton*, in that what they had up to then lived by faith, specifically, this final moment which had always been future, confirms that their history has been the history of the children of God. The "one far off Divine event,"[28] the moment which is not yet, confirms the believer's history as having been a history in the spiritual family.

Early in "The Conservation of Races," Du Bois writes, "Manifestly some of the great races of today—particularly the Negro race—have not as yet given to civilization the full spiritual message which they are capable of giving" (WDW 819). What the Negro race has to offer, in Du Bois's analysis, is a spiritual message that has not as yet been given; its arrival is still future at the time Du Bois is writing. Now, one way in which this can be understood is simply to say that even though Du Bois posits the message as arriving in the future, he has already identified a race of people as being Negro. This is semantically correct and conceptually mistaken.

The *Volk* whom Du Bois identifies as Negro are a people who have their identities as a question. They are not yet conscious of themselves; they have not, in Du Bois's view, achieved the self-consciousness and freedom that is their history. Like Augustine before him, Du Bois uses his autobiography to confess being a "problem" to himself: "*Mihi quaestio factus sum, et ipse est languor meus*" (I am now become a question to myself, and that is my infirmity).[29] It is thus impossible to make a hard and fast distinction between the people Du Bois wants to identify and the message that is "not yet" because the people, in this case, *are* the message. When the message is delivered in a time that has not yet come, it will be the message of a people who are themselves the message. This is one of the ways in which Du Bois situates the future as the essence of the present. In his language, the Negro is that being whose very identity is at issue, the Negro way of Being a Negro is a question, and, as such, is the determining feature of Negro existence. Insofar as the Negro is, for Du Bois, dialectically structured as a "problem," the Negro identity remains "open" and is not yet absolutely established or fixed; this is an identity that gains its confirmation in the *eschaton*. Thus, when Du Bois issues his "call" to the Negro people, it is with a restless refrain that is keenly aware that the identity of the Negro must necessarily be inexorably shaped by a future that has not yet been determined. The Negro, in Du Bois's formulation, is always already underway and not quite finished.

It is with this peculiar understanding that the notion of history in Du Bois's project becomes intelligible. Like the New Testament Christian living not by sight, but by faith, the Negro has a self-identification that projects itself toward the boundary of its horizon. The "now" for the Negro can never be simply "now," nor can it be a one-sided, isolated moment; it is an open-endedness toward the future in anticipation of what is yet to come. This is, of course, what is easily recognized in the relationship of *Geist* to history in Hegel. History, for Hegel, is the development in which Spirit comes to know itself, the process in which Spirit negates itself as other to itself. History is Spirit's self-realization through Freedom's actualization, which comprehends, since it is an actualization, not just what was, but also what can and what will be. There can be no mistaking the fact that for Du Bois the history of the Negro is *Geist* coming to know itself in the process by which *Geist* negates within itself the dialectic of "otherness"; this is the movement carrying the Negro to that moment when Negritude is no longer a self-questioning, but is, rather, self-realization of Freedom actualizing itself.

Under the weight of this heading Du Bois can look to Africa, a place he has never been, and find it *heimlich*. He remembers Africa as his "fatherland" through a tie that he can feel better than he can explain because his memory is the repetition of a future that *is* his becoming who he is. Du Bois had a vision that began with an end. He would eventually come home to Ghana as the place from where he started for the very first time.

> And the end of all our exploring
> Will be to arrive where we started
> And know the place for the first time.
> (T. S. Eliot, *Four Quartets*, "Little Gidding")

Notes

1. Maurice Merleau-Ponty, *In Praise of Philosophy*, trans. John Wild and James M. Edie (Evanston, Ill.: Northwestern University Press, 1963), p. 49. Henceforth PP.

2. Frantz Fanon, *The Wretched of the Earth*, trans. Constance Farrington (New York: Grove Press, 1968), p. 93.

3. James Baldwin, "White Man's Guilt," in *The Price of the Ticket: Collected Non-fiction, 1948–1985* (New York: St. Martin's/Marek, 1985), p. 410.

4. Du Bois was still striving to achieve this objective as late as 1947 in his capacity as the principal author of the NAACP's petition to the United Nations entitled *An Appeal to the World*. At that time this petition received international attention, which may have been due in no small part to the fact that Eleanor Roosevelt was on the NAACP's board of directors as well as a member of the American UN delegation. It has, however, been noted that Roosevelt "refused to introduce the NAACP petition in the United Nations out of concern that it would harm the international reputation of the United States." Cited by Mary L. Dudziak, "Desegregation as a Cold War Imperative," in Richard Delgado, ed., *Critical Race Theory: The Cutting Edge* (Philadelphia: Temple University Press, 1995), pp. 115–116.

5. W. E. B. Du Bois, "The Conservation of Races," in *W. E. B. Du Bois: Writings* (New York: Literary Classics of the United States, 1986), pp. 815–826. Henceforth WDW.

6. Hannah Arendt, *Lectures on Kant's Political Philosophy* (Chicago: University of Chicago Press, 1982), p. 8.

7. Hannah Arendt, *The Life of the Mind: Willing* (New York: Harcourt Brace Jovanovich, 1978), 45. Henceforth LM.

8. G. W. F. Hegel, *Vorlesungen über die Philosophie der Geschichte*, vol. 12, ed. E. Moldenhauer and K. Michel (Frankfurt am Main: Suhrkamp, 1971), p. 529 (henceforth VPG); trans. J. Sibree, *The Philosophy of History* (New York: Dover, 1956), p. 447 (henceforth PH). Translation modified.

9. David Levering Lewis, *W. E. B. Du Bois: Biography of a Race, 1868–1919* (New York: Henry Holt and Company, 1993), p. 131.

10. Hegel to Schelling. See LM, 45–46.

11. For the most part, my discussion of Hegelian appearances in the thought of Du Bois assumes a certain familiarity with the reflections pertaining to Du Bois and Hegel in Lewis, *W. E. B. Du Bois*; Joel Williamson, *The Crucible of Race: Black/White Relations in the American South since Emancipation* (New York: Oxford University Press, 1984) (henceforth BWR); and Shamoon Zamir, *Dark Voices: W. E. B. Du Bois and American Thought, 1888–1903* (Chicago: University of Chicago Press, 1995). Williamson's essay is the most important of these three sources with regard to the theme that I am pursuing here. I am disagreeing with his assertion that in Du Bois's writing "significant portions of Hegel's thought were ignored." What occurs with Du Bois's taking up of Hegel is an *aufheben*, a Hegelian "sublation" born out of the conviction that Hegel needs to be overthrown, if for no other reason than what he has to say about Africa. This difference aside, I agree with Williamson's assessment of the fundamentally Hegelian nature of Du Bois's "Strivings of the Negro People" and "The Conservation of Races." Referring to how these two pieces are woven together into the first chapter ("Of Our Spiritual Striving") of *The Souls of Black Folk*, Williamson writes, "First, it is Hegelian in its language. The ten pages are heavily laden with such favored Hegelian words as ideal, consciousness, strife, and self; spirit, soul, and genius; conflict and contradiction; Freedom (three times with a capital "F" as in *Freiheit*) and, of course, folk. Most relevant is his appropriation of the Hegelian view of history. Du Bois, like Hegel, sees the history of the world as the spirit of freedom rising to realize itself through specific world historical peoples. Consciousness is not achieved individually and one by one, but rather through the people, each people rising to a consciousness of itself, pursuing its *'Volkgeist,'* its spirit, its soul, its genius" (BWR, 403).

12. See a pertinent discussion related to this way of reading: Maghan Keita, "The Conservation of Races," in his *Race and the Writing of History: Riddling the Sphinx* (Oxford: Oxford University Press, 2000), p. 72. One of the claims that Keita makes is that in this particular essay "Du Bois does not begin by arguing the 'reality' of race. He argues the 'idea,' the 'spirit,' and the 'ideal' of race. He does this because he understands race to be an *invention*—a social construction."

13. Outlaw acknowledges Appiah's concerns but contends, "Du Bois was sufficiently insightful not to regard the relationship between physical characteristics, on the one side, and mental and cultural ('spiritual') factors on the other, as necessary such that the former determined the latter. More subtle still, Du Bois, as I read

him, did not define 'race' in an essentialist fashion, as a term for identifying natural kinds, by connecting the elements in the definition (physical characteristics, geography, cultural elements) conjunctively, making each element severally necessary and all together jointly sufficient." See Lucius T. Outlaw, Jr., *On Race and Philosophy* (New York: Routledge, 1996), p. 154.

14. The discussion of history found in Derrida presents an even more extreme and useful critique of the Hegelian concept of history. Derrida insists "that there is not one single history, a general history, but rather histories different in their type, rhythm, mode of inscription—intervallic, differentiated histories." See Jacques Derrida, *Positions*, trans. Alan Bass (Chicago: University of Chicago Press, 1981), p. 58; henceforth P. Also see David Wood's excellent discussion of Derrida's project in a chapter entitled "The Philosophy of the Future," in his *The Deconstruction of Time* (Atlantic Highlands, N.J.: Humanities Press International, 1989), pp. 361–383.

15. W. E. B. Du Bois, *The Souls of Black Folk*, ed. Henry Louis Gates Jr. and Terri Hume Oliver (New York: W. W. Norton and Company, 1999), pp. x–xi. Henceforth SoBF.

16. W. E. B. Du Bois, *The Souls of Black Folk*, in *W. E. B. Du Bois: Writings* (New York: The Library of America, 1986), 364.

17. Quoted in David W. Blight, "W. E. B. Du Bois and the Struggle for American Historical Memory," in Geneviève Fabre and Robert O'Meally, eds., *History and Memory in African-American Culture* (New York: Oxford University Press, 1994), p. 47.

18. Priscilla Wald, *Constituting Americans: Cultural Anxiety and Narrative Form* (Durham, N.C.: Duke University Press, 1995), p. 193. Henceforth CA.

19. Space will not permit extended remarks on Kant's philosophy of history. For a critical discussion of Kant that reassesses his philosophy of history, see Tsenay Serequeberhan, "Eurocentrism in Philosophy: The Case of Immanuel Kant," *The Philosophical Forum: A Quarterly* 27, no. 4 (Summer 1996): 333–356.

20. One other way of situating this forward gaze of Du Bois's Hegelian formulation of history is in terms of language that might be employed by Nietzsche, who gives us an exhortation of Heraclitean proportions when he writes, "You shall become the person you are" (*The Gay Science*, trans. Walter Kaufmann [New York: Random House, 1974], p. 219). The paradoxical tension between the future and present tense in this famous line of Nietzsche's is the very same tension that Du Bois attempts to work out: he sees a history in which African Americans become the people they are.

21. Stephen Houlgate, *Freedom, Truth and History: An Introduction to Hegel's Philosophy* (London: Routledge, 1991), p. 32. Henceforth FTH.

22. R. G. Collingwood, *The Idea of History* (New York: Galaxy Books, 1956), p. 118. Henceforth IH.

23. G. W. F. Hegel, *Reason in History* (Indianapolis: Bobbs-Merrill, 1953), pp. 89–90. Henceforth RH. The original is at VPG 99.

24. W. E. B. Du Bois, *The Autobiography of W. E. B. Du Bois: A Soliloquy on Viewing*

My Life from the Last Decade of Its First Century (New York: International Publishers, 1968), p. 171.

25. Derrida references some of these elements of history: "The metaphysical character of the concept of history is not only linked to linearity, but to an entire *system* of implications (teleology, eschatology, elevating and interiorizing accumulation of meaning, a certain type of traditionality, a certain concept of truth etc. . . .)." *Positions*, p. 57.

26. Kwame Anthony Appiah, *In My Father's House: Africa in the Philosophy of Culture* (New York: Oxford University Press, 1992), p. 30. Henceforth FH.

27. Immanuel Kant, *Critique of Pure Reason*, trans. Norman Kemp Smith (New York: St. Martin's Press, 1965), p. 310.

28. When Du Bois quotes the line "one far off Divine event," he is, of course, reciting a line from Tennyson's poem of 1850, *In Memoriam A. H. H.:* "That God, which ever lives and loves, / One God, one law, one element, / And one far-off divine event, / To which the whole creation moves."

29. Augustine, *Confessions*, trans. William Watts (Cambridge, Mass.: Harvard University Press, 1988), vol. 2, pp. 168–169.

Three

Douglass and Du Bois's
Der Schwarze Volksgeist[1]

Ronald R. Sundstrom

Frederick Douglass (1817–95) and W. E. B. Du Bois (1868–1963) are critical figures in the political and intellectual history of race in the United States, whose respective visions about race and its conservation remain germane and influential. Contemporary debates around the conservation of race, for example, can be seen to reflect the basic positions that Douglass and Du Bois laid out at the end of the nineteenth century. Just as those who argue that race ought to be conserved turn to Du Bois, those who disagree with Du Bois need to consider both Douglass's arguments and the historical reasons why Du Bois's and Booker T. Washington's strategies for racial justice eclipsed Douglass's. The works of Douglass and Du Bois are pieces of a conversation that must be considered in the context of early black political and intellectual movements, as well as in relationship to each other. This must be done for the sake of proper understanding, but also to avoid making the racist mistake of seeing Du Bois as merely the darker reflection of some European or American pragmatist philosophy.

Douglass, through his work for the abolition of slavery and the enfranchisement and uplift of African Americans, advocated a position of racial assimilation and amalgamation. His critics, such as Alexander Crummell (1819–98) and other early black nationalists, favored emigration, self-separation, and the conservation of black racial identity. Douglass, along with his critics, set the terms of the debate that Du Bois would engage with in his "The Conservation of Races."

Douglass

Although some of the particulars of Douglass's arguments have been rejected, his idealistic vision of human brotherhood, his skepticism about the political and moral value of race pride and self-segregation, his rejection of race as a political or social category, and his hope that assimilation and racial amalgamation would bring an end to racial oppression and result in a stronger America, more consistent with its founding liberal principles, remain influential in contemporary U.S. racial politics. Taking the progressive and egalitarian elements of Christianity very seriously, Douglass embraced the Biblical doctrine of human brotherhood and employed the combined strategy of assimilation and amalgamation, a strategy that sought to realize the divine ideal of human brotherhood on earth. Douglass, like many white and black intellectuals of his time, was, moreover, an Enlightenment thinker, a nineteenth-century modernist.[2] He believed in progress and the advance and mission of Western civilization. Douglass's modernism, additionally, was marked by a steadfast faith in the inevitability of Western Christendom's advance toward justice and universal human brotherhood:

> There are forces in operation, which must inevitably work the downfall of slavery. *"The arm of the Lord is not shortened,"* and the doom of slavery is certain. I, therefore, leave off where I began, with *hope.* While drawing encouragement from the Declaration of Independence, the great principles it contains, and the genius of American Institutions, my spirit is also cheered by the obvious tendencies of the age.[3]

Another element of Douglass's modernism, which is displayed in his use of Psalm 68:31, is the belief that non-white peoples, particularly in Africa and Asia, would "rise up" and join in this advance of civilization:

> The far off and almost fabulous Pacific rolls in grandeur at our feet. The Celestial Empire, the mystery of ages, is being solved. The fiat of the Almighty, *"Let there be Light,"* has not yet spent its force. No abuse, no outrage whether in taste, sport or avarice, can now hide itself from the all-pervading light. The iron shoe, and crippled foot of China must be seen, in contrast with nature. *Africa must rise and put on her yet unwoven garment. "Ethiopia shall stretch out her hand unto God."* (WSFJ 387)[4]

Human brotherhood, for Douglass, was a Christian doctrine that asserted that God created all the peoples of the earth out of "one blood." According to Douglass, this matter was unequivocally supported by Biblical text, and a rejection of it amounted to a rejection of the credibility of the Good Book. Obviously, for his audience and time, such a contention presented an argument against polygenists (who at the time were claiming that blacks were a separate and inferior species) and a powerful dilemma:

> The unity of the human race—the brotherhood of man—the reciprocal duties of all to each, and of each to all, are too plainly taught in the Bible to admit of cavil.—The credit of the Bible is at stake—and if it be too much to say, that it must stand or fall, by the decision of this question, *it is* proper to say, that the value of that sacred Book—as a record of the early history of mankind—must be materially affected, by the decision of the question.[5]

This doctrine, as used by Douglass and the abolitionist movement, was based on the Bible's creation story and Acts 17:26: "And hath made of one blood all nations of men for to dwell on all the face of the earth." Beyond an account of origins and unity, the doctrine of human brotherhood carried with it the moral injunction that since we are all equally human, we are all equally deserving of human rights.

Although he believed that the Biblical account was correct, for Douglass the doctrine was an essentially religious and moral one that held no matter the biological facts (CN 242–243). Given this position, he had little patience for the American school of polygeny and its argument—a non sequitur that commits the naturalistic fallacy—that the biological inferiority of blacks justifies their being denied human rights. Thus, Douglass takes special aim at the work of the American polygenists Josiah Nott, George Gliddon, Louis Agassiz, and Samuel Morton (CN). In addition to taking issue with their science, he argued that even *if* blacks are a distinct species and even *if* they are inferior, they are, as a part of humanity and children of God, entitled to full human rights:

> What, after all, if they are able to show very good reasons for believing the Negro to have been created precisely as we find him on the Gold Coast—along the Senegal and the Niger—I say, what of all this?—*"A man's a man for a' that."* I sincerely believe, that the weight of the argument is in favor of the unity of origin of the human race, or species—that the arguments on the other side are partial, superficial, utterly subversive of the happiness of man, and insulting to the wisdom of God. Yet, what if we grant they are not so? What, if we grant that the case, on our part, is not made out? Does it follow, that the Negro should be held in contempt? Does it follow, that to enslave and imbrue him is either *just* or *wise?* I think not. Human rights stand upon a common basis; and by all the reason that they are supported, maintained and defended, for one variety of the human family, they are supported, maintained and defended for *all* the human family; because all mankind have the same wants, arising out of a common nature. A diverse origin does not disprove a common nature, nor does it disprove a united destiny. (CN 231)

Douglass, obviously from his amalgamationist position, accepted the existence of biologically distinct races.[6] He accepted a climatist monogenism, which asserted the unity of the human species and that human diversity was due to the climates of the lands in which the races were isolated for centuries. His acceptance of races needs to be qualified, however, because he did not put great weight on what he characterized as merely "technical" distinctions in the brotherhood of humanity (CN). Although he did not deny these "technical distinctions," he believed that their existence ebbed and flowed, and that they were overshadowed by human fraternity.

Douglass supported the amalgamation of the biological races and assimilation of black and white Americans into what he imagined as a new sort of American. It is important to note the distinction between assimilation and amalgamation to understand Douglass's project. Assimilation and amalgamation are separate doctrines. Amalgamation does not follow by itself from assimilation, nor vice versa. Early black nationalists, such as Edward Blyden, Martin Delany, and Alexander Crummell, were separatists, but they also thought that blacks needed to assimilate by accepting Christianity and Western civilization (GA 15–31). Booker T. Washington, while not a black nationalist, also accepted an assimilationist-separatist strategy. Thus, Douglass's position, since he held that black and whites would not only assimilate with each other but also amalgamate into an "intermediate race," supported a program of assimilation and amalgamation.

Douglass began to advocate the controversial position of amalgamation during the 1860s. More than a strategy, he thought, it was a process that would naturally occur in the United States over time, eventually creating an intermediate race. He believed that amalgamation, combined with assimilation, would be the "only solid, and final solution" of race prejudice and division in this nation.[7] As he remarked to a reporter the day after his controversial second marriage to Helen Pitts, a white woman,

> There is no division of races. God Almighty made but one race. I adopt the theory that in time the varieties of races will be blended into one. Let us look back when the black and the white people were distinct in this country. In two hundred and fifty years there has grown up a million of intermediate. And this will continue. You may say that Frederick Douglass considers himself a member of the one race which exists."[8]

Douglass's stance on assimilation and amalgamation speaks volumes about his stance on the conservation of race. He equated the preservation of racial distinctiveness with the preservation of racial prejudice. The positions he took on many topics were informed by his stance against racial separatism and the conservation of the "races" in the United States.

Douglass reprobated attempts to build separate "negro pews, negro berths in steamboats, negro cars, Sabbath or week-day schools . . . churches," and so on.[9] He argued that attempts to separate blacks were in the interests of those in favor of slavery and would hinder black uplift. Likewise, he stood against the separatist, emigrationist visions of the American Colonization Society, founded by whites, and the African Civilization Society, founded by blacks.[10]

Although Douglass disfavored racial organizations, he thought it was necessary for African Americans to organize and unify to fight against slavery and racial prejudice, and to struggle for justice.[11] Nonetheless, for Douglass, this political organizing and unification was to be not for reasons of race or culture, but strictly for political reasons. While he expected blacks to unify to fight for the end of slavery and for justice, he railed against separatist accommodations, institutions, and organizations, and urged blacks to act "without distinction of color":

> It will be a long time before we gain all our rights; and although it may seem to conflict with our views of human brotherhood, we shall undoubtedly for many years be compelled to have institutions of a complexional character, in order to

attain this very idea of human brotherhood. We would, however, advise our brethren to occupy memberships and stations among white persons, and in white institutions, just so fast as our rights are secured to us.[12]

Douglass's "final solution" was the complete assimilation, dispersement, and amalgamation of blacks into the white population. To this end, he vigorously rejected notions of race pride, racial union, and black nationalism.[13] To those who argued that black race pride had to be cultivated to oppose oppression, he responded, "But it may be said that we shall put down race pride in the white people by cultivating race pride among ourselves. The answer to this is that the devils are not cast out by Beelzebub, the prince of devils" (ACP 317).

Race, according to Douglass, cannot be used to fight racism; likewise, self-segregation cannot be used to fight segregation.

Du Bois

Despite the fact that the nature of race and the question of its conservation had been topics of discussion in America at least since the mid-eighteenth century, and had been a principal subject of discussion among the black intelligentsia of the early and mid-nineteenth century, Du Bois, in his "The Conservation of Races," an address presented to the American Negro Academy, solidified and modernized the debate by linking a social conception of race with the question of its conservation.[14] Du Bois was responding to the devaluation of Africans by late-nineteenth-century racial science, the legacy of Douglass's assimilationist-amalgamationist politics, and the impending leadership of Booker T. Washington. Moreover, he was reaching out in intellectual affiliation to Alexander Crummell, early African nationalist leader, Episcopalian minister, Liberian missionary and colonialist, and co-founder and president of the Academy.[15]

One influence on Du Bois that would inform his comments before the American Negro Academy was, to a minor degree, pragmatism.[16] More important influences, however, were the idealism of European, especially Prussian, historiography and the tradition of intellectual and political activism for African American uplift of which Douglass and Crummell were paramount figures. Du Bois, like many intellectuals of his time, was an Enlightenment thinker who accepted the Western European mantra of progress, modernization, and civilization and who, as a member of the black diaspora, included African and African American uplift in this vision of world progress. Unlike Douglass, Du Bois, with the early black nationalists, embraced racial collective identity, racial destiny, and authoritarian collectivism. This package of ideologies, when bound together with the ideology of the advance of Western Christian civilization, formed Ethiopianism, a messianic vision of African civilization (GA).

Du Bois's acceptance of Ethiopianism, and civilizationism in general, is writ large in "The Conservation of the Races." His civilizationism is best displayed in his comment that

> The English nation stood for constitutional liberty and commercial freedom; the German nation for science and philosophy; the Romance nations stood for literature and art, and the other race groups are striving, each in its own way, to develop for civilization its particular message, its particular ideal, which shall help to guide the world nearer and nearer that perfection of human life for which we all long, that "one far off Divine event."[17]

And his Ethiopianism is evident in his comment that the

> complete Negro message of the whole Negro race has not as yet been given to the world: that the messages and ideal of the yellow race have not been completed, and that the striving of the mighty Slavs has but begun. The question is, then: How shall this message be delivered; how shall these various ideals be realized? The answer is plain: By the development of these race groups, not as individuals, but as races. . . . For the development of Negro genius, of Negro literature and art, of Negro spirit, only Negroes bound and welded together, Negroes inspired by one vast ideal, can work out in its fullness the great message we have for humanity. We cannot reverse history; we are subject to the same natural laws as other races, and if the Negro is ever to be a factor in the world's history—if among the gaily colored banners that deck the broad ramparts of civilization is to hang one uncompromising black, then it must be placed there by black hands, fashioned by black heads and hallowed by the travail of 200,000,000 black hearts bearing in one glad song of jubilee. (CR 487)

These comments ought not to be written off as rhetorical flourish or, as some have argued, the mere presentation of a political project.[18] The project was political, but it also was cultural. It advanced a mystical, messianic vision of African diasporic civilization.

It may be useful to compare Du Bois's talk of the "message" of each race in terms of J. S. Mill's "experiments in living," as Bernard Boxill does.[19] Mill's "experiments of living," however, were not what Du Bois had in mind. In *On Liberty*, Mill argues,

> As it is useful that while mankind are imperfect there should be different opinions, so is it that there should be different experiments of living; that free scope should be given to varieties of character, short of injury to others; and the worth of different modes of life should be proved practically, when anyone thinks fit to try them. It is desirable, in short, that in things which do not primarily concern others individuality should assert itself. Where not the person's own character but the traditions or customs of other people are the rule of conduct, there is wanting one of the principal ingredients of human happiness, and quite the chief ingredient of individual and social progress.[20]

Du Bois's conception of the "messages" of race is mystical and collectivist —not the individualistic, tradition- and culture-challenging experiments that

Mill had in mind. It is a conception influenced by the religious nationalism of Friedrich Schleiermacher and the historical idealism of Johann Gottfried von Herder, as filtered through the Ethiopianism of early black nationalism.[21] It is a reoccurring vision evident in his subsequent works such as *The Souls of Black Folk*, *Dark Princess*, and *Darkwater*, and in his pageant, *The Star of Ethiopia*.

As Moses argues, Alexander Crummell was an important influence on Du Bois. Many of the ideas within "The Conservation of Races," such as collective racial identity, the destiny of races, African civilizationism, African contributions to world civilization, the conservation of race, anti-assimilationism and anti-amalgamationism, and even the introduction of historical idealism in the language of black uplift, had already been introduced into the debate by Crummell and other blacks.[22] Crummell's works, such as "The Solution of Problems: The Duty and Destiny of Man," "Civilization: The Primal Need of the Race," and "The Race Problem in America," all of which Du Bois was familiar with, contained the above ideas as well as the familiar staples of Crummell's thoughts also apparent in "The Conservation of the Races": elitism and authoritarian collectivism, anti-individualism, and conservative Victorian values. In particular, we see the influence of Crummell when Du Bois, in his speech, goes on about the "heritage of moral iniquity from our past history"; when he urges the Academy to unite "to keep black boys from loafing, gambling and crime," and to "guard the purity of black women and to reduce the vast army of black prostitutes that is today marching to hell"; and when he enjoins the Academy "to sound a note of warning" to "echo in every black cabin in the land" that unless "we conquer our present vices they will conquer us; we are diseased, we are developing criminal tendencies, and an alarmingly large percentage of our men and women are sexually impure" (CR 489–491). In these passages Du Bois was explicitly declaring his affinity with Crummell's belief that moral guardianship played a central role in black uplift.

The idealism of German historiography was another important influence on Du Bois evident in "The Conservation of Races." Du Bois was first exposed to idealism through the works of Thomas Carlyle, and possibly those of Ralph Waldo Emerson, and then through his classes at Harvard with Josiah Royce and George Santayana. During his time at Fisk University, Du Bois had also shown an appreciation for Chancellor Otto von Bismarck, unifier of the Prussian states and victor in the Franco-Prussian war, who accounted for Germanic victory and ascendancy in ethnological and racial terms—a methodology in historiography with roots in the work of Herder and Hegel. His most influential exposure, however, came from his two-year stay at Friedrich-Wilhelm III Universität at Berlin, where he studied under Rudolph von Gneist, Gustav von Schmoller, Adolph Wagner, and, most importantly, Heinrich von Treitschke (1834–96), a prominent social theorist of Prussian unification.[23] Treitschke's view of Prussian history was presented in his seven-volume *Deutsche Geschichte,* the first volume of which was published in 1879. *Deutsche Geschichte* is an anti-Semitic treatise that put, in the tradition of Fichte, Herder, Hegel, and Humboldt, a racialized notion of *Volk* and *Völker-wanderung* at the center of Germanic historiography.

The link between idealism and German historiography is displayed in Du Bois's talk of history, progress, and his own use of racialized national identity.[24] Du Bois places racialized national identities, along with their individual contributions—an idea with links to Fichte and Herder—at the center of history, making their collective racial contributions the engine of historical progress. He expresses this conception of history most clearly when he remarks, "The history of the world is the history, not of individuals, but of groups, not of nations, but of races, and he who ignores or seeks to override the race idea in human history ignores and overrides the central thought of all history" (CR, 485).

Du Bois's characterization of the race spirit, idea, and ideal is directly comparable to the characterization of the *Volk* spirit, idea, and ideal evident in German historical idealism. For example, Hegel writes, in his *Vorlesungen über die Geschichte der Philosophie*, "The universal premise of this investigation is that world history represents the Idea of the spirit as it displays itself in reality as a series of external forms. The stage of self-consciousness which the spirit has reached manifests itself in world history as the existing national spirit, as a nation which exists in the present."[25] Applying this notion of history to Africa, Hegel claims,

> It has no historical interest of its own, for we find its inhabitants living in barbarism and savagery in a land which has not furnished them with any ingredient of culture. From the earliest historical times, Africa has remained cut off from all contacts with the rest of the world; it is the land of gold, for ever pressing in upon itself, and the land of childhood, removed from the light of self-conscious history and wrapped in the dark mantle of night. (VPW 214; PWH 174)

Thus, for Du Bois, a believer in an idealist notion of history, in which a *Volk* is measured by its participation in world history and its destiny is driven by its *Volksgeist*, it was imperative to invigorate *der schwarze Volksgeist* and lead it out of its slumber in "the dark forests" of Africa to become a "co-worker in the kingdom of culture"[26] and contribute "its particular message, its particular ideal" to the "broad ramparts" of world history: "We are Negroes, members of a vast historic race that from the very dawn of creation has slept, but half awakening in the dark forests of its African fatherland. We are the first fruits of this new nation, the harbinger of that black to-morrow which is yet destined to soften the whiteness of that Teutonic to-day" (CR 489).

In responding to the Hegelian judgment of Africa as a non-player in history, Du Bois was also rejecting the turn-of-the-century social Darwinist judgment of blacks as a people who were doomed to extinction or base servility. Du Bois argued that Africa and Africans had history-creating potential—Du

Bois seemed to think that Toussaint L'Ouverture was an "epitomized expression" of this potential that was to arise from New World blacks—and that it had already partially contributed to world civilization through ancient Egyptian civilization (CR 485).

Another connection between idealism and Du Bois's ideas in "Conservation" can be found in his ideas on the relation of individuals to races. According to Du Bois, given the centrality of race in an idealist conception of history, individuals are mere epitomes of the race to which they belong:

> Turning to real history, there can be no doubt, first, as to the widespread, nay, universal, prevalence of the race idea, the race spirit, the race ideal, and as to its efficiency as the vastest and most ingenious invention for human progress. We, who have been reared and trained under the individualistic philosophy of the Declaration of Independence and the laisser-faire [sic] philosophy of Adam Smith, are loath to see and loath to acknowledge this patent fact of human history. *We see the Pharaohs, Caesars, Toussaints and Napoleons of history and forget the vast races of which they were but epitomized expressions.* (CR 485)

The subsumption of individuals to races follows from Du Bois's idealist conception of history. There is more, however, than subsumption going on in the above passage. Du Bois is saying that important individuals, central to the history of each race, are "epitomized expressions" of their races. What Du Bois must mean by "epitomized expression," given his litany of historically "important" individuals, and his view that world history is the result of the expression of each *Volksgeist*, is that individuals are the "epitomized expressions" of *Volksgeist;* they are epitomes of the historically important expressions of each *Volk*, and thus the epitomes of each race's history.[27]

Understanding that he was influenced in important ways by Crummell and by German historical idealism is crucial for the correct exegesis of Du Bois, especially his early works. In asserting this I am minimizing the role of Jamesian pragmatism in "The Conservation of Races"; however, I am not arguing that it had no influence. Moses, on the other hand, takes a stronger position against a Jamesian reading. According to Moses, "The Conservation of Races" is

> a black nationalist manifesto. The document clearly placed the young Du Bois outside the tradition of American liberalism. It foreshadowed his lifelong penchant for racialistic collectivist dogmas, and presaged the Stalinist authoritarianism that would dominate the final years of his intellectual life. Nothing could be more incorrect than to view this young authoritarian mystic as an heir to the liberalism of Thomas Jefferson or the pragmatism of William James. (DCR 289)

Although I agree that "The Conservation of Races" is not a Jeffersonian document, and that it contains some illiberal ideas, I do not agree with Moses's position that James's pragmatism is not evident in Du Bois's speech. Moreover, I disagree with Moses's characterization of "The Conservation" as a "Crummellian essay" that was a restatement of a mystical Christian idea that Crummell had long preached, the idea that races were "the organisms and ordinance of God" (DCR 284).

Moses's *strict* Crummellian reading of Du Bois is wrong for two reasons. First, Crummell's definition of race, in his "The Race Problem in America," as the "organisms and the ordinance of God," and as "a compact, homogeneous population of one blood, ancestry, and lineage," is a religio-biological conception.[28] Race, for Crummell, was of "divine origin" and not something created by man. In contrast, Du Bois claimed that race was "the vastest and most ingenious *invention* for human progress."

Second, unlike Crummell's conception of race as an "ordinance of God," Du Bois's conception of race, as an invention, was something that groups, given the right circumstances, could not only ignore, but also be rid of: "It [is] the duty of the Americans of Negro descent, as a body to maintain their race identity until this mission of the Negro people is accomplished, and the ideal of human brotherhood has become a practical possibility" (CR 491).

Clearly, Du Bois's conception of race departs from Crummell's. Moreover, Du Bois's talk of race being an invention invites a Jamesian reading, but that is also where a Jamesian reading must stop.[29] There is little that is Jamesian about Du Bois's racial collectivism, his acceptance of authoritarianism, his black nationalism, his yoking of individuals with duties to their race, his talk of racial missions, messages, or ideals, or his claim that individuals are "epitomized expressions" of their races.

The influences of Crummell and idealism come to bear in Du Bois's responses to the ideas of Douglass and Washington. Du Bois has placed race in the center of history and individuals in the center of race; therefore, Douglass's assimilationist and amalgamationist policies were, for Du Bois, policies of "self-obliteration" (CR 488). Du Bois's rejection of Douglass's assimilationism-amalgamationism is explicit in his call for the conservation of race, and his rejection of Douglass's policies is explicit throughout the "The Conservation of Races." Du Bois argued that the destiny of African Americans

is *not* absorption by the white Americans: that if in America it is to be proven for the first time in the modern world that not only Negroes are capable of evolving individual men like Toussaint, the Savior, but are a nation stored with wonderful possibilities of culture, then their destiny is not a servile imitation of Anglo-Saxon culture, but a stalwart originality which shall unswervingly follow Negro ideals. (CR 487–488)

Moreover, Du Bois argues that the conservation of race is not only an integral part of black uplift but is the duty of each individual black American:

It is our duty to conserve our physical powers, our intellectual endowments, our spiritual ideals; as a race we must strive by race organization, by race solidarity, by race unity to the realization of that broader humanity which freely recognizes differences in men, but sternly deprecates inequality in their opportunities of development.

For the accomplishment of these ends we need race organizations: Negro colleges, Negro newspapers, Negro business organizations, a Negro school of literature and art, and an intellectual clearing house, for all these products of the Negro mind, which we may call a Negro Academy. (CR 489)

Du Bois's call for race organizations is a rejection of Douglass's position against black cultural unification and self-segregation. It is also, however, a retort to the anti-intellectualism of Booker T. Washington and to his call for the vocational education of blacks to the exclusion of academic education.

Du Bois thought that it was necessary to conserve race for cultural and political reasons. For Du Bois, the cultural reason that race needed to be conserved, given his idealism, was that each race was invested with a particular cultural "contribution" that arose from its race spirit, its *Volksgeist*, the spiritual and psychic differences that marked each group. The political reason for its conservation, according to Du Bois, was that human brotherhood was not yet a "practical possibility"; thus, racial solidarity was necessary in order for Africans and African Americans to attain justice and uplift. As Du Bois argued, African Americans must conserve race and strive in solidarity to bring about on the stage of world history "the realization of that broader humanity which freely recognizes differences in men, but sternly deprecates inequality in their opportunities of development" (CR 489).[30]

Considering all the influences that Du Bois was juggling in "The Conservation of Races"—black nationalism, idealism, and, to a lesser degree, pragmatism —it should not be surprising that the conception of race that he presented was, as Moses and Lewis remarked, confusing. Despite this confusion, and the worrisome elements of his idealism, I argue that Du Bois has presented a cogent sociohistorical conception of race. Near the beginning of the speech, he relates that it is "hard to come . . . to any definite conclusion" about "the essential" differences of the races. He relates that the visibly physiological criteria once used have been discovered to be too "exasperatingly intermingled" to be useful. Then, he remarks, "The differences between men do not explain all the differences of their history. It declares, as Darwin said, that great as is the physical unlikeness of the various races of man their likenesses are greater . . . " (CR 484–485).

Du Bois, twenty-nine years old, an idealist, under the spell of Crummell, and only three years removed from the nationalist stirrings in Germany, argued that despite the inability of science to define the races,

There are differences—subtle, delicate and elusive, though they may be—which have silently but definitely separated men into groups. While these subtle forces have generally followed the natural cleavage of common blood, descent and physical peculiarities, they have at other times swept across and ignored these. At all times, however, they have divided human beings into races, which, while they perhaps transcend scientific definition, nevertheless, *are clearly defined to the eye of the Historian and Sociologist*. (CR 485; my emphasis)

The "subtle forces" that Du Bois is referring to are social in nature and they divide humanity into races. Although these races escape biological explanation, they are apparent to the investigations of social scientists. As a result of this social dynamic, according to Du Bois, a race is "a vast family of human beings, *generally* of common blood and language, *always* of common history, traditions and impulses, who are both voluntarily and involuntarily striving together for the accomplishment of certain more or less vividly conceived ideals of life" (CR 485). Du Bois is using "generally" in the sense of "usually"; thus, for Du Bois, race usually follows the "cleavages" of biological difference, but it need not do so.[31] On the other hand, a race, Du Bois argues, always shares certain social features: a common history, traditions, strivings, impulses, and ideals of life.[32]

Du Bois's conception of race is purely social. Although it is not completely divorced from biology, it has, however, subordinated biological differences to the status of an epiphenomenon—sometimes they are there and sometimes not.[33] Therefore, his conception of "race" does not in any way rest on biology. Du Bois reiterates this point when he remarks, "While race differences have followed mainly physical race lines, yet no mere physical distinctions would really define or explain the deeper differences—the cohesiveness and continuity of these groups. The deeper differences are spiritual, psychical, differences—undoubtedly based on the physical, *but infinitely transcending them*" (CR 486).

A Defense of Du Bois's Sociohistorical Conception of Race

In opposition to this reading of Du Bois, K. Anthony Appiah argues that Du Bois has failed in his attempt to substitute "a sociohistorical conception of race for the biological one," and that *he* has instead buried the scientific conception below the surface of his sociohistorical conception.[34] Appiah argues that while Du Bois talks of a sociohistorical conception of race, his sociohistorical criteria do not hold up to examination, and thus at the core of his theory is the outmoded scientific conception of race. Appiah sees support for his argument in Du Bois's talk of "common blood." He asks, "If he has fully transcended the scientific notion, what is the role of this talk about blood?" (UA 25)

Du Bois's talk of "common blood" was figurative. He used the phrases "people of Negro blood" and "black-blooded people of America" as rhetorical devices near the end of his speech when he wanted to emphasize racial unity and collective identity. We should also keep in mind, however, that he was not trying to give a notion of race absolutely divorced from the biological. He thought, after all, that race occasionally did follow lines of physical difference, and he thought that "race," while social, was *based* on (i.e., inspired by) the physical. The presence of both a social conception of race and references to the biological conception of race does, however, create a tension between the two in his work.

I do not think that Du Bois thought, especially given the fact that he was of mixed racial heritage, that the lines of racial difference in the United States strictly followed lines of physical difference. Further, in his use of the term "blood," he seemed to have in mind the fact that in the United States race is assigned through birth and lineage.[35] Either way, if his talk of "blood" was figurative or if it communicated his belief in African American biological racial difference, it did not lessen his core claim that race is essentially a sociohistorical concept.

Appiah's main argument is aimed at Du Bois's definition of race as "a vast family of human beings, *generally* of common blood and language, *always* of common history, traditions and impulses" (CR 485). Each element of Du Bois's definition, Appiah argues, fails in turn to individuate members of the races—to assign an individual to some race—since each element is an a posteriori property of the various races and not a prior criterion for membership. According to Appiah, the use of "common history, traditions and impulses" to define the races would involve us in circularity. Hence, Appiah argues, what is at the bottom of Du Bois's sociohistorical definition, what Du Bois relies on to do the task of individuation, is the scientific, qua biological, conception. Arguing that Du Bois's sociohistorical notion collapses into a biological conception, and that race is not a legitimate biological category, Appiah then concludes that race is illusory: "The truth is that there are no races: there is nothing in the world that can do all we ask 'race' to do for us. The evil that is done is done by the concept and by easy—yet impossible—assumptions as to its application. What we miss through our obsession with the structure of relations of concepts is, simple, reality" (UA 36).

Appiah's claim that the races are illusory rests on the assumption of metaphysical monism—a school of thought that holds there is only one way for categories to be real—that admits the reality only of physical kinds or categories. Given this metaphysical assumption, "simple reality," for Appiah, does not include race or, probably, other social constructs. For race to "do all we ask" of it, given the criteria of metaphysical monism, it would have to be a real physical category; in other words, it would have to be a real biological kind. For it to be able to do the job of individuation, the races would have to be delineated by some biological "essence" such as distinct genetic codes. Since race lacks this biological essence, it is not a real biological category; further, as Appiah argues, since race is not a real biological category, then all that is left for it to be is an illusion.

To defend Du Bois's sociohistorical conception, we must dispense with the assumption of metaphysical monism in favor of a metaphysical pluralism that admits the reality of social kinds.[36] Metaphysical monism will not give us a fair or adequate assessment of the categories and dynamics of the social world; nor, for that matter, has it done so for the biological sciences. There is little hope, for example, of adequately accounting for biological categories such as "species" or "genes" with the standards of metaphysical monism.[37] Thus, not only does social science demand a shift toward pluralism, biological science demands it as well.

For race to be a real social kind at some site, given metaphysical pluralism, what has to be present are social forces—labels, institutions, individual intentions, laws, mores, values, traditions—combined in a dynamic with enough strength to give the category presence and impact at that site. This is the social view of race that Du Bois offers to us with his sociohistorical conception of race. Du Bois's consciousness about the role of social forces and their power to create categories and make them real in the world, or, if you will, their role in "world-making," is evident in his discussion of his sociohistorical conception of race. For example, in his discussion about what "binds" nations together to make races, he states, "The forces that bind together the . . . nations are, then, first, their race identity and common blood; secondly, and more important, a common history, common laws and religion, similar habits of thought and a conscious striving together for certain ideals of life" (CR 486).

The metaphysical pluralist reading of Du Bois's conception of race also addresses the problem of individuation that Appiah charged it with having. Du Bois's sociohistorical conception of race, given the framework of metaphysical pluralism, does do the job of individuation. It does not, however, do it in the manner of metaphysical monist frameworks—where exclusivity is expected—where for every "thing" in the world there is a constitutive answer to the question, "What is it?"

Metaphysical pluralist frameworks abandon the monist standard of exclusivity, and, thus, the mechanics of metaphysical monism, especially regarding the real kinds of biological and social sciences. In systematics, for example, whether some organism belongs to one or another species is ambiguous, and pluralist species conceptions recognize this ambiguity and do not demand clear-cut answers. Likewise, with the kinds of the social sciences, individuation is equally complicated.

To find out whether some person belongs to one or another race at a particular site, social scientists would have to investigate that site and determine what racial labels are in use at that site, what social forces serve in racial formation at that site, and how that particular individual fits into the racial dynamic at that site. In other words, scientists would need to determine how that person is racially labeled at that site, how racial laws, mores, values, and categories affect that person, and how that person labels herself. This system allows in the ambiguity and complexity of the social world, but ambiguity and complexity are what characterize our social worlds and are exactly what a proper ontology of our social worlds must capture.

Race, according to Du Bois, is a real category resulting from "subtle" forces, social forces, that have served through history to bind humans into various groups and divide them from others. Physical difference, although not absent, is not a constitutive part of Du Bois's sociohistorical conception. I conclude, therefore, that Du Bois's sociohistorical conception of race casts it as a real social category whose existence is due solely to social and historical forces; that this conception of race is not an essentialist one, in that it does not posit necessary and sufficient conditions for being a member of a particular race; and that Du Bois's conception of race is not biological.

Conclusion

Despite the success of Du Bois's conception of race, I reject what I see as the problematic elements of his arguments for the ontology and conservation of race. His sociohistorical conception of race is weighed down by superfluous biological beliefs. His idealistic and mystical notions that each race has its own, more or less, "vividly conceived ideals of life," that the "Pharaohs, Caesars, Toussaints and Napoleons of history" were but "epitomized expressions" of their races, and that each race has some specific mission or message serves to tie the bonds of "racial" identity to the point of suffocation.

It is important to note that Du Bois's understanding of race changed, despite Appiah's arguments to the contrary, throughout his life. As time went on, Du Bois's conception became more sociohistorical as he shed the idealism and racial science that marked "The Conservation of Races."[38] Appiah, after recent debates, has also changed his position. In his "Race, Culture, Identity: Misunderstood Connections," Appiah has moved away from a monist notion of race toward one that recognizes its social construction. He has been influenced by Ian Hacking's brand of pluralist metaphysics and his use of "dynamic nominalism" to account for the metaphysical status of social categories. This shift has also changed, somewhat, Appiah's reading of Du Bois.[39] All the same, Appiah, and the other philosophers of race who have similar racial nominalist or racial skeptic inclinations, favor a politic of race that owes its allegiance to Douglass.[40]

Douglass's assimilationist and amalgamationist vision of a world without race, however, has problems that must be attended to. His program is predicated on the positive valuation of European culture and Western progress, and although Douglass does not negatively value people of color, his program devalues their place in society and values the eradication of difference. Furthermore, it is not clear how democratic, equal, and extensive is his program of assimilation and amalgamation. From what we know of the history of American racial politics after the Civil War and Reconstruction, it is evident that the policies of assimilation and amalgamation would have resulted, as Du Bois said, in "self-obliteration" without delivering to this "intermediate race" the promise of human brotherhood. As can be seen in the racial politics of nations such as Brazil and South Africa, where intermediate races are recognized, amalgamation and mixture do not necessarily bring an end to race or to racial oppression.

The respective positions of Douglass and Du Bois are landmarks in the philosophy of race. In theorizing race, and criticizing the hegemonic racial politics of the United States and throughout the world, their legacies must be engaged.

Notes

1. The title of this chapter was inspired by Wilson Jeremiah Moses's reference to W. E. B. Du Bois's *The Souls of Black Folk* in the German in his "Culture, Civilization, and Decline of the West: The Afrocentrism of W. E. B. Du Bois," in Bernard Bell, Emily Grosholz, and James Stewart, eds., *W. E. B. Du Bois on Race and Culture* (New York: Routledge, 1996), p. 246.

2. For a detailed discussion of Enlightenment ideology among nineteenth-century black intellectuals, see the first chapter of Wilson Jeremiah Moses, *The Golden Age of Black Nationalism, 1850-1925* (Hamden: Archon Books, 1978). Henceforth GA.

3. Frederick Douglass, "What to the Slave Is the Fourth of July?" in *The Frederick Douglass Papers*, Series 1, vol. 2, ed. John W. Blassingame (New Haven, Conn.: Yale University Press, 1982 [1852]), p. 387. Henceforth WSFJ.

4. The psalm reads, "Princes shall come out of Egypt; Ethiopia shall soon stretch out her hands unto God." This verse was a centerpiece of "Ethiopianism" in Africa and throughout the African diaspora. See chapters 1 and 8 of GA for a discussion of Ethiopianism and its incarnation in the works of American black intellectuals. Douglass, as a believer in human brotherhood, rejected the racialist mysticism of Ethiopianism.For Douglass, this verse signified Africa's uplift, its coming role as a part of Western civilization. For others, such as Crummell or Du Bois, it had a racial message.

5. Frederick Douglass, "The Claims of the Negro Ethnologically Considered [1854]," in Howard Brotz, ed., *African-American Social and Political Thought, 1850-1920* (New York: Transaction Publishers, 1995), p. 231. Henceforth CN.

6. Douglass's "The Claims of the Negro Ethnologically Considered" is the best source for his position on race. See also his "The Future of the Negro," "The Future of the Colored Race," and "God Almighty Made But One Race," in *The Frederick Douglass Papers*, Series 1, vol. 5, ed. John W. Blassingame and John R. McKivigan (New Haven, Conn.: Yale University Press, 1995 [1884b]). See his "An Address to the Colored People of the United States [1848]," in Brotz, *African-*

American, pp. 208–213, for his arguments against the "Hammite" stories of the origins of non-whites. See his "Prejudice Not Natural," in Brotz, *African-American,* pp. 213–215, for his arguments against the position that racism is a biological fact.

7. Douglass, "The Present and Future of the Colored Race in America," in Brotz, *African-American,* p. 268.

8. Douglass, "God Almighty Made But One Race," p. 147. Douglass is equivocating with his use of race. Seemingly, he means by his first two and last uses of "race" something like species, if it is going to be consistent with his third use of race. I would argue that this equivocation was due to his intellectual struggle with race. He devoutly believed in human brotherhood, but the existence of race, which he felt that the evidence would not let him deny, was a stumbling block to the realization of that brotherhood. Thus, he begrudgingly accepted the "technical" divisions of race, all the while diminishing it in the "light" of human brotherhood. For Douglass, racial divisions existed, but in the big, divine picture they did not.

9. Douglass, "The Folly of Racially Exclusive Organizations," in *The Frederick Douglass Papers,* Series 1, vol. 2, pp. 109–111.

10. Douglass, "African Civilization Society" and "The Folly of Colonization," in Brotz, *African-American,* pp. 262–266 and pp. 328–331, respectively.

11. See Douglass's "What Are the Colored People," in Brotz, *African-American,* pp. 203–208, "An Address to the Colored People," and "The Union of the Oppressed for the Sake of Freedom," in *the Life and Writings of Frederick Douglass: Early Years, 1817–1849,* ed. Philip S. Foner (New York: International Publishers, 1950), pp. 399–401. Douglass's support of, and participation in, the Negro convention movement of the middle and late nineteenth century underscores this point.

12. Douglass, "An Address to the Colored People," p. 211. Henceforth ACP.

13. See Douglass's essays in Brotz, *African-American*: "The Present and Future of the Colored Race in America," pp. 268–271; "The Future of the Negro," pp. 307–308; "The Future of the Colored Race," pp. 309–310; and "The Nation's Problem," pp. 316–320. The severity of Douglass's assimilationism in his "The Nation's Problem" is amazing. To the argument that in black unity is strength, Douglass replied, "My position is the reverse of all this. I hold that our union is our weakness" (p. 319). In the paragraphs following that statement he advocates the dispersal of blacks among whites and the complete folding of black interests, identity, and activities into white society.

14. Benjamin Franklin, in his 1751 *Observations Concerning the Increase of Mankind,* ruminated about the future of whites and advocated for the exclusion of "blacks and tawneys." The nature of race and its conservation were discussed by nineteenth-century black intellectuals such as Edward W. Blyden, Alexander Crummell, Martin R. Delany, Frederick Douglass, and Henry Highland Garnet. See GA.

15. For the relationship between Crummell and Du Bois, see David Levering Lewis, *W. E. B. Du Bois: Biography of a Race, 1868–1919* (New York: Henry Holt and Company, 1993), henceforth BR, and Wilson Moses, "W. E. B. Du Bois's 'The

Conservation of Races' and Its Context: Idealism, Conservatism and Hero Worship," *The Massachusetts Review* (Summer 1993): 275–294, henceforth DCR.

16. Du Bois's contact with pragmatism occurred during his graduate studies at Harvard. In 1888, after earning a B.A. from Fisk University, Du Bois entered Harvard, where he received his M.A. in 1891 and his Ph.D. in 1895. He was the first African American to earn a Ph.D. from Harvard, where he studied, among other things, philosophy. He received instruction from William James, Josiah Royce, and George Santayana, and he developed a friendship with James that extended far beyond his years as a Harvard graduate student. See chapter 5 of BR.

17. W. E. B. Du Bois, "The Conservation of Races [1897]," in Brotz, *African-American*, p. 487. Henceforth CR.

18. See Lucius Outlaw, "Against the Grain of Modernity: The Politics of Difference and the Conservation of Race," in his *On Race and Philosophy* (New York: Routledge, 1996), pp. 135–158. Outlaw gives a political interpretation of Du Bois's notion of individual contributions of the races. According to him, Du Bois's notion of a "Negro message" was simply the political result of black American organization and community building. For Outlaw, this interpretation is key because he wishes to cast Du Bois as a liberal. His interpretation, however, ignores the authoritarian, illiberal, and civilizationist currents in Du Bois's "Conservation." At the time of "Conservation," Du Bois's thoughts on the contributions of the races were less than democratic. For more on Du Bois's illiberal tendencies, see William E Cain, "From Liberalism to Communism: The Political Thought of W. E. B. Du Bois," in Amy Kaplan and Donald E. Pease, eds., *Cultures of United States Imperialism* (Durham, N.C.: Duke University Press, 1993), pp. 456–473.

19. Bernard Boxill, "Du Bois on Cultural Pluralism," in Bell et al., *W. E. B. Du Bois on Race and Culture*, pp. 57–86. Henceforth DCP.

20. John Stuart Mill, *On Liberty* (Indianapolis: Hackett, 1978), p. 54.

21. Schleiermacher stated, "Every nation is destined through its peculiar organization and its place in the world to represent a certain side of the divine image . . . for it is God alone who directly assigns to each nationality its definite task on earth and inspires it with a definite spirit in order to glorify himself through each one in a peculiar manner" (as cited in GA 49). Lewis (BR 171) agrees with the Schleiermacher link. Herder, in his *Ideen zur Philosophie der Geschichte der Mensheit* (*Reflections on the Philosophy of the History of Mankind*, trans. Frank E. Manuel [Chicago: University of Chicago Press, 1968]; henceforth IPGM), states, "Nations modify themselves, according to time, place, and their internal character: each bears in itself the standard of its perfection, totally independent of all comparison with that of others. Now the more pure and fine the maximum on which a people hit, the more useful the objects to which it applied the exertions of its nobler powers, and lastly, the more firm and exact the bond of union, which most intimately connected all the members of the state, and guided them to this good end; the more stable was the nation itself, and the more brilliant the figure it made in history. The course that we have hitherto taken through certain nations shows how different, according to place, time, and circumstances, was the object for which they strove. With the Chinese it was refined political morality; with the

Hindoos, a kind of retired purity, quiet assiduity in labour, and endurance; with the Phoenicians, the spirit of navigation, and commercial industry. The culture of the Greeks, particularly at Athens, proceeded on the maximum of sensible beauty, both in arts and manners, in science and in political institutions. In Sparta, and in Rome, men emulated the virtues of the patriot and hero; in each, however, in a very different mode" (pp. 98–99). Du Bois encountered historical idealism from various sources, but the two most influential sources were the works of the early black nationalists and his studies in Germany.

22. Wilson Jeremiah Moses, *Alexander Crummell: A Study of Civilization and Discontent* (New York: Oxford University Press, 1989). See also DCR.

23. See BR for Du Bois's exposure to Carlyle (pp. 74–78; 115–116), to Bismarck (pp. 77–78), and to Goethe (p. 139), and for his time at the University of Berlin (pp. 130–149). See also Francis L. Broderick's "German Influence on the Scholarship of W. E. B. Du Bois," *Phylon* 19, no. 4 (1958): 367–371, and chapter 10 of Du Bois, *The Autobiography of W. E. B. Du Bois: A Soliloquy on Viewing My Life from the Last Decade of Its First Century* (New York: International Publishers, 1968; henceforth AD) for his discussion of his time in Berlin and his impressions of Treitschke; see chapter 8 for his impressions of Bismarck.

24. These "races" are the divisions of peoples that some nineteenth-century historians recognized as distinct peoples. They are clearly arbitrary, but to nineteenth-century historians they were the divisions that displayed distinct and clashing folk spirits. In the work of some social theorists, such as Humboldt, Hegel, Herder, Thomas Arnold, Matthew Arnold, Carlyle, Emerson, and Robert Knox, this historical notion of races was conflated with the biological notion of races. Thus, in the works of the Arnolds, Knox, and Emerson, for example, there are discussions of the physical mixing and degeneration of these historical/biological races. See chapters 7 through 9 of Ivan Hannaford, *Race: The History of an Idea in the West* (Washington, D.C.: The Woodrow Wilson Center Press, 1996).

25. G. W. F. Hegel. *Vorlesungen über die Philosophie der Weltgeschichte,* vol. 1 (Hamburg: Verlag Von Felix Meiner, 1996), p. 187; henceforth VPW; trans. H. B. Nisbet, *Lectures on the Philosophy of World History* (Cambridge: Cambridge University Press, 1975), p. 152, henceforth PWH.

26. W. E. B. Du Bois, *The Souls of Black Folk* (New York: Bedford Books, 1997 [1903]), p. 9. Henceforth SBF.

27. Ralph Waldo Emerson, in his essay "Fate" (in *The Conduct of Life and Natural History of Intellect and Other Papers* [New York: Houghton Mifflin Company, 1929]), makes a similar point: "The secret of the world is the tie between person and event. Person makes event, and event person. The 'times,' 'the age,' what is that but a few profound persons and a few active persons who epitomize the times?" (p. 39).

28. Alexander Crummell, "The Race Problem in America [1888]," in Brotz, *African-American*, pp. 184–185.

29. Bernard Boxill argues in "Du Bois on Cultural Pluralism" that Du Bois's conception of "race" is Jamesian (DCP 58).

30. An element of Du Bois's political reason for the conservation of race involved the maintenance of dignity, of self-respect, in the face of disdain and rejection.

See his comments, in his *Autobiography,* about his social separation from whites while at Harvard (AD 132–39).

31. Robert Gooding-Williams makes this point in his "Outlaw, Appiah, and Du Bois's 'The Conservation of Races,'" in Bell et al., *W. E. B. Du Bois on Race and Culture,* p. 49.

32. Du Bois's sociohistorical definition provides another link with German historical idealism. Du Bois's conception of race is similar, for both its dependence on sociohistorical indicators and its vagueness, to Herder's conception of *Volk.* According to Manuel, in his introduction to his translation of IPGM, "Herder's use of the term *Volk* is characteristically loose. It embraces the chosen people of Israel, the Greeks, the Egyptians, the Romans, the Germans, as well as tiny tribes of American Indians and Negroes in the African bush. A *Volk* is virtually any group that has a name and a culture. If there is a mythology, a folk poetry, a separate religion, a cuisine, a recognizably different pattern of sense perceptions, the *Volk* is identifiable" (IPGM xvii). Of course, Du Bois differs from Herder since he sees the people of Africa and of its diaspora as one, although, following Herder, he recognized a plurality of divisions among European and Asian peoples. Herder is a difficult figure in the history of the idea of "race." He denied the formal existence of the "races"—which he understood as the idea that groups of humanity were subspecies and had separate and distinct origins. However, he used a climatist notion of race to explain human diversity.

33. At one point Du Bois seems to suggest that the physical differences are ultimately the result of the social ones: "The whole process which has brought about these race differentiations has been a growth, and the great characteristic of this has been the differentiation of spiritual and mental differences between great races of mankind and the *integration* of physical differences" (CR 486).

34. K. Anthony Appiah, "The Uncompleted Argument: Du Bois and the Illusion of Race," in Henry Louis Gates Jr., ed., *"Race," Writing and Difference* (Chicago: University of Chicago Press, 1986) p. 34. Henceforth UA.

35. This interpretation is Michael Root's. See his discussion of Du Bois in chapter 8 of his forthcoming *How to Divide the World.*

36. The metaphysical pluralism I have in mind here is the kind defended by Root, "How We Divide the World," *Philosophy of Science* 67 (2000): 628–639; Ian Hacking, *The Social Construction of What?* (Cambridge, Mass.: Harvard University Press, 1999); and Ronald R. Sundstrom, "Race as a Human Kind," *Philosophy and Social Criticism* 28, no. 1 (2000): 93–117.

37. John Dupré, "Natural Kinds and Biological Taxa," *Philosophical Review* 90 (1981): 82–83. See also Philip Kitcher, "Species," *Philosophy of Science* 51 (1984): 309–333.

38. Appiah failed to see how Du Bois's understanding of race evolved because of his own commitment to a metaphysical monist framework. For Appiah, no matter how much Du Bois stressed the social, Du Bois's continuing use of the term "race" meant that he needed to continually rely, as an impossible referent, on the biological conception of race. For a discussion of how Du Bois's understanding of race evolved from his conception given in "The Conservation," see BR 173–174. Du Bois's growing commitment to a purely social conception of race is displayed

in the first chapter of his *The Souls of Black Folk*, and in the postscript, credo, and chapters 1 and 2 of *Darkwater*. In his *Dusk of Dawn*, a further commitment is seen in chapters 5 through 7, and from the postlude of his *Autobiography* comes one of his most powerful and moving statements about the social nature of race: "And then—the Veil, the Veil of color. It drops as drops the night on southern seas—vast, sudden, unanswering. There is Hate behind it, and Cruelty and Tears. As one peers through its intricate, unfathomable pattern of ancient, old, old design, one sees blood and guilt and misunderstanding. And yet it hangs there, this Veil, between then and now, between Pale and Colored and Black and White— between You and Me. *Surely it is but a thought-thing*, tenuous, intangible; yet just as surely is it true and terrible and not in our little day may you and I lift it. We may feverishly unravel its edges and even climb slow with giant shears to where its ringed and gilded top nestles close to the throne of Eternity. But as we work and climb we shall see through streaming eyes and hear with aching ears, lynching and murder, cheating and despising, degrading and lying, so flashed and flashed through this vast hanging darkness that the Doer never sees the Deed and the Victim knows not the Victor and Each hate All in wild and bitter ignorance" (AD 412).

39. A. Appiah, "Race, Culture, Identity," in A. Appiah and A. Gutman, eds., *Color Conscious* (Princeton, N.J.: Princeton University Press, 1996), pp. 30–105.

40. Ronald R. Sundstrom. "Racial Nominalism," *Journal of Social Philosophy* 33, no. 2 (2002): 193–210.

Four

On the Use and Abuse of Race in Philosophy
Nietzsche, Jews, and Race

Jacqueline Scott

In terms of race, Nietzsche is popularly dismissed as an anti-Semite. His views on race have either been used to reject his writings altogether or been ruled ancillary to the rest of his writings. As a result, little has been written on his concept of race and its role in his writings in general. I will investigate Nietzsche's use of race by looking at the way he contended with "the Jewish Question"—*the* race issue of his time. I will avoid evaluating either Nietzsche personally or his project as to whether he or it was anti-Semitic or racist.[1] Instead, my goal is to ascertain the role that race played in his philosophical projects. I will show that just as Nietzsche battled with the problem of decadence, he also battled with the problem that race (and in particular Jews) played in his call for cultural revitalization. As I have argued elsewhere, Nietzsche's positive philosophy can be characterized as attempts to treat himself and his culture for the disease of decadence, and in this paper I will further argue that his battles with the prevailing uses of "race" are an example of these attempted treatments.[2] There is a distinction between Nietzsche's public and private writings on Jews. In the public writings (those published in his lifetime), one witnesses his attempts to be diplomatic and to distinguish himself from the anti-Semitism of his time. In his private writings (his letters and unpublished notebooks), he is less diplomatic and his attacks are often *ad hominem*. Because my concern here is to analyze the role that Nietzsche assigned to Jews and race in his philosophical projects (as opposed to judging the extent of his racism and anti-Semitism), I will focus on references to them in his published works.

In the end, I will show that Nietzsche's theories of race, and his attempt to revalue the prevailing concept of it, are a telling example of his positive treatments for the ills of his culture. In other words, race and decadence are closely connected in Nietzsche's published works. Because decadence is integral to both his critical and his positive writings as a cultural physician, his concept of race must be taken seriously.

The Disease of Decadence

The organizing principle of Nietzsche's positive philosophy in the late works (those after *Thus Spoke Zarathustra*) is the problem of decadence. Nietzsche took up the "problem of decadence" with renewed vigor in the late works, especially in relation to the political aspects of his positive philosophy.[3] He viewed decadence as an organic, physiological disorder in which the "invisible, instinctual body" (in contrast to the physical body) is decaying due to an inability to organize properly the drives and impulses that are imposed on the individual human being by the outside culture.[4]

This decay of the instincts becomes manifest in the performance of our most human task: that of creating what I call rationales for existence—the values we create that lend meaning to our initially meaningless lives.[5] We create moralities (systems of values) so as to avoid the suicide-inspiring state of nihilism.[6] It is here that decadence becomes a problem: we have to create meaning in life, but any meaning that we create will eventually prove ineffective and will decay. The meaning that we create acts as an organizing principle and a catalyst for action. It gives us a reason to get out of bed in the morning, confront the myriad of life's daily challenges, and strive for a "better" life (as determined by the values derived from the meaning attributed to life). This meaning is created by or for a particular person in a specific time and place. As times, places, and the person change, the meaning will be less effective (will decay), and the individual will have to modify it or face nihilism.

This is the paradox of decadence. It then involves the decay of the values that we impose on existence to the point that we can no longer affirm our lives, and we begin the slide toward nihilism.[7] Because we cannot live in a state in which there are no values, the question posed by decadence is how we are to come to terms with the initial meaninglessness of life and the fact that any values that we create will decline. Traditionally, philosophers have responded by denying the meaninglessness of life, claiming to have "discovered" the Truth of it, and the objective, universal values based on this Truth. They have therefore denied the fact that their values would decay.

Nietzsche's positive philosophy, then, can be understood as an attempt to contend with the inevitable decline of meaning and values in life and with the inescapable fact that one who creates values is a decadent.[8] For Nietzsche, contending with decadence involves, first, recognizing the fact that, as a philosopher and moralist, one cannot "elude decadence" by making "war" on it. The only way to learn to affirm life again is by altering one's expression of decadence by still creating rationales for existence, but in a way that avoids the prime pitfalls of decadence. "It is a self-deception on the part of philosophers and moralists to imagine that by making war on *décadence* they therewith elude *décadence* themselves. This is beyond their powers: what they select as an expedient, as a deliverance is itself only another expression of *décadence* —they *alter* its expression, they do not abolish the thing itself" (TI "Socrates" 11). In passing through phases during which he was a weak type, Nietzsche fell victim to these pitfalls, but he claimed that he later managed to overcome these phases of weakness, learned from them, and was even grateful for them.[9] This is Nietzsche's concept of self-overcoming; it entails overcoming weak forces both within and outside of oneself.

As self-designated cultural physicians, Socrates, Wagner, Nietzsche, and the ascetic priest all assumed the task of treating the decadence of their respective cultures. The differences in their remedies are telling in that they reveal each cultural physician's view of decadence *as well as* the extent to which he suffered from the disease. In general, there are two categorizes of remedies: antidotes and cures. The problem with the second category for Nietzsche is that there can be no cure for decadence— for either an individual or a culture.[10] Decadence (the inevitable decay of values) is an inextricable part of the human condition, and to attempt to remove or avoid it is to deny a key fact of life and to fail to fulfill the human task of continually creating rationales for existence. This is why Nietzsche always associated nihilism— the lack of rationales for existence—with suicide. It is a state of being that human beings are unable to maintain. His self-appointed task was to find a healthier way of contending with the disease of decadence. He accepted the fact that there is no cure for it.

In the late works Nietzsche attempted to distinguish himself from traditional approaches to the problem of decadence by making an implicit distinction between strong and weak decadents.[11] he did not explicitly make such a distinction, but he implicitly used it as a criterion in his evaluation both of himself and of others who grappled with decadence.[12] Strong decadents are able to contend with decadence by changing the value they place on it.[13] As opposed to denying the fact that all values are subjectively created, and will eventually decay, the strong decadent celebrates these facts.

Nietzsche's contention was that we must move away from attempting to discover Truth and instead should try to create values that do not deny their subjectivity. These values would celebrate and affirm the life of the individual and others like him or her, and their purpose would be the enhancement of the creator (a celebration of his or her flourishing) and, by extension, of the species. In turn, cultures are evaluated based on the strong types they are able to produce (A 3).[14] The type who creates such values is a strong decadent because he or she is creating values in the face of the meaninglessness of life, and is therefore a decadent, but this individual is considered "strong" in that he or she acknowledges this decadence and affirms it as part of life. Strong decadents, like their weak decadent counterparts, are afflicted with the disease of decadence but, unlike these counterparts, are not debilitated by it. I want to argue that while Nietzsche did admit to the fact that one cannot "elude" decadence, there are differences as to how one might respond to this inevitability (TI "Socrates" 11). For Nietzsche, the goal of civilization is the creation of a "more valuable type" who, in turn, would create the life-affirming values that would help the community to flourish (A 3). One of the primary effects of weak decadent morality had been that this more valuable type was not being bred and had in fact been vilified. Nietzsche's response was that one should question the values that led to the breeding and survival of a large group of mediocre types.[15] The primary way that he suggested instituting this treatment of revaluing values was to persuade his readers that the prevailing values were ones that led not to flourishing but instead to nihilism, and then to convince "all the sciences" (e.g., linguistics, physiology, medicine, and philosophy) to determine new values and, based on the connection that he had made between values and human types, new types of people.

Nietzsche on Jews and Judaism

Nietzsche wrote during a fertile time in the history of the concept of "race." Beginning in the century before, the modern concept of race had come to prominence with the writings of Arthur de Gobineau, Ernst Renan, and Kant.[16] With them, race became accepted as a biological term that also had implications for anthropology, psychology, physiology, and philosophy.[17] Since he cited nationalism as a pernicious example of the chief problem of his time, and since this nationalism emerged in large part from a new understanding of the Jewish problem as a racial problem, his criticisms and proposed solutions to the problems of his time are intimately connected to issues of race. While he did not frame the issue *primarily* in terms of race, he did write about race, the role that races play in cultural development, and even specifically the roles that Jews, as a race, have played and continue to play in European cultural development.

Before I can fully substantiate this claim about Nietzsche and race, I need to make a slight digression. In this section, I analyze how Nietzsche contended with the turbulent race issues of his time by examining the way in which he wrote about Jews and the role that they played in his critical and positive philosophy. Since he did not systematically write about race in the published works, in order to establish the fullest possible picture of his theories of race, I will generalize from his writings about Jews as a race, and then connect those ideas to his general comments about race.[18] My claim in this section is that Nietzsche's writings about Jews and Judaism provide an excellent case study for his theories of race, culture, and cultural health. I do not want to overstate the case in claiming that his views on Jews are integral to understanding his philosophical thought.[19] In studying Nietzsche on Jews and Judaism, one does not learn much about Judaism or actual Jews; instead, one gets an insight into Nietzsche's own philosophical battle with the prevailing ideas of his time about race and its relationship to the culture.

While Nietzsche praised Jews, he also was critical of them. There has been much scholarship on his seemingly ambivalent view of Jews, and the best of it aims at parsing out this ambivalence by understanding that he divided the Jews into three historical groups and evaluated each group differently.[20] In *The Antichrist*, he briefly traces the history of the Jews and divides it into five stages: 1) the Kingdom ("the *great* epoch"), 2) anarchy, 3) the rise of the priests, 4) the altering of Jewish morality by the Jewish priests and making it the antithesis of life, and 5) the rise of Christianity from the "soil" created by the priests (A 25–27). It is from these five stages that he derived three types of Jews. I want to use this tripartite division to create a portrait of how he wrote about Jews as a race and to describe the historical role that he assigned to them. The first group of Jews he wrote about, which I will label Old Testament Jews, comprises pre-eighth-century Jews. The second group is the Priestly Jews, which refers to those Jews who instituted rabbinic Judaism (eighth century to Nietzsche's contemporaries). These are the historical Jews who came about during the time of the Second Temple, and who, after its destruction, reconstituted Judaism to fit the needs of Jews in the diaspora. The third group is the Contemporary Jews of Nietzsche's time.[21]

Nietzsche was most complimentary about the Old Testament Jews, in large part because they were similar to his beloved ancient Greeks.[22] Like the Greeks, the Old Testament Jews were representatives of a superior race because they were a mixture of races. In the case of Greeks, it was a mixture of Mongolians, Semites, and Thracians, and it was only by organizing this "chaos" of foreign cultures that the Greeks were able to become a pure race. In Nietzsche's theory of race, there are no naturally pure races. It is only by carefully harnessing the energies of various peoples that a race, like the Greeks, can become pure—meaning "stronger and more beautiful" (D 272).[23]

Nietzsche also praised Old Testament Jews because of their relationship to God. Like the Greeks, whose gods reflected human, all-too-human characteristics, the "angry holy Jehovah" of the Jews was modeled on the "angry holy [Jewish] prophets" (D 38). For Nietzsche, such a depiction of a people's deities demonstrated that their religion was natural, and therefore healthier. In fact, he saw in the Jewish conception of God an expression of the will to power. Their God was a type of worthy opponent against whom they wrestled to bring out the best in themselves (A 16). He also claimed that Old Testament Jews contributed the Old Testament, which he described as a "book of divine justice" and the "mightiest book" rivaling Greek and Italian literature (HH I 475; BGE 52). He called it a sin to partner the Old Testament with the far inferior New Testament (BGE 52).

While Nietzsche had many positive things to say about the culture and characteristics of Old Testament Jews, he was critical of many aspects of the content of their religion. They lacked the Greek sense of sin—namely, that

sacrilege could be noble and thus tragic.[24] He also was critical of Jewish mono-
theism because it lacked a sense of individuation, and thus led to stagnation—
unlike Greek polytheism, which prevented it (GS 143).

Another positive similarity between the Greeks and Old Testament Jews
was that both were forced to contend with a cultural deterioration brought
about by an internal crisis. Unlike the Greeks, because of their instinct for
preservation, the Jews avoided the consequences of the weakest decadence (as
exemplified by Socrates) (A 24; TI "Socrates" 2, 11).[25] The deterioration of
this instinct for preservation characterizes the next group of Jews. In short,
Nietzsche deemed Old Testament Jews "a people" (GM III 22). He liked
those aspects of Old Testament Jews that were closest to his ancient Greeks:
their attitude toward life, which was vital, natural, this-worldly, and self-
affirming.[26]

Nietzsche's Priestly Jews came to dominance in response to a cultural crisis. During the time of the Assyrians there was internal disorder, and the
strongest types in Judaism decided that the traditional concept of God no
longer provided adequate meaning in life and so they carried out a revaluation
of values (A 25). Self-preservation became the goal, and life took on a "novel
and dangerous attraction" that lasted for two thousand years (BGE 195). In
order to preserve Jewish culture, these strong types altered the meaning of
"natural causality" into an "anti-natural causality": one was to blame for all
events in one's life; all events could now be explained in religious terms (A
25). These strong types, "the priestly agitators," turned Judaism into an
"anti-natural" religion, and made their role in it "*everywhere indispensable*" (A
26). According to Daniel Ahern's understanding of the account, Nietzsche's
claim was that unlike the Greeks, the Jews were never dominated by their
weakest types because the Jewish priests had established a hierarchy by creating a pathos of distance between the priests and the weak types.[27] The priests
might be understood as strong types because they acted as cultural physicians,
they created new values, and they understood and maintained the pathos of
distance. In short, they were willing to give up the naturalness of their religion for the survival of their people. These priests were not unlike Nietzsche's
Socrates, who "falsified" ancient Greek values in hopes of saving a declining
culture, but the distinguishing feature between the two, by Nietzsche's account, is that the priests voluntarily gave into decadent instincts without believing in them, and used them as a means to an end (TI "Socrates" 9).

> Considered psychologically, the Jewish nation is a nation of the toughest vital
> energy which, placed in impossible circumstances, voluntarily, from the pro-
> foundest shrewdness in self-preservation, took the side of all *décadence* instincts
> —not as being dominated by them but because it divined in them a power by
> means of which one can prevail *against* "the world." The Jews are counterparts
> of *décadents*: they have been compelled to *act* as *décadents* to the point of illu-
> sion, they have known, with a *non plus ultra* of histrionic genius, how to place
> themselves as the head of all *décadence* movements . . . so as to make of them

something stronger than any party *affirmative* to life. For the kind of man who desires to attain power through Judaism and Christianity, the *priestly* kind, *décadence* is only a *means:* this kind of man has a life-interest in making mankind *sick* and in inverting the concepts "good" and "evil," "true" and "false" in a mortally dangerous and world-calumniating sense. (A 24)

They introduced decadent instincts to preserve their culture without becoming "dominated" by them. They used decadence as an illusion in which they never fully believed, and this is why Jews maintained their tough "vital energy."

While these Jewish priests might have preserved their own culture, a subgroup of priests (headed by Saul/Paul) became infected with decadence, took revenge on "ruling Judaism," repudiated the laws of the main group, and created an outgrowth of Judaism that had brought about the decline of nineteenth-century European culture—Christianity: "For precisely this reason the Jews are the most *fateful* nation in world-history: their after-effect has falsified mankind to such an extent that today the Christian is able to feel anti-Jewish without realizing he is the *ultimate consequence of the Jews*" (A 24).[28]

Nietzsche's assessment of Priestly Jews, then, is decidedly ambivalent. While they were strong, noble types who resisted the most heinous effects of decadence while still using it successfully to preserve their culture, they also laid the foundation for a virulent form of decadence in the form of Christian values. For Nietzsche, then, Priestly Jews were closely tied to Christianity, and this view ran directly counter to the prevailing views of his anti-Semitic contemporaries: "Wagner is Schopenhauerian, for example, in his hatred of the Jews to whom he is not able to do justice even when it comes to their greatest deed; after all, the Jews are the inventors of Christianity" (GS 99).[29] Anti-Semites were attempting to depict Jews and Judaism as aberrant because of their differences from the Aryan Christian norm, and Nietzsche claimed that that which was most damning about Christianity was precisely its inheritance from a Jewish source (Paul), and its further sullying of this inheritance.

While Nietzsche reserved most of his venomous criticism for Priestly Jews, in the published works, his discussions of Contemporary Jews was on the whole positive. For him, Contemporary Jews were distinct from Priestly Jews in that they were inheritors of the Judaism created by the strong priests but unclouded by Paul's *ressentiment.* These Jews had managed to maintain their purity by refusing to be assimilated by lesser cultures and by using negative external forces to consolidate themselves into "the strongest, toughest, and purest race now living in Europe" *(*BGE 251). Similar to characters in Greek tragedy, Contemporary Jews contended with suffering and were still able to affirm life. Nietzsche also contended that Jews had a "grand style in morality," were logical, had "cleanlier intellectual habits" than Germans, and had enviable customs regarding honoring parents and children as well as marriage (GS 348; D 205). It is because of these "racial" characteristics that he contended that Jews were necessary for the healthy revitalization of European culture (D 205; BGE 251). In fact, he called for the breeding of Jews with European nobility in order to mix these positive Jewish characteristics with those of Europeans and thereby create a new, healthier European type (HAH I 475).[30] He wanted, then, for Jews to assimilate into European culture, and thus strengthen it, while also "select[ing]" out their less desirable traits (e.g. usury, "the romanticism and sublimity of moral questionabilities" [BGE 250–251]).[31] Contemporary Jews, according to Nietzsche, were the descendants of the Old Testament Jews and not the Christian Jews, and so they represented the European hope for a revival of the best of ancient Greek culture. He accepted the stereotypical anti-Semitic "racial" traits of Jews, but then assigned a high value to these traits and proclaimed them as indispensable in the breeding of a healthier European race.

In taking a broad view of Nietzsche's three categories of Jews and, in particular, his revaluation of them, I read Nietzsche as carrying out a revaluation of the term *Verjudung*. Anti-Semitic nationalists had charged Jews with attempting to "Judaize" Europe, and they called for a flourishing of Aryan German culture to thwart this supposed Jewish conspiracy. Nietzsche was trying to take this claim and turn it on its head: it was the Christians who were "Judaizing" Europe, and in fact, they were using the wrong Jews (GS 135).[32] As opposed to drawing inspiration from the vigorous Old Testament Jews or even the hardy Contemporary Jews, the Christian nationalists focused on the morality of the Priestly Jews who had brought about the birth of Christianity. In his attempts to "revalue" the term *Verjudung*, Nietzsche placed a higher value on the very Jews whom the nationalists reviled—namely, Old Testament Jews and Contemporary Jews.[33] In addition, as we shall soon see, he wrote about *Verjudung* not only as a positive event, but as one on which the very health of European culture depended.

Nietzsche on Race

What, then, did Nietzsche mean with his idiosyncratic view of Jews and Judaism? One may dismiss it as having little philosophical importance and being of interest solely to those who wanted to evaluate Nietzsche's anti- or philo-Semitism. I want to argue that because his discussion of Jews in the published works was accompanied by (often in the same section of text) a theory of race, his views of Jews and Judaism not only have philosophical significance in general, but are also important in getting a full picture of his criticisms of, and proposed solutions for, the European culture of his time.

First, a disclaimer: Nietzsche did not present a fully comprehensive theory of race in his books, and the racial theory that is there is not indispensable for understanding him. It does serve to highlight his theories about cultures:

their evolution, their health, and the treatment for unhealthy cultures. He was influenced by the theories of de Gobineau, Renan, and Paul de Lagarde, and as a result the philosophical health of individuals and culture was not just a metaphor for him.[34] For Nietzsche, cultures are evaluated based on the people they produce, and they also evolve as the people that characterize them evolve. In short, cultures are organic and have a physiological component to them. The physiological constitution of human beings affects the character of a culture, and once established the culture will in turn affect the groups of people or races that characterize it.

> Europe's *democratic* movement: behind all the moral and political foregrounds to which such formulas point, a tremendous *physiological* process is taking place and gaining momentum. The Europeans are becoming similar to each other; they become more and more detached from the conditions under which races originate that are tied to some climate or class. . . . The tempo of this process of the "*evolving European*" may be retarded by great relapses, but perhaps it will gain in vehemence and profundity and grow just on their account: the still raging storm and stress of "national feeling" belongs here, also that anarchism which is just now coming up. (BGE 242)

European culture, then, was undergoing a "physiological process" that caused Europeans to become similar because the cultural conditions that caused people to differentiate, to form races, had been removed. R. J. Hollingdale defined Nietzsche's notion of race as "a group of people who had to live together a long time and as a result had certain needs and certain characteristics in common."[35] Using this definition and the way in which race operates in the above quotation by Nietzsche, groups of people (nations) make races, and the characteristics that emerge from these races, when combined with the characteristics of other races, coalesce into cultures.[36] While the aim of cultures is stability, they evolve as the various races that constitute them vie for dominance. Races, then, can be understood as catalysts for cultural change. Democracy resisted that change by assigning a high value to similarities between its people and thus undercutting the growth of races. In Nietzsche's time a "national feeling" was trying to eliminate all races that were not Aryan, thus causing the culture to stagnate.

It was this stagnation which Nietzsche claimed was a primary symptom of the "sickness" of his culture (BGE 201–203, 242). This is the reason that he prescribed a fresh infusion of healthy races (e.g., Contemporary Jews) as a treatment. He, then, was agreeing with his contemporaries that their culture was physiologically ailing and that the introduction of healthier "blood" was required. The difference between them was the type of "blood" that each prescribed. This reading of Nietzsche is contentious because there are some who claim that he divorced his racial claims from any biological assumptions.[37] In part, they do this to remove the stain of anti-Semitism from him.

Others admit that there might be some links to biology, but that Nietzsche "rejects value difference linked to biology alone," and therefore he accepts race but rejects racism.[38]

On my reading, Nietzsche's race talk is a mixture of the biological and the sociological—one cannot be divorced from the other without ignoring many references. On the biological side, Nietzsche diagnosed the sickness of Europe as due to a sudden mixing of races that created a generation that "has inherited in its blood diverse standards and values" (BGE 208). He claimed that "the problem of race" was that each individual cannot help but inherit the "qualities and preferences of his parents and ancestors in his body" (BGE 264). Wayne Klein interprets both of these sections as referring to a "figurative," as opposed to "literal," transference of characteristics and values.[39] I agree that a strictly literal, biological reading of these passages is too simplistic, but understanding Nietzsche's references to "blood" and "body" only metaphorically would make the same error. He seems to be playing with his nationalistic counterparts' obsession with biological determinism.[40]

I want to propose that Nietzsche's use of biological terms was meant to refer to his physiological concern for the culture and the types (or races) of people that it produced, but it should not be understood as being *purely* biological. In his discussions of various races, it is clear that they are determined by psychological as well as physical traits and that the inheritance of these traits can be manipulated—both internally and externally. Both Klein and Sarah Kofman understand Nietzsche's races as being characterized by types of human beings as opposed to biological races—with the understanding that types are sociologically produced.[41] There is certainly a typological component in Nietzsche's race theory, but it does not override the biological. Returning to BGE 264, he further claims that though the "problem of race" damns the child with the "qualities and preferences" of the parents, biological inheritance can be fooled:

> If one knows something about the parents, an inference about the child is permissible: any disgusting incontinence, any nook envy, a clumsy insistence that one is always right—these three things together have always constituted the characteristic type of the plebian—that sort of thing must as surely be transferred to the child as corrupted blood; and with the aid of the best education one will at best *deceive* with regard to such heredity. (BGE 264)

Certain psychological traits may be inherited by way of "corrupted blood" and they constitute a type of person, but one can reduce the effects of the corrupted blood via deception. The deception does not change the physiological inheritance, but it does alter its effects such that one may develop a "second nature": "[W]e are the outcome of earlier generations . . . it is not possible wholly to free oneself from this chain. . . . The best we can do is to confront our inherited and hereditary nature with our knowledge of it, and through a new, stern discipline combat our inborn heritage and implant in ourselves a new habit, a new instinct, a second nature, so that our first withers away . . . always a dangerous attempt because . . . second natures are usually weaker than first" (UM II 3). Returning to Hollingdale's definition of Nietzsche's races, the common characteristics of a given race come about through a complex combination of heredity, conscious and unconscious adoption of characteristics, and external forces which affect the needs of the group—they are organic. Races, then, are created over time from both within and without, and Nietzsche's division of Jews into three distinct groups is an excellent example of this notion of race.

In Nietzsche's transition from the Old Testament Jews to the Priestly Jews, one sees his depiction of a race adopting a second nature. The Priestly Jews who saved their culture by making the priestly class the rulers instilled "the art of adaptability" in the Jews.

> As for the *Jews*, the people who possess the art of adaptability par excellence, this train of thought suggests immediately that one might see them virtually as a world-historical arrangement for the production of actors, a veritable breeding ground for actors. And it really is high time to ask: What good actor today is *not*—a Jew? The Jew as a born "man of letters," as the true master of European press, also exercises his power by virtue of his histrionic gifts; for the man of letters is essentially an actor: He plays the "expert," the "specialist." (GS 361)

Jews, then, developed the characteristics of the actor so as to adapt to the challenges of maintaining their culture while being forced into a life of continuous wandering. This artistic trait had become an instinct among Contemporary Jews. The Priestly Jews bred a particular type of Jew and brought about an organic change in the race (I will have more to say about breeding below). Perhaps it was this adoption of this second, weaker nature, which also caused Saul/Paul's sect to adopt such unhealthy characteristics: "Such human beings of late cultures and refracted lights will on the average be weaker human beings: their most profound desire is that the war [brought on by the indiscriminate mixing of races] they *are* should come to an end. Happiness appears to them, in agreement with a tranquilizing (for example, Epicurean or Christian) medicine and way of thought" (BGE 200).

Races, then, are a combination of physiological and psychological traits that are primarily inherited but can also be affected by the individual's will to deceive or by external forces. The prime catalyst for racial evolution, though, is race mixing, which is generally brought about by blood. This blood mixing can come about in two ways: discriminant and indiscriminant race mixing. Nietzsche referred to the first type as breeding or cultivation (*Züchtung*). As is the case with "blood," *Züchtung* is another word that was used by the nationalists in their attempts to render Germany an Aryan nation.[42] For Nietzsche, breeding is an aspect (*Fall*) of morality, and it had been used badly by Christianity.[43]

Züchtung plays an important role in defining who has the "right to philosophy." That right is determined at least in part by "one's origins; one's ancestors, one's blood," and several generations are required to ensure that the correct virtues have been "acquired, nurtured, inherited, and digested singly" (BGE 213). One can then see that cultivation (in both a biological and sociological sense) is intimately tied to morality and the philosopher. This cultivation involves not only a biological inheritance but also the instilling of virtues by way of education, religion, politics, and economics (BGE 61). It is not always conscious or voluntary. The creation of meaning in life (the creation of values or moralities) is undertaken for the sake of survival (at the worst) or flourishing (at the best), and in this way, this creation of values is part of the process of cultivation—of breeding (*Züchtung*)—particular human beings who will be able to hold off the suicidal nihilism by embodying this meaning (GM III 28). "Now look for once at an aristocratic commonwealth . . . as an arrangement, whether voluntary or involuntary, for breeding [*Züchtung*]: human beings are together there who are dependent on themselves and want their species to prevail, most often because they *have to* prevail or run the terrible risk of being exterminated" (BGE 262). In the best case, that of an aristocracy, the breeding is used to instill particular traits or virtues (e.g., hardness) into the people by forcing them to struggle against "unfavorable conditions." When those unfavorable conditions change, then the struggle for flourishing diminishes, and individuals emerge who, because of fear, try to breed a type who wants primarily to survive. With such "turning points in history," the mediocre majority comes to the fore and a type resembling them is bred.

Besides breeding, another way in which races mix and are created is through incidental contact (e.g., trade). In a well-known section in *Human, All-Too-Human*, Nietzsche claimed that the decline in isolated European nations and the resulting mixing of races was inevitable. Germany was so dominated by the morality of mediocre types that its goal was the artificial preservation of the Aryan type as opposed to an active breeding of new types. It was this desire for preservation that, according to Nietzsche, explained the rise in national hostilities whose goal was to encourage Germans to bond together and keep themselves from being "contaminated" by other races—particularly Jews. In response to this nationalism, Nietzsche called for the reader to "work for the amalgamation of nations" (HAH I 475). In particular, he called for the mixing of positive Jewish characteristics ("their energy and higher intelligence, their capital in will and spirit") with those of Europeans so as to breed a new mixed race—the Good European.[44]

> As soon as it is no longer a question of the conserving of nations but of the production of the strongest possible European mixed race, the Jew will be just as usable and desirable as an ingredient of it as any other national residue. . . . Christianity has done everything to orientalize the occident, Judaism has always played an essential part in occidentalizing it again: which in a certain sense

means making of Europe's mission and history a *continuation of the Greek*. (HAH I 475)

Nietzsche admitted that, like all races, Jews also had negative characteristics (those of the "youthful stock-exchange Jew" who is the "most repulsive invention of the entire human race"), but it was worth the risk of involving those qualities in the process of breeding because Jews held the key to a continuation of the "enlightenment of Graeco-Roman antiquity" (HAH I 475). In other words, if a creation of a modern strong European type to rival those of the ancient Greeks and Romans were possible, then a new type must be created by mixing races. The German nationalists who claimed to be breeding a strong, pure Aryan race by excluding Jews were actually merely preserving a mediocre type, calling for the elimination of a strong race, and were thus endangering the culture.[45]

In fact, in BGE 251, Nietzsche claimed that the primary motivation for German anti-Semitism was the weakness of German culture. The "physiology" of the German culture could not digest any more Jews. For this reason, he called for the mixing of German "blood" with that of Italians, French, and English because they had "stronger digestive systems." Only then could Europe digest the blood of the Jews, who were the "strongest, toughest, purest" race and who wanted to be "absorbed and assimilated by Europe."

> To that end it might be useful to and fair to expel the anti-Semitic screamers from the country. Accommodated with all caution, with selection; approximately as the English nobility does. It is obvious that the stronger and already more clearly defined types of the new Germanism can enter into relations with them. . . . It would be interesting in many ways to see whether the hereditary art of commanding and obeying . . . could not be enriched with the genius of money and patience (and above all a little spirituality, which is utterly lacking among these officers). But here it is proper to break off my cheerful Germanomania and holiday oratory; for I am beginning to touch on what is serious for me, the "European problem" as I understand it, the cultivation of a new caste that will rule Europe. (BGE 251)

Nietzsche was referring to the possibility of mating German officers with Jews so as to bring about a combination of the qualities which characterized each race: commanding/obeying and genius of money/patience. This was his suggested remedy for the European problem of cultivating a new ruling caste. This caste of mixed-race people who would aid in addressing the decline of values that was plaguing his contemporaries.[46]

One of the tasks of cultures or nations, then, is the cultivation of types of human beings who will create meaning in life that will, in turn, ensure its continuation and, hopefully, its flourishing. Nations, for Nietzsche, are not static entities; they are "*res facta*," something made: "something evolving, young, and easily changed." Eventually, a nation might take on "race" status if it can prove its strength through long endurance ("an *aere perennius*"—more enduring than bronze). This endurance is not attained by attempting to survive, but by a combination of hostile external forces and the attempt to flourish despite them. As demonstrated above, Nietzsche's Contemporary Jews were such a race (BGE 251). For him, "there are probably no pure races but only races that have become pure," and even these *res facta* races are "extremely rare" (D 272). A race becomes pure by mixing with other races, taking the energy produced by the resulting contradictory qualities and channeling them so that they "will stand at the command of the total organism." In other words, like Nietzsche's strong types, a pure race is able to master its forces and unify them within a single organism such that both are "stronger and more beautiful."[47] It was in this section that he cited the Greeks as a race that had become pure, and later, in BGE 251, he called the Jews the "strongest, toughest, purest race." At the end of section 272 of *Dawn,* he expressed the hope that there would one day be a "pure European race and culture."

Once again we see the ways in which Nietzsche viewed race as being both intimately intertwined with the decline and the only hope for a revitalization of European culture. The survival of European nations, particularly Germany, depended on their evolution into a new race, and this evolution was to come about by way of the deliberate mixing of established races—in other words through the process of breeding. Breeding would bring about, as it had done with the Greeks, a combination of characteristics in these new, "good Europeans" such that they would create more vital, affirmative values. These values would counter the weak decadent values that were leading nineteenth-century Europe to nihilism. In other words, they would aid in treating Europe for the disease of decadence which had plagued it for centuries.

This racial mixing had to be done carefully, because it also represented the danger of further degeneration. It is precisely an indiscriminate mixing (of various classes) that had brought about the weakening of the will with which Nietzsche had diagnosed his own culture.

> [It is] the most spiritual expression of a certain complex physiological condition that in ordinary language is called nervous exhaustion and sickliness; it always develops when races or classes that have long been separated are crossed suddenly and decisively. In the new generation, that as it were, has inherited in its blood diverse standards and values, everything is unrest, disturbance, doubt, attempt; the best forces have an inhibiting effect, the very virtues do not allow each other to grow and become strong, balance, a center of gravity, and perpendicular poise are lacking in body and soul. But what becomes sickest and degenerates most in such hybrids is the *will:* they no longer know independence of decisions and the intrepid sense of pleasure in willing—they doubt the "freedom of the will" even in their dreams. (BGE 208)[48]

Europe, then, had tried to treat itself for the disease of decadence, caused by the introduction of Socratic values, by mixing classes—in other words, by adopting democratic values. Within the organisms of European nations, this mixing had introduced "opposite drives and value standards that fight each other and rarely permit each other any rest." This struggle among drives and values had in turn led to a further weakening of the cultures. Again, "such human beings of late cultures and refracted lights will on the average be weaker human beings: their most profound desire is that the war they *are* should come to an end" (BGE 200). Returning to my previous discussion of pure races, Nietzsche's predecessors had been unable to organize the oppositional forces brought on by race mixing, and as a result, they had led to the further decay of the culture.

Conclusion

Because of this close connection between the problem of decadence and the breeding of races, race, and in particular Nietzsche's attempted revaluation of it, is an important component of his call for cultural revitalization. He tried to carry out a revaluation of the function of race in this revitalization. He was particularly well suited for this task because he had suffered from the symptoms of the weak decadence of his time (e.g., nationalism) and had overcome them.[49]

> What does a philosopher demand of himself first and last? To overcome his time in himself, to become "timeless." With what must he therefore engage in the hardest combat? With whatever marks him as the child of his time. Well, then! I am, no less than Wagner, a child of his time; that is, a decadent: but I comprehended this, I resisted it. The philosopher in me resisted. Nothing has preoccupied me more profoundly than the problem of decadence—I had reasons. (CW Preface)

Both the weak decadence and nationalistic racism that would mark one "a child" of nineteenth-century Germany were personified in Wagner. In "overcoming" Wagner, Nietzsche had also overcome or recovered from the most virulent symptoms of the disease of his time and thus had become timeless. Because decadence is integral to understanding both Nietzsche's diagnosis and his proposed treatment for his ailing culture, one cannot blithely dismiss his discussion of race. In fact, as I have tried to argue in this essay, his concept of race and his proposed revaluation of it serve as excellent examples of his revaluation of decadence. For Nietzsche, race, like decadence, had become a problem in his time, but the solution was not to eliminate them; instead, one was to change the values assigned to them and use their revalued forms to invigorate the culture. Because weak decadence involved a physiological and philosophical decay, he contended that nineteenth-century Germans required rejuvenation by way of a fresh infusion of blood and values. In short, a breeding of Germans with stronger races was the only hope that he saw for halting the German decline into weak decadence and the inevitable nihilism that had been brought about by the breeding of mediocre types. The infusion of strong decadent blood would alter the type of Germans being produced, and this new type would in turn produce different values. Nietzsche argued, contrary to the views of his contemporaries, that Jews were needed for the culture—but it had to be the right Jews. *Züchtung* was also to be a part of revitalization, but it would not involve excluding other races from Germany. Instead, a mixed race of Europeans needed to be bred, and in particular, this breeding required the physiological and social traits of Contemporary Jews. Race and its revaluation for Nietzsche is an example of his prescription for contending with the problem of decadence.

Notes

1. This type of project has been undertaken by a myriad of scholars, and there seem to be three dominant schools of thought: Nietzsche as anti-Semite, as philo-Semite, and as ambivalent regarding Jews. For the Nietzsche-as-anti-Semite group, see Hubert Cancik and Heldegard Cancik-Lindemaier, "Philhellénisme et antisémitisme en Allemagne: Le cas de Nietzsche," in D. Bourel and T. Rider, *De Sils-Maria à Jérusalem* (Paris: Cerf, 1991), pp. 21–46; Marc de Launay, "Le juif introuvable," in Bourel and Le Rider, *De Sils-Maria à Jérusalem,* pp. 353–385; Daniel Conway, "The Great Play and Fight of Forces," in Julie K. Ward and Tommy L. Lott, eds., *Philosophers on Race* (London: Blackwell, 2002), pp. 167–194; Sarah Kofman, *Le mépris des juifs* (Paris: Editions Galilée, 1994).

   For Nietzsche as philo-Semite, see Jacob Golomb, "Nietzsche's Judaism of Power," *Revue des études juives* 147, no. 3–4 (July–Dec. 1988): 353–385; Harry Neumann, "Nietzsche's Interpretation of the Jewish Instinct," in James O'Flaherty, Timothy F. Sellner, and Robert M. Helm, eds., *Studies in Nietzsche and the Judeo-Christian Tradition* (Chapel Hill: University of North Carolina Press, 1985), pp. 29–46; Walter Kaufmann, *Nietzsche: Philosopher, Psychologist, Antichrist,* 4th ed. (Princeton, N.J.: Princeton University Press, 1974); Weaver Santaniello, *Nietzsche, God, and the Jews* (Albany, N.Y.: SUNY Press, 1994).

   For Nietzsche as ambivalent toward Jews, see Arnold Eisen, "Nietzsche and the Jews Reconsidered," *Jewish Social Studies* 48 (Winter 1986): 1–4; Robert Holub, "Nietzsche and the Jewish Question," *New German Critique* 66 (Fall 1995): 94–122; Yirmiyahu Yovel, *Dark Riddle: Hegel, Nietzsche, and the Jews* (Cambridge: Polity Press, 1998).

2. Jacqueline Scott, "Nietzsche and Decadence: The Revaluation of Morality," *Continental Philosophy Review* (formerly *Man and World*) 31 (January 1998): 59–78.

3. Friedrich Nietzsche, *The Case of Wagner,* trans. Walter Kaufmann and R. J. Hollingdale (New York: Random House, 1967). Henceforth CW.

4. Daniel Conway, *Nietzsche's Dangerous Game* (Cambridge: Cambridge University Press, 1997), pp. 24–31. While Nietzsche did not explicate his theory of decadence in a comprehensive way, Conway provides a careful catalogue of the myriad of references to decadence, instincts, and drives and explicates clearly the implicit relations between these terms in the late works. However, he falters in his account of Nietzsche's personal relationship to decadence.

5. Scott, "Nietzsche and Decadence," pp. 60–61.

6. Friedrich Nietzsche, *On The Genealogy of Morals*, trans. Walter Kaufmann (New York: Random House, 1967), III, sec. 28. Henceforth GM.

7. Friedrich Nietzsche, *The Antichrist*, trans. R. J. Hollingdale (London: Penguin Books, 1968), sec. 6. Henceforth A.

8. See also Conway, *Dangerous Game,* pp. 107–116. Conway contends that decadence is destiny, and that in the late works (especially in *Twilight of the Idols*), Nietzsche admitted that there was "no real hope for an antidote to the instinctual disarray to which Nietzsche now trace[d] the problem of morality." In *Twilight of the Idols* (trans. R. J. Hollingdale [London: Penguin Books, 1968]; henceforth TI), Nietzsche claimed that there was no point in attempting to treat the culture for decadence, and so the only hope was to wait out this stage until the culture was ready to move on to the next one. During this waiting time, one could attempt to "*retard* this development and through retardation, dam and gather up degeneration itself and make it more vehement and *sudden:* more one cannot do" ("Skirmishes" 43). While I agree with Conway to a certain extent regarding the comprehensiveness and inevitability of decadence, my reading of Nietzsche's response to the problem it posed for his culture is different.

9. "Where one can no longer love, there one should pass by" (Friedrich Nietzsche, *Thus Spoke Zarathustra*, trans. Walter Kaufmann [London: Penguin Books, 1954], sec. 3, "On Passing By"; henceforth Z). See also TI "Maxims" 42: "For me they were steps, I have climbed up upon them—therefore I had to pass over them. But they thought I wanted to settle down on them . . . "

10. I am using the terms "cure" and "antidote" in very specific senses. A cure permanently heals a disease, and an antidote treats the symptoms without radically affecting the disease itself.

11. In *Dangerous Game*, Conway makes a distinction between passive and active nihilists that is analogous to my strong vs. weak decadence dichotomy (pp. 114–116). Conway has argued that Nietzsche portrayed himself as "our best example of an active nihilist" (p. 114). While I agree with Conway that Nietzsche did make a distinction between active and passive nihilism, they are only *symptoms* of decadence. It is clear (as I will argue later) that it is the *disease* itself with which Nietzsche attempted to contend, and that is why in the late works he emphasized decadence and the fact of his own decadent status. Nihilism is only one of the many symptoms of decadence (e.g., timeliness, bad conscience, dogmatism, etc.), and while it is arguably one of the most problematic for Nietzsche, his attempt at a revaluation of values was meant to be an antidote for the most rabid symptoms of decadence, and not for nihilism alone. His primary task involved a revaluation of decadence (weak to strong decadence) and not nihilism.

12. Scott, "Nietzsche and Decadence," pp. 63–68.

13. Friedrich Nietzsche, *The Gay Science*, trans. Walter Kaufmann (New York: Vintage Books, 1974), sec. 382. Henceforth GS.

14. There is a school of thought that Nietzsche abandoned his cultural physician status in the late works. See Alexander Nehamas, *Nietzsche: Life as Literature* (Cambridge, Mass: Harvard University Press, 1985) as an example.

15. "The question: what is the *value* of this or that table of values and 'morals?'"

should be viewed from the most divers perspectives; for the problem *"value for what?"* cannot be examined too subtly. Something, for example, that possessed obvious value in relation to the longest possible survival of a race (or to the en-hancement of its power of adaptation to a particular climate or to the preservation of the greatest number) would by no means possess the same value if it were a question, for instance, of producing a stronger type. The well-being of the ma-jority and the well-being of the few are opposite viewpoints of value: to con-sider the former *a priori* of higher value may be left to the naiveté of English biologists.—*All* the sciences have from now onto prepare the way for the future task of the philosophers: this task understood as the solution to the *problem of value,* the determination of the *order of rank among values"* (GM I 17).

16. Arthur de Gobineau, *The Inequality of Human Races,* trans. Adrian Collins (New York: Howard Fertig, 1967); Immanuel Kant, "On the Use of Teleological Prin-ciples in Philosophy," trans. Jon Mark Mikkelsen, in *Race,* ed. Robert Bernasconi (Oxford: Blackwell, 2001), pp. 37–56, and "Of the Different Human Races," trans. Jon Mark Mikkelsen, in *The Idea of Race,* ed. Robert Bernasconi and Tommy L. Lott (Indianapolis: Haskette, 2000), pp. 8–22; Ernst Renan, *Le judaïsme comme race et comme religion* (New York: Rand School of Social Science, 1943).

17. In fact, Richard Wagner read Gobineau, introduced him to members of his Bayreuth circle, and aided in forming the Gobineau Society, whose goal was to publish Gobineau's theories of racial inequality (Paul Weindling, *Health, Race and German Politics between National Unification and Nazism, 1870-1945* [Cam-bridge: Cambridge University Press, 1989], pp. 57, 107).

18. Marc de Launay, in his essay "Le juif introuvable," claims that there is no sys-tematic treatment of Judaism in Nietzsche's works, no particular role assigned to it, nor even evidence of effective knowledge about Judaism (p. 82). While I agree that Nietzsche does not display extensive knowledge of Judaism, I disagree with the other two claims. Throughout Nietzsche's published writings not only does he write about Jews and Judaism frequently, but they play a specific role in both his critical and positive philosophy.

19. Jacob Golomb ("Nietzsche's Judaism of Power," p. 354) argues that "Jews [are] an important yardstick for determining the meaning and integrity of Nietzsche's philosophical thought," and in particular for understanding Nietzsche's psy-chology of power. Weaver Santaniello argues that "Nietzsche's philosophy . . . as-signed to the Jews a privileged status not on a biological basis, but on the basis of psychology and history" (*Nietzsche, God and the Jews,* p. 108). Both Golomb and Santaniello misstep in the importance that each assigns to Jews in Nietzsche's philosophical thought and the role that they understand Jews as playing in his thought. While Jews were not central in Nietzsche's philosophical thought, they are a good example of a particular theory. I disagree that they only exemplify his psychological theories; in fact, they exemplify an application of the intersection of his theories on psychology, physiology, race, cultural health, and cultural devel-opment.

20. Yirmiyahu Yovel claims that he was the first to publish this grouping of Jews ("Perspectives nouvelles sur Nietzsche et le judaïsme," *Revue des études juives* 137 [July–Dec. 1979]: 483), but see also D. Bechtel, "Nietzsche et le dialectique de l'histoire juive," in *De Sils-Maria à Jérusalem,* p. 69; Golomb, "Nietzsche's

Judaism of Power," p. 376; Santaniello, *Nietzsche*, p. 104; Eisen, "Nietzsche and the Jews Reconsidered," pp. 1–14; Sander Gilman, "Heine, Nietzsche and the Ideas of the Jews," in Jacob Golomb, ed., *Nietzsche and Jewish Culture* (New York: Routledge, 1996), p. 76; Michael Duffy and Willard Mittelman, "Nietzsche's Attitudes towards the Jews," *Journal of the History of Ideas* 49 (April–June 1988): 302.

21. I have borrowed this characterization of the three groups from both Santaniello (*Nietzsche*, pp. 104–105) and Yovel (*Dark Riddle*, pp. 152–153).

22. Contrary, then, to some claims, Nietzsche's praise of Hellenism was not *always* meant to serve as a counterpoint to his criticism of Jewish and Christian values. He drew many points of similarity between Greeks and Jews, and as we shall soon see, he did argue that Jews might be indispensable for a revitalization of a European culture that would rival that of the ancient Greeks; see Friedrich Nietzsche, *Dawn*, trans. R. J. Hollingdale (Cambridge: Cambridge University Press, 1982), sec. 205 (henceforth D); Friedrich Nietzsche, *Human, All-Too-Human*, trans. R. J. Hollingdale (Cambridge: Cambridge University Press, 1986), vol. 1, sec. 475 (henceforth HAH); Friedrich Nietzsche, *Beyond Good and Evil*, trans. Walter Kaufmann (New York: Vintage Books, 1955), sec. 251 (henceforth BGE). The key difference between the ancient Greeks and the ancient Jews was that they each represented a different type of genius. The Greeks, along with the French, were the type of culture that "begets" or forms others, while the Jews, along with the Romans, were the type that are fertilized and thus give "birth" to other cultures (BGE 248). According to Nietzsche, it is via these procreative functions that dynamic cultures become stronger—namely by interacting with other cultures. Nietzsche tended to prize the Jewish, Greek, Roman, and French cultures in part because of their tendency to "parent" other cultures.

23. Hubert Cancik, "Mongol, Semites, and the Pure-Bred Greeks," in Golomb, *Nietzsche and Jewish Culture*, p. 55; Kofman, *Le Mépris des juifs*, p. 74. See also Friedrich Nietzsche, *Untimely Meditations*, trans. R. J. Hollingdale (Cambridge: Cambridge University Press, 1983), II, sec. 10. Henceforth UM.

24. According to Nietzsche, tragedy is "essentially and profoundly foreign to the Jew, in spite of all of his poetic gifts and his sense for the sublime" (GS 135).

25. Daniel Ahern makes a similar point in *Nietzsche as Cultural Physician* (University Park: Pennsylvania State University Press, 1995), p. 91.

26. Yirmiyahu Yovel, "Nietzsche and the Jews," in Golomb, *Nietzsche and Jewish Culture*, p. 127.

27. Ahern, *Nietzsche*, p. 93.

28. "The whole fatality was possible only because there was already in the world a related, racially-related megalomania, the *Jewish*: once the chasm between Jews and Jewish Christians had opened up, the latter were left with no alternative but to employ *against* the Jews the very self-preservative procedures counseled by the Jewish instinct, while the Jews had previously employed them only against everything *non*-Jewish. The Christian is only a Jew of a *'freer'* confession" (A 44).

29. Israel Eldad notes that for Nietzsche, Christianity is a double inheritor of decadence: Priestly Jewish and Socratic ("Nietzsche and the Old Testament," in O'Flaherty et al., *Nietzsche and the Judeo-Christian Tradition*, p. 50).

30. I will analyze this call for breeding in the next section.

31. There are two occasions in the published works on which Nietzsche claims that, if they wanted, Jews could "conquer" Europe. In *Dawn* 205, he argues that Jews would not carry out such a conquest, but to do so they would need to "distinguish themselves in every domain of European distinction and to stand everywhere in the first rank," then Europe "may fall into their hands like a ripe fruit," and it would benefit from the resulting "great men and great works." Later in *Beyond Good and Evil*, he claims that Jews could master Europe, but won't because they would prefer "to be absorbed and assimilated by Europe" (251). The latter reference is clearly less strident than the first, and the change can best be attributed to his desire to make a clear separation between his views of Jews and breeding and those of the anti-Semitic nationalists of his time.

32. "Sin, as it is now experienced wherever Christianity holds sway or has held sway, is a Jewish feeling and a Jewish invention. Regarding this background of all Christian morality, Christianity did aim to 'Judaize' [*verjüdeln*] the world" (GS 135).

33. Weaver Santaniello, "A Post-Holocaust Re-examination of Nietzsche and the Jews," in Golomb, *Nietzsche and Jewish Culture,* p. 24.

34. Santaniello, "Post-Holocaust Re-examination," p. 40.

35. R. J. Hollingdale, *Nietzsche: The Man and His Philosophy* (Baton Rouge: Louisiana State University Press, 1965), p. 224.

36. It would seem, then, that nations are mere political units that, due to time and circumstance, might progress to become races and cultures (see BGE 251 and the discussion of breeding below).

37. Kofman, *Le mépris des juifs*, pp. 18–19, and Wayne Klein, *Nietzsche and the Promise of Philosophy* (Albany: SUNY Press, 1997), p. 165.

38. Yovel, *Dark Riddle*, p. 135.

39. Wayne Klein, *Nietzsche*, pp. 163–165.

40. For instance, as Klein has pointed out, in BGE 213, Nietzsche made another mention of "blood" and its role in constituting the characteristics of an individual along with "one's origins" and "one's ancestors." In this section the word "blood" [*Geblüt*] is in quotation marks, and Nietzsche's use of quotation marks around a word almost always signals to the reader that he was assigning a different meaning or value to it.

41. Klein, *Promise of Philosophy*, p. 67; Kofman, *Le Mépris des juifs*, pp. 18–19.

42. Walter Kaufmann claimed that the terms *Zucht* and *Züchtung* appear occasionally in *Will to Power*, and that there are even fewer references to either word in the published works. He further claimed that "[i]f one looks for a philosophic precedent for Nietzsche's strange concern with breeding, one will have to seek it not in his German predecessors but in Plato" (*Nietzsche: Philosopher*, pp. 304–305). There are actually quite a few references to *Zucht* and *Züchtung* in the published works, and they are not "throwaway" lines. Contrary to Kaufmann, I think that Nietzsche, at least in part, was borrowing from "his German predecessors" in his use of the terms, but it was not a wholesale borrowing.

43. Unlike their true Aryan predecessors of "Indian morality," Christians were

breeding "the poor and lowly." According to this account, the Indian Aryans' task was the breeding of four races, with the "virtuous . . . people of race" (the Aryans) at the top of the hierarchy (TI "Improvers" 3). These Aryans were of "pure blood," but the Christians inherited the "Chandala" (Untouchable) values, and as such, they are "the *anti-Aryan* religion *par excellence*" (TI "Improvers" 4). In short, breeding is a part of morality, but some breeding is preferable to others.

44. "We who are homeless are too manifold and mixed racially and in our descent, being 'modern men,' and consequently do not feel tempted to participate in the mendacious racial self-admiration and racial indecency that parades in Germany today as a sign of a German way of thinking and that is doubly false and obscene among the people of the 'historical sense.' We, are in a word—and let this be our word of honor—*good Europeans*, the heirs of Europe, the rich, oversupplied, but also overly obligated heirs of thousands of years of European spirit" (GS 377).

45. See also GS 377.

46. Earlier in *Dawn* 205, Nietzsche has also called for an absorption of Jewish values by Europe, and there he said after this assimilation had brought about the creation of "great men and great works," then the Jews would have "transformed its eternal vengeance into an eternal blessing for Europe." In other words, then they would have atoned for having produced Paul and, by extension, Christianity. Nietzsche also suggested that Europe could use Chinese blood to counteract the restlessness and fretfulness of Europeans (D 206).

47. In BGE 200, Nietzsche offers the following description of the process of purifying, and thus strengthening, individuals and nations: "But when the opposition and war in such a nature have the effect of one more charm and incentive of life—and if, moreover, in addition to his powerful and irreconcilable drives, a real mastery and subtlety in waging war against oneself, in other words, self-control, self-outwitting, has been inherited or cultivated, too—then those magical, incomprehensible, and unfathomable ones arise, those enigmatic men predestined for victory and seduction, whose most beautiful expression is found in Alcibiades and Caesar . . . "

48. See also BGE 224 and 200 for further discussions of nineteenth-century Europe as a degenerating culture due to the indiscriminate mixing of races.

49. "Let us articulate this *new demand:* we need a critique of moral values, *the value of these values themselves must first be called into question*—and for that there is needed a knowledge of the circumstances in which they grew . . . What if a symptom of regression were inherent in the 'good,' likewise a danger, a seduction, a poison, a narcotic, through which the present was possibly living *at the expense of the future*? Perhaps more comfortably, less dangerously, but at the same time in a meaner style, more basely?—So that precisely morality would be to blame if the *highest power and splendor* actually possible to the type man was never in fact attained? So that precisely morality was the danger of dangers?" (GM Preface 6).

Five

Heidegger and Race

Sonia Sikka

For anyone acquainted with Heidegger's writings, the question of Heidegger and race is likely to seem, prima facie, a little peculiar. Given that the idea of race is generally associated with a biologically based species of anthropology, and given that Heidegger's thought is, in its fundamental principles, opposed to any such anthropology, one would not expect him to grant any validity to the idea of race. That expectation appears to be confirmed by a survey of his works. Nowhere in those works is there any theory of racially distinct groups, or any affirmation of a hierarchical ranking of such groups. Thus, George Steiner is right to note that "there is in Heidegger's voluminous writings no spoor of biological racism."[1] One might conclude, then, that the idea of race, to the extent that it is present at all in Heidegger's thought, functions only in a negative way, as something he opposes.

However, in light of Heidegger's political engagement with Nazism, there seems to be something unsatisfactory about the claim that his relation to race is purely critical. If Heidegger grants no validity of any form to the idea of race, one might ask, how could he have supported a political regime that not only was incidentally racist, but was founded upon racist principles? Granted, he could not have endorsed any concept, purporting to apply to the fundamental constitution of human beings, that was based on the alleged findings of a natural science such as biology. But is there, in his thought, some notion parallel to that of race, which might explain some part of his attraction to Nazi ideology? If so, is there also some sense in which he could be described as a "racist" after all?

This essay takes up all of these questions. It explores, first, the nature and extent of Heidegger's sustained, if often covert, critique of race and associated ideas within Nazi ideology in his lectures during the late 1930s and over the course of the war. As one would expect, anti-biologism forms a staple component in this critique, but it functions as part of an opposition whose aim is always correction rather than destruction. His criticisms of elements in Nazi ideology consistently seek, that is, to bring National Socialism back to what he thinks is its proper form or "essence," saving it from the corruption that he believes it has undergone as a result, in part, of contamination with biologistic ideas. The second part of the essay focuses on this alleged "essence," locating the Nazi views revolving around the idea of race to which Heidegger would have been sympathetic, in spite of his antipathy toward biologism, because he himself held non-biologistic versions of these views.

As one might expect, the results of my analysis in these first two parts of the essay suggest that the non-biologistic parallel notions that Heidegger espoused belong to the sphere of "culture" rather than "race." In the final part of my analysis, however, I reconsider the issue of the relation between race and culture in Heidegger's thought and point out that there actually is a sense in which "biology," conceived in a certain manner, enters into his conception of the identity of peoples. But I also maintain that, if one adds some modifications and caveats, this conception is right. It acknowledges one dimension of the reality of race and presents one reason why race and culture cannot be as clearly distinguished as is sometimes thought.

Heidegger's Anti-biologism

In his interview with *Der Spiegel* in 1966, Heidegger is asked whether his relation to the NSDAP changed after his resignation as rector, and he responds as follows:

> After my resignation from the Rectorate, I confined myself to my teaching responsibilities. In the summer semester of 1934, I delivered the lectures on "Logic." In the following semester, 1934/35, I held the first lecture course on Hölderlin. In 1936 began the lectures on Nietzsche. Everyone, who could hear, understood that these lectures were a confrontation with National Socialism.[2]

One can see, in the published text of the courses that he mentions here, an increasingly critical relationship to Nazi ideology, including those elements which concern or underpin Nazi race-theory. In the lecture course called "Logic,"[3] Heidegger is clearly still hopeful about the future of Germany under Nazi rule. His choice to illustrate his analysis of history by presenting a meeting between the Führer and Mussolini as an example of a genuine historical happening (L 83) demonstrates that these two figures and what they represent still constitute, for Heidegger, a positive historical force. To be sure, given the context of this reference, in which Heidegger is drawing a contrast between the unfolding of events with human significance and mere sequences of occurrences, thereby distinguishing the realms of "history" (*Geschichte*) and "nature," a meeting between Hitler and Mussolini would count as genuinely historical regardless of how it were judged. Nonetheless, it seems that, at this juncture, Heidegger views such events as promising rather than ominous.

Heidegger's rare explicit remarks on race, in this work, appear within the context of his analysis of history as definitive of being human and as essential to membership in a *Volk*.[4] These remarks are, on the surface, neither positive nor negative in their attitude toward race, seeming merely to describe a dimension of what the term is generally held to mean. For instance, Heidegger claims at one point that "'race,' like 'people,' is ambiguous," because "it concerns that aspect of a people which is connected, in its genetically determined drive to life, with blood and with the physical," but can also connote rank (L 65). Considering the highly charged climate of ideas within which he is speaking here, one could complain that even pointing out these features of the idea of race, and particularly the connection between race and rank, without critical comment is problematic, as it implicitly lends credence to an idea that ought, rather, to be discouraged. One would not, however, wish to make too much of this. After all, considering this same climate, what is *not* said in this passage, or anywhere else in the published text of the lectures, is considerably more significant. Heidegger does not endorse any notion of "blood" as determining the character of a people, or any doctrine regarding the superiority of one biological race to another, or any idea of degenerate races. He does mention sickness and blood at one point, but maintains that these are actually historical rather than purely biological phenomena (L 153). Again, one could justifiably believe that, at the time these lectures were delivered, affirming *any* notion of sickness and blood, however revised and transformed, was sure to do more harm than good. Nonetheless, Heidegger's intent is critical. He rejects an obvious biological construal of "blood," claiming instead that what is called "blood" is determined by disposition and character, and not the other way around (L 153).[5] In general, his analyses consistently insist that the elements which "determine" the character of a people, and which present at the same time the possibility of superiority and degeneration, belong to the realm of history rather than nature. They concern cultural rather than genetic inheritance, and decision rather than causation.

With respect to the constitution of individuals and peoples, Heidegger's fundamental thesis in these lectures is that history is essential to, and definitive of, being human. It is in arguing this thesis that he makes the by now somewhat notorious statements about "negroes" having no history. These statements occur as part of his consideration of a possible objection to the thesis that he has been arguing, the thesis that history is the defining characteristic of being human. He imagines that someone might point out that "there are human beings and human groups (negroes, for instance Xhosa) who have no history" (L 81). The racism of these remarks has a number of components. First, there is the dubious supposition that some unitary and distinct group is named with the term "negroes," a group identified, presumably, by biological characteristics, by skin color and lineage, perhaps, or by the same types of characteristics, whatever these may be, that distinguish biological species and subspecies. This is not at all the way in which Heidegger would normally define a *Volk*, but he shows here no awareness that there are African peoples, nor does he acknowledge any distinction between such peoples and people of African descent living elsewhere. Second, the idea that "negroes" have no history is of course racist in its assertion that they have no historical consciousness or traditions, and really belong more to nature than to culture. Finally, people who hold such ideas can usually be taken to task for making absurd and denigrating generalizations about people of whom they know little or nothing, and an important aspect of racism consists in this unthinking, and frequently ill-willed, manner of passing judgment. However, even if, in his references to "negroes," Heidegger is guilty of racism in all of the above-listed ways, this does not per se provide evidence of a general biological racism, or of sympathy with the racist side of Nazi ideology. Heidegger would hardly be alone in excluding Africans from his conception of humanity at the cost of being inconsistent, and, in 1934, this sort of exclusion was not limited to opponents of the liberal democratic "West."[6]

By the time he delivers the first set of lectures on Hölderlin (winter semester, 1934/35), Heidegger's disillusionment with the actuality of Nazism is palpable. Whereas, in the "Logic" lectures, he had still tended to support this actuality while wanting to help shape and purify it, by now he is less inclined to believe that it can be redeemed. He never ceases to affirm what he sees as the ideal form or "essence" of National Socialism, but he progressively loses faith in the possibility that the actual movement can be brought back into conformity with this essence, and certainly in the possibility that his own participation could be effective in bringing about such a redemptive return. This disenchantment is evident in the overtly critical remarks in the Hölderlin lectures, which suggest that, in its current form, Nazi ideology is not genuinely revolutionary, but is largely continuous with the decadent course of Western history, characterized, Heidegger thinks, by subjectivism and nihilism. For instance, in criticizing the conception of poetry as an "expression of experiences," he claims that all conceptions of this sort move within the same manner of thinking, regardless of whether one interprets the expressed experiences as "the experiences of an individual—'individualistically'—or as the expression of a collective soul [*Massenseele*]—'collectivistically'—or with Spengler as the expression of a cultural soul, or with Rosenberg as the expression of the soul of a race or of a people."[7]

The same genre of disenchantment is evident in other critical remarks:

The author Kolbenheyer says: "Poetry is a biologically necessary function of the people." It does not take much intelligence to see that this is also true of digestion. (HHG 27)

Not long ago, one searched for the hidden bases of poetry through psychoanaly-sis, now it is all about national character [*Volkstum*] and blood and soil, but everything remains as it was. (HHG 254)

Heidegger's disgust with the reductive biologism that characterized so much Nazi literature is obvious in the remark about Kolbenheyer. The second com-ment shows that Heidegger is no longer likely to speak positively, as he had in his inaugural address as rector, about "the forces rooted in the soil and blood of a *Volk*."[8] Nonetheless, the 1934–35 Hölderlin lectures are thematically con-tinuous with the lectures on logic in their focus on historicality, and in their interpretation as historical of phenomena that Nazi ideologues interpreted as physical, phenomena constitutive in some way of the identity and character of a people. For instance, Heidegger claims that in Hölderlin's poetry, *Heimat* is "not a mere place of birth, nor only a familiar landscape," but is "the power of the earth, on which a person 'dwells poetically' at any given time, in ac-cordance with his historical existence" (HHG 88), and that "earth and home-land [*Erde und Heimat*] are meant historically" (HHG 196). Correspondingly, *Vaterland* has nothing to do with any "doubtful and noisy patriotism," but means "the land of the fathers, it means us, this people of this earth as his-torical, in its historical being" (HHG 120).

Max Müller is not quite right, therefore, in saying that "Heidegger was not concerned with Hölderlin's conception of the fatherland, which was what es-pecially interested the National Socialists about this poet,"[9] nor in his claim that, after 1934, "as far as a nonparticipant can tell, not a single political word was spoken in [Heidegger's] courses" (MHNS 191). The Hölderlin lectures are still deeply political, at least in the sense that their themes are directly related to the social and political ideology of Nazi Germany. The shift that occurs in 1934 is not a shift away from the realm of "politics," construed broadly, but toward a distinctly more critical assessment of what is actually occurring within that realm. But the substantive content of Heidegger's phi-losophy does not undergo any significant change in 1934. His understanding of the nature of human existence and of the role of national identity within that existence remains fundamentally unaltered. What has changed is his view of the relation of Nazi ideology, in its effective actuality, to his own under-standing of these issues and to its own "essence."

Heidegger remains critically concerned with biologistic ideas, along with other features of Nazi ideology, throughout the lecture courses he gives in the late 1930s and early 1940s. In the 1942 summer semester lectures on Hölder-lin,[10] he still attempts, at times, to oppose such ideas by interpreting differ-ently the phenomena that underlie them. He again refers to the term "blood," construing it as a label for "physical life" (*leibhaftes Leben*), and claims that the connection between human beings and blood is "first determined by the relation of human beings to being itself" (HHI 147). "Blood," that is, names an aspect of being human, which, precisely because it is an aspect of being *human,* cannot be analyzed in the terms appropriate to the investigation of "nature." In that case, "blood" has to be understood in terms of the structure of being human. For Heidegger, the heart of that structure consists in a reflexive relation to being. Likewise, the relation to what is one's own, as opposed to what is foreign, is constituted by—and therefore must be interpreted through—this structure; it "is never merely the self-assured affirmation of the so-called 'natural' and 'organic'" (HHI 179). Heidegger maintains that "all the simply 'organic' of nature is foreign to the law of history, as foreign as is the 'logical' of reason" (HHI 179). He thereby challenges a dichotomy prevalent within Nazi writings, while at the same time guarding himself against the anticipated objection that anyone who criticizes one side of this dichotomy must be promoting, instead, the decadence of an abstract reason that has become increasingly divorced from the realities of concrete human existence.

One can also see this challenge at work in *Beiträge zur Philosophie* (composed 1936–39),[11] in which Heidegger claims that the absolutization of spirit within German Idealism achieves a suppression of individuality and an alienation of being that actually expedites the fall into positivism and biologism. He adds that "the present 'confrontation' with German Idealism, if it deserves to be called that, is only 're-active' . . . it absolutizes 'life' with all the indeterminacy and confusion that it can conceal in that term" (BP 315). According to these claims, the emphasis that Nazi writers placed on "life," with its accompanying biologism, belongs, for Heidegger, to the falling movement of Western thought, a movement through which reality, in the modern age, has exclusively become that which the subject can place before itself and represent (*Vor-stellen*) as an object. In opposition to the Nazi self-interpretations, then, with their rhetoric of overcoming decadence by a return to life over spirit, Heidegger is proposing that this glorification of a vague notion of "life" is in fact a continuation of Western decadence. Any attempt to characterize a *Volk* on the basis of this notion must then also belong to the same decadence. Heidegger insists, by contrast, that in truth the essence of a people resides in historicity, and that "'life' and body, breeding [*Zeugung*] and lineage [*Geschlecht*], descent [*Stamm*], stated in a basic word: the earth, belong to history" (BP 399).

By this point in the development of his thought, Heidegger sees Nietzsche's emphasis on life and on biological forces as a part of this merely reactive movement of decline (BP 315). In the text of his first lecture course on Nietzsche, on the other hand, *The Will to Power as Art,* delivered in 1936,[12] he is a little more charitable in his interpretation. He already sees in Nietzsche's thought a culmination, rather than an overcoming, of the declining movement of Western metaphysics, and his antagonistic stance toward any form of biological reductionism is pervasive and consistent. Heidegger's dominant view of Nietzsche in these lectures, however, is that Nietzsche is fundamentally *not* a biological reductionist, if one takes care to understand properly what he means by "life" and related notions, but that, unfortunately and to his own discredit, he does sometimes, in his analyses of aesthetic phenomena, use a false and misleading reductive vocabulary drawn from physiology and biology.[13]

It would be wrong to assume, though, that any attempt to dissociate Nietzsche from biologism constitutes per se a critique of the Nazi appropriation of Nietzsche. Alfred Bäumler, whose *Nietzsche der Philosoph und Politiker* (1931) is fully part of this appropriation, also rejects the idea that Nietzsche's thought is biologistic and sees his attempt to root consciousness in life-functions as a hyperbolic reaction to the overvaluation of consciousness by other philosophers.[14] Heidegger criticizes Bäumler's reading of Nietzsche for being guided by politics rather than metaphysics,[15] but he praises Bäumler for being one of the few who goes against "the psychological-biologistic interpretation of Nietzsche through Klages" (NI 25). However, Bäumler's rejection of the biologistic understanding of Nietzsche does not prevent him from applauding Nietzsche for emphasizing the origin of the individual within concrete unities such as race, people, and class (NPP 179), and for the fact that "before his eyes stood again the old task of our race: the task, to become the leader of Europe" (NPP 182). Heidegger, too, emphasizes the role of cultural membership in shaping historical existence, and he believes in a special mission for Germany within Europe—topics about which I will have more to say in the next part of this essay—but he never speaks of these in terms of race, nor is the language of race present in what he sees as positive about Nietzsche.

Moreover, in general, a central component of the Nazi literature on Nietzsche did of course concern biologically based racial theory, and one should not underemphasize the enormous distance between this literature and the views expressed in Heidegger's lecture courses. Consider, for instance, the following statement from Heinrich Härtle's *Nietzsche und der Nationalsozialismus*: "Since the knowledge of race is fundamental for our political world, nothing distances us from, and binds us more strongly with, Nietzsche as those ideas whose truth or error is rooted in his understanding or misunderstanding of the problem of race, an understanding in which he is bound to his times."[16] Heidegger, on the other hand, sees the issue of race as central neither to "our political world" nor to an interpretation of Nietzsche. Although he does sometimes speak positively of the idea of rank, one cannot imagine Heidegger saying with Härtle that "Nietzsche shows the error and dangers of a doctrine teaching the equality of all that bears a human face" (NN 24). He clearly never promotes the view that Nietzsche was anti-Semitic, let alone *rightly* anti-Semitic (cf. NN 38, 44, 49 50, 54), nor is there any trace of anti-Semitism in his own lectures. One might also compare Heidegger's subtle interpretations of notions such as "life," "body," and "blood" with Härtle's claim that "as a thinker of life and of the body, Nietzsche had to run up against the race-question" (NN 55). For Härtle, Nietzsche adopts the right position on this question when he remarks, in *The Will to Power*, that "there is only nobility of birth, nobility of blood,"[17] and the wrong position in believing that the character of a people is determined by "external" factors.

Härtle's description of the essential difference between Nietzsche and National Socialism on this point is worth quoting at length for the light it sheds on how Heidegger's notion of a *Volk* might be situated in relation to the Nazi one:

> The National Socialist concept of a *Volk* is not only historical or intuitive, but has a scientific and biological basis.
>
> Nietzsche once attempted to explain the development of a *Volk* in this way: "When people have lived for a long time together under similar conditions (of climate, of soil, of danger, of needs, of work), then something arises, in which there is a certain 'agreement,' a *Volk*." Something is lacking here, which for us is central, *race*. Only because Nietzsche—in conformity with his times—does not understand the *Volk* racially as well could he distance himself to such an extent from the *Volk*.
>
> For us too is *Volk* not only race. We recognize the "steady modification" of our inherited condition through place and history, landscape and destiny. The accent, however, lies on the racial. A Jew may live for a thousand years in the German community, with its place and destiny, but he will never become a member of the *Volk* [*Volksgenosse*]. But the Huguenots, who are classified as nordic, would become full members of the *Volk*. (NN 82)

Given that Heidegger disagrees that any concept essential to a description of being human "has a scientific and biological basis," and given his own insistence that all such concepts are in fact grounded in historicity, it would seem reasonable to conclude that his thought on this subject also lacks what is central to Nazi ideology, the idea of race, and that his concept of *Volk* is quite close to the description given here of Nietzsche's.

Moreover, in a context in which Härtle's picture of Nietzsche is a representative sample of the authorized Nazi version, Heidegger's claim, in the *Der Spiegel* interview, that there is a critical engagement with Nazism in his Nietzsche lectures is highly plausible, and certainly with respect to the issue of race. In *The Nietzsche Legacy in Germany 1890–1990*, Steven Aschheim claims, on the other hand, that even if their intent was critical, many passages in Heidegger's Nietzsche lectures "could have been taken as validating the regime's self-conception and aims."[18] This is probably true with respect to some aspects of those lectures, and it is also true that Heidegger does not provide any extended critique, as he might have done, of those Nazi ideas from which he distances himself, including the idea of race (NLG 267). Aschheim's remarks are directed against interpretations of the Nietzsche lectures which claim that they intentionally do not contribute to the political reading of Nietzsche within the Nazi context. As an example of such an interpretation, Aschheim quotes David Krell's claim that what students in these lectures would have heard "was in fact totally out of context" (NLG 266). "But within the contours of the Third Reich and Nietzsche's authorized role,"

Aschheim notes, "the very use of Nietzschean categories and terminology formed part of an already-charged political context informing the audience's receptivity and predispositions" (NLG 267). Within that same context, however, taking into account the nature of the literature being published defining and promoting the Nazi Nietzsche, the critical force of the Nietzsche lectures is clear, at least on the topic of race. Given what is generally being said, and said emphatically, about Nietzsche and race at this time, what Heidegger does not say is once again significant, and would have been perceived as such, as would his statement of a view of Nietzsche incompatible with the Nazi one.

If my analysis so far is largely right, and if it follows that Heidegger opposes any biological concept of race, and instead sees the defining features of a *Volk* as stemming from its history, it would seem that he could not in any way have agreed with Härtle's statement that a Jew cannot become a member of the German nation. In that case, Heidegger would have had to oppose Nazi anti-Semitism, along with every other facet of Nazi ideology having to do with race. But then one has to ask how Heidegger could have supported such a virulently, and openly, racist regime. This is the topic of my next section.

Race and Culture

In *Heidegger and Modernity*, Luc Ferry and Alain Renaut pose these questions about Heidegger's support of Nazism:

> Is it really credible that a sensible and responsible person who joined the National Socialist Party in 1933 could do so without at least "concealing" the anti-Semitic "component" and by being so naive or blind as to imagine it "possible to separate the racism from the movement"? Who—above all, what intellectual who is in principle an attentive analyst of ideas and texts—could imagine that racism in the Germany of 1933 was merely one aspect of Nazism, one not consubstantially bound up with it and its constitutive principles? Rather than dreaming up an unlikely compromise with the unacceptable and attacking what is despicable in this compromise, isn't it more plausible to suppose that Heidegger knew what he had to about Nazism and hence could recognize a *certain* anti-Semitism in himself? Certainly he never subscribed to a biological basis for it (nor to the exterminative fate), but in some of its fantasies, anti-Semitism readily linked up with the idea that a lack of rootedness, in whatever sense one understands rootedness, was not exactly a sign of authenticity.[19]

Nazi anti-Semitism did indeed frequently link Judaism with a lack of rootedness. Härtle finds in Nietzsche a seed of the hypothesis that "the Jews are neither a *Volk* nor a race, but the human anti-race, the parasites of the human species" (NN 47). Alfred Rosenberg, in *The Myth of the Twentieth Century* (1930),[20] also refers to the Jews as a parasitic anti-race (M 437), seeing in Judaism a variety of "raceless universalism" (M 39), which he in turn associates with Bolshevism, communism, Marxism, democracy, liberalism, and international finance. For Rosenberg, these are all instances of the same de-

generate way of thinking. They are all based on an idea of man which is simultaneously individualistic and universalistic. Supposedly, according to this
idea, the species is composed of atomic individuals who are equal and alike,
and who form no significant community except that of humanity in general.
Within Rosenberg's anti-Semitism, then, the Jews are actually identified as a
Volk by the very fact that they lack the features identifying a *Volk*, so that they
are a sort of race/*Volk* that is not one.

It is possible that Heidegger felt some sympathy for the view that Jewish
identity involved, as one of its features, a lack of rootedness, due to the fact
that Jews in the diaspora did not, in a simple manner, belong to and identify
themselves with a single nation and locale. He may well even have felt that this
lack of simple belonging to one nation inclined Jews toward thinking of man
as "man," toward universalism and cosmopolitanism, and thus toward the
politics allegedly associated with these, liberalism and Bolshevism, about
which Heidegger frequently also makes negative remarks. Presumably, he
would only have believed, in contrast with Nazi ideology, that this feature of
the Jewish soul was rooted in history rather than biology. The biographical
evidence concerning Heidegger's personal attitudes and behavior toward Jewish colleagues and students is, on the whole, unclear, but there is enough in it
to render plausible Ferry and Renaut's suggestion that Heidegger recognized
in himself "a certain anti-Semitism."[21] Thus, on the issue of anti-Semitism,
there might well have been a non-biological parallel in Heidegger's thought to
the biologically based anti-Semitism of Nazi ideology. I want now to examine
other elements, pertinent to the issue of race, within the expressed ideology
of National Socialism, to which Heidegger would have been sympathetic because he himself held similar views, but ones grounded in "history" rather
than biology.

First of all, Heidegger would have been attracted to some version of the
idea that a *Volk* forms, or should form, an "organic unity." In his rectoral
address, and in his political speeches and writings during his time as rector,
Heidegger calls for precisely such a unity. For instance, in a speech supporting labor service (January 23, 1934), he affirms "the fact that all belong together in an ethnic-cultural [*volkhaft*] unity,"[22] and maintains that "there is
only *one single* German 'estate' [*Lebensstand*]" (HC 54). "The goal," then, he
claims, is "to become strong for a fully valid existence as a *Volksgenosse* in the
German *Volksgemeinschaft*" (HC 56). For this, it is necessary to know "where
one stands as a member [*Glied*] of this *Volk*" and to know "how the *Volk* is
structured [*sich gliedert*] and renews itself in this structure [*Gliederung*]."[23]
Although, after his resignation as rector, Heidegger no longer uses specifically
Nazi terms like *Volksgenosse* and *Volksgemeinschaft*, he remains committed to a
notion of the organized unity of a *Volk* as something desirable. In the "Logic"
lectures, to the question of who "we" are, he answers, "We stand within the
being of the *Volk;* we are ourselves the *Volk*" (L 57), where "the *Volk* is
created by history" (L 85). Moreover, he still supports a national brand of

"socialism," meaning one which does not aim at "an empty leveling [*Gleichmacherei*]," but which involves "concern for the measure and essential structure of our historical being" and therefore wants "ranking according to calling and work" (L 165).

Heidegger was thus opposed to what he took to be the liberal picture of society as a mere collection of atomic individuals. He could have agreed with the view, expressed in an article in *Volk im Werden*, the journal edited by Ernst Krieck, that "the liberal theory of an industrial society does not recognize the *Volk*, but knows only the free being next to one another of producers, that is, capitalists, the owner of property and the worker."[24] He could have agreed with Rosenberg that "this atomistic world-view was and is the precondition for the political doctrine of democracy" (M 190). And against Marxism, or any brand of international socialism, Heidegger affirmed the belonging of the worker to a national identity in which he would play a central and defining role, and within which he would not be divided from, or against, other classes, a recurring theme within Nazi speeches and writings. In general, Heidegger's ideal *Volk* is always one with a single character and a single destiny. In *Being and Time*, he had already stressed that the historicality of *Dasein* is fundamentally bound up with the destiny of a *Volk*.[25] Ernst Krieck is thus entirely wrong to claim, in "Germanischer Mythos und Heideggersche Philosophie" (1934), that the concepts of *Volk* and destiny do not exist within Heidegger's philosophy.[26] No one who had actually read the relevant sections of *Being and Time* could have believed this. In fact, Heidegger could at any time have supported Krieck's statement that "action, way of life, world-view, and poetry belong inextricably together and bring to expression the line of destiny of a *Volk*,"[27] although doubtless he would have wanted to subject some of the terms in this statement to a deeper scrutiny. What he could *not* have supported was Krieck's view that the constant and basic character of any ethnic group was granted by race, as a biological category (VW II/5 289). It is granted, rather, for Heidegger, by history, in which place and landscape are intimately involved, in a way that he analyzes in his lectures on Hölderlin. Heidegger would therefore also have been attracted to the Nazi emphasis on the link between national identity, and particularly German identity, and a relation to landscape. He would not have been hostile to the notion that "landscape is the native ground, from which each *Volk* takes its origin,"[28] and he probably saw such notions as naive expressions of something that in a more sophisticated version was nonetheless true.[29] His emphasis on the role of decision and resolve in bringing about the unity of a *Volk*, specifically the German *Volk*, and in bringing that *Volk* into its destiny, forms part of this notion of an essential unity which is somehow both present and achieved. It is also consonant with an often-repeated theme in Nazi writings, which frequently referred to the necessity of the Germans "becoming" a *Volk*.[30]

To be sure, by the time Heidegger composes the *Beiträge zur Philosophie*, he is considerably less enthusiastic about the idea of individuals being incorporated into a greater national entity:

> The most dangerous are those in whom the worldless "I" has apparently been abandoned and delivered over to another, which is "greater" than it and to which it is assigned as a part or a member. The dissolution of the "I" in the "life" of the *Volk*—here an overcoming of the "I" is initiated without its first condition: namely, a reflection on being-a-self and its essence. (BP 321)

By this point, Heidegger sees incorporation into the *Volk* as nothing more than a greater assertion of the "I"-subject. It is therefore not in tune with the essential belonging to being toward which his own reflections on selfhood, starting with the "Logic" lectures, are meant to gesture. However, although Heidegger ceases to affirm the language of organic unity and incorporation, since he does not support what this language actually means within Nazism, he retains a strong version of this belief in the unity and identity of a *Volk*, the nature of which he explores in his various lecture courses.[31]

Some of Heidegger's views on the specific nature of the German people also accord with assertions common in Nazi literature. In the 1934–35 Hölderlin lectures, he connects the character of German thought, as manifest in Hölderlin, Nietzsche, and Meister Eckhart, with Heraclitus, and claims that the latter stands for "the original power of occidental-germanic historical existence, in its first confrontation with the Asiatic one" (HHG 133–134). Hölderlin is supposed to have overcome the Asiatic conception of fate, as the ancient Greeks first did in their development as a people (HHG 173). These statements echo ideas frequently expressed by Nazi authors: the belief in a special link between Germany and Greece, the praise of Heraclitus, against Parmenides, as a thinker of becoming rather than being, and, above all, the description of the character of the German *Volk* as determined by a Heraclitean form of becoming. "The German is not, he *becomes*, he develops," says an article in the *Völkischer Beobachter*, citing Nietzsche, and "development is therefore the authentic German discovery and contribution within the great realm of philosophical formulations."[32]

For Heidegger, the identity of a people is bound up with its destiny, its historical mission, the unique role that it is supposedly called upon to play in virtue of its character and situation. Although he becomes increasingly skeptical about the possibility that this can be accomplished at the level of politics, in 1934 he firmly believed that the state was the proper expression and vehicle of the singular historical character and mission of the *Volk*:

> The "state," not as an abstraction and not as derived from an invented right related to a timeless human nature, but the state as the essential law of historical being through whose structure the *Volk* first secures its historical continuity, and that means the preservation of its mission and the struggle to accomplish its task. The state is the historical being of the *Volk*. (L 165)

Like other National Socialists, then, Heidegger opposes the notion of the state as founded upon any conception of universal human rights in that, as one author writes, "For National Socialism the state is not a mere external form, but simultaneously the expression of the essence and will of the *Volk*."[33] Heidegger at this point agrees. Clearly, this idea of the state entails that it should be a monoethnic one—and one, moreover, whose "ethics" are tailored to suit the character of its specific ethnic population.

It is significant that Heidegger maintains, in the "Logic" lectures, that "there is no absolute truth," since "we are for now only human beings and not gods," while insisting that "a truth is no less a truth just because it cannot be held by everyone" (L 79). He does not explicitly say here that ethical principles are expressions of a particular *Volk* rather than absolute truths binding upon all people. But his remarks are nonetheless suggestive of this idea, since they are made against the backdrop of a political context in which Nazi authors were in fact deriding claims to absoluteness with the intention of promoting the alternative view that moral principles are specific and variable, rooted in the characters of different peoples rather than in the nature of a universal humanity. Nazi interpretations of Nietzsche often focused on precisely this point. Härtle, for example, uses Nietzsche in support of the claim that "there is no meta-ethic . . . morals spring from the conditions of life and the will to growth of estates, peoples, races" (NN 10), and Kurt Kaßler, in *Nietzsche und das Recht* (1941), claims that the Nietzschean point of departure maintains that "right is *immanent*, not transcendent."[34] Kaßler's claim that this right is "anthropocentric and biological" (NR 32) would have been anathema to Heidegger, but in his first set of lectures on Nietzsche, Heidegger does point out, and without criticism, that Nietzsche understands the "should" as immanent: "If what-is is conceived as will to power, then there is no need for a should which would first have to be imposed upon what-is, so that what-is could be measured against it. If life itself is will to power, then it is itself the foundation, the principle of any value-positing" (NI 38). I have argued elsewhere that there is, in Heidegger's writings, a form of ethics that is more than merely local and particular, and that is not relativistic.[35] Nonetheless, Heidegger would always have been hostile to any discourse that embraced the idea of universal or transcendent human rights, or, indeed, of rights at all. Although he is only interpreting Nietzsche in the above passage, Heidegger was probably sympathetic to the notion that the character of obligation is immanently rooted in the "life" of a people. At least, he does not take care here to distance himself from that notion, nor, more importantly, from the implications that Nazis drew from it.

Heidegger's sense of the appropriate relations between different peoples or nations also corresponds to some Nazi statements—hypocritical and mendacious, to be sure—on this point. His conception of the singular character and destiny of each people was accompanied by the idea that peoples should be independent of one another and should confront one another from this independent position. Such a relation between peoples is supposed to respect the different identity of each one, while promoting the fulfillment of its unique destiny. As he says in a speech supporting Germany's withdrawal from the League of Nations,

> The will to a true community of nations [*Völkergemeinschaft*] is equally far removed both from an unrestrained, vague desire for world brotherhood and from blind tyranny. Existing beyond this opposition, this will allows peoples and states to stand by one another in an open and manly fashion as self-reliant entities. . . . Our will to national [*völkisch*] self-responsibility desires that each people find and preserve the greatness and truth of its destiny [*Bestimmung*]. (HC 48)

Accordingly, in the second of his lecture courses on Nietzsche, Heidegger suggests that "the future mission of Europe," in which he believes Germany has a special role to play, "can only find its answer through the exemplary and decisive historical shaping of individual peoples in competition with each other" (NH 107).

Although it is questionable in itself, this notion of a creative and respectful competition between peoples who are different but not unequal may seem to be far removed from the reality of Nazism. But it is not at all removed from the claims that Nazi officials and supporters sometimes made, at least in the earlier years of the regime. For instance, in an October 1934 article in *Wille und Macht*, Friedrich Lange writes,

> Hitler-Germany, which places the *Volk* at the centre of thinking, feeling and acting, also respects the character of other peoples. "In that we adhere to our own character with unlimited love and faithfulness," explains the *Führer* in his well-known peace speech of May 17, 1933, "we also, on the basis of the same consideration, respect the national rights of other peoples, and wish from the depths of our hearts to live with them in peace and friendship."[36]

On February 17, 1934, an article in *Völkischer Beobachter* proclaims that "the German racial laws do not wish to pass any judgement over the worth and value of other peoples and races," and that Hitler himself says this in *Mein Kampf*.[37] A few days later, another article supports Nazi policy toward the Jews by stating, "it is self-evident that the Jewish race is not of lesser value [*minderwertiger*] than many other races . . . but one thing is clear, that it possesses a different value [*anderswertig ist*] and . . . is therefore completely unsuitable for a cultural cross-breeding with the German people."[38] And although Ernst Krieck was contemptuous of Heidegger's thought, his own vision for Europe, in 1935, is actually much like Heidegger's one year earlier. "The new Germany," he writes, "is built upon *Volksgemeinschaft*, Europe will be built upon the *Gemeinschaft* of individual European peoples [*Volksindividualitäten*]."[39]

In sum, while Heidegger did not support, and indeed opposed, any biologically based concept of race, he held a strong view of the unity and identity of every particular *Volk*. This view included the idea that each people has a single, unique character and destiny and a set of obligations rooted in that character and destiny. At one time, Heidegger also believed that the nature of a people, with its will to achieve its proper historical mission, was ideally expressed in the form of the state. These arguably essentialistic beliefs certainly form a kind of "cultural" parallel to the equally essentialistic beliefs that underlay biologically based Nazi race ideology. Moreover, while Heidegger combines these beliefs with the idea that different nations can, and should, respect one another in their unique identities, where an important part of that respect consists in the possibility of creative confrontation, his understanding of the nature and mission the German people does suggest that it is in some way special, and that Germany has a particularly important role to play in shaping the future of Europe. And his views about *völkisch* identity could also support the idea that Jews do not belong fully to the German *Volk*, and that they are not able to be full members of any European *Volk*.

Should one conclude from these observations that Heidegger is a "racist" in *some* sense, perhaps a "cultural" racist? Since the term "racism" usually connotes a belief in the superiority of one group over another, Heidegger's essentialism about cultural groups does not by itself qualify him as a racist. It can be argued, on the other hand, that such an essentialism feeds cultural racism, and that it is in any case false. It assumes the homogeneity of each culture, whereas cultures are in fact internally diverse. It also underestimates the extent of interaction between cultures, while misrepresenting the nature of that interaction by interpreting it as an exchange between wholly distinct and independent individual entities. If cultural essentialism is mistaken in these ways, then an attempt to promote its view of ideal peoples and their relations to one another is bound to be oppressive, even if it does not involve any "racism" in the sense of a belief that peoples are hierarchically ordered with respect to one another. A liberal analysis would naturally want to add the moral necessity of respecting certain basic rights that are universal, and to insist on the dangers of ignoring individual rights in the name of any group-identity, a danger made much worse by the presence of a strongly authoritarian state with the power to enforce that identity.

One can, however, agree with all of these criticisms, while maintaining at the same time that there is such a thing as a *Volk*, that cultural identity is not purely a fiction, and that political theory and practice does need to recognize this identity, in one fashion or another. In *Heidegger's Crisis: Philosophy and Politics in Nazi Germany*, Hans Sluga claims that German philosophers in the 1920s and 1930s who raised questions about German identity "failed to consider the possibility that nations are only temporary formations, that their identities are fortuitous and their boundaries shift, that they are discursive constructs with no reality outside the speech that defines them."[40] But if, by "nation," Sluga means not only a state but also a *Volk*, this complaint fails to consider the possibility that peoples can have a genuinely distinct identity without it being the case that one could, for instance, specify that identity firmly through a list of necessary and sufficient conditions. There are hardly any types of things that meet such stringent criteria, and these criteria are clearly not suitable for all kinds of identification and sorting. One should not implicitly posit false alternatives here. It is possible to affirm the reality of cultural identity, in some measure, and still to agree with Sluga in rejecting the "binary logic" whereby one simply "is a member of a particular nation or one is not," and with his suggestion that "the social reality that such political distinctions are meant to regulate consists of an infinitely complex web of relations with all kinds of gradations and variable degrees of closeness and distance" (PPNG 123). And it should be kept in mind that "our" liberal political culture increasingly acknowledges the importance of recognizing cultural membership as a component of the respect due to individuals. I have argued elsewhere that aspects of Heidegger's thought, with the requisite modifications and caveats, can make a positive contribution to an analysis of cultural identity[41] and that an approach which recognizes the identity and difference of peoples has some ethical advantages over one that does not.[42] Such an approach *can* feed cultural racism, but it need not do so, and it can also promote a respect for the other that includes, rather than attempting to overlook, the role of cultural membership in defining his or her identity.

What of the possibility, though, that there is some brand of racism evident in Heidegger's privileging of German identity? I noted two features of this privileging: Heidegger's belief in the power of the German language, and his belief in Germany's historical mission within Europe. Heidegger never says that the German language is superior to all other European languages in every respect, and his view of Germany's mission is combined with the idea that every *Volk* has a unique destiny, but the tenor of some of his remarks might nevertheless raise the suspicion that although he believed that every *Volk* was special, he was inclined to think of the Germans as especially special. This is probably true, and it does point to some cultural bigotry in Heidegger's psychological makeup. I do not mean to suggest that any positive appraisal of an element in one's own culture, and any criticism of an element in another culture, amounts to racism. But there are good reasons to suspect the motives behind the claim that one's own *Volk*, by virtue of its language or manner of thought, has some kind of manifest destiny in shaping the future character of a continent. One wonders how, even if this were true, Heidegger, or anyone else, could be in a position to know it, and if he is not in a position to know it, the question recurs about his motives for asserting it. In that case, the accusation against Heidegger of a degree of personal cultural bigotry is legitimate, although it has only a minor significance for an assessment of his general view of ethnic and cultural identity.

From my analysis so far, then, it would seem that Heidegger embraces a strong view of cultural identity, where that identity is grounded in whatever belongs to the realm of "history," and has nothing to do with biological descent. However, this analysis still does not fully account for the idea that Jews are not quite "rooted" in the German *Volk*, or any *Volk*, if Ferry and Renaut are right to maintain that Heidegger is sympathetic to this idea, as I believe they are. After all, if identity is determined by history rather than descent, why *would* a German Jew have a different manner of thought than any other German? Moreover, on my analysis to this point, his views should entail that within a couple of generations, any people from anywhere could become members of any given *Volk*, and this suggestion simply does not fit well with the language of Heidegger's descriptions of *völkisch* identity. In the next, and final, part of this essay, I propose to ask whether there might not be a "biological" component in Heidegger's view of *Volk* after all.

Race Reconsidered

In March of 1934, Heidegger gave a broadcast lecture entitled "Creative Landscape: Why Do We Stay in the Provinces?" in which he explains his refusal of a second offer from Berlin University. The lecture celebrates the simple existence of Black Forest farmers, and it does so in a highly romanticizing language. Given how closely this language, and the sentiments underlying it, resembles the blood-and-soil rhetoric of the Nazi regime, the lecture has understandably been widely criticized. In it, Heidegger says, "The inner belonging of my own work to the Black Forest and its people comes from a centuries-long and irreplaceable rootedness [*Bodenständigkeit*] in the Alemannian-Swabian soil."[43] Statements like this one pose something of a problem if one wishes to claim that Heidegger's concept of *Volk* has *nothing* to do with "biology." It has indeed nothing to do with *genetics*, but it does not exclude the idea of lineage, of biological descent. It is fair to say that within Heidegger's thought, there is no sense in which the character of a people is transmitted by means that the discipline of biology could describe in terms that are proper to it. And yet, when speaking of *Volk* and related matters, Heidegger always writes under the assumption that the members of the *Volk* possess *Bodenständigkeit*, and that this possession is acquired through their having dwelled in the same place over generations. He always assumes, that is, that the members of the *Volk* are *eingeboren*, native. A *Volk* is constituted by history, certainly, but the possession of that history by its members is linked to descent, to hundreds of years of *Bodenständigkeit* in a particular place.

In the *Logic* lectures, when considering the important role of decision in forming the "we" of the *Volk*, Heidegger adds, "Yet it is not up to us, whether we belong to a *Volk* or not. For that has already been decided, independently of our will, on the basis of our descent [*Abstammung*], which we did not ourselves choose. One can perhaps will citizenship, but never membership in a *Volk*" (L 60). The point seems to be that one can resolve upon the essence, the highest potential, of the *Volk* to which one belongs, and can win that essence, thereby becoming the genuine "self" of that *Volk*, just as *Dasein*, in *Being and Time*, can choose itself authentically or lose itself in the "they" (*das*

Man). But membership in the *Volk* whose essence can be won or lost is not itself a product of decision. In the language of *Being and Time,* one could say that it is part of the facticity of *Dasein.* It is given, and Heidegger always seems to assume that it is given by descent. This assumption is rarely made explicit—the above-cited remark from "Logic" is an isolated instance—but it is hard to imagine how any German resident who did not identify himself or herself with a long line of German descent could feel quite comfortable with the language of *Erde* and *Heimat* and *Vaterland* in the Hölderlin lectures. And in the place of which Heidegger writes in "The Pathway"[44]—where, he says, "more frequently through the years, the oak by the wayside carries me off to memories of childhood games and early choices" (HMT 69), where at times "the east wind is blowing up a storm where mother's home village lies" (HMT 70), where "behind the castle, rises the tower of St. Martin's Church" (HMT 71)—in this place, there does not seem to be any room for a latecomer, an immigrant. The language in which this village is described simply does not welcome the presence of anyone who could not unambiguously locate herself in that place, in virtue of a past that extends well beyond her actual arrival there.

The question then is, How can Heidegger's thoroughgoing anti-biologism be reconciled with his assumption that the members of a *Volk* are defined by descent? Heidegger does not, to my knowledge, confront himself with this question, but the most plausible hypothesis consistent with his views is that descent becomes a determining factor through the way that biology enters "history"; that is, through the inevitable role that it plays in *self-*identification. He could claim that someone who is not located within a particular line of descent will not identify himself or herself completely with the history of the *Volk* whose intergenerational continuity is bound up with certain lines of descent. This claim could justify the belief (supposing that Heidegger did have this belief) that German Jews are never full members of the German *Volk* and that they think somewhat differently than those who are, without attributing this difference to any strictly biological factor. The difference would occur because, due to their awareness of their own descent, Jews would never identify fully with the history of those who do identify themselves unambiguously with a certain physical place, and with the "destiny" that is unfolding there.

But if this is Heidegger's implicit view, he is in some measure *right,* even if he is still very wrong in some of the social and political implications he draws from this view. It is simply a psychological fact that, for certain purposes, people do identify themselves with a history that is tied to their biological line of descent. To the extent that this is a psychological fact, it is even true that, regardless of language or nation or "culture," a Jew may still remain a Jew. Heidegger might have been slightly anti-Semitic, but this assertion is not by itself anti-Semitic. It seems to me that Emmanuel Lévinas, for instance (who is not an anti-Semite), indicates the possibility of a Jew remaining a Jew by suggesting, with Heidegger and Nazi *völkisch* ideology very much in mind, that the identity of being Jewish is linked to the consciousness of the face beyond any homeland, the face that is "absolute" and "without any cultural ornament."[45] For Lévinas, it is this culturally non-specific face that forbids all violence. Lévinas could agree, then, that there is a universalizing tendency in the Jewish mind, that it is linked to a lack of *völkisch* rootedness, to an awareness of belonging to a people without a homeland, and that it inclines Jews to maintain precisely the "error" that Härtle sees Nietzsche as exposing—namely, "the equality of all that bears a human face" (NN 24).

I am maintaining, then, that there is some truth in the idea that one identifies with a *Volk* in part through self-identification with a line of descent, and that this idea is not by itself racist. Nor is it necessarily politically noxious, at least not per se. The thesis that states should be monoethnic, for instance, does not follow from it without additional premises. It can just as easily further one dimension of the recognition of various identities that is required for harmonious and just relations within a multiethnic state. One might object that to identify people in terms of their descent in any way, or to legitimate this kind of self-identification, is dangerous simply because it provides a framework for distinguishing between "races," a distinction which is a necessary condition for racism. This is true, but, returning to a point that I made earlier, while this distinction *can* feed racism, it need not do so. It can also promote a respect for others that recognizes this aspect of the way in which they identify themselves, as opposed to a relation to them that covertly attempts to absorb and assimilate. There is something objectionable in the notion that the only way to maintain harmony, the only way to defeat "racism," is to refuse to admit the reality of any dimension of race, as if it were impossible to respect others while acknowledging difference.

One might also object that if the "reality" of race is established only by contingent psychological and social facts—self-identification by descent being one of these—then the best strategy is to work to eliminate these facts, rather than granting them some permanent, or semi-permanent, status. However, self-identification by descent for certain purposes is a *stubborn* psychological fact, and social ideals must take stubborn psychological facts into account, just as moral and political theories must take into account the general facts about human psychology. If the stubbornness of this fact is invisible to many people, this is because those who locate themselves within the historical lines that predominate in a given society have a tendency to fall into the illusion that they are not locating themselves anywhere, that race and culture are not important features of their identities or, therefore, of anyone's identity. But they fall into this illusion only because their own historical identity is reflected so broadly in the culture and institutions of their society that it seems not to be there at all. As Linda Alcoff points out, "When your own particular and specific attributes are dominant *and* valorized, they can be taken for granted and ignored."[46] It is dislocation that makes one aware of location. In fact, one has no choice but to locate oneself somewhere in history, and if that is so, then self-identification by descent, within certain contexts, is inevitable. Consider the psychological unfeasibility, as well as undesirability, of an African American identifying himself or herself entirely with the history of a majority European population, a history that includes slavery. To quote Alcoff again,

> Systems of oppression, segregated communities, and practices of discrimination create a collective experience and a shared history for a racialized grouping. It is that shared experience and history, more than any physiological or morphological features, that cements the community and creates connections with others along racial lines. And that history cannot be deconstructed by new scientific accounts that dispute the characterization of race as a natural kind. (AMR, 272)

I would add that, given the "historicity of *Dasein*," the fundamentally narrative character of being human, we naturally situate ourselves among stories that extend beyond our birth and that tell us who we are. We therefore cannot help but place ourselves within racially defined historical communities, even when the conditions which brought those communities into being have changed substantially. Furthermore, the existence of a few people, if there are some, who do not in any circumstances identify themselves in terms of descent does not disprove the generalization that most people do, and that social ideals need to take account of this. After all, the existence of few people who do not have the usual needs and desires does not invalidate the generalizations about these needs and desires upon which moral and political theories are based, nor does it suggest that the unusual psychology is the one that should form the foundation of moral and political reasoning.

I have argued in this essay that Heidegger has a strong view of cultural identity as determined by "history" rather than "nature," that he is therefore not a biological racist, and yet he does suppose that descent plays a role in determining membership in a *Volk*. I have speculated that Heidegger could consistently maintain this through the claim that descent enters history through people's self-identification, and that this is a legitimate claim. I emphasize, however, that one cannot directly derive from this claim the further theses that states should be monoethnic, that there is no basis for universal rights, or that cultures and/or races are homogeneous units that can be clearly distinguished from one another. All of these theses require further premises, and ones which do not, I believe, hold up under examination.

But the claim that people do, as a matter of stubborn psychological fact, identify themselves in terms of descent explicates one dimension of the *reality* of race, a dimension that is linked to physical facts but is not describable in physicalist terms. It also suggests one reason, among other possible ones, for why a clear line between "race" and "culture" cannot in practice be drawn. In *Multicultural Citizenship*, Will Kymlicka treats the terms "culture," "people," and "nation" as synonymous, and he provides for them the following definition: "An intergenerational community, more or less institutionally complete, occupying a given territory or homeland, sharing a distinct language and history."[47] A few pages later, he distinguishes cultural groups, thus defined, from "racial and descent groups" (MC 23). If, however, people identify themselves partly on the basis of descent, and if this self-identification plays a role in their location of themselves within a certain intergenerational community and history, then the distinction cannot be so neatly made. With respect to the categories of "history" or "nature," it might be that this aspect of culture/race could in fact be reabsorbed into the sphere of history, since, although it is linked to biological facts, it fundamentally has to do with *Geist*, with a human activity and form of awareness. Perhaps, however, it would be better just to say that some phenomena resist being classified under one these two domains.

Notes

Unless otherwise indicated, all translations are by the author.

1. *Times Literary Supplement,* Jan. 29, 1999, no. 5000, p. 4.
2. "Nur noch ein Gott kann retten uns" (Only a God can save us), *Der Spiegel,* May 31, 1976, pp. 203–204. This interview took place in 1966, but, at Heidegger's request, it was not published until after his death.
3. *Logik: Als die Frage nach dem Wesen der Sprache* (henceforth L), in *Gesamtausgabe* (henceforth GA), vol. 38 (Frankfurt: Klostermann, 1988).
4. There is no precise English equivalent for the German word *Volk.* In different contexts, it can usually be translated either as "nation" or as "people." I will use these translations where appropriate, but will often leave the term in German, to avoid misleading implications.
5. It is nonetheless apparent from remarks like this one that Heidegger is aiming for a revised understanding of biological categories, not a simple rejection of them. On this point, see R. Bernasconi, "Heidegger's Alleged Challenge to the Nazi Conceptions of Race," in T. Faulconer and M. Wrathall, eds., *Appropriating Heidegger* (Cambridge: Cambridge University Press, 2000), pp. 50–67.
6. Interestingly, however, having described the Xhosa as not having a history (*geschichtslos*) (L 83), Heidegger points out that a people without a history is still capable of entering history, so that "a *Volk* without a history, which then enters history, is without history in a totally different sense than the earth is without history" (L 84). He does not say where "negroes" finally fit in terms of this framework, as he simply does not give the matter much thought, but it is not clear that he means unambiguously to support the claim that they are fully part of nature and therefore not human.
7. *Hölderlins Hymnen "Germanien" und "Der Rhein"* (winter semester, 1934/35), in GA 39 (1980), p. 26. Henceforth HHG.
8. "The Self-Assertion of the German University" (1933), trans. William S. Lewis, in Richard Wolin, ed., *The Heidegger Controversy* (Cambridge, Mass.: MIT Press, 1993), pp. 33–34. Henceforth HC. German text: *Die Selbstbehauptung der deutschen Universität, Das Rektorat 1933/34* (Frankfurt: Klostermann, 1983), p. 14.

9. Max Müller, "Martin Heidegger: A Philosopher and Politics—A Conversation," in Günther Neske and Emil Kettering, eds., *Martin Heidegger and National Socialism* (New York: Paragon House, 1990), p. 190. Henceforth MHNS.

10. *Hölderlins Hymne "Der Ister"* (summer semester, 1942), GA 53 (1984), p. 147. Henceforth HHI.

11. *Beiträge zur Philosophie (Vom Ereignis)*, GA 65 (1989). Henceforth BP.

12. *Nietzsche I: Der Wille zur Macht als Kunst*, GA 43 (1985). Henceforth NI.

13. See, for example, NI 113–114.

14. Alfred Bäumler, *Nietzsche der Philosoph und Politiker* (Leipzig: Reklam, 1931), p. 28. Henceforth NPP.

15. He makes this point when criticizing Bäumler's attitude toward Nietzsche's doctrine of eternal recurrence. Heidegger feels that Bäumler rejects this aspect of Nietzsche's thought as unimportant only because "the doctrine of eternal recurrence does not fit with his politics, or at least he thinks it does not fit" (NI 25).

16. Heinrich Härtle, *Nietzsche und der Nationalsozialismus* (Munich: Zentralverlag der NSDAP, 1937), p. 8. Henceforth NN.

17. Cited in NN 55. The full quotation from *The Will to Power* reads: "There is only nobility of birth, only nobility of blood. . . . When one speaks of 'aristocrats of the spirit,' reasons are usually not lacking for concealing something; as is well known, it is a favorite term among ambitious Jews. For spirit alone does not make noble; rather, there must be something to ennoble the spirit.—What then is required? Blood." *The Will to Power*, trans. Walter Kaufmann and R. J. Hollingdale (New York: Vintage Books, 1968), § 942, pp. 495–496.

18. Steven E. Aschheim, *The Nietzsche Legacy in Germany 1890–1990* (Berkeley: University of California Press, 1992), p. 268. Henceforth NLG.

19. Luc Ferry and Alain Renaut, *Heidegger and Modernity*, trans. Franklin Philip (Chicago: University of Chicago Press, 1990), pp. 24–25.

20. Alfred Rosenberg, *Der Mythus des 20. Jahrhunderts* (Munich: Hoheneichen, 1930). Henceforth M.

21. On this point, see Rüdiger Safranski, *Martin Heidegger: Between Good and Evil* (Cambridge, Mass.: Harvard University Press, 1998), pp. 248–263: "Is Heidegger Anti-Semitic?"

22. "Political Texts, 1933–1934," trans. William S. Lewis, in HC 53.

23. *Nachlese zu Heidegger*, ed. Guido Schneeburger (Bern: Suhr, 1962), p. 199. Henceforth NH.

24. Andreas Pfenning, "Zur Soziologie der Volksidee," *Volk im Werden* (henceforth VW) 8, no. 1–2 (1940): 28.

25. See *Sein und Zeit*, 16th ed. (Tübingen: Max Niemeyer, 1986), p. 384.

26. Ernst Krieck, "Germanischer Mythos und Heideggersche Philosophie," VW 2, no. 5 (1934): 248–249.

27. Ernst Krieck, "Das rassich-völkisch-politische Geschichtsbild," VW 2, no. 5 (1934): 291.

28. Hans Rolf Sprengen, "Landschaft und Volksgemeinschaft," VW 2, no. 7 (1934): 434.

29. Within Nazi racist ideology, reconciling a strictly biologistic understanding of the character of a people with this emphasis on landscape poses something of a problem. How can one maintain, on the one hand, that race determines character in such a way that centuries of living in a certain milieu cannot change the ethnic identity of an individual, while maintaining, at the same time, that there is a deep connection between relation to a particular landscape and ethnic identity? In an article in the *Völkischer Beobachter,* "Wirkt die Landschaft auf die Rasse ein?" (Nov. 24, 1935), Ewald Banse offers an ingeniously absurd solution to this problem, suggesting that a race's "*Urlandschaft*" leaves irremediable biological traces in its "idioplasm," which is passed on from one generation to the next.

30. For example, Adolf Hösel, "Der romantische Seher," *Völkischer Beobachter,* July 17, 1934 (n.p.): "When Novalis pronounces: 'The *Volk* is an idea—we must become a *Volk,*' he says a hundred years earlier that which today belongs to the firm content of our knowledge and will." Cf. Waldtraut Eckhard, "Novalis als Urheber der organischen Staatstheorie": "In this sense the words of Novalis can still engage us today: 'We should become' a *Volk,*' or, as Schelegel expressed it: 'Being German lies not behind, but before us.'" VW 9 (1941): 107.

31. For a detailed analysis of Heidegger's thought on this issue, see my "Heidegger's Concept of *Volk,*" *Philosophical Forum* 26 (1994): 101–126.

32. Arthur Rathje, "Nietzsche und das neue Werden," *Völkischer Beobachter,* Jan 22, 1934. Cf. Rosenberg: "This continually 'becoming' (*werdende*) struggle for 'being' (*Sein*) is the Germanic religion, which is present even in those forms of mysticism that are most detached from the world" (M 131).

33. *Völkischer Beobachter,* Jan. 26, 1934.

34. Kurt Kaßler, *Nietzsche und das Recht* (Munich: Ernst Reinhardt, 1941), p. 32. Henceforth NR.

35. In my "Questioning the Sacred: Heidegger and Lévinas on the Locus of Divinity," *Modern Theology* 14 (1998): 299–323; see pp. 300–304.

36. Friedrich Lange, "Was gehen uns Volksgruppen an?" *Wille und Macht* 2, no. 20 (October 1934): 11.

37. "Der Sinn der Rassegesetzgebung des Dritten Reiches," *Völkischer Beobachter,* Feb. 17, 1934.

38. Eugen Fischer, "Rasse und Kultur," *Völkischer Beobachter,* Feb 23, 1934.

39. Ernst Krieck, "Ein neues Europa?" VW 3, no. 6 (1935): 330.

40. Hans Sluga, *Heidegger's Crisis: Philosophy and Politics in Nazi Germany* (Cambridge, Mass.: Harvard University Press, 1993), p. 84. Henceforth PPNG.

41. "Heidegger's Concept of *Volk*"; see note 32.

42. I made this point in the context of an assessment of Emmanuel Lévinas. See my "How Not to Read the Other: 'All the Rest Can Be Translated,'" *Philosophy Today,* Summer 1999, pp. 195–206.

43. "Warum bleiben wir in der Provinz?" (NH 216–218).

44. "The Pathway," trans. Thomas F. O'Meara, revised by Thomas Sheehan, in Thomas Sheehan, ed., *Heidegger: The Man and the Thinker* (henceforth HMT) (Chicago: Precedent Publishing, 1981), pp. 69–72.

45. E. Lévinas, "Meaning and Sense," in *Collected Philosophical Papers,* trans. Alphonso Lingis (The Hague: Martinus Nijhoff, 1987), pp. 95, 96.

46. Linda Alcoff, "Mestizo Identity," in Naomi Zack, ed., *American Mixed Race* (henceforth AMR) (Lanham, Md.: Rowman and Littlefield, 1995), p. 271.

47. Will Kymlicka, *Multicultural Citizenship: A Liberal Theory of Minority Rights* (Oxford: Clarendon Press, 1995), p. 18. Henceforth MC.

Six

Ethos and Ethnos
An Introduction to Eric Voegelin's Critique of European Racism

David J. Levy

As my title indicates, the purpose of this essay is to offer a historical and philosophical introduction to Eric Voegelin's critique of European racist ideology. That critique is contained in two books, *Race and State* and *The History of the Race Idea: From Ray to Carus,* both published in Germany in 1933, and now reissued, in English translation, as volumes 2 and 3 of the thirty-four volume *Collected Works of Eric Voegelin.*[1] In addition to these works, the reader can be referred to an article, "The Growth of the Race Idea," which Voegelin published in *The Review of Politics* in 1940 following his emigration from Austria in 1938 in the wake of the *Anschluss* and in which he summarized for an American audience some of the analytical ideas he had advanced seven years before. This essay also has now been republished, in volume 10 of the *Collected Works,* and though generally it summarizes many of the ideas of the earlier books it also draws upon insights developed in the last book that Voegelin published before his escape from Austria, *Political Religions.* Between them, these works provide a unique contribution to the study of a phenomenon that has rarely, if at all, been analyzed with the philosophical and historical acuity that Voegelin provides. There is nothing like them in the literature on racism, and they remain to this day indispensable, if difficult, reading for anyone seeking to understand the essential character of the phenomenon that they treat.

In *The Origins of Totalitarianism,* Hannah Arendt refers to Voegelin's race books as providing "the best account of race-thinking in the pattern of a history of ideas available,"[2] and in a long, perceptive review of the German edition of *Rasse und Staat* that Helmuth Plessner published in 1934 in the Vienna-based journal *Zeitschrift für öffentliches Recht,* the already exiled philosophical anthropologist judged that Voegelin's work represented a significant advance in understanding the phenomenon of racial ideology in a philosophically adequate way.[3] Nor was it only opponents of National Socialism who perceived the merits in Voegelin's work. For while the Nazi lecturer in international and constitutional law Norbert Gürke described *Rasse und Staat* as contradicting "in its general thought, the National Socialist concept of the people and the state" and as "neither a scholarly nor a meritorious book, but a collection of intellectual constructions that serves to question the basic idea of race," the young Arnold Gehlen, already on his way to making his career within Hitler's New Order as successor to the dismissed Paul Tillich, praised it. He described it in a review in the January 4, 1934, edition of *Die Erziehung* as a book which, despite its political shortcomings, was "an important work" that provided a "first decisive approach to a philosophical analysis of the race problem."[4] Indeed, in his massive polemical tirade against National Socialism, *The War against the West* (1938), the Jewish-born Catholic philosopher Aurel Kolnai—a thinker who was, like Voegelin, deeply indebted to the philosophical anthropology of Max Scheler—classified Voegelin's book among the works that contributed to the ideological climate of Nazi thought—"the work of a shrewd thinker of a counter-revolutionary society whose greatness is only partially due to his stupendous erudition," and who, if "too fastidious to be a National Socialist himself," was still in general terms a theorist "representative of Nazism or at least of its general trend and atmosphere."[5]

As I hope to show, Kolnai's verdict on Voegelin's race books was profoundly mistaken, but the mere fact that he could so misjudge their significance is symptomatic of the difficulties that attended a proper contemporary reading of what Voegelin was trying to show in his analyses of the ideology of race. And if Voegelin's two books created such confusion at the time of their publication, today they present problems that are no less great in an age when any objective discussion of the phenomenon of race and racist ideology is made more difficult still by a climate of opinion in which the cool yet ultimately merciless tone in which he advances his analyses, and the relative merits that he perceives in the work of some race theorists, can all too easily be misunderstood as evincing a degree of sympathy for ideas which the author never felt. Which is to say that Voegelin's two race books require no special ideological pleading. Read with the care that they demand and require, they can scarcely be seen as anything other than the condemnations of National Socialist ideology that they are intended to be. And yet, at the same time, they are, for various reasons, exceptionally difficult texts to understand at all adequately. Only part of this difficulty lies in the fact that their tone in dealing with the phenomenon of racist thought is cold and objective to a degree that will be neither familiar nor agreeable to an audience more used to condemnatory polemics in issues of race. In addition, that audience not only sees no possible merit in theories that once commanded respect in circles that could in no way be considered sympathetic to the Nazi cause, it also thereby fails to perceive the deep intellectual roots and resonances of racist thinking in the mainstream of Western philosophy and science.

In part, these difficulties reflect problems that Voegelin had in organizing his material. This is because he wanted, within one work, both to provide a systematic philosophical analysis of current race theory and to develop an anthropologically informed historical genealogy of what was then a potent, omnipresent climate of political ideas. But there is the further problem that his mode of discourse depends in both style and content on two traditions—the specifically German political thinking that goes by the name of *Staatslehre* and the characteristic interpretive perspective of post-Schelerian philosophical anthropology—neither of which is at all familiar even to students of twentieth-century Continental philosophy.

Moreover, there is the fact that even though *Race and State* and *The History of the Race Idea* are two separate books, published by different publishers—the first by J. C. B. Mohr in spring 1933 in Tübingen, the second by Junker and Dünhaupt somewhat later in Berlin—they form a single analytical unity directed toward the clarification of a unitary spiritual, political phenomenon—that of Nazi racial ideology. Furthermore, the division between the two works does not exactly correspond to the different modes of analysis which each, at first, seems to exemplify. The first book, *Race and State,* is the longer and, at first sight, more explicitly philosophical of the two. However, it not only provides a philosophically systematic analysis of race theory and a critique of its pretensions to provide a scientifically acceptable account of human existence based broadly on the principles of Scheler's philosophical anthropology, but, in its second part, it embodies an account of the political significance of racial theory as a formative political idea that draws on Voegelin's presentation of the relatively recent history of racial thinking. The second book, *The History of the Race Idea,* is a more exclusively historical inquiry that traces the developmental mutation of racial thinking from its inception in the formative changes undergone by biologically oriented thinking in Western thought during the period from the late seventeenth century, as exemplified in the works of the English botanist John Ray, to the nineteenth century, when the theorist Carl Gustav Carus, in his 1849 study of Goethe, uses the image of his hero both to exemplify a theory of the psycho-physical perfection possible to humankind per se and to advance a notion of the intrinsically unequal capacity for perfection attainable by folk of differing individual and ethnic composition.

Many of the authors whom Voegelin discusses in his books are little known today, and even in the work of those who are more familiar to the educated reader, such as Herder, Kant, and Schelling and, among the non-Germans to whom he refers, Buffon, Gobineau, and Darwin, the themes on which Voegelin focuses in furthering his genealogical purpose are ones that usually pass unnoticed among other commentators. And yet nothing could be more mistaken than to assume that Voegelin's apparently eccentric approach to the intellectual history of the West is motivated by any sort of mystificatory intent. Writing in 1933, and from the heartland of the civilized Western tradition, he is trying to analyze a movement of thought which in his own day threatens to displace and overwhelm a conception of what it is to be properly and fully human and to set in its place an idea of man based upon a supposedly scientific sense of the unalterable conflict between races, some of which are desired and even destined to triumph, and the others to wither and perish in an apocalyptic struggle between the earthly powers of good and evil.

Today, it is easy enough to dismiss Nazi racial ideology as an ad hoc confection of atavistic myths and tendentious pseudo-scientific theories, but what Voegelin's studies, and they perhaps alone, allow us to do is to understand, historically and philosophically, how such an otherwise inexplicable ideological complex as National Socialism was able to wreak the havoc that it did both in the minds of those who accepted it and on the bodies of those who were its victims. *Mein Kampf* and Alfred Rosenberg's *The Myth of the Twentieth Century* are intellectually shoddy stuff—that goes without saying—but one cannot even begin to understand the influence that they exerted on the history of a murderous age unless one also understands that, however crudely, they drew upon and developed ideas that not only had a more respectable ancestry but were, in an identifiable sense, central to the self-understanding of the civilization that permitted the murderous regime of Nazi Germany to emerge and all but triumph. It was Eric Voegelin's privilege and pain that, in the 1930s, he was in a time and place that allowed him to do just this.

In recent years, and especially since his death in 1985, Voegelin's work has been the object of considerable attention in the English-speaking academic world. There have been several solid books dealing with the overall structure and content of his thought;[6] and a number of studies that examine particular aspects of his contribution to various areas of twentieth-century thought. However, apart from Thomas Heilke's estimable 1990 work *Voegelin on the Idea of Race*,[7] none of these has discussed Voegelin's contribution to the clarification of the nature and significance of European racial thinking with the attention that it deserves. Even Barry Cooper's compendious study of Voegelin's early writings, *Eric Voegelin and the Foundations of Modern Political Science*,[8] devotes only a few sentences to his two race books, preferring to concentrate on an extended analysis of the multi-volume *History of Political Ideas* and the other writings that he composed after his emigration to the United States.

In part this neglect reflects the fact that, until recently, not only were the two books on race untranslated but, for reasons connected with the circumstances of their first publication, even the German texts were generally unavailable. As already mentioned, both volumes were first published in Germany in 1933, and though, at the time, *Rasse und Staat* received a considerable number of reviews, *Die Rassenidee in der Geistesgeschicte*, which Voegelin in his *Autobiographical Reflections* (1989) modestly designates as "one of my better efforts," was, for understandable political reasons, withdrawn from circulation by the publisher soon after its publication and the remaining copies of the book destroyed. But, significant though these circumstances may be, they are insufficient to explain the neglect that the volumes have suffered even at the hands of otherwise thorough students of Voegelin's work. To some extent we must understand the silence with which, in particular, *Race and State* is surrounded not only in terms of the difficulties of the text but by reference to the pervading embarrassment that surrounds all objective discussion of issues of race in philosophical and political circles. For while *Race and State* is resolutely condemnatory of Nazi racial theory, and especially of its scientific pretensions, it is also very much a book of its time, and, by that token, treats seriously both the phenomenon of race as a possible object of scientific inquiry and the significance of racial or, as we prefer to call it today, "ethnic" consciousness as a mobilizing factor in the constitution of political communities. In a period, such as the present, of increasing ethnic awareness throughout the world this alone would seem to justify its more careful study not only as an item in the history of ideas but as a presently relevant contribution to our self-understanding as political beings.

In order to develop this point, we must look with care at the way in which Voegelin himself approaches the issue of racial thought. Only thus will we be able to understand the distinction that he draws between, on the one hand, the *concept* of race as a potential object of scientific investigation and, on the other, the *idea* of race as a formative political notion capable of engendering feelings of solidarity within communities and thus equip them for action in the world. On the first Voegelin, at least in *Race and State,* is, so far as I can see, intellectually agnostic. By this I mean that it is not entirely clear from the book whether or not he believes that it is possible to construct a philosophically adequate concept of what a race may be. For while he is, for reasons to be clarified below, quite clear that a biologically determinist notion of race is worthless as a means of identifying, still less evaluating, existing human groups or individuals, his relatively appreciative discussion of the race theories of Ludwig Clauss and Othmar Spann suggests that, in 1933, he believed it at least possible that an ontologically adequate concept of race—one that, in Plessner's terms, acknowledges man's "multi-layered existence as a physical, vital, psychic and intellectual being"—might, in time, be conceived. Thus, though critical of aspects of the theories of both Clauss and Spann, Voegelin contrasts their work favorably with the work of other, more exclusively biologically oriented race theorists, such as Fritz Lenz and Friederich Gunther; he does so because, despite their deficiencies, at least Clauss and Spann admit the fact that human identity is not a product of biological heritage alone, but must be construed in anthropologically broader terms, as that of a being possessing, besides its body, a mind and soul from whose combining agencies the reality of both the individual and the political-cultural community are formed historically as units able to survive in the world.

As for the political *idea* of race, the issue is rather simpler. We need not place ourselves in Voegelin's situation, in Austria in the 1930s, in order to note that race is a potent symbol around which communities frequently construct their identities. Here Voegelin's point is that the potency of an idea of race as a politically mobilizing notion at any point in history depends not on its correspondence with any biologically identifiable unit to which it supposedly relates—its real or imagined scientific value—but on historical, cultural factors that make it a preferred label for a group anxious to define the boundaries of its identity. Thus the fact that, in modern times, the biologically derived term "race" is often used in political discourse has less to do with the empirical existence of identifiable, scientifically distinct groups than with the derived prestige which a seemingly scientific term enjoys in a secularized world that identifies science with truth.

In his 1940 article "The Growth of the Race Idea," Voegelin makes explicit the non-cognitive, essentially political, and even quasi-mythic function of the idea of race in National Socialist ideology; in view of the great importance that he attaches to his distinction between the political *idea* and the purportedly scientific *concept* of race—notions potently elided in the self-understanding of Nazi theorists within an environment especially susceptible to the supposed political significance of "hard science"—it is worth quoting what he says at length:

> As a matter of fact, the race idea with its implications is not a body of knowledge organized in systematic form but a *political idea* in the technical sense of the word. A political idea does not attempt to describe social reality as it is, but sets up symbols, be they single language units or more elaborate dogmas, that have the function of creating the image of a group as a unit. The life of social groups in general, and of a political group in particular, when understood in behavioristic terms, dissolves itself into individuals, their actions, and the purposes and motives of such actions. The group as a unit is not found on this level. What welds the diffuse mass of individual life into a group unit are the symbolic beliefs entertained by the members of a group. Every group has its symbols that serve to concentrate into an emotional and volitional substance that which, if viewed empirically, is a stream of human action, articulated by behavior patterns and purposes, of highly questionable unity. A symbolic idea like the race idea is not a theory in the strict sense of the word. And it is beside the mark to criticize a symbol, or a set of dogmas, because they are not empirically verifiable. While such criticism is correct, it is without meaning, because it is not the function of an idea to describe social reality, but to assist in its constitution. An idea is always "wrong" in the epistemological sense, but this relation to reality is its very principle, and there is no point in proving it for every given instance. (VCW X 27–28)

Nevertheless, the choice of a particular symbol, though historically contingent, is not arbitrary; for while

> A political idea is not an instrument of cognition . . . this does not mean that it has no relation to reality, or that any product of a fertile imagination can serve as a political symbol. History shows that social symbols, even when they move very far away from empirical reality, have at least their starting point in it, and

that the link to reality cannot be broken without their function being destroyed. And history also shows that not just any part of reality will be used for the development of symbols but that certain basic universal experiences regularly tend to become the material starting point from which the transformation into a symbol begins. (VCW X 27–28)

In the case of the race idea, the relevant "basic universal experience" in question is man's experience of belonging to a biological unit of descent, and much of the historical material, both in the race books and in the 1940 article, aims to show why this particular source of political symbolization came, in early-twentieth-century Germany, to have the special potency it did. Here Voegelin argues that the political unity of the German state was forged during an age—the late nineteenth century—in which the explanatory value of biological science was widely perceived as having a preeminent cognitive value in explaining the essential character of individuals and peoples as a function of organic inheritance. By contrast, the unity of the nations of Western Europe had been constituted earlier, in a historical era when the sense of group identity was perceived as associated with processes of cultural formation that were understood as stemming from factors other than biological descent alone. It was this historical factor, above all, which, in Voegelin's view, explained the greater susceptibility of German political consciousness to the claims of racist ideology in comparison with the political cultures of the Western nations, which had, as a result, remained relatively resistant to the explanatory pretensions of racist thought.

This does not mean that similar ideas did not exist elsewhere; on this, Voegelin cites the works of Lothrop Stoddard and Madison Grant to illustrate the presence of forms of thinking analogous to Nazi ideology in the political culture of the United States.[9] However, neither in America nor in Britain or France could such symbolic constructs ever attain either the intellectual preeminence or the political impact of their German equivalents.

Voegelin's thesis is not that the ideology of race was, in any sense, a uniquely German creation. Rather, the history of the race idea shows it to be a more general product of the gradual transformation of European thought that followed the dissolution of the spiritual unity of Western Christendom, one of whose effects was the displacement of a spiritually conceived sense of group identity—one founded in shared belief in a world-transcendent God— by one derived from the world-immanent, reductionist explanations of science. In *The History of the Race Idea*, Voegelin traces this process in detail and with a subtlety at which, in this essay, I can only hint. What, in this view, sets the German case apart is only the fact that the political formation of the nation state coincided in time with the point at which this transformation was all but complete.

In his *Autobiographical Reflections*, Voegelin observes, "The motivations of my work . . . are simple. They arise from the political situation" (VCW X 93).

Given this, it is surprising neither that Voegelin, writing in Vienna in the 1930s, should have been drawn to the study of race theory and ideology, both in its scientific aspect and with regard to its political impact, nor that he should focus on the German literature. Not only was this literature more extensive than anything to be found elsewhere, but it was much more influential in forming the political consciousness of the nation. Furthermore, this literature then seemed, to its critics and proponents alike, to provide a plausible, scholarly, and scientific legitimation for a movement, National Socialism, that Voegelin found both morally repugnant and politically threatening.

It was for these reasons that Voegelin believed that simply to contradict the dogmatic assertions of Nazi ideology would be not just intellectually inadequate but politically ineffective as well. For the racist world-view of the Nazi movement not only drew upon elements deeply ingrained in German thought, it also stemmed from the broader process by which, since the Reformation, and more especially since the scientific revolution of the seventeenth century, European man had come increasingly to define his nature and existence in terms derived from the concepts of natural science. This made it necessary to provide an intellectual critique of racist ideology not at the level of political polemic, but in terms of a philosophical anthropology—a theory of the nature and condition of man—that was more hermeneutically adequate than any which a solely natural science of man, still less biology alone, could ever, even possibly, attain.

For this critique, Voegelin drew primarily on the late writings of Max Scheler, whose essay *Die Stellung des Menschen im Kosmos* he read with care when it first appeared in 1928.[10] In *Race and State,* Voegelin refers to Scheler, alongside Helmuth Plessner, Bernhard Groethuysen, Karl Jaspers, and Martin Heidegger, as being among the thinkers who were, in his own day, developing a more critically adequate anthropology. What Voegelin found in Scheler, and may have noted in Plessner's work as well, was a theory of man that, as the latter put it in his review of Voegelin's book, recognized that *Homo sapiens* was not just a creature of his biological heritage but possessed a "multi-layered existence as a physical, vital, psychic and intellectual being" and that, therefore, any attempt to interpret and explain humanity solely in terms of any one of these levels was bound to be reductive and, so, intellectually misconceived. While Voegelin did not adopt Scheler's position in full, this perspective gave him a sufficient starting point for the philosophically radical critique of racist thought that he endeavored to develop.

This is not the occasion to give a full, overall account of the philosophical anthropology that provided Voegelin with the means of advancing his radical critical analysis not only of Nazi-oriented racial thinking, but of every other perspective, including economistic Marxism, that purported to explain the totality of human affairs by reference to what was, in truth, only a single, partial element in the constitutive form of human existence.[11] What interests us here is only the use that Voegelin made of Scheler's anthropology in furthering his own criticisms of the fundamental philosophical assumptions that concerned him. And here it is worth noting that, even in terms of the contemporary state of knowledge of biology and of the mechanics of the genetic transmission of characteristics intergenerationally between individuals and groups, Voegelin had been sensitized to the strictly scientific deficiencies in the literature on which Nazis drew by studies that he himself had made in genetics, when, in 1924–25, in the laboratory of Thomas Hunt Morgan at Columbia University, he had participated in the research that young biologists such as Kurt Stern were conducting on the biology of the *Drosophila* fruit fly.

Thus, quite apart from the philosophical deficiencies which, on grounds drawn from the Schelerian theory of man as a unitary yet stratified being, Voegelin noted in his critique of the biologically determinist tenor of German racial thinkers, he was also able to point to the strictly scientific shortcomings of the ill-conceived biological theories to which these theorists claimed to refer. These thinkers were, he observed, not only bad philosophers but, generally, poor scientists as well. This is significant in conveying the particular importance of his critique; even if, in overall terms, it is, perhaps, a less fundamental matter than his philosophically informed verdict on the necessary inadequacy of *any* construct that claims to explain, as most of the then influential race theorists did, the nature and character of man in exclusively biological terms.

This part of his critique, in the first section of *Race and State*, Voegelin calls "The Systematic Content of Race Theory," and if attention therein to the scientific deficiencies of the theories co-opted by the Nazis is secondary to a broader, Schelerian critique of every such attempt to explain the composite unity of man in terms of any one of his component parts, this must be seen as a function of the defining nature of Voegelin's own line of engagement with his theme, which is to analyze, in terms of an integral political anthropology, the very real political role that scientific theories, whether true or false, may play in forming or deforming political life.

As I see matters, it is this essentially philosophical aspect of the critique of racism in the race books, even more than the subtlety of the historical analyses they deploy, that gives them their claim to our lasting attention. Aside from its merits in contributing to, in Arendt's words, our understanding "of race-thinking in the pattern of a history of ideas," it is this philosophical content that gives to *Race and State*, in particular, its current pertinence in an environment newly awakened to the relevance of biology to human social and political affairs—albeit one presented no longer in the discredited form of a biologically determinist theory of racial constitution and conflict, but now under the more neutral, even benign guise of the biological or genetic engineering of the human substance. This pertinence exists despite the organizational problems of the book and the unfamiliar, perhaps forbidding, discursive framework in which the work is cast. This, then, is why, despite forgoing the ambition of providing a comprehensive presentation of Voegelin's post-

Schelerian anthropological theory, I shall dwell a little longer and in modest detail on what I believe its philosophical structure and significance to be.

Voegelin's anthropological theory is important in this context for two related reasons. First, despite the fact that the presently philosophically well-known figure of Heidegger is mentioned by Voegelin as among those contributing to the new and more differentiated form of anthropology, we know that, in contrast to Scheler, and indeed to Plessner, one of whose works Voegelin had extensively reviewed in 1931, Heidegger's particular variant of anthropological analysis—the fundamental ontology of *Dasein* presented in *Being and Time* (1927)—which Voegelin read in 1929, had left him philosophically unmoved. Second, Heidegger himself regarded his ontology of *Dasein* not just as distinct from but as opposed to the sort of Schelerian anthropology that Voegelin endorsed in 1933. Indeed, in 1928, Heidegger, in *Kant and the Problem of Metaphysics,* had offered what he saw as a refutation of philosophical anthropology and its crucial claim, endorsed by Voegelin, to embody a philosophically foundational science of man. These are important issues which I hope to address in a forthcoming work but which cannot be fully treated in this context. Nevertheless, it is important to say something about the aims and thematic form of Scheler's philosophical anthropology, not least because one of the main effects of Heidegger's current status in philosophical circles has been not just to eclipse the reputation of his once equally, if not more, famous colleague, for whom he always expressed the greatest respect, but to cast doubt on the philosophic credentials of the very enterprise with which, in his last years, Scheler was associated and on whose philosophical framework Voegelin relied.

While not losing sight of the primarily expository, historical interpretive intention of this essay, it would seem both remiss and contrary to the spirit of Vogelin's own conception of his philosophy to neglect, in the context of a presentation of his critique of racist thought, what seems to me the abiding philosophical and political significance of what he has to say. But to do this I must, perforce, also say something about the general character of the intellectual school in which his relevant work is, self-identifyingly, placed. And this is the ideal form of philosophical anthropology—in its structure, its content, and its purpose—as expounded by Max Scheler and then employed, for his own particular and topically distinctive ends, in Voegelin's books on race. The difficulty in doing this is that Scheler died in 1928 and never lived to write the systematic treatise on anthropology that he had promised. What we have from his pen, aside from some fragments in his now published *Nachlass,* is the brief if intellectually pregnant essay *The Place of Man in the Cosmos*—not man's "place in nature" as Meyerhoff's translation of the title would, misleadingly, have it—and the programmatic statement of the range and goal of philosophical anthropology that, somewhat earlier, in 1924, Scheler gave in "Man and History." In this essay, he defines philosophical anthropology as "a fundamental science which investigates the *essence* and *essential constitution* of man, his relationship to the realms of nature (organic, plant and animal life) as well as the source of all things, man's metaphysical origin as well as his physical, psychic, and spiritual origins in the world, the forces and powers which move man and which he moves, the fundamental trends and laws of his biological, psychic, cultural and social evolution, along with their essential capabilities and realities."[12]

This ambitious characterization is typical of Scheler's ever-encyclopedic intentions for his own thought; no one can say how successfully this project would have been attained if he had ever written the treatise he envisaged. Nonetheless, we do have the essay on man's place in the cosmos, which, while compact, does at least contain a sketch of the way he perceives man as an essentially multi-layered being, who, as a unit, actively participates, with every level of his compositional structure, in both the spiritual and the material destiny of the cosmos. Though we can say with confidence that Voegelin always rejected the metaphysical overview that pictures this process in terms of a gradual cosmic inter-penetration of two primordial, metaphysically distinct principles of "spirit" (*Geist*) and "drive" (*Drang*), it is this conception of the ontological range and cognitive scope of philosophical anthropology that Voegelin has in mind when, in the race books, he endeavors to develop his own anti-naturalist critique of racist thought.

We now know, from Barry Cooper's research on Voegelin's early writings, that in his copy of *Die Stellung* Voegelin inscribed a careful note summarizing his own understanding of Scheler's characterization of man as both a being of nature and one who, no less essentially, encompassed, through his possession of "spirit" (*Geist*), a world-transcending dimension as the distinctive mark of his own special nature.[13] What is fascinating in Voegelin's note is the scrupulous way in which he lists the humanly distinctive features that characterize the composite structure of human nature as one that encompasses, within its own essential form, features of every other level of being in which, by virtue of his worldly existence, his act of living, he necessarily participates —not just the distinctively human, but also the animalistic, the vegetative, and the inorganic. This note, while in itself no more than suggestive and even a trifle obscure, as we might expect in a fragment intended only for the author's personal use, gives us at least some idea why it was on Scheler's characterization of philosophical anthropology, rather than on the much more systematic and thorough treatment of the topic that, in the same year that *Die Stellung* appeared, 1928, Plessner had published under the title of *Die Stufen des Organischen und der Mensch* (The levels of organic being and man), that Voegelin relied in developing his critique of racist naturalism.

At several points in *Race and State* Voegelin seems to refer, though without explicitly naming it, to Plessner's book. One of these is when, alongside Scheler's, Plessner's anthropological ideas are given the dubious privilege of being compared, unfavorably, with the treatment of the problem of the relationship, within man, between body, soul, and mind in the much earlier anthropology of Immanuel Hermann von Fichte. Therefore, there can be no question that Voegelin knew Plessner's masterly treatise when he wrote his books on race theory. Furthermore, we also know, from Voegelin's 1931 review of Plessner's essay on the anthropology of power, *Macht und menschliches Natur,* that he appreciated Plessner's thought. In view of Voegelin's note in his copy of *Die Stellung* and his recourse to Scheler's idea of anthropology in *Rasse und Staat,* I can only surmise, albeit tentatively, that Voegelin was, to put it as neatly as I presently can, preferentially drawn to the older man's concept of anthropology as a result of his greater elective affinity for the overt, if ill-defined, religiosity present in the closing sections of Scheler's text. Whether or not this conjecture is correct I cannot say, though, for reasons that I need not expand upon here—connected with the even greater relative ignorance of Plessner's important work compared with that of Scheler among Anglophone students of philosophy—Voegelin's option for preferring Scheler seems to me, at least heuristically and educationally, regrettable. At any rate, the issue is not of central pertinence to either the topic or the argument of this essay. This is because whether Voegelin had chosen to base his critique on Scheler, as he did, or on Plessner, as he did not, the upshot, given the creativity with which he appropriates the principles of a philosophical anthropology embody-ing the conviction that man must be understood as an innately stratified, world-participating being, would have been, so far as I can judge, much the same. This is both because Voegelin does not crudely apply the tenets of Schelerian anthropology to race theory but adapts them, as he needs, to his critical topic and purpose, and because, as he notes of Scheler but might have noted of Plessner as well, there was, before *Rasse und Staat,* nothing in the relevant and substantively adequate anthropological literature that dealt topi-cally and directly either with the philosophically substantive or, soberly, with the political aspects of race theory—a fact that he admits to finding quite shocking in a literary and academic environment awash, as Germany was, in widely disseminated discussions of race by apparently scholarly men purport-ing to be scientists and/or "philosophers."

Judged by the high criteria of his own notions of scientific and philosophi-cal adequacy, the actual race literature was, despite occasional insights, all but worthless. The real philosophers left issues of race alone, and the publicists of racial "science," many of whom held university chairs even before January 1933, were not, in the true sense, philosophers at all. Despite Voegelin's stud-ied tone of objectivity, which I have noted above, we cannot escape the con-tempt with which this devoted student of Max Weber, but not of Weber alone, regards the vast majority of the literature with which he has to deal. That he had to deal with it at all is a function of the historical age of political disorder and intellectual confusion in which he lived and to which he, as a philosopher, tried to respond. But what I admit to finding disconcerting in the position adopted in *Race and State* is the Olympian detachment with which Voegelin seems to hold open the question of whether or not a cognitively valid philosophical theory of race, a particularizing hermeneutics of humankind, could ever, in fact, be attained. As both Plessner and Gehlen agree in otherwise differing estimations of Voegelin's book, this work truly raises issues of race theory to higher levels, but it never quite answers the central question that it seems implacably to raise.

Nevertheless, there is, besides the historical issue of why the race idea came, in modern Germany in particular, to occupy the position it did, a great deal that *Race and State* does indeed clarify. But, in order to say what this may be we must distinguish, with care, for reasons of space more schematically than Voegelin does himself, a number of related notions that were, in his view, confused in the then current literature of race, but which must be separated if the clarification at which he aims is to be achieved. These are, first, the empirical fact of race, or ethnic, difference within the general body of mankind; second, the political idea of race as a mobilizing principle of group formation and identification; third, the notion of an explanatory science of race; and fourth, the concept of a philosophically adequate theory of race. Of these, it is the last that Voegelin finds the most interesting but also the most complex and, in a definable way, mysterious. Here my use of the term "mystery" must be taken in its strict, technical sense, as it is used, familiarly enough, by theologians to analyze aspects of religious experience and belief where the matters involved may be linguistically explicated but not exhaustively explained. In treating such issues, the role of the linguistic concepts used by the theologian is to identify, define, or delimit in what their mysterious element consists—or, put another way, what it is in the phenomenon to be clarified and communicatively conveyed that can be empirically identified as a reality of the believer's experience or faith but that cannot be explained in terms of world-immanent cause and effect between materially existing, empirically identifiable objects.

Two relevant theological examples of such mysteries are, first, the Catholic doctrine of transubstantiation, in which, at the moment of consecration in the Mass, the bread of the host actually becomes the body of Christ and the wine his blood; second, the doctrine of divine creation from nothing that, in Biblical religions, is held to occur once only, at the moment of cosmic inception resulting from an act of creative will enacted by a world-transcendent, eternal God. These are, in the only authentic sense of the term, theological *mysteries* because, though they can and must be identified and described in conceptual language drawn from man's experience of the world, they cannot be explicated in terms of processes otherwise familiar in our mundane experience. In the first case, transubstantiation, bread and wine become, really and not just symbolically in the mind of the believer, flesh and blood: in the second, creation, something existent emerges from a prior void. In transubstantiation, bread and wine ontologically become flesh and blood. At the moment of creation, something real and experienced, the cosmos, begins to be where nothing was before in an otherwise ontologically unparalleled event of cosmogenesis.

Although I invoke here the theological concept of mystery to clarify issues in Voegelin's anthropological theory, the reader must bear in mind that he or she is not being asked to share with the religious believer acceptance of the truth or falsehood of the examples given. These are matters pertaining to the region of faith alone. Theological mysteries, in this sense, are real, definable items within the regional ontology of religion; as such, they are the business of the theologian, who is, as it were, the scientific analyst, or regional ontologist, of the religious realm. In this same sense, the philosophical anthropologist must be the regional ontologist of the sphere of human nature. Therefore, in adopting the concept of mystery for anthropological purposes, what is brought to our attention is the existence, within the realm of anthropology—the science of man—of issues concerning the relationship of body, soul, and mind that are, in the same or, at least, a sufficiently analogically identical sense as in the mysteries of theology, truly mysterious—issues that, therefore, may be conceptually clarified by a theory of ontological stratification even when the causal connections between the levels cannot be exhaustively explained.

What this implies is that though a philosophical anthropology can identify the levels of being present in the ontological composition of human nature—bodily material and form, psychic or mental processes, and spiritual or ideational impulses that give sense and direction to human life—it cannot give an explanatory account of how any one of these acts on or reacts with the others. That, as a matter of fact, they do, we know from our fellow human beings, in our present experience of both ourselves and others, and from the records of the historical past. But quite how or why things should be as they are we cannot, thus far, say. Whether, in the future, we will able to give an exhaustive explanation of the informing structure of human nature is an open question, on which the scientifically proper attitude is honest agnosticism. What is, however, an object of present knowledge is the enduring existence, within the phenomenon of man, of the complex, internally differentiated whole, the human composite, that we observe and experience in our own and other selves. In this sense, a philosophical anthropology, an ontology of man, is a descriptive but not, or not yet in full, an explanatory science. It describes phenomena that it cannot completely explain. And the accuracy of its descriptions must, Voegelin insists, be judged in accord with the ways we experience human beings to be, without prejudice toward any hypothesis that purports to explain how or why this may be. So seen, philosophically, the major problem in what purported to be a science of race was that its claims to provide a biological explanation for mental and spiritual phenomena were both conceptually and empirically flawed.

Let us take each of these two aspects of the deficiencies in racial science, the conceptual and the empirical, in turn. In *Race and State* Voegelin characterizes race science as one, if among the most currently influential, of what he calls "super-power constructions." If this term evokes memories of the well-known Marxist distinction between base and super-structure, these memories should be speedily set aside. As Voegelin uses the term "super-power construction" he means by it quite the reverse of what super-structure means in Marx. While Marx sees the super-structure as an epiphenomenon of the causal base, Voegelin designates as the super-power the level within a phenomenon to which a privileged causal status is attached. In this view, Marxist economism is, like race science, a super-power construction. The difference between the two is that while Marxism explains the generation and content of ideas by reference to a causal base, in Voegelin's terms, a causal super-power, identified with the economic process, race theory goes a step further along the road of determinist materialism by explaining the cultural, psychic, and ethical field in terms of the biological composition of the group that produces it.

This comparison between Marxism and scientific racism, which Voegelin makes gleefully explicit, was almost guaranteed to infuriate the Nazi sympathizers among the practitioners of race science—who were the vast majority —and that was at least part of his intent. However, his more serious philosophical point is to argue that *every* super-power construction is conceptually flawed because it ignores the fact that each level within a human phenomenon has its own intrinsic lawfulness—is subject to an innate dynamic of its own— and that, therefore, no one level can be identified as the formative cause of any other. At most we can say that the existence of one is the ontological condition for the existence of another; in this sense it is obviously true that there can be no cultural, ideational, or moral sphere without the prior existence of a group of biologically formed individuals who may, or may not, be the historical bearers of particular systems of values and spiritual qualities. Only to this extent can we speak of a hierarchical relationship between levels of human being in which the biological individual and group must be seen as the ontological precondition for the historical, cultural and moral values with which he or they are empirically and historically associated. However, it is pure superstition and a conceptual fallacy to move from this elementary descriptive observation of any particular historical association—Welshmen with rugby and West Indians with cricket, for instance—to the claim that it is their being, in terms of their biological descent, either Welshmen or West Indians, that causes them to pursue the sport they do. Yet this is just what race science inevitably does.

As this example is intended to indicate, the logical fallacy involved in the typical race scientist's illegitimate transition from the observation of the historical fact of a group's cultural affinity for an activity or attitude—sometimes merely impressionistic, sometimes decked out in the armor of "empirical" research—to the claim to have discovered a racial, causal connection is obvious, and may even, as in the case given, seem even a trifle comic. Furthermore, the simple consideration of the fact that a Welshman born in Barbados might well be culturally drawn to take up cricket, while a West Indian raised in Pontyprydd might be similarly predisposed to take up rugby, clearly exemplifies what Voegelin means by his observation that each level—in this case, the cultural—is subject to an innate, autonomous dynamic of its own. Yet, as the example of German race science's obsession with the contrast between the honest, brave "Aryan" and the shifty, exploitative "Jew" indicates, when associated with atavistic prejudices and political fears, this logical shift may, at times, be fraught with sinister consequences, especially when, as here, it becomes, for specific historical reasons, bound up with a group's perceived need to define its identity over and against that of another, regarded as embodying the supposedly threatening presence of an alien, hostile power. And, as Voegelin illustrates in his chapters detailing the trend within race science to counterpose the self-affirming idea of the innate nobility of the in-group with the evil integrally embodied in the counter-idea of the character of the out-group—an idea that draws tacitly on Carl Schmitt's theory of the inherent tendency, within communities, for political identity to be structured around a conflictual opposition between the "Friend" and the "Enemy"—the result can easily be, as it was in Nazi racism, to associate all valuable qualities with those attributed to the self-chosen valued "race," and all evil with the supposedly hostile character of those defined as pertaining to the enemy-other, regardless of the actual empirically identifiable qualities actually observable in each. This is the fearful logic that leads implacably to the practice, first, of exclusion, and then potentially, as historically it did, to genocide.

Here we see, in exemplary form, the mechanism by which the conceptual and empirical fallacies of an explanatory race science can, under certain conditions, come to be associated with both the mobilizing role of a political idea of race and the empirical existence of ethnically diverse groups within a state, to murderous effect. This is something that Voegelin observes, with prophetic acuity, in his philosophical critique of race thinking—based, as it is, on a theory that allows for the reality of identifiably different groups that may be bound by ethnic descent and also be the historical bearers of certain ethically diverse qualities. Hence my title, "Ethos and Ethnos."

Notes

1. Eric Voegelin, *Race and State*, trans. Ruth Hein, intro. Klaus Vondung (Baton Rouge: Louisiana State University Press, 1997); idem, *The History of the Race Idea: From Ray to Carus*, trans. Ruth Hein, intro. Klaus Vondung (Baton Rouge: Louisiana State University Press, 1998). All references to Voegelin's *Collected Works* (henceforth VCW) refer to the edition in thirty-four volumes now published by the University of Missouri Press, 1989. For a general study of Voegelin's race books, see Thomas Heilke, *Voegelin on the Idea of Race: An Analysis of Modern European Racism* (Baton Rouge: Louisiana State University Press, 1990).

2. Hannah Arendt, *The Origins of Totalitarianism* (New York: Harcourt Brace Jovanovich, 1973), p. 158 n. 3.

3. *Zeitschrift für öffentliches Recht* 14, no. 3 (1934): 407–414.

4. Full references to these reviews of *Rasse und Staat* can be found in Klaus Von-
    dung's introduction to the English translation of the book, Voegelin, *Race and
    State*.

5. Aurel Kolnai, *The War against the West* (London: Viking, 1938). I have discussed
    Voegelin's debt to Scheler in David J. Levy, *The Measure of Man* (Columbia: Uni-
    versity of Missouri Press, 1993), esp. pp. 44–50.

6. See especially Ellis Sandoz, *The Voegelinian Revolution* (Baton Rouge: Lousiana
    State University Press, 1981); Eugene Webb, *Eric Voegelin: Philosopher of History*
    (Seattle: University of Washington Press, 1981); Kenneth Keulman, *The Balance
    of Consciousness* (University Park: Pennsylvania State University Press, 1990); and
    Glenn Hughes, *Mystery and Myth in the Philosophy of Eric Voegelin* (Columbia:
    University of Missouri Press, 1993).

7. Thomas Heilke, *Voegelin on the Idea of Race* (Baton Rouge: Louisiana State Uni-
    versity Press, 1990).

8. Barry Cooper, *Eric Voegelin and the Foundations of Modern Political Science* (Co-
    lumbia: University of Missouri Press, 1999).

9. See Lothrop Stoddard, *The Revolt against Civilization: The Menace of the Under-
    man* (New York: C. Scribner's Sons, 1922), and Madison Grant, *The Passing of
    the Great Race; or, The Racial Basis of European History*, 4th ed. (New York:
    C. Scribner's Sons, 1932).

10. Max Scheler, *Man's Place in Nature*, trans. Hans Meyerhoff (Boston: Beacon
    Press, 1961).

11. Readers who are interested in exploring this issue further may refer to my book
    Political Order: Philosophical Anthropology, Modernity and the Challenge of Ideology
    (Baton Rouge: Louisiana State University Press, 1987).

12. Max Scheler, "Man and History," in *Philosophical Perspectives*, trans. Oscar A.
    Haac (Boston: Beacon Press, 1958), p. 65.

13. Cooper reproduces, in translation, the first part of this note in *Eric Voegelin and
    the Foundations*, p. 169.

Seven

Tropiques and Suzanne Césaire
The Expanse of Negritude and Surrealism

T. Denean Sharpley-Whiting

Born in 1913 in Trois-Ilets, Martinique, the picturesque village where Napoleon's Joséphine spent her adolescence, Suzanne Roussy was a philosophy student in Paris in the 1930s. Her philosophical debut would not occur until the onset of World War II. In 1937, Suzanne Roussy became Suzanne Roussy Césaire. She returned with then aspiring Negritude poet Aimé Césaire to their native land of Martinique in 1939 and took a teaching position at the Lycée Victor Schoelcher. Among the lycée's students were the future theorist of global oppression Frantz Fanon and the creator of the concept of *Antillanité* Edouard Glissant. On the teaching faculty was the philosopher René Ménil, a contributor to the Marxist-Surrealist pamphlet of 1932, *Légitime défense*.

The mounting discontent of the French right during the 1930s, expressed most fervently in the *cri de coeur* "La France aux Français" (France for the French), Germany's rapid rebuilding in the *après-guerre* years, and the attendant rise of fascism in Italy, Spain, and Germany would have grave consequences for France and Martinique. In June 1940, France, under the leadership of Marshal Henri Philippe Pétain, hero of Verdun in the Great War, signed an armistice with Germany. Under the terms of the armistice, France was arbitrarily partitioned and occupied by Germany and paid a daily indemnity of four hundred million francs. After toppling the Third Republic, and thereby ridding a sinful France of its perceived excesses, a right-wing Nazi-collaborating *État FRANÇAIS* at Vichy with Pétain at its helm administered France and its colonies. Names such as Pétain and Admiral Robert would forever be associated with the Axis powers and Hitlerism. Under Pétain's Vichy government, there was very little cover for organizing among progressive cultural and political dissidents. The label of "Communist" was hurled at liberals and other leftists with frequency and swiftness. The democratic principles

115

of liberty, equality, and fraternity that had been held sacrosanct in France were quickly dispensed with during the Nazi collaboration era of 1940–44. A repressive intellectual climate reigned on the island of Martinique under Admiral Robert and in France proper. Freedoms of the press were stamped out in favor of censorship; and groups and individuals committed to human freedom and transformation were routinely persecuted, imprisoned, or exiled. At the lycée, Suzanne, who frequently skipped the school's morning *La Marseillaise* ritual in protest of the tyrannical and racist nature of the state, was repeatedly threatened with dismissal from the faculty.[1]

Inspired by a visit to his homeland in 1937 while still a student in Paris, Aimé Césaire published *Cahier d'un retour au pays natal* in 1939 in the periodical *Volontés* with no literary fanfare. The work encapsulated the discontent of the race-conscious, metropolitan-educated black intelligentsia returning en masse to Martinique at the dawning of the war. The rose-colored glasses, as the cliché goes, came off, and the horrendous facts of Martinican existence were poetically laid bare. The island of Martinique and its people, mired in dire poverty because of colonialism and choking from their imbibing of bilious stereotypes of intellectual and cultural inferiority, continued to look toward France as the model of cultural excellence—one to be appropriated and imitated. Criticisms of West Indian literature as imitative, servile, sterile, and inauthentic began nonetheless in 1932 with Paulette Nardal's essay "Awakening of Race Consciousness," quickly followed in June 1932 by the publication of *Légitime défense*. In this manifesto, Etienne Léro and René Ménil challenged their West Indian literary forebears and contemporaries to create an original literature. Primarily taken to task were such notables as the Guadeloupean Emmanuel Flavia-Léopold and the Martinican Gilbert Gratiant, on the basis of their perceived pedantic poetic mediocrity, for their strict adherence to the Romantic and French Parnassian schools of poetry. As Ménil writes in "General Observations about the Colored 'Writer' in the Caribbean,"

> [T]he Antillean of color makes the tour of ideas (broadminded, he says) and finds himself among the last who appreciate the artificial character of the infatuation with Greco-Roman bric-a-brac, the Parthenon. . . . *This abstract and objectively hypocritical literature interests no one: not the white because it is only a poor imitation of French literature of yesteryear, nor the black for the same reason.* . . . Boredom, condemnation of the self by the self, weighs upon the shoulders of the black Caribbean writer. His works are bored and boring; depressed and depressing. (Ménil's emphasis)[2]

Less the sardonic tone, Ménil's commentary echoes that of Paulette Nardal. At the heart of Ménil's polemic is an analysis of the depersonalization inherent in the West Indian writer's prose and poetry. The black Caribbean writer was so thoroughly alienated, so enamored with French-centric cultural practices, thus suppressing passions and emotions that could be construed as outside of that tradition, that he was blinded to "the feeling of the cane cutter before the implacable factory, the feeling of solitude experienced by blacks throughout the world, the revolt against injustices which he suffers above all in his own country, the love of love, the love of alcohol dreams, the love of inspired dances" (GE 8). The genius of the New "American" Negro writer, whose focus on folk and folklore seemed to convey a sense of originality, is also cited as inspiration for their Francophone counterparts. Committed to re-creating this dynamism in Martinican literature and culture, Suzanne Césaire, Aimé Césaire, and René Ménil founded the cultural review *Tropiques.*

In the review's fourth issue, in January 1942, Suzanne Césaire offered her own critique of West Indian literature in "Misère d'une poèsie: John Antoine-Nau":

> Talent? Certainly for those whom it interests. But what a pity! He looks. But he has not "seen." [H]e does not know the Negro soul. . . . It is graceful. It is overdone. Literature? Yes. Literature of the hammock. Sugar and vanilla literature. Literary tourism. Blue Guide and C. G. T. Poetry, not so. . . . [T]rue poetry is elsewhere. . . . Martinican poetry will be cannibal or it will not be.[3]

In her use of the word "cannibal," Suzanne Césaire issues a literary decree regarding the orientation, and even existence, of Martinican poetry, and plots conceptually the course of an original West Indian literature. The Martinican writer would assimilate, cannibalize, and appropriate white Western culture, its various theoretical tools, and its language, in the exploration and articulation of the specificities of Martinican experiences and reality. In this new cannibalizing mode, the writers of *Tropiques,* more specifically both Césaires, adopted as their critical and artistic tools of choice a Negritude inflected with surrealism—a poetic movement steeped in Hegelian dialectics and Freudian psychoanalysis and equally committed to human freedom. For her part, Suzanne Césaire's use of surrealism allowed her to push the envelope of Negritude's Africanist parameters as espoused by Aimé Césaire, to include the specificity of the Martinican situation. She theorized a Negritude that recognized the racial and cultural *métissage* of the island, its history of "le brassage le plus continu" (the most continuous intermingling), as she writes in "Malaise d'une civilisation." Africa has its place in the Martinique sun, but, as she writes in "1943: Surrealism and Us," the time has come to "transcend finally the sordid antinomies of today: whites–blacks, Europeans–Africans, civilized–savages."[4] "[D]elivering the bread of its depth" (SN 18), Suzanne Césaire's Negritude set in motion the idea of the multiplicity of Martinican origins as a result of historical processes, a Negritude that would definitely offer intellectual sustenance to the hybridizing theories of race and writing Antillanité, and later to the Creolité of Martinicans Patrick Chamoiseau, Raphael Confiant, and Jean Bernabé.

Tropiques: revue culturelle: The Remedy for
the Martinican Cultural Void

The cultural review *Tropiques* made its debut in Fort-de-France, Martinique, in April 1941. The quarterly could be purchased at 12 francs per issue or 40 francs for a year's subscription, increasing to 20 francs and 75 francs, respectively, by 1945. Yearly subscriptions were rare, as the readership was composed mostly of students. The review was funded primarily out of the pockets of the Césaires and Ménil, and its conceptual depth, breadth, and subversive artistic politics did not escape Vichy officials on the island. The island's bourgeoisie also opposed the review and pressed for its discontinuation. In 1943, an explosive standoff occurred between the editors and Vichy officials. In a letter to Aimé Césaire, dated May 10, 1943, Lieutenant Bayle, chef du service d'information, informed him that he was forbidding publication of the review by withholding printing paper. In returning the manuscripts scheduled for publication, he accused the contributors of "poison[ing] minds, sow[ing] hatred, and destroy[ing] morals." *Tropiques* was not a "literary or cultural review," he continued, but a "revolutionary, racial and sectarian review."[5] Disconcerted by the review's republication of Schoelcher's texts, Bayle insisted that since the abolitionist era, "France has engaged in a politics of racial equality that it has not just proclaimed, but which it has more sweepingly put into practice." Bayle deduced that Schoelcher "would be quite surprised to see his name and words used for the profit of such a cause" (T xxxviii). Undeterred by Bayle's letter and refusal to grant the paper necessary to print *Tropiques*, Aimé and Suzanne Césaire, Georges Gratiant, Aristide Maugée, René Ménil, and Lucie Thésée responded in a laconic one-page letter two days later, on May 12, in which they catalog all and sundry invectives used by Bayle to describe the review and its editorial collective: "racists," "sectarians," "revolutionaries," "ingrates and traitors to the fatherland," "poisoners of minds."[6] The collective drew comparisons between their agenda and that of other revolutionary thinkers. If they are "ingrates and traitors," then they are in the spirit of Zola, who denounced the "reactionary press"; "revolutionaries like Hugo of "Châtiments"; "sectarians, passionately so, like Rimbaud and Lautréamont" (T xxxvix). Their racism, they conclude, is the racism of Toussaint Louverture, Claude McKay, and Langston Hughes rather than that of Drumont and Hitler. Volumes eight and nine of *Tropiques* were published in October of that year. And in that sixth issue that so rattled Lieutenant Bayle, Suzanne Césaire had defiantly challenged the authoritarian state of affairs on the island and declared that surrealism was in the service of liberty "in 1943, when liberty itself is threatened throughout the world."[7]

April 1942 marked the one-year anniversary of *Tropiques*. In its first year of existence, Suzanne Césaire published in it four articles on varied topics from

Frobenius's ethnology to André Breton's surrealist poetry. For the anniversary issue, although it was not proclaimed as such, Suzanne Césaire wrote the first of three of the most pioneering and provocative essays of her short-lived literary career, "Malaise d'une Civilisation." The theme of cultural sterility expressed in the domain of Martinican art and literature predominates, and World War II functions as an analytical backdrop. Césaire situates the dilemma within the critical interstices of Frobenius's theories on culture, race, and ecology and Breton's automatic writing. The former, a German ethnologist, made a significant impression on young black students in Paris upon their first reading of his reprinted essay on spiritism in Central Africa in *La Revue du monde noir*. As Negritude author Léopold Senghor admits in his preface, "Lessons of Leo Frobenius," to *Leo Frobenius: An Anthology*, "We knew by heart Chapter II of the first book of the *History*, entitled 'What Does Africa Mean to Us,' a chapter adorned with lapidary phrases such as this: 'The idea of the "barbarous Negro" is a European invention, which in turn dominated Europe until the beginning of this century.'"[8] Senghor continues, "Leo Frobenius was the one, above all others, who shed light for us on concepts such as *emotion, art, myth, Eurafrica*" (LF vii).

Frobenius combined the four branches of science—history, archaeology, ethnography, and cultural morphology—in his study of the meaning and phenomena of culture. For the Negritude writers, Frobenius's valuing of concepts such as emotion, intuition, and so on, are "concepts," as Senghor asserts, "or synonyms which we confront when we are considering Negroes. . . . It is easy to guess the consequences of this discovery and the increased self-confidence which it gave us" (LF x–xi). By creating such terms as *paideuma*, the "spiritual essence of culture in general" or the "*soul*," Frobenius divided civilizations into two categories, Ethiopian and Hamitic. These civilizations subscribed to different methods of interpreting reality—"intuitive" or "mechanistic."[9] Such a division was neither racial nor quantified as superior or inferior, for Frobenius maintained that the German soul approximated the Ethiopian essence or style, and that all cultures possess degrees of one or the other:

> The mechanistic approach is nowadays very much in vogue, and the intuitive correspondingly rare. . . . Both, in their way, are comprehensive, penetrating, almost compulsive modes of thought, with their own claim to interpret reality. Nor am I suggesting that there is anything especially new or superior about the intuitive method. As for novelty, Goethe himself took a thoroughly intuitive view of the world . . . so that he was not wrong in predicting that his work would never be popular—even though tags from *Faust* are on everybody's lips. As for superiority, every culture we know has oscillated between the two poles of mechanism and intuition. . . . However, in advancing the theory that we are moving into a new cultural era, the advent of which can be felt rather than proved, I am bound to support the revival of an intuitive attitude.

It must also be stressed that there is no such thing as an absolutely mechanistic or an absolutely intuitive outlook. It is a question rather of the predominance of one or other of two tendencies. . . . [10]

Hence the Ethiopian style apprehends reality intuitively rather than mechanistically, and is prone to emotion and given over to the creation of myths, art, and poetry. The Ethiopian style is one of abandon, of harmony with nature, while the Hamitic style, preoccupied with the domination of nature, is one of struggle. Moreover, according to Frobenius, civilizations do not progress in a linear fashion from primitivity to modernity, nor does mankind create or perfect civilization. Civilization develops in manifold directions, in a nonlinear fashion through the shock or surge of the *paideuma's* interaction with living species. Each shock, writes Frobenius in his *History of Civilization*, occasions "new sentiments of life," and "the history of civilization is the history of transformations of the sentiments of life."[11]

In following Frobenius's morphology of cultures, Suzanne Césaire's premise in "Malaise d'une civilisation" is that the war is a *paideumaic* surge or shock, an "inexorable pressure of destiny" that "will dip the whole world in blood in order, tomorrow, to give it its new face." As imperialist and catastrophic as these "troubling times" are,[12] they are, importantly, the horrific catalyst of a new humanism, of a new art in Martinique in which the "suffering, sensitive, sometimes mocking being" pervasive in Martinican folkloric traditions would be represented "in Martinique's ordinary literary products" (MuC 43). The present war-torn age, Césaire seemingly contends, cannot but reshape Martinican destiny in terms of the self and culture. But before this new date with destiny can be realized, Martinique, so long in the shadow of Frenchness that a malaise has gripped its soul, must be cured via an unearthing of its true self. Frobenius again proves useful as Suzanne Césaire begins "Malaise d'une civilisation" by exploring the topographical nature and geographical position of the island and their relationships to the Martinican personality and the paucity of authentic art and literature.

Martinique is "the Tropics," she notes. Thus, despite reprehensible living conditions and obscene mortality rates, imported Africans adapted because of the similarity rather than dissimilarity of the island's climate to that of their homeland. And yet this adeptness of Martinican people at climatic adapting, at survival over the course of centuries of economic, social, and political depravation, has not resulted in a similar production of "authentic works of art." How, Césaire asks, "is it that over the centuries no viable survivors of the original styles have been revealed—for example, those styles that have flowered so magnificently on African soil? Sculptures, ornate fabrics, paintings, poetry?" (MuC 44) Refuting the imbecilic claims that attribute "climate," "inferiority," "instincts of laziness, theft, wickedness" to Martinican artistic torpor, Césaire insightfully argues:

[I]t is explained I believe as follows:

1. The horrific conditions of being brutally transplanted onto a foreign soil; we have too quickly forgotten the slave ships and the sufferings of our slave fathers. Here, forgetting equals cowardice.
2. An obligatory submission, under pain of flogging and death, to a system of "civilization," a "style" even more foreign to the new arrivals than was the tropical land.
3. Finally, after the liberation of people of color, a collective error about our true nature, an error born of the following idea, anchored in the deepest recesses of popular consciousness by centuries of suffering: "Since the superiority of the colonizers arises from a certain style of life, we can access this power only by mastering the techniques of this 'style' in our turn."

Let's stop and measure the importance of this gigantic mistake. (MuC 44–45)

Martinican cultural inertia is multiply rooted. The horrors of the Middle Passage are evoked; the life-threatening and "style"-altering cultural immersion processes that required a repression of one's name, country, family, clan, language, and culture, and the atrocities of chattel slavery are cited as explanations, but perhaps the most damaging, in Césaire's view, has been the mastery of the French "style" as a result of centuries of compelled submission. For her, there are apparent inconsistencies between the Martinican's authentic style or self and the life that he leads in 1942 as a result of slavery and colonialism. The conflict in the Martinican psyche must be ferreted out for a better understanding of just who the Martinican really is and who he has become as a result of various historical processes. Again turning to Frobenius, she asks, "What is the Martinican?" "A human plant" is the response (MuC 45). The Martinican coexists peacefully rather than antagonistically with nature; the Martinican abandons himself to the "rhythm of universal life." In this comparison, Césaire debunks at once the stereotype of the "lazy" Martinican. The Martinican "vegetates"; his favorite expression is "Let it flow" (MuC 45). In heading off any assumptions regarding Martinican passivity, Césaire follows up by relating that independence and tenacity are also characteristics of the plant—thus, the Martinican. Despite being trampled upon, yanked and pulled out of the land by its roots, the Martinican cum plant persists. The plant as a leitmotif for the Martinican way of life further reflects, according to Césaire, island folklore: after the birth of a child, the placenta is interred among the coconut or banana trees; grass growing on a grave is that of the dead protesting death (MuC 45). The Martinican has forgotten his nature, his true self; hence, for Césaire, the cultural malaise, sterility, and discontent of the civilization. She continues, "The Martinican has failed because, misrecognizing his true nature, he tries to live a life that is not suited to him. A gigantic phenomenon of collective lying, of 'pseudomorphosis.' And the current state of civilization in the Caribbean reveals to us the consequences of this error. Repression, suffering, sterility" (MuC 46).

The loss of the self naturally occurred as a result of the adaptation to oppressive socio-historical and economic conditions. In providing a brief overview of Martinican history, Césaire reminds her reader that the Martinican, *métis* class and black, was socially, politically, and culturally disenfranchised. Assimilation was initially strictly forbidden but deference to whites was demanded as early as 1764. By 1788, the only occupation open to free men of color was manual labor, "the hoe and the cutlass." The abolition of slavery did not result in the opening up of economic avenues for the Martinican on the island. Under the colonial system, the island was still deeply wedded to a plantation-like, agrarian economy; its primary function continued to be the export of primary products. The Martinicans, although resistant to the circumscription of their labor and talents, were again tied to the field as low-paid wage laborers. As Joseph Zobel wrote in his coming-of-age novel *La rue cases-nègres*, the *patron*, or boss, has merely replaced the master. Work permits were required for those wishing to indulge in other occupational areas. The attendant effect of systematic second-class citizenship was the desire for first-class citizenship, with the macabre twist that the latter became narrowly defined through a prism of Frenchness. An almost slavish desire for assimilation to Frenchness preoccupied the psychic impulses of the Martinican. "Liberation" disastrously became equated with "assimilation."

The psychic drive for assimilation, most evident among the "colored bourgeoisie," according to Césaire, definitively suppressed the Ethiopian sentiment of life, the desire for abandon, and replaced it with that of the Hamitic desire for struggle. In Freudian terms, the Martinican true self, the Ethiopian sentiment, is buried deep within the unconscious, the id, whereas the Hamitic desire for struggle occupies the conscious and preconscious, the ego and super-ego. As Césaire remarks, "The race to riches. To diplomas. Ambition. Struggle reduced to the level of the bourgeoisie. The race to monkey-like imitations. Vanity fair" are representative of Hamitic culture. But more troubling is that the imitative desire clearly perceived among those conscious Martinicans is wholly repressed in the unconscious of those in hot pursuit of Frenchness. Like a clinician observing and diagnosing her patient, in this case, Martinican civilization, Césaire concludes:

> No "evolved" Martinican would accept that he is only imitating, so much does his current situation appear natural, spontaneous, born of his legitimate aspirations. And, in so doing, he would be sincere. He truly does not KNOW that he is imitating. He is *unaware* of his true nature, which does not cease to exist. . . .
>
> Just as the *hysteric* does not realize that he is merely *imitating* a sickness, but the doctor, who cares for him and delivers him from his morbid symptoms, knows it.
>
> Likewise, analysis shows us that the effort to adapt to a foreign style that is demanded of the Martinican does not take place without creating a state of

pseudo-civilization that can be qualified as *abnormal, teratical*. (MuC 47–48; emphases are Césaire's)

Suzanne Césaire uses the French concept of *évolué* to describe the imitating, assimilated Martinican, who believes sincerely that he has "evolved" to Frenchness, that he is French when he is instead imitating Frenchness. The energy that the Martinican has expended in this struggle against himself has been rewarded with the creation of an imitative civilization; a France in the Caribbean that is not really French but a copy; therefore a mere *shadow* of the original.

The lengthy analysis of Martinican civilization's psychosis naturally concludes where it began—in a turn toward the cultural. In searching for the cure to cultural sterility, Césaire endeavors to determine if the "essence" of the Martinican buried in the unconscious, the primacy of the plant and the Ethiopian sentiment, can be rechanneled to create "a viable, hence imposing, cultural style." She calls upon her readers, future artists, poets, and intellectuals, to recognize their true selves, their inner selves, to become inspired by these tropical lands and produce an authentic culture and arts. Surrealism is evoked here as a means by which to tap that inner self. Surrealism, with its emphasis on writing from the unconscious, "gave us back some of our possibilities," Césaire writes. "It is up to us to find the rest. By its guiding light." Surrealism will become a tool for the exploration of what is authentically Martinican, while Negritude will initiate the coming into race-consciousness of these potential bards of Martinican culture. Despite recognizing the connection to Africa—that Ethiopian sentiment essential to tapping into the self—here Suzanne Césaire makes a critical theoretical move toward cultural and racial *métissage*, hitherto repressed by the privileging of the Hamitic culture, that best characterizes Martinican civilization:

Understand me well:

It is not a question of a return to the past, of resurrecting an African past that we have learned to appreciate and respect. On the contrary, it is a question of mobilizing every living force together in this land where race is the result of the most continuous intermingling; it is a question of becoming conscious of the tremendous heap of various energies that we have until now locked up within us. We must now put them to use in their fullness, without deviation, without falsification. (MuC 48)

Césaire's emphasis is on the present realities, not the past. And yet the conscious recognition of that past is essential to reaching the inner self and recreating a new postwar world.

Liberatory Poetics, *Métissage*, and Diversity

In her essay in the 1945 issue of *Tropiques*, which marked the end of the cultural review's publication run, and of Suzanne Césaire's contributions to

Martinican letters and apparently to public life, the enigmatic Césaire interestingly has the last word. Her essay closes out volume 13–14 of *Tropiques*. Whether domestic responsibilities overtook her activism, or her husband's increasing presence and celebrity in French and Martinican political and literary life during the postwar period became the family priority, her essay "Le Grand Camouflage" represents her final effort to expand the theoretical parameters of Negritude's Africanist identity politics. This last essay professed that the originality, diversity, and plurality of Martinican culture and its people were well embodied in the "femmes-colibris, femmes-fleurs tropicales, femmes aux quatre races et aux douzaines de sang" (hummingbird-women, flower-women, tropical women of four races and dozens of bloodlines).[13] It also presented the dismal social and political realities in the Antilles in general and Martinique in particular.

"Le Grand Camouflage" could very well be entitled "The Great Smokescreen," as Césaire takes the reader on a rather violent but sublime tour of Caribbean topography and the productive life forces of exploding volcanoes, turbulent cyclones, earthquakes, and "the beautiful green waves [belles lames vertes]" (GC 267) of the Caribbean Sea. From Puerto Rico to Martinique to Haiti, a billowing and swirling cyclone pummels the islands. But this is, we are to understand, nature's way, the ebb and flow of life on the islands. When the storm passes, the beauty of the islands reappears. This incomparable splendor, "perfect colors and forms," is what the Caribbean has come to represent. With eyes of an enraptured tourist, a blind Antillean native, Césaire writes,

> Nevertheless, fifteen years ago, the Antilles was revealed to me from the flank of Mount Pelée. From here I discovered, though still very young, that Martinique was sensual, coiled up, extended, distended into the Caribbean sea, and I thought about the other islands that are so beautiful.

> Once again in Haiti, during the summer morning of 1944, I experienced the presence of the Antilles, more perceptible in places from which, as at Kenscoff, the mountain views are of an unbearable beauty. (GC 267–69)

And yet there is, and has always been, trouble in these paradisiacal isles—pain and pangs accompanying their beauty. A legacy of slavery and colonialism effectively altered the balance between humanity and the island's natural beauty, harnessing the slave and, then, the worker to the land; fusing racism, wage labor and class exploitation into modern capitalism. The naive vision of a Martinican girl and the cataract-filled eyes of a woman in Haiti in 1944 are replaced with the wide-eyed sagacity of a pan-Africanist theorist: "And now total lucidity. Beyond these perfect colors and forms, my gaze detects the inner torments in the Antilles' most beautiful face" (GC 269). The complex history of the Americas, the New World—if such a term is appropriate in light of the New World's newness only to Europe and not to its indigenous populations of Carib and Arawaks—is laid out for the reader's contemplation. From the conquistadors importing the technology of firearms to the "infamy of the slave trade" and colonialism, the Americas and their annihilated aboriginal and forcibly imported populations have been reduced to the economic, social, psychological, and political whims of a European-descended population of "adventurous demons," "convicts," "penitents," and "utopians" "belched forth" to various corners of the New World (GC 269).

Césaire's diasporic accounting of black exploitation and affliction moves through the Caribbean to the United States and then back to the Francophone West Indian situation in 1945. The ideals of the abolitionist Victor Schoelcher regarding the status of blacks in the post-plantation economies of the colonies are contrasted with the reality of the "refined forms of slavery" masked in its "degrading forms of modern wage labor." The Francophone Caribbean is, according to Suzanne Césaire, "a stain" on France's face (GC 269). Her historical analysis of the coming-into-being of an exploited black world paves the way for a sociological analysis of the island of Martinique. She provides the reader with greater insight into the interlocking and complex race, color, and class structure dominating Martinique. Martinique is composed of *békés*, or white Creoles, white French "metropolitan officials," "a colored bourgeoisie," and the black working class ("les travailleurs") (GC 270–72).

"[T]he human depravation in the Caribbean" is attributed to the *békés*. Born on the island, they do not feel wholly French because of their "drawling accent," "unsure French"—almost assuredly a result of their intermingling with their patois-speaking "black *da[s]*"—and they certainly did not feel Martinican because of its "colored" connotations (GC 270). The *békés* belong primarily to the merchant and managerial classes, those "false colonizers" (GC 270) whose exploitation of the black working class amounts to drastically low wages in the plantation economy of factories and drastically high prices for goods purchased in the marketplace. The moral bankruptcy and cowardliness of this class is, for Césaire, handily demonstrated through their collaborationist past:

> Ready to betray any and all in order to defend themselves against the rising tide of blacks, they would sell themselves to America were it not that Americans claim that the purity of their blood is highly suspect, just as in the 1940s they devoted themselves to the Admiral of Vichy: Pétain being for them the altar of France, Robert necessarily became the "tabernacle of the Antilles." (GC 270)

Césaire delivers a two-pronged critique—one of the United States and the other of the *béké*. The race-purity-obsessed narratives of America confirm the very fears of the white Creoles—the perception that they are not white by virtue of their proximity to blacks. The U.S. narrative is necessarily fraught with contradictions given the associations of blacks and whites during chattel slavery in the North and South and despite the legalized segregation of the *Plessy v. Ferguson* era. The end of slavery in the United States led to a rise in black women domestic workers, the equivalent of the "da" in the Antilles, in white American households. The *béké* class also suffers from French exoticism whereby they are rendered strange because of their place of birth, yet familiar because of their "white" skin. The white Creole bears the brunt of American perceptions of France's racial liberalism—a liberalism that importantly encompassed, in the American mind, sexual intimacy, thus "colored" ancestry. Césaire infers that the *béké* is a man or woman with no veritable country, no feeling of belonging, no concept of patriotism or of *la République* FRANÇAISE, which would explain why they could unabashedly pledge themselves to the wrong France—*L'État* FRANÇAIS of Vichy.

The island's other white racial and class grouping consists of metropolitan French functionaries. For them, Césaire cynically suggests, color prejudice is nonexistent. And yet, there is a fear and loathing upon contact with "our old French lands":

> When they look into the maleficent mirror of the Caribbean, they see a delirious image of themselves. They dare not recognize themselves. . . . They know that the *métis* share some of their blood, that they are also, like them, part of Western civilization. . . . But their colored descendants fill them with dread. . . . They did not expect that strange burgeoning of their blood. Perhaps they didn't want to answer the Antillean heir who does and does not cry out "my father." (GC 270–271)

The Antillean human landscape of racial *métissage* and cultural assimilation is overwhelming for the metropolitan. The Martinicans are importantly the "unexpected sons" and "charming daughters" of France. Césaire begs the question regarding France's unexpectedness in light of centuries of intermingling (sexual and social), coercive and consensual, and cultural importation, also coercive, at least initially. The Martinicans are French, yet they do not hold the "title of citizen" (GC 269–271). Their muffled voices but voluminous-speaking *métis* existence demand recognition in its most literal sense of paternity from *la Patrie* and *le Père*. France has inseminated the island. Césaire's patriarchal emphasis, the masculinized embodiment of France, is undeniably deliberate; neither *mère* (mother) nor *mère-patrie* (motherland) is evoked. The Hegelian master-slave dialectic is color-coded and sexualized, with France representing the white male master and Martinique the subjugated black female slave. Indeed, Frantz Fanon would write, "In the colonies, in fact, even though there is little marriage or actual sustained cohabitation between whites and blacks, the number of hybrids is amazing. This is because the white men often sleep with their black servants,"[14] and Suzanne Césaire would certainly elaborate this theme in her discussion of the *naissance* of the colored bourgeoisie.

"Here is an Antillean," she writes. "The great grandson of a colonist and a black slave woman" (GC 271). He has inherited the "courage" of "African warriors" in their eternal life-death struggles, and the "greed" of the colonists. This West Indian tussles with his identity. He is not white, although he desires complete immersion in whiteness, and he will not "accept his Negritude": "Here he is with his double force and double ferociousness, in a dangerous equilibrium" (GC 271). He is a member of the "colored bourgeoisie"; running the island with a smooth efficiency, he placates and attends to white interests by exploiting the needs of the black workers—a true comprador. "So blossoms in the Antilles," she concludes, "that flower of human baseness, the colored bourgeoisie" (GC 271).

And the black working class, indubitable slaves to the machine, is varyingly seduced by the "automobile de grand luxe" (luxury car), the "usines-claires" (brightly lit factories). Returning to the Frobenius-inspired vegetal imagery regarding Martinicans and articulating a Marxist zeal, Suzanne Césaire visualizes "an invisible vegetation of desire" within the black workers from whom a "Revolution will spring forth" (GC 271). As a plant people, a vegetal people, who at once flow seamlessly with life and resist systematic destruction, the worker and the land are one; the land exists, suffers, and resists as do the masses of people. That poet who merely passes by will nonetheless continue to be ensnared by the beauty of the tropical landscape, "the sweet sound of palms," while "the Antillean serf lives with misery and abjection on the grounds of the 'factory' and the mediocre state of our cities-towns is a nauseating spectacle" (GC 270).

By the concluding paragraphs of "Le Grand Camouflage," Césaire imagines that the Antillean poet will take his place as an *engagé,* that he will catch a glimpse of that "vegetal fire," his head reeling, and contrast that wondrous *paysage* of cicadas, frangipani, canna, gerbera, hibiscus, and bougainvillea and those who work the land, see "the hungers, fears, hatreds, and ferocity that burn in the hollows of hills" (GC 273). Only the poet, whose "eyes" alone are "able to see," will unmask the game of "cache-cache," hide-and-seek, the "great camouflage" (GC 273). The poet's "tongue," as Aimé Césaire writes in *Cahier,* will "serve those miseries which have no tongue," his "voice the liberty of those who founder in the dungeons of despair,"[15] the interpreter, interlocutor, of the collective conscience, a liberatory resource who will present the island's history, pain, and exploitation. And that day when the smoke has cleared, the fog has lifted, and the silent vapors of the Caribbean Sea evaporated via the will of the masses and the poet's pen and voice, will certainly, Suzanne Césaire concludes, "be too enchanting for us to see" (GC 273).

Notes

This essay is excerpted from the volume *Negritude Women: Race Women, Race Consciousness, Race Literature, 1917–1945* (Minneapolis: University of Minnesota Press, 2002). All translations are by the author unless otherwise noted.

1. Lilyan Kesteloot, *Black Writers in French,* trans. Ellen Conroy Kennedy (Washington, D.C.: Howard University Press, 1991), p. 237.

2. René Ménil, "Généralités sur 'l'écrivain' de couleur antillais," *Légitime défense* 1 (June 1932): 8. Henceforth GE.

3. Suzanne Césaire, "Misère d'une poèsie: John Antoine-Nau," *Tropiques* 4 (Jan. 1942): 49–50, in *Tropiques: collection complète 1941–1945* (Paris: Jean-Michel Place, 1978).

4. Suzanne Césaire, "1943: Le Surréalisme et nous," *Tropiques* 8–9 (Oct. 1943): 18. Henceforth SN.

5. "Lettre du Lieutenant de Vaisseau Bayle, chef du service d'information, au directeur de la revue *Tropiques*," *Tropiques: collection complète* (henceforth T), p. xxxvii.

6. "Réponse de *Tropiques*" (T xxxvix).

7. Suzanne Césaire, "1943: Le surréalisme et nous," *Tropiques* 8–9 (Oct. 1943): 15.

8. Léopold Senghor, "Lessons of Leo Frobenius," in *Leo Frobenius: An Anthology*, ed. Eike Haberland, trans. Patricia Crampton (Wiesbaden, Germany: Franz Steiner Verlag GMBH, 1973), p. vii. Henceforth LF. See also Léo Frobenius, *Histoire de la civilisation africaine*, trans. H. Back and D. Ermont (Paris: Gallimard, 1952).

9. Leo Frobenius, "On the Morphological Method of Studying Cultures" and "The Nature of Culture," in *Leo Frobenius: An Anthology*, pp. 15, 20–21.

10. Frobenius, "The Nature of Culture," p. 20.

11. Quoted in Suzanne Césaire, "Léo Frobenius et le problème des civilisations," *Tropiques* 1 (April 1941): 34, 35.

12. Suzanne Césaire, "Malaise d'une civilisation," *Tropiques* 5 (April 1942): 43. Henceforth MuC.

13. Suzanne Césaire, "Le Grand Camouflage," *Tropiques* 13–14 (1945): 268. Henceforth GC.

14. Frantz Fanon, *Peau noire masques blancs* (Paris: Seuil, 1952), p. 37 n; *Black Skin, White Masks*, trans. Charles L. Markmann (New York: Grove Press, 1967), p. 46 n.

15. Aimé Césaire, *Return to My Native Land/Cahier d'un retour au pays natal* (Paris: Présence Africaine, 1960), pp. 60–61.

Eight

Losing Sight of the Real
Recasting Merleau-Ponty in Fanon's Critique of Mannoni

Nigel Gibson

The specific subject of *Black Skin, White Masks*[1] is the disalienation of the Antillean who, mired in a "dependency complex," wishes to turn white. We will consider this issue in Fanon's critique of Octave Mannoni's *Caliban and Prospero*.

What does Fanon mean by alienation? The root of his conceptualization is a medical one, meaning a neurosis (cf. BSWM 204), but he employs it in a social context so that donning a white mask is equated with a false self, an inauthentic self in Sartre's terms, or a self with a false consciousness in Marxian terms. Establishing a process of "disalienation" moves Fanon away from a medical model toward a radical social conception of praxis, which is based on a belief that human beings are reflective and actional, beings of praxis. However, he keeps coming back to psychoanalytical interpretations of "the Black problem" and "the colonial problem," and *Black Skin* can be seen as a painstaking examination leading in myriad ways to the same conclusion, namely the necessity to uproot the social conditions that cause alienation. Disalienation calls for a nihilation, the ripping away of the masks (or the false consciousness) and a *reintegration* of the human being's presence:

> I have been led to consider their [the Blacks'] alienation in terms of psychoanalytical classifications. The Black's behavior makes him *akin* to an obsessive neurotic type, or, if one prefers, he puts himself into a complete *situational* neurosis. In the man of color there is a constant effort to run away from his own individuality, to *annihilate* his own presence. (BSWM 60, my emphasis)

Fanon's critical approach to psychoanalysis is expressed in the first few pages of *Black Skin*. First he states that "only a psychoanalytical interpretation of the Black problem can lay bare the anomalies of affect that are responsible for the structure of the complex." On the very next page he declares that because the Black's alienation is not an individual question his approach will be "sociodiagnostic," which "entails immediate recognition of social and economic realities" (BSWM 11). It is necessary to understand racism both as a psychology of colonialism and as its socio-economic product. Applying this method to psychoanalysis would mean highlighting its Eurocentric and bourgeois assumptions which are passed off as universals, as well as the social-economic reality produced by European colonialism.

Black Skin is in part, like Octave Mannoni's *Caliban and Prospero,* a psychology of colonization: "The Black enslaved by his inferiority, the white man enslaved by his superiority alike behave in accordance with a neurotic orientation." Additionally, like *Caliban and Prospero, Black Skin* is a work of the author's experiences and observations dating back to his army days. But it is also a book that attempts to offer an answer to a problem that is only "akin" to an obsessive neurotic type. Despite all the references to psychoanalytic theory, therefore, Fanon's interest in *Black Skin* is not to polemicize among Freudians (or the varying disagreements within the psychoanalytic schools, Lacan's included) but to understand the person of color's view of self in the world and to map out ways to change that consciousness and the world. While Fanon takes psychoanalytic theory seriously, every time he engages a psychoanalytic theorist, be it Freud, Jung, Adler, Mannoni, or Lacan, there is an immediate qualification that questions assumed Eurocentric universals. All psychoanalytic theory comes up short. Neither Freud, nor Adler, nor Jung gave serious thought to racism in his research, nor did Lacan or his circle give any hint that race mattered in France.

Dissatisfied with the basic psychoanalytic unit of analysis, the individual and the family, Fanon finds in the colonial context that one has to move toward the wider social situation. If there is a question of internalization—"or better epidermalization"—of the inferiority complex (a veiled reference to Mannoni) it is not an obsessive neurotic type but *akin* to it (BSWM 60). Fanon wanted to get behind the similarities to the root of the symptom.

Psychoanalysis had revealed the symptom, but Fanon's quest for disalienation leads him away from a purely psychoanalytic answer because the alienation of the Black is not simply a product of an individual neurosis but is caused by a racist society. Thus, the end of alienation necessitates the end of the society that produces it. Unlike Freud and Lacan, then, Fanon says that it is not the human condition but the social reality that has caused the alienation, and thereby his conception of alienation must be read in intersubjective and social terms. "It will be seen that the Black man's alienation is not an individual question" (BSWM 11), he states in the introduction to *Black Skin,* adding that it is absolutely essential to root the work in its own time.

Black Skin, White Masks is "valid only for the Antilles—at least the Black man at home," (i.e., Martinique [BSWM 16]), Fanon declares, but the dialectic pushes him further: "In the beginning I wanted to confine myself to the Antilles. But, regardless of consequences, dialectic took the upper hand

and *I was compelled to see* that the Martinican is first of all a Black" (BSWM 172; my emphasis). This dialectic is crucial to the sweep and limitation of *Black Skin* as a work of a specific context.

We shall see later that under the pressure of Mannoni's dependency complex Fanon's inclusion of the Malagasy in his dialectic reveals the strengths and weaknesses of his approach, which also takes a whole people as the subject of "destructuration." The Martinican is a "crucified person," declares Fanon, who "has no culture, no civilization, 'no long historical past.'" Thus stripped, the existence and being of the Martinican is in an inferiority complex[2] (BSWM 216, 34). Such a complex is created in *every* people that experiences the death of its own local cultural originality (BSWM 18). Such a death is a process of destruction and of the civilizing mission of the colonial regime. For example, in the public health service "Arabs or Blacks" are systematically dehumanized, and language, which is the subject of chapter 1 of *Black Skin*,[3] plays a crucial role. In Paris the Martinican is particularly upset. He turns to the white doctor and pleads, "We're not like them, we're French" we're not a "pidgin-nigger-talker" (BSWM 32). A tension is evident in the dialectic of *Black Skin* between the decultured but "civilized" Martinican and the uncivilized but cultured Arab, Senegalese, or Malagasy who has a written culture, poetry, and an art that can be *translated* into French. In the Manichean world of French colonialism, civilization is solely French. On the scale of humanity, those who write and speak proper French are more civilized. This becomes clear to Fanon in Paris, where he finds that the Martinican is at the top of the Black pecking order, but it is a *Black* pecking order. This is an important ambiguity within Manicheanism. In Paris the Antillean is seen as Black, but the distinction of a divisive ordering, inspired by colonial Manicheanism,[4] means that the Guadeloupan tries to "pass" as Martinican. The Senegalese, on the other hand, tries to "pass" as Antillean.

Fanon began *Black Skin, White Masks* with the experience of the Martinican in France: Here was a group of people who had grown up speaking, thinking, and looking French. How could Martinicans look French? Because they believed they were French. They had fully internalized French culture, growing up reading Tarzan stories and talking about "our ancestors the Gaul" and identifying themselves not only "with the exploiter and the bringer of civilization," but with "an all-white truth" (BSWM 146–147). At school in Martinique, children acted like little Parisians in essays about what they did on vacation: "I like vacations because then I can run through the fields, breathe fresh air, and come home with *rosy* cheeks" (BSWM 162 n.25).

"As late as 1940 no Martinican found it possible to think of himself as a Black [*nègre*]."[5] The war had a tremendous effect on Martinican values—the fall of France, the Vichy regime, and the arrival of racist French sailors all created what Fanon called a metaphysical experience—but it was Aimé Césaire, a schoolteacher, an educated man worthy of respect, who created a scandal when he proclaimed that it was "good to be a Black" (BSWM 21).

After the war there continued the belief among students arriving in France that they would find their real white face (BSWM 153 n.15). On being seen as Black, they had two choices: either continue a stand with the white world or reject Europe and "go native," becoming comfortable in the "*Umwelt* of Martinique" (BSWM 37). Fanon found these choices particularly unbearable and left Paris. He was twenty-two years old.[6]

Fanon's critique of Mannoni provides an opportunity to clear away (dis-alienate?) some of the confusion that has evolved with the overly psychoana-lytic readings of Fanon by postcolonial critics. My discussion of Fanon's cri-tique of Mannoni will be grounded in his critique of Merleau-Ponty's notion of the body in the social world, but the silent interlocutor will be the one hundred thousand Malagasy slaughtered in 1947.

Not under My Skin: On Sartre and Merleau-Ponty

Sartre's influence on Fanon's *Black Skin* is well known and is found in its multiple references to *Anti-Semite and the Jew* and *Being and Nothingness* as well as to "Orphée Noir," the introduction to *L'Anthologie de La Poésie Nègre et Malagache*. Sartre's conflictual account of reciprocity between self and other and his account of human relations, characterized by "The Look" (part 3, section 4, of *Being and Nothingness*), appear powerfully reaffirmed in the colonial situation as well as by Fanon's account of phobogenic anxiety re-flected in the phrase of a white child to its mother that begins chapter 5 of *Black Skin, White Masks:* "Look a Black [*Nègre*]"—"The Black [*Nègre*] is a phobogenic object" (BSWM 151). Sartre's description of "the Look" pro-vides a conceptual language, but what is of equal importance is the influence of Merleau-Ponty's notion of "bodily schema" and subject/object on Fanon's thought.[7] According to Simone de Beauvoir, Fanon attended Merleau-Ponty's philosophy classes in Lyon, though she adds that Fanon found him distant and rather cold.[8]

The literal translation of the important chapter 5 of *Black Skin, White Masks,* "L'expérience vécue du noir," as "The Lived Experience of the Black" clearly indicates the influence of Merleau-Ponty.[9] Fanon's focus on lived experience of a "body-subject" facing the world explicates how colonial racism has affected the corporeal existence of the colonized Black and pre-sented "him" with "difficulties in the development of his bodily schema" (BSWM 110).[10]

The idea of "lived experience" alerts us to Fanon's appreciation of different starting points in the philosophies of Sartre and Merleau-Ponty. For example, where Sartre argued that the fundamental struggle between consciousnesses creates social relations, for Merleau-Ponty it is the social nature of conscious-ness that creates the possibility of conflict. One can see in *Black Skin* the importance Fanon puts on the *social* basis of *non*-recognition in an anti-black racist society.

Fanon opens "L'expérience vécue du noir" with a statement that ontology alone does not "permit us to understand the being of the Black man," because there is not really a black being or essence (BSWM 110). "Being," in Merleau-Ponty's sense, is a body in a spatiality of situation, or, as Fanon puts it, "a definitive structuring of the self and of the world—definitive because it creates a real dialectic between my body and the world" (BSWM 111).

What is problematic, however, is when the situation is saturated by color. Where for Merleau-Ponty "the body image is finally a way of stating that my body is in-the-world" (PP 101), for Fanon there are times when the Black is not in the world but "locked into his body" (BSWM 225). Where for Merleau-Ponty, "one's body is the third term . . . as far as spatiality is concerned" (PP 101), for Fanon the fact that the Black "must be black *in relation* to the white" means that the consciousness of body for the person of color is not only a "third-person consciousness," but a person triply split.

When "the Black man is among his own," Fanon argues (which assumes a certain level of equality and recognition of identity and difference), Merleau-Ponty's conception of intersubjectivity appears correct, yet in a colonial society "every ontology is made unattainable" (BSWM 109). In other words, among "their own" the Black is another person. In a racist society in which the image of whiteness has been powerfully internalized, Sartre's notion of the objectifying power of the gaze (internalized by all), his conflictual and dualistic philosophy, appears to be a powerful explanatory tool for understanding the causes and effects of the child's statement: "Mama, see the Black [*Nègre*]! I am frightened!" (BSWM 112).

Driven back, as it were, into "race," an ontology based on reciprocity is, by definition, sealed off. Though the existence of the Black is dependent on the white, the Black man has no ontological resistance in the eyes of the white. And thus while it is true that for Fanon, as for Sartre, existence precedes essence, the Black's existence is defined by the essence of Blackness. (In Fanon's survey of five hundred white Europeans [BSWM 166], this essence was expressed by the words "biology, penis, strong, athletic, potent, boxer, Joe Louis, Jesse Owens, Senegalese troops, savage, animal, sin.") The Black's being is reduced to a corporeal malediction. The body has been snatched away, and in its place is put a "racial epidermal schema." In contrast to what Merleau-Ponty describes as being aware of the body as a "third person,"[11] Fanon replies, my body is "a triple person. . . . It was not that I was finding febrile coordinates in the world. I existed triply. I occupied space" (BSWM 112). Blacks are not simply individual actors responsible for themselves, they are responsible for their race (culture) and their ancestors (history). This existential baggage produces dread and nausea.

From the perspective of "the Black," Sartre's proposal of an absolute freedom in *Being and Nothingness*, projecting a consciousness which can tear through inferiority complexes and the layers of meaning that have structured one's life, as an act of sheer will, appears eminently concrete. In the

Manichean world of colonialism there is no other perspective, and no need to quibble about shades of gray.

Merleau-Ponty's perspective that the lived body cannot be divorced from the world as experienced complicates things. These relationships are, according to Merleau-Ponty, "the third term between the for-itself and the in-itself" (PP 122). For him, freedom is rooted in the world and mediated through the body. The body appears to limit the possibility of freedom, but it actually makes such a possibility concrete in that it is in relation to other bodies, and thus freedom and the limits to freedom are confirmed through intersubjective relations. Freedom is a social act, not simply an act of individual will (itself a product of social relations) just as values are socially constructed and thus changing and changeable. Where the social world is crucial to Merleau-Ponty's conceptualization of freedom and intersubjectivity, for Sartre all intersubjective relations are the same: "The essence of relations between consciousnesses is not *Mitsein*, but conflict."[12] On the other hand, Merleau-Ponty views the relationship between ourselves and other people as already a result of intersubjectivity. Relationships might be alienated. Indeed the truth of others as hellish is understanding that the perceiving subject is already an interrelation of subject and object, body and mind, and is already "open" and possibly hurt and deformed by others.

Although consciousness is mediated by lived experience in a social environment, it does not mean that *mutual* recognition exists. In his reading of Hegel's master/slave dialectic, for example, Merleau-Ponty sees the necessity of the struggle for recognition to get beyond "unilateral recognition."[13] Unlike Kojève, and indeed Sartre, who makes unilateralism an ontological principle, Merleau-Ponty recognizes the dialectical character of Hegel's master/slave conflict. The conflict is a *moment* that must be experienced (indeed, the drama of *Phenomenology* is the drama of consciousness of experience). At the same time, the goal of "mutual recognition" is given content by the drama that consciousness experiences in getting there.

One's experience of the body is part and parcel of one's experience of the world, argues Merleau-Ponty. This is exaggerated for the Black who, "walled in by color," has two different experiences of his body and his being in the world. When race is added to the dialectic of body in the world, the dialectic seems closed off and replaced by a dualism that looks like Sartre's ontology. In the Manichean colonial world there are no choices, only a series of double binds. If Blacks renounce their bodies as products of their internalization of the gaze of the other—in other words, the third (who in this case is white)— they are forced into a Sartrean bad faith either by creating a solipsistic community before consciousness or by creating a make-believe world of assimilated colorless angels (WE 218). In such a bind, how does one become conscious of oneself and, in doing so, change the world? Merleau-Ponty had understood this flaw in Sartre's philosophy as a closed dialectic. Rather than an individual consciousness that results from the gaze of the other and that always resists intersubjectivity, by grounding consciousness in the social world Merleau-Ponty offers a different way out. For Fanon, Sartre's dialectic in "Orphée Noir" leads to an intellectualized, rather than existential, project. Privileging the subjective existential over the objective dialectic, Fanon accuses Sartre of forgetting concrete Black experience. Sartre had forgotten that "The Black suffers in his body quite differently from the White man" (BSWM 138). Though Fanon had almost essentialized the difference between the body experiences of the Black and the White, this difference was grounded in a social and historical context and was the result of a lived experience, not an ontological flaw: one is not born Black but becomes Black, to paraphrase de Beauvoir.

Fanon's response to Sartre's "Orphée Noir," shouting at him "in the paroxysm of my being and my fury" (BSWM 138), was broadcast in another ontological register. Fanon was reminding Sartre that in terms of the movement of dialectical negativity, "a consciousness committed to experience is ignorant, has to be ignorant, of the essences and the determinations of its being" (BSWM 134). Dialectic for Fanon, as for Merleau-Ponty, remained "open-ended," not predetermined. On the other hand, Sartre, the existentialist, had jumped over experience. Thus when Fanon criticized the possibility of reciprocity in Hegel's master/slave dialectic when color was added, he also rejected Sartre's radical dichotomy between being-for-self and being-for-others. Instead Fanon, *the existentialist*, reminds Sartre of the lived situation, "the white man is not only The Other but also the master, whether real or imaginary" (BSWM 138n). In other words, there is a power relation making it appear that Sartre's radical dichotomy between myself and others, which he posits as an absolute, seem correct. On first blush this may seem a useful way of thinking about Fanon's critique of Hegel's master/slave dialectic, but Fanon's position is purely contextual. Sartre precludes my *ever* experiencing the other as intersubjective and reciprocal. In fact such a belief in mutual rather than conflictual reciprocity is an expression of inauthenticity and bad faith, and it leads to an end of the dialectic, and to reifying alienated relations.

Sartre cannot account for a yes-saying intersubjectivity. Like Merleau-Ponty's articulation of intersubjectivity, Fanon's vision is of the possibility of mutual recognition (BSWM 109). When Fanon writes of "on their own," it assumes an Other to "their own," but the conception is not completely determined by the reality, image, or internalization of the white. In the colonial situation, this notion of "among one's own" is already shot through with contradictions. The "Black on Black" violence described in *The Wretched*, for example, is a result of the colonial situation and already complicates the situation of being "on their own." The Black is walled in by the colonial regime, a walling that is multidimensional—political, economic, social, cultural, and spatial. The violence of the ghetto, as well as its grinding poverty, introduces uncertainty and danger. The ideal of "among one's own" is a place where consciousness of the body in the world is "subject/object," in the Merleau-Pontyan sense, and is not "solely a negating activity" as it is for the Black in the white world. Yet it is from this negating activity that "among one's own," when turned outward to the source of the violence and human destructuration, becomes for Fanon the basis of the dialectic of decolonization. In terms of the Hegelian dialectic, such a conceptualization could already be found in the master/slave dialectic, in which the slave's finding his own mind is exactly the mental liberation that Fanon found to be a necessary condition for independence. Fanon would have to wait until his involvement in the Algerian revolution to see how "being on one's own" could work, but in his critique of Mannoni's notion of dependency we already see the conception employed.

In his 1965 foreword to *Psychologie de la colonisation (Prospero and Caliban: The Psychology of Colonization)*, Mannoni tells us that Madagascar had fascinated him for many years and that before the war he had carried out a number of ethnographic studies. *Prospero and Caliban* presented a significant change in focus, reflecting a wish to get behind the ethnographic to "more disturbing psychological problems" which included his own self-analysis. At the time of writing, Mannoni claimed that he was more interested in his own psychological make-up than in the "psychology of the subjects under observation who presented a less complex problem." It was his Madagascar experiences, he claimed, that cured his obsessional neurosis, and it was this self-understanding that was "an essential preliminary for all research in the sphere of colonial affairs" (PC 5, 34).

Interviewed by Elisabeth Roudinesco for her book *Jacques Lacan & Co.*, Mannoni reports that he spent twenty years in Madagascar, from 1925 to 1945, "as an ethnologist and director general of the information service."[14] Two years later in Paris, he interrupted his psychoanalytic studies and his analysis with Jacques Lacan and returned to Madagascar. His return coincided with an anti-colonial rebellion that resulted in the brutal massacre of one hundred thousand Malagasies by French troops. For Mannoni the rebellion tore aside a veil, "and for a brief moment a burst of dazzling light enabled one to verify the series of intuitions one had not dared to believe in" (PC 6). The series of intuitions were developed into a psychology of colonization that could explain Malagasy life and the dynamics of the rebellion. In short, the colonizer overcompensated for an inferiority complex that was the result of feelings of abandonment, and the colonized, mired in a dependency complex, were prone to feelings of abandonment by the colonial father figure.

A few essays by Mannoni had whetted Fanon's appetite, and he was thinking of writing to Mannoni to find out more before his book was published in 1950, when Fanon began working on *Black Skin*. Particularly arresting and new was submitting the colonizer's behavior to psychoanalytic inquiry. However, when it was published Fanon was disappointed and subjected it to harsh criticism.[15] Apparently shared conclusions about dependency are based on very different notions of human subjectivity, very different analyses of roots of colonialism and racism, and very different ideas about what constitutes being and existence.

In his largely critical foreword to the English edition of *Prospero and Caliban,* the anthropologist Maurice Bloch mentions that Fanon's critique of Mannoni, though "deserved," was "very general" (PC vii). Fanon has little to say about life in Madagascar. Lacking the necessarily empirical knowledge, he does not criticize Mannoni's ethnographic observations and makes no claims about indigenous life, such as the possible meanings of ancestor worship and Malagasy spirit worlds. Fanon's lack of knowledge has led to a view that he takes too much of Mannoni's argument on board. For example, Jock McCulloch thinks that Fanon's critique of Mannoni is based on a kind of sibling rivalry. "There is *nothing* in Fanon's theory of colonial man," suggests McCulloch, "which was not first suggested to him, in his encounter with *Prospero,*" and there is not much in Fanon's conception of post-independence society, continues McCulloch, that hasn't already been suggested by Mannoni.[16]

While it is true that one can find a resonance between Mannoni and Fanon, not least in the dehumanizing effect of colonialism on the European, McCulloch's positing of an affinity between the two is mistaken. For example, whereas Fanon saw the possibility of self-determination, Mannoni (logically from his theory of dependence) predicted that political independence would inevitably bring corruption, forced labor, arbitrariness, and political oppression. In fact, Mannoni's projection of a slow decolonization based on the revival of the village councils was taken over by the French colonial administration in an attempt to avoid granting independence.[17] Such a view of mixing the "traditional" and the "modern" was already a typically colonial form of rule (mapping the colonial administration on top of perceived traditional forms of rule) and was far from Fanon's view of the future society. Mannoni's administrative mentality is discerned in his celebration of the "modernizing" effects of issuing identification cards, for example, without seeing their more ominous side. In terms of psychological development, Mannoni praises the transference of dependence to a "remote, abstract and almost imaginary object" as material for the creation of a different personality (PC 152), but he ignores both the economic and political reasons for Malagasy individuals to identify themselves as members of ethnic groups. These identifications were often necessitated by colonial taxation and labor polices as well as by the larger structural, economic, military, and political realities of French colonization in Madagascar.

The apparent similarity between Fanon's and Mannoni's conceptions of "dependency" works only if one collapses cause and effect. Just as Sartre's idea of (non) reciprocity describes Black–white relations, so Mannoni's conception of dependency powerfully describes the colonized *evolué.*[18] Additionally, Mannoni describes the difficulties of the Malagasy taking on the "persona" of a "European" being complicated by the color of the skin: "The difference in skin-color is enough, in fact, for the European colonial society to refuse to receive these evolved natives. . . . Paradoxically the more 'civilized' the colonial inhabitants become, the greater is the awareness on both sides of *irremovable racial differences*" (PC 75, my emphasis). But behind Mannoni's insight lies the assumption that the cause of the problem is the Malagasy's dependency, not the colonial structure.[19] In response, Fanon called Mannoni's thesis an inversion of reality, titling his chapter "the *so-called* [*prétendu*] dependency complex of colonized peoples."

Ideas of "dependency" and reciprocity loom large in Fanon's work but the crucial difference between Fanon and Mannoni was the differentiation between being and existence: Fanon argued that dependency was a *result* of colonial rule, whereas for Mannoni it was in the Malagasy's very being to be colonized. According to Mannoni, the Europeans quite easily became as revered as the ancestors, and in fact took their place. The colonized are not made dependent because they are colonized but are colonized because they are dependent. In fact the colonized "unconsciously expected—even desired" such a development (PC 86): "To my mind there is no doubting the fact that colonization has always required the existence of the need for dependence. Not all peoples can be colonized: only those who experience *this need*" (PC 85).

However one understands dependency, it changes with the appearance of the European on the island. Yet for Mannoni, the psychological and economic consequences of this action realize rather than change the different typological psychologies of the colonizer and the colonized. While the first colonizers are "pioneers of civilization," the colonized become true to form, expressing the inferiority complex. For Mannoni, the dependent and the inferior find their true personalities in the colonies. It is in the colonies that each population realizes its allotted place! Prospero or Caliban: "It is obvious that the white man acts in obedience to an authority complex," Fanon adds sarcastically, "a leadership complex, while the Malagasy obeys a dependency complex. Everyone is satisfied" (BSWM 99).

This dualism of inferiority complex and dependency complex as a mutually exclusive "alternative" (PC 40) characterizes the Manichean colonial set-up and is also at the root of the 1947 rebellion. Dependent Malagasy consciousness determines Mannoni's political prescriptions. The rebellion is a result of a fear of abandonment, and thus the solution is not political independence but a controlled process in which a newly enlightened colonial regime brings the Malagasy beyond dependency. Such a solution can be engineered only by metropolitan France, "unquestionably one of the least racially-minded countries in the world" (PC 110).

By applying a classical psychological typology developed in Europe directly onto the Malagasy, Mannoni's insight led him toward portraying the Malagasy as the child of Europe. Fanon quoted: "The fact that when an adult Malagasy is isolated in a different environment he can become susceptible to the classical type of inferiority complex *proves almost beyond doubt* that the germ of the complex was latent in him from childhood" (PC 40, quoted in Fanon BSWM 84, my emphasis). In times of crisis the Malagasy's main concern was "not to feel abandoned" (PC 49). Mannoni's theory of Malagasy dependency echoes dominant sociological theories of the time and repeats views of social evolutionism in the social sciences, in classical psychoanalysis,[20] and in colonial practice. In these theories "primitive" societies correspond to earlier phases of "advanced" societies. Maurice Bloch points out that "Mannoni's argument combines European history, ontogeny, and evolutionary anthropology" (PC viii): The child first experiences life in a state of dependence on his parents; he or she does not think of them as his equal but expects succor from them; dependency is finally broken by the adolescent, though this can lead to a feeling of abandonment if not handled correctly by the parent, and thus to an "inferiority complex" in which there is a wish to dominate others. The modern colonizers are examples of people who suffer an inferiority complex. Europeans who go to the colonies carry with them a latent inferiority complex. In the colonies the "Prospero complex," the "inner pressures of the man's own personality" becomes manifest (PC 108). Additionally, the history of the individual is also the history of Europe. "Primitive" Europe is depicted as being dependent and egalitarian; feudalism represents the domination of dependency and the end of egalitarianism, while the French revolution once again re-establishes the importance of egalitarianism, independence, and individualism.

Mannoni's unabashedly Eurocentric view of development explains the African. Africa is mainly in a "primitive" state of dependence and egalitarianism, or in some cases, like the Malagasy, at the feudal level of dependency with lifelong pseudo-parents in the form of elders and ancestors. Faced with colonization, the Malagasy transfer their dependence onto the colonials, who become a type of father figure. Abandoned by their parents, the colonials, on the other hand, are dominated by an inferiority complex and need to dominate the natives. This is the "psychology of colonization."

Despite his use of scare quotes, Mannoni cannot find another word for primitive "because the alternatives, such as 'isolated,' 'unevolved,' 'archaic,' 'stationary,' and 'backward,' are in fact no better" (PC 22), he confesses. All express the model of development from which he cannot escape. The linearity from primitive to civilized, as a kind of recapitulation of an individual's development from dependency to independence (with the possibility of inferiority), absolutely determines his project: He finds "the wholly 'phantastic' world which Melanie Klein has found in infants, and has attributed to persecution, is also to be found in 'primitive peoples'" (PC 34).

Manonni's Apologia

Mannoni recognizes that racism exists and is genuinely appalled by it, but he maintains that European civilization, its best representatives, and its colonial policy are not responsible for it (PC 24). Mannoni divides French colonial policies, which he says are not racist (but are produced by the best representatives of French culture and rationalism), from the type of people who become colonists—those with an inferiority complex and with a will to superiority over others.

Is Mannoni simply an apologist for colonialism? In his foreword to *Prospero and Caliban*, Bloch argues that, in the final analysis, with a "degree of hesitation [Mannoni] makes himself the apologist" for the colonial power (PC vii). Fanon never uses the word apologist,[21] and whether Mannoni is an "apologist" for French colonialism or not,[22] his naiveté is apparent in a passing reference to South Africa. Ignoring the then recent establishment of apartheid (1948), he states that poor whites and petty officials are more contemptuous of the Blacks than are those in the ruling class, thus proving that the inferiority complex is really a petty bourgeois and white-working-class (for Mannoni the mediocre and uneducated European) phenomenon. Fanon's response was to remind him of the racist structure of a society like South Africa's.

Although Fanon stresses the importance of the social structure, it is actually Aimé Césaire's poetry[23] that provides him with the most powerful expression of racist dehumanization and the experience of living in a colonial economy. To Mannoni's claims of Europe's humanism Fanon quotes Césaire implicating Western civilization in Nazism. To the so-called dependency complex of the Malagasy, he quotes Césaire's speaking of the wretched pain of poverty. To the Malagasy's depersonalization, he quotes Césaire's ventriloquizing dehumanization, "I am a brute beast . . . I have no use in the world" (PC 98). To Mannoni's claim that "colonial exploitation is not the same as other forms of exploitation and colonial racialism is different from other kinds of racialism" (PC 27), he quotes Césaire: "When I turn on my radio, when I hear that Blacks have been lynched in America, I say that we have been lied to: Hitler is not dead" (BSWM 90).

Fanon's criticism of Mannoni is not that he avoids economics but that he avoids lived experience, which is better described by the Negritude poet from Martinique than by psychoanalytic types. No one is better than Césaire in representing the material reality of poverty in the colonies.[24] What Mannoni has forgotten is the lived reality of the Malagasy. Fanon repeats this even if he knows little about the details of concrete life and employs a Martinican poet to describe reality. Partly Césaire can be employed because for Fanon there are not different types of racism. The existential point is the existence and nonexistence of personhood. In other words, the appearance of colonialism sounds the fragmentation of Malagasy intersubjectivity, which is in fact already multicultural, reflected in language and developed over hundreds of years of interactions between various peoples, namely the existence of, invention of, and the being "among one's own."

General Gallieni's[25] "pacification" of Madagascar at the turn of the century included French soldiers taking young *ramatoa* as "temporary wives." Though aware of the charged atmosphere of sexual excitement and unconscious notions of the Black's sexual potency among Europeans (cf. PC 111 n.1), Mannoni doesn't ask why these unconscious tendencies are directed toward the Malagasy. Instead he claims that relations between soldiers and their "temporary wives" were "healthy" and unmarred by complexes, and he concludes that "this goes only to show that racial conflicts develop gradually and do not arise spontaneously" (PC 122). The truth was quite different: it was the pacification campaign, the murder and the domination of the Malagasy by the French, that was the fruitful site in which racial conflicts developed quickly and "spontaneously." Racial conflicts coexisted with the war: "Let us not exaggerate," answers Fanon in *Black Skin*, "when a soldier of the conquering army went to bed with a young Malagasy girl, there was undoubtedly no tendency on his part to respect her entity as another person. . . . The fact that Algerian colonists go to bed with fourteen-year-old housemaids in no way demonstrates a lack of racial conflicts in Algeria" (BSWM 46 n.5).

According to Mannoni, the Malagasy are sealed into their own customs and become Malagasy only in relation to the European. In contrast, Fanon argues that the Malagasy have ceased to exist in their Malagasyhood since the time of Gallieni (BSWM 94). In other words, before colonialism the Malagasy were in-themselves and for-themselves Malagasy. Gallieni's campaign interrupted Malagasy life and culture, sealed it, and then attempted to petrify it into local forms of rule and custom: "A new element having been introduced, it became mandatory to seek to understand the new relationships" (BSWM 97). One aspect of this new element is ideological. The government functionaries, school inspectors, and missionaries play an important role, creating programs in the effort to make the chosen (Merina) elite French: "In the end they dropped him and told him, 'You have an indisputable complex of dependence on the white man'" (BSWM 216). To be emptied and then refilled with the civilizing mission, only to be "abandoned." That might very well create complexes described by Mannoni, but even if correct Mannoni's descriptions might be applicable to only a very small number and not everyone, as he assumed, including his tennis coach.[26]

How does the phenomenological critique of the racial gaze work when speaking of a national body? The move from the dialectic of race to that of national liberation parallels the deepening social and political maturity of the Continental anti-colonial movement that emerged after World War II (and even during it, such as the 1943 revolt in Madagascar). There is a concomitant shift in Fanon's focus (especially after the Algerian war of independence began) from a phenomenology concerned with lived experience in a racist society to that of the lived experience of anti-colonial revolt and thereby an investigation of what he calls the dialectics of liberation (see TAR 186). His critique of Mannoni expresses his working out of this problematic.

Unaware of—or perhaps, better, phenomenologically bracketing off—internal power divisions in Malagasy society, which could raise problems in an independent Madagascar, Fanon posited French colonialism as an absolute dividing line. It is the absolute shock to Malagasy life, to its being and existence. The loss of Malagasyhood is a result of French colonialism. "Robbed . . . of all worth, all individuality," the Malagasy are told that they are human only insofar as they are in step with the white world. The logical move, then, is to become French. Perhaps Mannoni will counter, "But you cannot do it because deep within you there is a dependency complex" (reminding us that those who had taken part in the revolt were not fully assimilated), but Fanon would reply that all such attempts are already doomed because the colonizer qua master who remains the subject of actions is also white. Fanon would posit Césaire's articulation of a new rebellious Negritude consciousness in place of Mannoni's Prospero, the bestial, betrayed, and abandoned native (cf. PC 108).

The problem of racism is not simply that of Blacks living among whites but of systematic exploitation. Mannoni had begun with an assumption that colonial exploitation is not the same as other forms because "the colonizing peoples are among the most advanced in the world, while those which undergo colonization are among the most backward" (PC 27). Fanon rejected such a precondition. The similarity between racisms was exploitation: "Blacks exploited, enslaved, despised by a colonialist capitalist society that is only accidentally white" (BSWM 202). Thus we are back to socio-economic realities: it is the colonial condition that creates the colonial type.[27] Perhaps colonialism does attract people with neuroses, but, Fanon quickly adds, the majority of Europeans go to the colonies to get rich as quickly as possible. If one concentrated on a socio-economic type—that is, the colonial as "trafficker"—one could grasp the "psychology of the man who arouses in the autochtonous population 'the feeling of inferiority.'"

Fanon has been accused of ignoring the economic and the political while not himself developing a clear articulation of the relations between economics and psychological types. In Mannoni's defense, he does explain at the beginning of *Caliban and Prospero* that the colonial "problem," which is "one of the most urgent of those confronting the world today—and France in particular," can be considered from many different points of view, but he will choose a psychological approach. The psychological offers a new perspective because it gets behind the received view to introduce "two entirely different character types."[28] Mannoni's attempt to develop a psychoanalytic explanation of the colonial situation seems to fit with Fanon's stated project at the beginning of *Black Skin*. But in his critique of Mannoni it becomes very clear that Fanon finds a psychoanalytic interpretation increasingly problematic. Is Fanon, then, too quick, as Homi K. Bhabha insists, to name the Other?[29]

Fanon argues that Mannoni has not understood the "real coordinates" of the colonial situation. But what are its "real coordinates"? What is the R/real? The lure of Lacan may seem to have a resonance in Fanon's use of the term "the real" and "the imaginary" in *Black Skin,* yet it would be jumping the gun to argue that Fanon is employing the Lacanian "real" as a desiring reality inaccessible to subjective thought and beyond the reach of reason.[30] Let us stick closer to the context (BS 108).

First, Fanon does not disagree with Mannoni's claim that only a psychological analysis can "place and define . . . the colonial situation," but he wonders why, if this is the point of departure, Mannoni tries to "make the inferiority complex something that antedates colonization" (PC 85). It is in fact because Mannoni has a "unilateral analysis" (BSWM 94). The real has to fit the typology.

Second, rather than clarify the theoretical basis of Mannoni's analysis, Fanon explicates the logical conclusion of Mannoni's argument—namely, that "the Malagasy has ceased to exist" (PC 94). Sealed into their own customs, the Malagasy are described by Mannoni as living within a closed circle. Such a static society characterizes dependency. Where Mannoni views French colonialism as breaking the circle positively, Fanon sees the arrival of the French as breaking the Malagasy. In fact the "real" history of the Malagasy is anything but a closed circle. The subjugation of Malagasy by the French,[31] and the subsequent colonization and economic expropriation of the Island, is not only the historical real—namely, that the Malagasy exist historically—but also the present real (i.e., 1947) that is under scrutiny:

> What M. Mannoni has forgotten is that the Malagasy alone no longer exists; he has forgotten that the Malagasy exists *with the European.* The arrival of the white man in Madagascar shattered not only its horizons but its psychological mechanisms. As everyone has pointed out, alterity for the Black man is not the Black but the white man. (BSWM 97)

Is Fanon's phrase "as everyone has pointed out" a red flag? Indeed, what has "everyone" understood? That such alterity is both absolute but situational? That it requires in response not a "Bantu Philosophy" (BSWM 184–86) but an uprooting in the most materialistic of terms? Fanon's critique of Alioune Diop's introduction to Placide Tempels's *La philosophie bantoue* illuminates his refusal to construct the method or goal of a philosophy of liberation, outside of the context of "the real": "Be careful! It is not a matter of finding Being in Bantu thought, when Bantu existence subsists on the level of nonbeing . . . Now we know that Bantu society no longer exists" (BSWM 186). On the other hand, realizing that Bantu society had been destroyed did not mean falling into Mannoni's teleological trap. Fanon instead sensed new beginnings in the emerging continental anti-colonial movements. What comes out strongly is Fanon's belief in the ability of the subaltern's conscious activity to change the world and to realize freedom as self-determining human beings.

Mannoni includes six dreams as an epilogue to part 1 of *Prospero and Caliban* as evidence of his theory of dependency. In a footnote he informs us that the dreams have come from different sources, "but in the main they have been collected in schools in the form of French homework" (PC 91 n. 2). He is not concerned that the dream recollections were written in language foreign to the students, even though he attached a great importance to the choice of words. His analysis is further problematized through translation; for example, he takes note of the use of the singular and plural nouns where in Malagasy singular and plural are not indicated.[32]

Mannoni does not engage in a thorough analysis of and gives very little background to each dream, seeming to be content with dream symbolism, dominated by notions of protection and danger associated with the mother and the more symbolically rich father: Mother = tree = security; Father = rifles/bull's horns = phallus = sexual danger = Senegalese troops = lack of protection. But what is particularly striking about his interpretations is his insistence that even though the dreams "were recorded at the time of public disturbance . . . their authors had seen nothing of the disorders and knew nothing of the disorders" (PC 89). In contrast, for Fanon the dreams had everything to do with the rebellion. Fanon's approach to criticizing Mannoni's dream interpretation is to view dreams socially. In other words, Fanon believes that we should follow the manifest surface meanings rather than seeking meaning in the unconscious: "What must be done is to restore this dream to its proper time, and this time is the period during which eighty thousand natives were killed" (only after 1956 was the estimate one hundred thousand) (BSWM 104). It is quite impossible to state that Malagasy whose dreams Mannoni used knew of the rebellion only through hearsay. Be that as it may, what is central to Mannoni's dream analysis is the Malagasy's supposed reversion to routine, which equates Malagasy adults with a childish need for security. "To depart from routine is to wander in pathless woods; there you will meet the bull who will send you helter-skelter home again" (PC 70). The love of routine is nothing other but the routinization of colonial rule—namely, the pacification of Madagascar: "Settle down Malagasies, and stay where you belong." This is exactly how Fanon characterizes the Mannoni's psychology of colonialism throughout *Black Skin:* The colonized better keep in their place (BSWM 107, 34). To which Fanon responds, "Certainly not! . . . I will tell him, 'The environment, society are responsible for your delusion'" and must be changed (BSWM 216).

What is the meaning of the dream imagery?
The rifle of the Senegalese soldier is not a penis but a genuine rifle, model

Lebel 1916. The Black bull and the robber are not *lolos*—"reincarnated souls"—but actually the irruption of real fantasies into sleep. (BSWM 106)

In the circumstance of the massacre of 1947 the *socius*, the intersubjective, is more important than the individual or the symbolic. The Senegalese soldier is not the smiling consumer of breakfast cereal, but part of the military intelligence terror machine. It is the reality of torture, and the Senegalese soldiers often used as torturers, that haunt the dreams. Fanon records a testimony at a trial in Antananarivo (Tananarive) in which a witness, Rakotovao, spoke of torture at police headquarters. The Senegalese soldiers had been instructed to use different methods, including repeatedly holding the head under water and beatings with a bullwhip. The witness denied the charges but was sentenced to death. Fanon concludes, "When one read such things, it certainly seems that M. Mannoni allowed one aspect of the phenomena that he analyzes to escape him: The Black bull and the Black men are neither more nor less than the Senegalese police torturers. . . . The discoveries of Freud are of no use to us here" (BSWM 106 n. 32, 104).

Before he records Mannoni's dream analysis Fanon questions Mannoni's use of the unconscious as the basis to answer why the Malagasy was prone to colonization. For Mannoni, it is the unconscious that accounts for why the Malagasy welcomed the shipwrecked Europeans and strangers (*vazaha*). But he could have easily given an answer in "terms of humanity, of good will, of courtesy" rather than in terms of unconscious desires. Fanon replies to Mannoni, "Yes, the unconscious—we have got to that. But one must not extrapolate." Fanon then describes a Black patient's dream of a long exhausting walk: "I had the impression that something was waiting for me I came into an empty hall, and behind a door I heard a noise. I hesitated before I went in, but finally I made up my mind and opened the door. In this second room there were white men, and I found that I too was white" (BSWM 99). How do we understand this dream as a wish fulfillment? What is the significance of the long, tiring walk? Could the second room be a tomb? Could the white men be ancestors or father figures?

How easy it is to follow a Mannonian interpretation. But, like any good analyst, we need more information: the dream "in itself" has multiple meanings, we need to know who told it, how and under what circumstances it was told, and we need to know more about the analysand. Fanon at least informs us that the analysand has problems in his career, so the dream fulfills an unconscious wish. But "outside my psychoanalytic office," he says, indicating that he had such an office and practiced psychoanalysis, "I have to incorporate my conclusions into the context of the world" (BSWM 100). In Mannoni's world the informants knew nothing of the 1947 revolt and thus it was not the "uprising" that was fundamental but unconscious deeper motivations. For Mannoni this "real" was expressed in irrational terms and could only be read psychoanalytically. That is exactly what he does in *Prospero and Caliban*. In contrast, Fanon's argument clearly advocates a radical humanist psychology: the Black should no longer be confronted by the predicament "turn white or disappear" but "should be able to take cognizance of a possibility of existence." In other words, if society makes it difficult to exist because of color, then the psychoanalyst, whose task is to help the analysand bring the real to self-awareness, should not encourage the analysand to adjust to that difficulty but "put him in a position to *choose* action (or passivity) with respect to the real source of the conflict—that is, toward the social structures" (BSWM 100). Fanon is also painfully aware of the limits of psychoanalysis in its own terms. Citing Anna Freud, he notes that sometimes analysis makes the problem worse; sometimes "the result of analysis is to weaken the ego still further and to advance the pathological process" (quoted in BSWM 59). This observation can lead Fanon in only one direction: not only to understand the world but to change it. He provides not a sophisticated conceptualization of hegemony and ideology but a belief translated into political praxis that better knowledge of reality is part of the process of action that gets beyond reaction and Nietzschean *ressentiment* (BSWM 222). Confronting the alienated anti-black world meant conscientizing it (to allude to Steve Biko's Black Consciousness Movement[33]) to effect change in the direction of human freedom.

Fanon's ability to speak of the Malagasy and Malagasyhood is as much indebted to Merleau-Ponty's notion of lived experience. "Disalienation" is equated with the removal of French colonialism, though internal social relations could be as repressing and alienating. What has interested us here is Fanon's argument against Mannoni's social evolutionism, which is really what his conception of dependency becomes. Fanon concludes, "[of] this original complex in its pure state that supposedly characterized the Malagasy mentality throughout the whole precolonial period, it appears to me that M. Mannoni lacks the slightest basis on which to ground any conclusion" (BSWM 108). But what of cultural specificity? In his work at the hospital in Blida, Algeria (1953–56), Fanon challenged his own theoretical and cultural limitations in his practice of socio (or milieu) therapy.[34] In the end, under the pressure of the war of liberation and in the atmosphere of French torture, psychological work itself was impossible. Even if *Black Skin* is less clear, Fanon already understood culture as always something coming to be.

Fanon kept coming back to the quandary that the colonial world had sealed Blacks into their Blackness, while insisting that he wanted to find a concrete way beyond such a confinement. The lived experience of revolt and social movement in Setif, Algeria, in 1945 and Madagascar in 1947 marked a new opening. The French drama would be best expressed by colonial revolt, and Fanon's thought is in many ways a product of this situation. Thus, in many ways the limitations to *Black Skin*, like those to any great theoretical work, are historical. Whereas, for France, Madagascar and Algeria had been experimenting colonies, for Fanon, Algeria, as we can see in *A Dying Colonialism*, became the laboratory for what he hoped would be a revolutionary transformation. What had been Merleau-Ponty's problem—the leap from lived experience to revolutionary consciousness—became for Fanon the lived experience of the revolution and opened up new problematics.[35] Thus Fanon transcended Merleau-Ponty. Rather than nationalism or a celebration of nationhood, it was the ways in which the oppressed experience, through action and thought, a radical mutation in consciousness that illustrated how anti-colonial national consciousness is a necessary but not sufficient condition for freedom. Self-consciousness does not close the door of communication but guarantees that it stays open (WE 247).

It is this notion of openness of thought, which is found in Merleau-Ponty's *Phenomenology of Perception*, that remains contested and allows Fanon to stay attuned to the continuing change in social reality and consciousness. We need to remind ourselves that for Fanon, living in the epoch of anti-colonial struggle, "dialectic took the upper hand" because there was no great dividing line between consciousness and reality.

Notes

1. Frantz Fanon, *Peau noire, masques blanc* (Paris: Seuil, 1952); trans. Charles Lam Markmann, *Black Skin, White Masks* (New York: Grove Press, 1967). Henceforth BSWM.

2. Fanon uses the term "inferiority complex" here not in a Mannonian sense. This does not mean that he misunderstands Mannoni's conception of "inferiority" and "dependency" (as McCulloch asserts), but that he is also referring to other conceptions of inferiority and abandonment (cf. Fanon's references to G. Geux in BSWM, pp. 73–80).

3. "The Black and Language." One must be careful of the term "Negro" in Fanon (see note 5). Markmann's translation makes no differentiation between Fanon's use of *noir* and of *nègre*. Chapter 1, "Le Noir at le langage," should obviously be translated "the Black," not "the Negro." This leaves us with a different angle on chapters 6 and 7, in which Fanon adopts the word *nègre* in the title.

4. He mentions that "for some reason or other" Guadeloupe was "considered to be a country of savages." Frantz Fanon, "West Indians and Africans," in *Toward the African Revolution: Political Essays*, trans. Haakon Chevalier (New York: Grove Press, 1967), henceforth TAR, p. 21.

5. Fanon uses the term *nègre* throughout *Black Skin*. It can mean either "Negro" or "nigger," and Fanon uses both. He also uses the terms *noir* (black) and "l'homme de couleur" (man of color). Each of these terms is used in chapter headings. The term "negro" is also significant because of Negritude's (negro-tude, or "nigger" attitude) positive recasting of the term. Thus when Fanon uses the term there can be a number of meanings and confusions. I have tended to use the term "the

Black" instead of "the Negro" and he indicated Fanon's use of the term *nègre*. I think "Black" reinforces the idea of a Manicheanism, but also, after "Black power" and "Black consciousness," it carries the ambiguity without the offensiveness. Where needed I have altered Markmann's translation.

6. In terms of his intellectual development, Fanon's move from Paris to Lyon was particularly important. Paris was the intellectual center and also the center of psychoanalytic theory in France. In Lyon there was no psychoanalytic institute and psychoanalysis did not permeate the curricula of medical schools.

7. See Ato Sekyi-Otu, *Fanon's Dialectic of Experience* (Cambridge, Mass.: Harvard University Press, 1996).

8. A phrase of Simone de Beauvoir's. *Force of Circumstance,* vol. 2 (New York: Paragon House, 1992), p. 314.

9. This translation traces its philosophic pedigree to Merleau-Ponty's translation of the German *Erlebnis* (indicating a Husserlian influence) and in English "lived experience." See Ronald A. Judy, "Fanon's Body of Black Experience," in Lewis R. Gordon, T. Denean Sharpley-Whiting, and Renée White, eds., *Fanon: A Critical Reader* (Oxford: Blackwell, 1996), p. 54.

10. Whereas the retranslation of "L'expérience Vécue du Noir" emphasizes the existential lived experience, Markman's translation, "The Fact of Blackness," caught the facticity of blackness both as a social and historical construction and as a constructed fact that emphasizes not "the Black" qua being but blackness qua existence, as a lived fact. What Markmann's translation signals (which could be lost in a mere accounting of lived experiences) is Fanon's concern with creating a new fact and a new way of life. Such a conceptualization is attained by thinking of lived experience not only as a social construct reflecting reality but also dialectically (a subject/object in Merleau-Ponty's terms, of the body in the world, of touching and being touched, of seeing and doing) (Maurice Merleau-Ponty, *Phenomenology of Perception,* trans Colin Smith [London: Routledge, 1962], henceforth PP, pp. 94–95) embodying tensions and contradictions that necessitate struggles to shape new realities.

11. Namely, an awareness of the other's awareness of my self, the third term that mediates and makes concrete "in-itself" and "for itself."

12. Jean-Paul Sartre, *Being and Nothingness,* trans. Hazel Barnes (London: Methuen, 1957), p. 555.

13. Cited in Kerry Whiteside, *Merleau-Ponty and the Foundation of an Existential Politics* (Princeton, N.J.: Princeton University Press, 1988), p. 88.

14. Elisabeth Roudinesco, *Jacques Lacan & Co.,* trans. Geoffrey Mehlman (Chicago: University of Chicago Press, 1990), p. 234.

15. A criticism that Jock McCulloch views as almost pathological. He believes that Fanon is forced to violently separate himself from a position akin to his own (see McCulloch's *Black Soul, White Artifact: Fanon's Clinical Psychology and Social Theory* [Cambridge: Cambridge University Press, 1993]).

16. McCulloch, *Black Soul,* pp. 214 (my emphasis) and 234 n. 7.

17. A point that Mannoni acknowledges and regrets in his second foreword to the book.

18. Mannoni notes that the 1947 revolts were led by many "whose assimilation had been incomplete" (PC 76).

19. The problem was an individual not a social one. In this, Mannoni is in line with other "Africanists" of the time who complained that the "evolved" African was thin-skinned and oversensitive to issues of race. The source of the sensitivity was the dependency complex. *Black Skin, White Masks* provides an exhaustive critique of this view.

20. For example, the subtitle of Freud's *Totem and Taboo*, "Some Point of Agreement between the Mental Lives of Savages and Neurotics."

21. McCulloch thinks that this was "at the heart of Fanon's critique of *Prospero*" and that "Fanon was wrong . . . Mannoni was not an apologist for colonialism." McCulloch, *Black Soul*, p. 219.

22. Mannoni seems to be aware of this problem in "The Decolonization of Myself," *Race* 7 (April 1966): 327–335.

23. In contrast to Mannoni's use of Shakespeare, Césaire's version of *The Tempest* was set in the Caribbean.

24. In fact, Fanon declared "Césaire's description of [Fort-de-France] anything but poetic" (BSWM 21).

25. Perhaps one of Mannoni's "best minds," he was part of a new generation of radicals on colonial policy who was an intellectual freethinker and admirer of Herbert Spencer.

26. Mannoni explains an experience with his tennis coach which he believes highlights the dependency complex. Mannoni gave the coach some anti-malarial drugs; instead of showing gratitude, the coach expected more presents (DC 42). Fanon might immediately ask Mannoni for more information on the social context.

27. Once again McCulloch flattens Fanon's argument, claiming that Fanon simply accepts Mannoni's characterization of the modern colonial as a "Prospero type" (McCulloch, *Black Soul*, p. 218).

28. Mannoni offers an attempt to explain the "pathology" of colonialism not as one between native and colonialist (as McCulloch believes; see *Black Soul*, p. 214), but in terms of the white colonial's motivation to "put an end to a feeling of unsatisfaction on the level of Adlerian overcompensation" (Fanon, BSWM, p.84).

29. Homi Bhabha, "Remembering Fanon: Self, Psyche, and the Colonial Condition," in Nigel Gibson, ed., *Rethinking Fanon* (Amherst, N.Y.: Humanity Books, 1999), pp. 179–194.

30. By the time Fanon had completed *Black Skin*, Lacan's topography "The Real, the Symbolic and the Imaginary" had not been published.

31. Mannoni states that when Madagascar "was first conquered, the Malagasies fled at the first shots being fired." This is far from the truth. But he contrasts this with the revolt of 1947 to emphasize the different reactions of the dependency complex. First, the open armed embrace of the white qua the Malagasy's own ancestor; second, the feeling of abandonment by the white's so-called liberalization (DC 86).

32. See Maurice Bloch's introduction to *Prospero and Caliban*, p. xv.

33. See Nigel Gibson, "Black Consciousness in South Africa," *Africa Today* 35, no. 1 (1988).

34. See Hussein A Bulhan, "Revolutionary Psychiatry of Fanon," in Gibson, *Rethinking Fanon*, pp. 161–175.

35. See Nigel Gibson, "Radical Mutations: Fanon's Untidy Dialectic of History," in Gibson, *Rethinking Fanon*, pp. 408–446.

Nine

Fanon Reading (W)right, the (W)right Reading of Fanon
Race, Modernity, and the Fate of Humanism

Lou Turner

My intention in this essay is to provide something of a metareading of the dialectic of race and racism—that is, to read the meaning of that logic by which the social construction of "race" is aggravated and distorted in the value judgments posited in the lived experience of individuals of dominant and subordinate groups at the end of late modernity. My "reading" of this dialectic is by way of an intertextual reading of a seldom-considered intellectual relationship between the Francophone radical psychiatrist Frantz Fanon and the Anglophone radical writer Richard Wright. That the texts of both of these men rely heavily on the narratives and performances of a phenomenological psychology should not make us lose sight of the essentially liberatory enterprise in which they are engaged. On the contrary, the existential psychology of their work, instead of being counterposed to their aims to liberate "modern man" of racial alienation, is evidence of their radical—that is, critical—appropriation of Western humanism for the purpose of positing a "new humanism." Wright and Fanon believed that this was not only a justly creditable response to the enormity of the historical-material consequences of Western racism, but that the "other" posited in the philosophical anthropology of Western humanism was indispensable to the creation of a "new humanism."

Given the significance accorded each of these men with respect to closing the circle of modernity with the formation of this "new humanism," it is surprising that little or no serious discussion has taken place on the relationship of the thought of Frantz Fanon to that of Richard Wright.[1] Quintessential diasporan intellectuals of black modernity, Wright and Fanon share a common intellectual genealogy of the postwar, Third World, liberatory era: Marxism, French and German phenomenological existentialism, post-Freudian social

151

psychology, modernist literary trends, Negritude, critical discourses on Western civilization and humanism, and intimate participant knowledge of the dialectics of African decolonization. In short, they moved in the same intellectual milieu. Evidence exists that each was deeply aware of the other's work. And in the case of Fanon, there is the note to Wright, 6 January 1953—"I am working on a study bearing on the human breadth of your works."[2] Wright, as the principal organizer of the 1956 Congress of Negro Writers and Artists, invited Fanon to speak at the Congress, and it was the last time Fanon would speak in public in France.

In common, too, was the fact that the mind of each man was othered by the racial barbarism of Western civilization. Notwithstanding Elizabeth Fox-Genovese and Eugene Genovese's paternalistic estimation of Fanon, Wright and Fanon were among "those black intellectuals who were unwilling to repudiate their blackness and unwilling to forgo their rights and dignity as men."[3] Why one should exclude the other is never made clear by the Genoveses. Fanon's eagerness "to circumscribe in the most complete way" the "human breadth" of Wright's message transcends any suggestion that the blackness and the humanity of that message are in any way exclusive of each other. What, however, is apparent upon "reading" Fanon is that his reading of Wright is evident throughout *Black Skin, White Masks*, then less than a year off the press when Fanon refers to it in his letter to Wright. The two died a year apart in circumstances that had all the "black ops" trappings of the Cold War era—Wright unexpectedly in 1960, in France, rumored to be a target of U.S. intelligence operations, Fanon in December 1961, at Bethesda Naval Hospital, under CIA watch. Radical intellectuals of the African diaspora whose lives and work embodied that global identity, Wright died in a country that Fanon could never return to, and Fanon died in a country from which Wright had exiled himself.

Fanon Reading Sartre and Merleau-Ponty (W)right

The role that Wright played in Fanon's thought ushers us into that phenomenology of black mind that both men were so instrumental in radicalizing and encrypting with modernity. Sartre's relationship to Wright and Fanon was seminal in this regard. It is not that Fanon needed Sartre to read Wright; on the contrary, Fanon turns to Wright in the course of his reflexive critique of Sartre, at the penultimate moment of the chapter "The Fact of Blackness" in *Black Skin, White Masks*. Fanon's strategy of critically handling Sartre's syllogistic subsumption of Negritude under a proletarian dialectic of class struggle, in "Black Orpheus,"[4] was not in order to deny the objectivity of Sartre's argument, but to remind him that the racial alienation that he dramatizes in his play on the sexual and violent content of race relations in American society, *The Respectful Prostitute,* finds its resolution neither in a Senghorian

Negritude of recollecting a lost black innocence, nor in a doctrinaire Marxism. While hardly a resolution of the alienations of racial modernity, Fanon turned to Richard Wright's *Native Son* and the genre, both literary and cinematic,[5] that it spawned, including Sartre's *The Respectful Prostitute,* to explore the unique existential situation of the "lived experience of the black," in part elided by Sartre's "Black Orpheus." Wright articulated a language of violent refusal of racial domination, one that did not compromise with that reality and with which compromise could not be made.

Wright appears at the unresolved climax of "the lived experience of the black," which began with Fanon frozen in the glare of a white child's gaze on a Paris train. Breaking the immobility brought on by that experience meant shedding a gallery of masks, beginning with the "ideal Negro type" whose professional status could not inoculate him against racial dread and despair, and culminating in the revolution in consciousness that Wright's character Bigger Thomas experiences in *Native Son.* Either the black accepts the spiritual-existential amputation of racial modernity, or he or she explodes. Every attempt to find the right mask is a futile effort to postpone the violence that sleeps restlessly in every black.[6] Reading Wright reinforced the language in which Fanon wanted to speak to the alienated black.

Fanon sought to comprehend the psychological rigidity, so recurrent in the work of African-American writers such as Wright, that was a modern condition seemingly absent from Negritude writers, but that he experienced himself. Merleau-Ponty, whose lectures Fanon attended, describes this psychological rigidity as what Freudians call "reaction formation," or "a façade interposed by the subject between his psychological reality and others who are there to examine him."[7] As Fanon's (and Wright's) concern is with the aggressivity underlying racial violence, Merleau-Ponty's reading of the work of Dr. Else Frenkel-Brunswik, a principal author of the massive Authoritarian Personality study headed by Theodor Adorno, is not without interest.[8] Keeping in mind the distinction that whereas Merleau-Ponty and the Freudians, including those associated with the Berkeley Authoritarian Personality project, emphasized the affectivity of individual psychology, Fanon's theoretical framework is irreducibly sociogenic and compatible with Merleau-Ponty's observation that "If the individual is very aggressive he conceals his aggression under an acquired veil of politeness, and often the most apparently polite people are, at bottom, the most aggressive" (PPOE 101). Merleau-Ponty's terms of the problem—that is, the "reaction formation," or affective response to examination—gives Fanon's narrative of his train experience its quasi-experimental character. The black (Fanon) comes under the examination of the white train passengers, his politeness concealing temporarily an aggressivity whose source is located not, as it is for Merleau-Ponty's subject, in the family, but in racial modernity. Merleau-Ponty nonetheless recognizes the sociogenesis of aggressive reaction formation, alluding to "the legends in America and French Africa concerning the sexuality of Negroes" in which

[s]ubjects project onto the Negro (considered to represent a "natural" sexuality that is stronger and more violent than their own) something of themselves that they would like not to have. The same mechanism is called into play with the Jews; the construction of the Jewish character often proceeds by a division of this kind. The anti-Semite throws off onto the Jew the part of himself he does not want and is most ashamed of, as others do with the Negro. . . . Simone de Beauvoir has analyzed a mechanism of the same kind in the phenomenon of the "battle of the sexes." (PPOE 103)

Were it possible to reduce the sociogenetic character of the racist to the individual psychological schema of the family, one would have to begin with the most overlooked agent in Fanon's narrative of his train experience, viz., the child. No one among Fanon's commentators seems to have asked, How does it happen that a French child is intuitively frightened of a "polite Negro" on a Paris train? This is what gives Fanon's experience its quasi-random character. A child does not imitate others, but rather the conduct and action of others (PPOE 117). Fanon's problem, as set forth by Merleau-Ponty, is that

knowing how conduct can be transferred from another to me is infinitely less difficult to solve than the problem of knowing how I can represent to myself a psyche that is radically foreign to me. . . . What is essential, however, is to see that a perspective on the other is opened to me from the moment I define him and myself as "conducts" at work in the world, as ways of "grasping" the natural and cultural world surrounding us. (PPOE 117)

This, in fact, is Fanon's problem on the train, fixed in the gaze of a white child. For adults, Fanon's black presence (body) presents no problem because there is nothing in his *proper conduct* to cause alarm. This is because for white adults, the significance of conduct—that is, decoding it, to use Merleau-Ponty's term (PPOE 115)—has been sublated by the problem of representing to themselves the *psyche* of an-other who is "radically foreign." For the white child on the train confronted with Fanon's black bodily presence, on the other hand, the problem exists at the actional level of conduct. Radical foreignness is not easily sublated, nor apparently sublimated, in the child's relations with the other. The child, in other words, grasps the "psyche that is radically foreign" to her, and thus her own natural and cultural surroundings, by the conduct of the other. In a word, the child hasn't developed a comprehension of the "radically foreign" as a representation, so the emotional response—in the case of the child on Fanon's train, fear—expresses a grasping for self-defining conduct. The *look* of the Negro, elicited by "Look, a Negro . . . " becomes a spontaneous piece of conduct that the child anxiously grasps to situate the psyche of Fanon's radical foreignness. With the startled gaze of a white child Fanon is lifted from his corporeal schema and plunged into the historico-racial schema that was always already there . . . waiting for him.

With his Negritude "outed," the private internal sensations and outward perceptions that should situate him and his body in the world are sublated by a *public* postural schema. The private suffers the privation of the public in the lived experience of the black; indeed, this privation *is* the lived experience of the black, *is* black social being. *Black* is ever a public postural schema for which the gallery of masks that are supposed to mask the irreducible mask of Western civilization appear always already unmasked. There is, in other words, beneath the gallery of masks, an irreducible mask—*the* mask, for which the existence of the black is forever providing the date and occasion for a violent unmasking. Marx calls the appearance of appearance *time,* by which he means the appearance of the appearance of Being's being. Black lived existence in this way is trans-historicized—in other words, is lived impossibly, or is *lived impossibility.* One's very experience is lived irony; that is, the black is cast as ahistorical in order that he assume the trans-historicized role that is always already there for him. He is *an* unknown who is made to play *the* unknown. And in the role of *the* unknown, the black is object of the absolute knowing of Western civilization; he is its *thing-in-itself.* It is simply impossible to know black subjectivity on such a stage, however, which is why its fate or, less dramatically, its existence is a permanent performance.

Sartre's Respectful Prostitute, Wright's Savage Puritans

Fanon's and Wright's concerns rendezvous at Sartre's performance of the American racial (and sexual) drama scripted in his 1946 *La Putain Respectueuse.* Not only do we have Wright's introductory note to Sartre's *The Respectful Prostitute,* in addition to his critical annotations on a draft of Sartre's screenplay adaptation of the play,[9] we also have a brief response to the play by Fanon in *Black Skin, White Masks.* At the time of his commentary on Sartre's *The Respectful Prostitute,* Wright, writes Michel Fabre, began to change "his concept of the racial question, which he had already begun to see in a broader perspective," a change which impelled him to "look elsewhere [than Europe] for reasons to believe in mankind" (UQ 326). He had come in search of the wellsprings of Europe's humanist tradition in 1946; by 1948 he was revolted by its retrogression "before the advance of Americanization" (UQ 326). Whereupon the emancipatory fate of the Third World became his last best hope for rekindling humanism, "just as the liberation of the American Negro would be the salvation of America" (UQ 326). The 1948 crisis of humanism impelled Wright's decision to journey to Africa.

The Euro-American side of the crisis, viz., the Cold War, motivated Wright's writing *The Outsider;* its African-American dimension elicited his interest in Sartre's *The Respectful Prostitute* the same year. Wright's and Fanon's readings of Sartre's script are, respectively, farcical and tragic. In his introductory note, Wright tells us that in Sartre's America the race problem is not a "Negro problem" but a "White Problem" that the existentialist views "in terms of farce" (RWBW 237). The characterization is significant and provides a clue to why Wright scholars are so often at sea in assessing his later work, or what they contend is a shift in his view of the race question.[10] As a consequence of his expatriate position *outside* of America, and not only in Paris or Europe, Wright elevates America's race "Problem" to the international level of what Nietzsche called "great politics."[11] In Wright's case this meant the Cold War struggle between the American and Russian superpowers for a single world hegemony over the mind of humanity. *The Respectful Prostitute*, Wright argues, "is a calculated challenge to those who feel that America is a finished democracy" (RWBW 236).

From the "great politics" vantage point, Sartre elected not to place the "traditional Negro protagonist in the foreground" (RWBW 236) of his play, thus suppressing the "unnatural method of placing the moral blame of the Negro problem upon the Negro himself" (RWBW 236), in order to expose America's race problem as a "moral comedy of the white American character" (RWBW 237). The idea of a white working-class prostitute gaining the respectful gentility of a Southern belle, or being convinced that she could, by displaying her willingness to the powers-that-be to play the South's deadly sexually charged game of racial charades may or may not have actually been farcical in Sartre's view. Wright, nonetheless, found Sartre's morality play inherently farcical because the comic contradictions of the South's silly racial and sexual taboos stripped the great World War II savior of the "free world" of all pretense of being a democracy at its soft southern underbelly. *The Respectful Prostitute* is a burlesque moral striptease, as only French existentialism could perform it, whether Sartre was fully aware of it or not.[12] Only a black Southern writer such as Wright, having delved into the violent terrain of this world without a shred of self-conscious tragic pathos—the very hallmark of Wright's black modernity—could register the farcicality of America's Southern burlesque as the opposite side of the "natural-born killer" guise that white supremacy usually masquerades as.

For Fanon, the drama does not turn so much on a so-called black inferiority complex as it does on an existential ontology of nonexistence.[13] Sartre's black is caught in the historico-racial schema from which there is "no exit." The paralysis that sets in as a consequence of the hegemony of this schema can be broken only by action, according to Fanon, the violent action that becomes Bigger Thomas's meditation on his personal emancipation in Wright's novel *Native Son*. Already in Wright's *Black Boy*, with which Fanon was familiar, the appearance of Wright's impersonal style gestured toward existentialism. But, as Raya Dunayevskaya notes, the impersonal writing style of so individualistic a writer as Richard Wright is less an instance of existentialism and is "in reality the *personality of a people*" (RDC 9039; emphasis in the original). Wright, not Sartre, disclosed for Fanon the black man as "a non-man." *Native Son*, not *Being and Nothingness*, made Fanon aware of the fact that if whites are "to understand the Negroes a revolution must occur in *their own* lives" (RDC 9040; emphasis in the original). Wright, not Sartre, convinced Fanon that the formal end of action is *to feel*. And in the end, Wright's "anguish is deeper than that of [the] existentialists" (RDC 9042). Though there is no solution to the problem of black freedom in modern capitalist society, modern racism exposes just how universal the psychological disintegration of the individual personality is. Existentialism explains Wright, and Wright explains existentialism (RDC 9042).

Fanon's is a tragic, not farcical, reading of black lived experience, not so much from a moral point of view—a condition that, while modern, would make it captive of the old humanism—instead as a consequence of having been marked by the fateful undoing of one's own *situation*. Race is viewed by Fanon in the manner of ancient tragedy, that is, as a fateful condition that weighs upon black lived experience in the sense in which inevitability attaches to all of one's actions. Black lived experience is robbed of its free will, or deluded by the false appearance of free will, which accounts for its violence: both the violence of its existential condition of being black and the violence of liberating itself from this "fact of blackness." It is this tragic violence, or violence of tragedy, that Richard Wright examines in the lives of his savage puritans.[14]

Wright wrote *Savage Holiday*, a psychological crime thriller, on the heels of the publication of *The Outsider*, in 1952–53. While the theories of the prominent, though unorthodox, Freudian Frederic Wertham were of use to Wright, and he had undergone psychotherapy with Wertham, *Savage Holiday* does not involve black characters but instead a white man, Erskine Fowler, haunted by his Oedipal past, who like Brewer (see note 14) inexplicably murders a woman he loves.

Wright's interest in individual and social psychology developed in very sophisticated ways in the decade following *Native Son*. The influence of the University of Chicago sociological theorist Louis Wirth on Wright's writing of *12 Million Black Voices* evinced the sociogenic dimension of Wright's thought, one which Communist ideologues such as Herbert Aptheker dismissed as "too sociological" and not sufficiently "Marxist." *The Outsider* was written around Wright's social psychology of the totalitarian personality (left and right), from which black consciousness fatally asserts its independence. After *Savage Holiday*, the second novel in Wright's trilogy of savage puritans is "Strange Daughter," which while involving a black character, a Nigerian, has as its protagonist a white woman (Peggy Vinson) who, like Erskine Fowler in *Savage Holiday*, is sexually repressed by the puritanical values of her parents. The savage intimacy of modernity's worlds in collision asserts itself in "Strange Daughter" in the form of an alleged Nigerian taboo against having the spirit of ancestors reincarnated in a non-African form. The tragic turn at the climax of the novel, leading to the murder of the pregnant protagonist, exhibits the social psychology of African (and Third World) religion and culture that becomes the framework of the third novel of what Wright projected as his "Celebration of Life" modal trilogy. "When the World Was Red" was to be a novel exploring the social psychology of religion behind the conquest of the Aztecs by the Spanish conquistador Hernan Cortes. The protagonist, the Aztec emperor Montezuma, is a Mannonian figure, while the Aztec elite display the social psychological characteristics that Wright criticized in his analysis of contemporary African elites in *Black Power* and *White Man, Listen!* Wright's non-fictional writings on Africa and its elites are integral to his concerns in the innovative, unrealized "Celebration of Life" that his agent's and publisher's lapse in imagination discouraged.

Finally, what should not be overlooked upon considering Wright's savage puritans is the role that his trips to Spain, in 1954–55, and his travel essay *Pagan Spain* played in the dialectic of his fictional and non-fictional social psychology. Spain, the psychological repressiveness of Catholicism, and the political repression of Franco's fascist state, however, suggest only one side of the relationship to the Spanish conquest of the New World in "When the World Was Red." Octave Mannoni's social psychology of colonialism, *Prospero and Caliban*, represents the other.

De-Colonizing Mannoni

Richard Wright's notion of mood, or what I would call modality, is, from the little written about it, highly susceptible to misinterpretation. Discerning the origins of Wright's late experiment in narrative expression would entail as comprehensive an approach as Wright's own ambitious construction of a modal writing form. That his agent, Paul Reynolds, and his former editor at Harpers, Ed Aswell, to whom he wrote extensive explanations of what he had in mind, and to whom he submitted rather complete story lines of the three small novels he envisioned making up the modal trilogy that he called "Celebration of Life," found Wright's idea unmarketable is perhaps understandable. That Wright scholars still dismiss Wright's project as an unrealizable piece of avant-garde literature exhibits a certain poverty of imagination.

This, however, is not the venue either to critically delve into this lacuna in Wright scholarship or to mount a full-scale excavation of the various sources of Wright's mood concept in which he invested so much of his intellectual energies and on which he was apparently prepared to gamble his literary prestige near the end of his life. Although that enterprise is the only proper one in which to comprehend the rich philosophical implications of his experiment in psycho-existential narrative, my more immediate concern with the simulacra of Fanon and Wright suggests several conceptions that might otherwise go unexplored. For example, Wright and Fanon exhibited seemingly divergent attitudes toward Mannoni's *Prospero and Caliban*. The title of chapter 4 of *Black Skin, White Masks* left no doubt as to Fanon's attitude, referring to Mannoni's 1950 work as "The So-Called Dependency Complex of Colonized Peoples." A version of Wright's 1956 review of Mannoni's *Psychology of Colonization*, which appeared under the title "Neuroses of Conquest,"[15] is reproduced by Fabre in his biography of Wright (RWBW 223–225) with a title that is an apparent allusion to Fanon: "White Faces: Agents Provocateurs of Mankind." However, we aren't told whether "White Faces" is Wright's allusion to Fanon, or Fabre's (UQ 434). Fortunately, there are other allusions to Fanon by Wright, indicating that he was well aware of Fanon's critique of Mannoni when he wrote his review.[16]

Fabre reports that Wright's reading of Mannoni's book also provided material for his speech at the 1956 Congress of Negro Artists and Writers and for his lecture "The Psychological Reactions of Oppressed Peoples" that appears as the first chapter of *White Man, Listen!* In fact, perhaps with the exception of his essay "The Literature of the Negro in the United States," the whole of *White Man, Listen!* is representative of Wright's reading of Mannoni, with important allusions to Fanon.

A comparison of Wright's "Celebration of Life," extensively outlined in his 1956 correspondence with Reynolds and Aswell, with Fanon's *Black Skin, White Masks*, especially chapter 4 on Mannoni and chapter 5, "The Lived Experience of the Black" (substituted in the English translation by the title "The Fact of Blackness"), reveals intriguing simulacra not only on the question of existentialism but concerning the influences of Negritude and surrealism. Both, moreover, display Marxist commitments in their approaches to the liberation of men and women from the psychological suffering of modern alienation. While there are various sources of Wright's concept of mood for his experimental trilogy "Celebration of Life," Mannoni figures as the most significant for our purposes.

Thanks to Maurice Bloch's critical forward to a new English translation of Mannoni's work, we are provided with a helpful and brief summary of Mannoni's argument which avoids the almost hagiographic misreadings of what Mannoni meant by the dependency and inferiority complexes and, in the case of the latter, *who* exactly has one. Whatever other usages the inferiority complex may have, Mannoni locates its origin in the European, not African, personality. The first point that Bloch clears up is that Mannoni's debt is to Adler, not Freud, for the dependency and inferiority complexes. And while Mannoni does rely on Freud (and, apparently, Lacan), the influence of Levy-Bruhl's Eurocentric theories of the African's so-called irrational, savage mind is apparent.

Using the overworked schema of childhood development for societal and cultural evolution, Mannoni borrowed Adler's concept of dependency and abandonment to explain the lived experience of peoples. For now, we must set aside problems of translating individual psychology into terms of social psychology, except to note that this philosophical infantilism underlies the racial mythology of Enlightenment anthropology and humanism, as well as later positivism. In Mannoni's view, societies, like individuals, begin in a state of childhood dependence. With civilization this dependency is broken, leading to feelings of abandonment by the parent, especially father, figure(s). Because the break was initiated by the child/subject, the ensuing feeling of abandonment creates a reflexive feeling of guilt over the lost dependency. This self-reflexive feeling of abandonment and guilt results in an "inferiority complex" for those individuals who are unable to make a "healthy" transition to modernity and civilization, or who experience modernity as an irresolvable crisis of European civilization. These individuals and segments of modern European society experience their inferiority complex as an unsatisfied desire to dominate others. In Adlerian terms, this aggressivity is over-compensation for feelings of guilt over lost dependency and abandonment. These individuals and segments of European society seek the satisfaction of this seemingly insatiable desire in "brave new world(s)"—that is, in worlds without (civilized) men. This corresponds, of course, to the colonial personality, who in seeking satisfaction of his desire to overcome an inferiority complex (i.e., feelings of inadequacy in the face of modernity) undergoes a transformation into the dominating father figure who had originally elicited feelings of guilt. While the violence of this dominance is motivated by feelings of guilt and is itself the over-compensating resolution of those feelings, they (the feelings) create their own dehumanizing moral crisis and seek its resolution through the cultivation of dependency among those dominated.

Now, this last moment in the logic of dependency is not Mannoni's but Fanon's, his point being that given the logic of Mannoni's insights, he should have gone there but did not. Instead, Mannoni fabricates what meso-American scholars call "the myth of the myth" when they refer to the alleged Aztec myth that the Europeans were the anticipated gods of former times returned to assume their positions of authority over the people. Although there is no lack of theorizing the connection between race and sovereignty, Mannoni was one of the first to psychologize that relationship. Both Fanon and Wright, no matter how different their assessments of Mannoni, responded to this endeavor. Fanon, in some sense, never stopped responding, from *Black Skin, White Masks*, through *A Dying Colonialism*, to *The Wretched of the Earth*. The psychological connection between race and sovereignty demanded the creation of "a new man and a new woman," or at least that is what decolonization entailed. Fanon's was not an ego psychology in this regard but a psychology of consciousness; that is, he was less interested in, and in fact critiqued, the idea of an African personality and Senghorian Negritude, and was more taken with comprehending the conditions which make the transformation of social consciousness possible. And from works such as *A Dying Colonialism* and *The Wretched of the Earth* it is clear that those conditions were not reducible to violence alone. The question of what happens after the revolution, after national independence, after the first act of decolonization was as much, even more, a question of what conditions are necessary and adequate for the transformation of consciousness.

Colonialism was for Mannoni and Fanon the contact and interaction of two distinct personalities, or "two differently-constructed types of personality."[17]

Mannoni, moreover, rather plainly states the psychosocial fact that the socialized individual is equivalent to what he takes to be the personality, insofar as its social environment is stable (PC 25). And while colonialism is the self-evident destabilization of that social environment, and Mannoni and Fanon are both interested in mapping the psychodynamics of the disintegration of the "native" personality, Mannoni is interested in stabilizing that personality within a more rational colonial context than the one that inaugurated the process of disintegration, whereas Fanon sees the further destabilization of the colonial environment, viz., the revolution, as the process by which the native transcends the ego-personality formed by the colonial environment. When Fanon, at the outset of his critique of Mannoni, judges his work as "too exhaustive," a characteristic that Mannoni shared with current psychological research, it is at the cost of "los[ing] sight of the real" (BSWM 83). It is "the real" which is both at risk of subsumption by the exhaustiveness of psychological analysis of the colonized, and more broadly, "modern man," and upon which Fanon will rely in his phenomenological critique of Mannoni and the exhaustiveness of current research.

That Fanon commences this critique with singling out two important elements in Mannoni's research, for which he "deserves our thanks," should not come as too much of a surprise. Mannoni, after all, was in debt to many of Fanon's own philosophical influences, most notably existentialism and psychoanalysis. The two elements that Mannoni introduces are 1) the importance of the objective human situation, in this case, the "colonial situation," and 2) the importance of human attitudes toward the objective conditions of that situation. Fanon also found useful Mannoni's view that the pathology of the colonial conflict was produced by the European colonial mentality in search of satisfying its desire to find *a world without men*. Principal among Mannoni's contributions is that of the "colonial situation"—that is, the situation produced by the confrontation of "civilized" and "primitive" peoples. This confrontation produced both the colonial situation and illusory and mistaken attitudes about the other.

Despite his comprehension of the phenomenology that lay at the source of real everyday relations of the colonial situation and its attendant attitudes, Mannoni still lapsed into racial relativism and racial essentialism, the former as a result of his own French colonial status and the latter as a consequence of his Enlightenment inheritance. His racial relativism assumed the form of an attitude which maintains the illusory perception that racism is differentiated according to class status and culture. For instance, he thought that "racism is the work of underlings and hence in no way involves the ruling class, that France is one of the least racist countries in the world" (BSWM 85), and that the north of France is more racist than the south. A society, Fanon declares, is either racist or it is not. European civilization and its best representatives were not responsible for colonial racism, according to Mannoni. In line with his social psychology of the white colonial personality, he attributes "colonial racialism" to "the work of petty officials, small traders, and colonials who have toiled much without great success" (BSWM 90 n. 11).

To this Fanon adds what he calls the "racial distribution of guilt" (BSWM 103)—that is, the formation of a hierarchy of peoples of color who are responsible for oppressing each other, with the black relegated to the lowest rank. The white man, Fanon argues, "sloughs off his responsibilities" (BSWM 103) onto the shoulders of racial and ethnic groups below him as the cause of their respective sufferings. The European concept of race becomes distributed among the peoples who have come under the hegemony of European civilization. The subordinate ranking of the black in this hierarchy is not accidental: Africans used by the French to suppress the colonial revolts of their other non-European subject peoples inscribed the black on the native consciousness as a phobic representation identified with repression and fear. Racial relativism and its corollary, the racial distribution of guilt, represented two sides of a phenomenological dialectic of racialism—the former, the externality in which reality is made illusory, and the latter, the interiority in which the illusory is invaded (colonized) by the real. In the case of the racial distribution of guilt, real fantasies (real because of the historical trauma of colonial subjugation) irrupt in the illusory dream world of sleep, not laden with the Freudian symbolism that Mannoni attributed to the dreams of Malagasy children traumatized by the violent incursion of Senegalese troops into Madagascan society at the time of the 1947 revolt and colonial genocidal suppression, but with these real historical traumatic events. To restore the trauma of the real fantasies that broke out in the dreams of Malagasies to their real historical time and place of the colonial situation, in Fanon's estimation, underscores the significance of the *socius* as the key to alienation of the individual.

Importantly, the racial essentialism of Mannoni's work preoccupied Fanon and the literary imagination of Richard Wright in quite different ways. Fanon indicates the catastrophic consequences of European toying with racial relativism. The "Great Generation" that fought Nazism would have to be "great" indeed, inasmuch as it was fascism's accomplice before it became its enemy, or the threatened object of its barbaric power, the very power whose use against non-European peoples Europe sanctioned. In any event, it is Césaire's critique, following Fanon, of Mannoni's racial essentialism that finally brings us face to face with Richard Wright's most imaginative decolonization of the philosophic anthropology that lies at the heart of European humanism, a project that, by 1948, Wright (and, it seems, Fanon) found had come to a teleological dead end. No progress could be made without decentering the role of the European and privileging that of the "other" on whose degradation and for whose "education" Western humanism had been constructed. The lead would have to be taken by the non-European other in rethinking the humanist canon, an impossible project without deconstructing it. That Hegel, Freud, and Marx were being rethought prior to the postmodernist turn by "postcolonial" writers and artists such as Wright, Césaire, Fanon, and C. L. R. James is evident from their all-out assault on the old humanism.

To be sure, this is only part of the story; less recognized or "read" is the story of the "new humanism" and the formation of demythologizing myths of the Western world and its world-without-men other. The "dossier," as Césaire calls the catalogue of atrocities of Western "civilization," is indeed over-whelming.[18] It begins, however, with the ontotheological cum ontoanthro-pological exercise of apprehending what exactly makes men different. Outer cultural appearances, according to Mannoni, are expressions of innate person-ality traits that differentiate men as "civilized" and "primitive." Because the dependency complex of the black supposedly antedates colonization, Mannoni contradicts his own best insight that the formation of the "colonial situation" arises from the confrontation of two distinct group personalities. Mannoni's contradiction displaces the subject from his or her situation, and the attitudes of the black and the European responsible for its construction, and instead substitutes innate psychological essences that allegedly predate the "colonial situation." In Jock McCulloch's view, one which he devotes an expanded ap-pendix to arguing at the end of his Fanon book, this results from "Mannoni's rendering of the ahistorical model of psychopathology fashionable among the descendants of Freud and Adler."[19] Like the Genoveses, McCulloch is less interested in the racial essentialism that results from the ahistoricality of Freudian and Adlerian models of psychopathology than in positing a specious amalgam of Fanon and Mannoni. Accordingly, race achieves its ideological transcendence over the historical-material situation of colonialism proximately responsible for its formation, a transcendence marking the virtual inversion of reality.

Mannoni reasserts the ahistoricism of the psychopathological model, re-gardless of the phenomenological (colonial) situation. This is what Fanon critiques despite the fact that he recognizes, with Mannoni, the existential reality of modern racial alienation, that is, that the social alienation of moder-nity is visited upon the African in the form of colonialism, complete with dependency and inferiority complexes. Fanon wishes to liberate blacks from this alienation, while Mannoni wishes to humanize their alienation within the colonial context. The two positions that Fanon and Mannoni arrive at are not, however, attributable merely to their respective subjectivities, but arise instead from the conceptual regress made by Mannoni into a racial essentialism that vitiates the phenomenological approach upon which he premised his original point of departure, viz., the importance of comprehending the phenome-nology of the "colonial *situation*." Far from "the shadow of [Mannoni's] *Prospero* fall[ing] across all of Fanon's writings" (BSWA 213), or the fact that Mannoni, "more than any other single figure, set for Fanon the boundaries of his life's work" (BSWA 214), Fanon's sharp critique of Mannoni's re-gress into racial essentialism, a regress that in important respects replicated Senghorian Negritude, which Fanon would also come to critique, constitutes a profound philosophic divide. Without Fanon's critique, Mannoni's regress would vitiate both any comprehension of the existential reality of black alienation and the articulation of the liberatory perspectives needed to overcome it.[20] Thus, the mistaken claims of the Genoveses and McCulloch for a congruity between Fanon and Mannoni, because both acknowledged the pathology of racial alienation, proceeds on grounds of not having recognized this critical moment in Fanon's treatment of Mannoni. Such claims either are premised on the same kind of regress into racial essentialism, or are unmindful that the warrant for such claims is only possible upon such a premise.

Mannoni's racial essentialism explains the humanity of the native/other toward the European as a desire, inscribed in his collective unconsciousness, to be mastered. Fanon's dialectical humanism, that "new humanism" in which "[t]he future of every man [and woman] today has a relation of close dependency on the rest of the universe" (BSWM 126), does not begin with the emancipatory project of decolonization. Fanon was well aware of the "pitfalls of national consciousness" before writing *The Wretched of the Earth*. It begins, first of all, with colonialism's challenge to the humanity of the African by its incursion into the reality in which she lived her authenticity—that is, lived the particularity of her humanity as a universal. Second, it is only because of the degradation to her humanity that the black experiences that she desires to assert her humanity in the self-alienated form of desiring recognition from the one who deprives her of it. It is this dialectic that Mannoni misread as a dependency complex that the native possesses in her cultural and psychological essence, and as one that white colonialism and supremacy supposedly satisfies.

Mannoni's problem in colonizing the African's pre-colonial past, as Fanon points out, is that the closed ontology of a so-called African authenticity, one which seals the African in her customs and culture and then inserts her into the bilateral totality (BSWM 94) of an overlapping African/European world, ceased to exist. So where the African may have exhibited traits of dependency —for instance, toward ancestors in the form of the "cult of the dead," or in submissive attitudes toward ruling elites—that must not suddenly be taken out of its original ethnological context and represented as the phenomenological situation of colonialism. Mannoni's distortions of the African personality are equally distortions of African history: colonialism destroyed the African personality; it is not the persistence of it through a supposed transference of dependency to European authority. The bilateral totality of colonialism (i.e., its Manicheanism) can have no other result than dependency and inferiority. "In his first novels," Fanon told the delegates to the 1956 Paris conference of Negro writers and artists, "[Richard] Wright gives a very detailed description" of the black guilt complex that results from this (TAR 35). Colonialism does not leave African authenticity intact. On the contrary, "The social constellation, the cultural whole, are deeply modified by the existence of racism" (TAR 36).

For Richard Wright, Mannoni's distortions of personality and history are of less importance than is the complexity of guilt that the individual suffers as a consequence of the cultural distortions of her social existence inaugurated by colonialism and racism. To apprehend the symbiosis of individual guilt and the cultural distortions of a society, Wright sought to capture the mood in which the organism flourishes.

"When the World Was Red"

And if I told you I like Freud and Marx, not in terms
of politics but because they are poets . . . [?]
—Richard Wright, interview, September 1960

[M]an philosophizes in order to live.
—Miguel de Unamuno

The organism in Wright's "Celebration of Life" is *race,* for which he articulates a literary imaginary or mood as its domain. In the shuttle back and forth between Spain and France (he made a total of three trips to Spain) in 1954 and 1955 for the writing of *Pagan Spain,* followed immediately by his attendance at the 1955 Bandung Conference of Non-Aligned Nations, for which he wrote *The Color Curtain,* Wright, according to John Reilly, "began to sense a deep and organic relation . . . between race and religion, two of the most powerful and irrational forces in human nature."[21] However, neither Reilly nor Anthony Appiah's "A Long Way from Home: Wright in the Gold Coast" mentions Mannoni as a crucial source of Wright's views on African religion, psychology, and colonialism.

It may be that Wright's approach to Mannoni through the mediation of his modal literary device accomplished a more successful decolonization of Mannoni's psychosemantics than did his non-fictional works, such as *Pagan Spain, Color Curtain, Black Power,* and *White Man, Listen!* At this point, though, it is necessary to consider, if only speculatively, some sources of what Wright refers to as "mood." His interest in French cinematography in the 1940s and 1950s, as well as experimentations in modern jazz with modal concepts in music, in the same period, suggest possible influences.[22] However, what Ralph Ellison recollected in an interview with Horace Cayton, 8 September 1968, for an unrealized biography of Wright on which Cayton worked at the end of his life, suggests that the idea had been germinating in Wright since his first trip to Paris in the early 1940s. "[H]e was reading [Miguel de Unamuno's *Tragic Sense of Life*]," Ellison recalled.

Dick was excited about it[.] I had come across [Unamuno] by reading Malraux[.] Unamuno appears as a character in [Malraux's] "Man's Hope," so I had a good sharpened and developed interest in existentialism and by this time Sartre began to show up. [I]n talking to Dick about this he said we don't want to get mixed up in this. I had already seen in my own mind that the blues had prepared me for existentialism and Malraux had handled this better as a novelist than Sartre. But before I knew it RW is writing an existentialist novel—*The Outsider*. A bad novel.[23]

It was this Spanish precursor of modern existentialism, whose work as philosopher, novelist, and poet suggested the formal possibilities of the literary form, that Wright spelled out in a very long letter to Ed Aswell in 1956, after he visited the Gold Coast, Spain, and Bandung. The dialectical tension between faith and reason that Unamuno sustains in his philosophy of life resides naturally in Wright's considerations of the dialectic between race and religion. Like Hegel's objective idealism and Marx's naturalism, Unamuno and Wright saw man's externalization of his being outside himself into the realities of others, including into nature and its processes, as constitutive of a naturalism or humanism that Wright, and from a different direction, Fanon, found irresistible in the first postwar decade. What is more, Wright's Whitmanesque poetic interludes afford us further insight into the modality of race at work in his literary experiment.

Merging and expiration, sexuality and death, are tropes of Wright's "Celebration of Life," whether represented by the protagonist in *Savage Holiday* who kills the object of his sexual love, or by the young white woman in "Strange Daughter" who in finally coming to terms with her sexuality loses her life to her African lover because of the role strain placed upon him by the religious prohibition of his "cult of the dead" against the spirit of black ancestors being reborn into new life in a "white skin," or by the enormity of the blood sacrifices made by the Aztec god-king Montezuma to assuage the guilt of his own conscience for having succumbed to a new "cult of the dead"—Christianity. Wright's interest in the relationship between race and religion is itself constitutive of a critique of the ontotheology of modernity, one whose humanism is transcended by a "new humanism." The strains of longing and unsatisfied desire that Mannoni attributes to both the anti-democratic European-cum-colonialist and to the dependency-bound African "dissolve themselves in their universality of race."[24]

However, the species-being—that is, the racial process—of man is not purely organic or genetic in virtue of his reproductive activity, it is productive by virtue of the means by which man's labor merges him with inorganic nature. As a consequence, Marx viewed alienated labor not only as the alienation of man from the product and the activity of his labor, but from his species- or racial-existence. Having had torn away from him the object of the activity that constitutes his species-life, man is relegated to the level of animal existence—that is, he is cheated of the advantage that he had over animals. As a consequence of the loss of his inorganic body—that is, through the loss of the product of his symbiotic relation with nature—his transcendence of the racial process of propagation by his conscious productive activity is itself suspended, casting him back into an animal existence.

This is the move that Fanon makes in *Black Skin, White Masks* when differentiating his master-slave dialectic from Hegel's.[25] Before Marx, Hegel had already postulated the transcendence of the species-life of the race on the basis of the productive consciousness of man's practical laboring activity. Fanon saw, seemingly tautologically, that the racial character of the master-slave dialectic also suspends this transcendence for the black, relegating him to the level of animal species-life. Fanon's logic is only seemingly tautological because in it labor never manages to raise the black above the racial-animal level to the human level; specifically, the black appears only in the guise of racial- or species-being. The black is never afforded the emancipation won through Hegel's concept of labor because the *actual concept* of race never allows the black to be anything but *black*. This is the *fact* of blackness, a fact, to paraphrase Hegel, that *is* before it enters into existence. Productive labor, which constitutes the objectification of his species-life as a man, is torn away from *the black man*, not only as a consequence of the product of his labor being alienated from him, but because at a more fundamental level his species-being as a man is alienated (as if it were a possession) from him.

In wresting *the black man* from his nature—from that which constitutes the objectification of his species-life as a man—racism, by a dialectical inversion, objectifies him as an element of nature. Where Marx saw the tearing away of that which represents the objectification of man's species-existence as a man, viz., the product of his labor, Fanon comprehends the tearing away of man himself from the objective conditions of his species-existence—that is, from his "native land." As the genesis of the reprobate materialism that signaled the "rosy dawn" of capitalism's primitive accumulation, these two forms of alienated labor represented the twin discontents of modern alienation on a monumental scale: man's estrangement from the object of his labor (i.e., from his social needs), and his estrangement from his own species-being (i.e., in order for man to oppress man wherever he finds him, he must make him[-self] a stranger to himself). In the latter instance, man's body undergoes a Cartesian estrangement from his mind, by being made "strange" to him, as the phenomenological condition of the corporeal alienation of man—that is, the proprietorship of man by man.

Marx locates the religious halo of these forms of estrangement, these strange formations of man's relation to man, in posing the originary question, To whom does all of this belong? From whom does it issue?

The gods? In the ancient world(s), the monumental products of social production, such as temples, pyramids, and public works, in Egypt, India, and Mexico served the gods. The gods were never the masters of labor, however; they instead served man as the mediating expression (i.e., imaginary objectification) of his relationship to other men. If his relationship to his labor, to the product of his labor, and even to the species-being of his race, is alien, hostile, awesome, and overpowering, then man's relationship to other men is alien, hostile, awesome, independent, overpowering, and fearful. Such a relationship is a master-slave relationship, if also from the other side these same men relate to their own labor as bonded and under the rule of another man. The world is red with the blood of our time, whose stain won't wash away. This reflects the materiality of religious estrangement—that is, man's production of a lost reality, of a product by virtue of his symbiosis with a (N)ature that does not belong to him and, finally, of the human essence of the species-being of the race that he has commodified.

Just as Montezuma is the absolute expression of this estrangement and, in Wright's "myth of the myth," is the sacrificing (and sacrificial) blood sovereign over this religious materiality, so it is Montezuma's sovereign right as lord and master to bestow upon strangers (Cortes and the conquistadors) that which does not belong to him. As against the traditional tale (myth) about the demise of Aztec civilization, and the one Wright tells of religious worlds in collision, the crisis was fundamentally an internal one already afoot when Cortes arrived and was bred by the irresolvable contradictions of religion and sovereignty or by the contradiction between possession (communal) and proprietorship (sovereignty). Was Montezuma empowered to confer to others, by virtue of alienating from the Aztec people, that which did not belong to him, or did not Aztec religion, of which he was supreme lord and mediator, as the very terms of this religious estrangement, confer on Montezuma the intercessionary powers to confer by alienation the sovereign possession of the Aztec world, as his property, to strangers, especially if, according to the "myth of the myth," he believed that the strangers were themselves returning gods with sovereign rights to this world? The gods are not the cause of this confusion but the effect. Nonetheless, at the culminating point of the crisis in Aztec civilization, reached at the time of Cortes's incursion into the Yucatan, not only does the secret behind this confusion reveal itself but the intrusion of Christianity marks the inversion of its (the confusion's) cause-effect relation.

When the World Was Read: Americanism and the Phenomenology of Black Modernity

Not till the sun excludes you do I exclude you.
—Walt Whitman, frontis to Richard Wright's *Black Power*

The confusion of the colonial situation did not, in Wright's view, emanate from the anxiety and aggressivity surrounding the supposed abandonment complex of the non-European native. It issued from another (third) side. Wright's myth of the myth of Montezuma apprehends the appearance of the modern personality at the birth of the modern world: not European man but non-European man is forced into the *habitus* of two worlds. At opposite ends of modernity's historic spectrum, Montezuma and Wright himself share a bi-chromatic mythology ("myth of the myth"). Where Wright celebrates his rootlessness, which he assures us makes him neither psychologically distraught nor in need of idealistic allegiances, nor bothered by any sense of abandonment, Montezuma, first emerging into the red world, experiences the dread and fascination of all these feelings. Like his protagonists, from Bigger Thomas to Erskine Fowler of *Savage Holiday,* Wright himself breaks out of the straitjacket of expectations formed by his situation.

In his letter of 21 August 1955 to Ed Aswell, Wright refers to the exhilaration of having to forge his own meanings of the world after his celebrated break from the Communist Party in 1942. Fanon identifies the Marxian moment in which Jean-Paul Sartre syllogized Negritude and class struggle in similar though inverted terms, writing, "It is not I who make a meaning for myself, but it is the meaning that was already there, pre-existing, waiting for me. It is not out of my bad nigger's misery, my bad nigger's teeth, my bad nigger's hunger that I will shape a torch with which to burn down the world, but it is the torch [Marx's philosophy of revolution] that was already there, waiting for that turn of history" (BSWM 134). Despite being critically disposed to pre-existing interpretations of the world, it is Marx*ists*—post-Marx Marxists—not Marx, whom Fanon and Wright have in mind. For regardless of their distance from organized Marxism—that is, the Party—Marx's *philosophy* figured centrally in the way in which Wright and Fanon read the world.

After a five-year hiatus from fiction, Wright's real writing interests began to manifest themselves. The "Celebration of Life" trilogy is the result of this self-rediscovery. Among the surprising effects of this is Wright's profession of his Americanness in light of his expatriate existence in France. What is more, the tone, or mood, of his Americanism is Whitmanesque. There is nothing remotely nationalistic or patriotic about it. Langston Hughes had also, in his leftist radical days, professed this kind of Whitmanesque Americanism. Hence, it is this Americanism that suffuses Wright's literary invention of mood in the "Celebration" trilogy. Even its name—"Celebration"—is evocative of Whitman's Americana. Wright's twelve-year association with the Communist Party had armed him against America's racial problem and, as he notes, subsumed it. His break left him finally to confront the phenomenology of the racial problem by his own means and on his own terms. The situational environment for transcendence of the race problem was provided by Wright's expatriation in France, a condition which was necessary for his discovery of a "new humanism" that would be the dialectical counterpart of the black modernity that had already found expression in his pre-expatriate work. Wright, then, is transcendentally American in his letter to Aswell. For a "Mississippi-born Negro" that is a cause for "celebration."

What, however, is one to make of Fanon's view that in being embattled, the American Negro is a thoroughly modern sensibility? Wright in no way transcends this modern black sensibility without in some way conserving it. Preoccupied with the *socius* and the *psyche,* he writes in and outside of America's racial box *as* an American writer. His new humanism is a response to the making and breaking of individuals in and by society, often in the very same process. Its dialectic underwrites, almost pantheistically, the continuity and discontinuities of experience. Wright's Negritude, in a certain sense, reaches that ontology of being the world that Fanon discovers in his phenomenology of the "lived experience of the black": " . . . raining . . . poetic power on the world, 'open to all the breaths of the world[,]' I embrace the world! I am the world" (BSWM 127). Rocked by the shock of recognition that the world he possesses, or seeks to possess as master, is a world brought into being by the black man, the white man discovers that the world is "forever lost to him and his" (BSWM 128). This mystical essence of the world is the black man's fortune, his *Negritude.*

Through the mediation of his Americanness, Wright nonetheless transcends Negritude. For he knows, as Fanon recognized, that white men "have had earth mystics such as you [the black man and his Negritude] will never approach. Study our [Western] history and you will see how far th[e] fusion [of reason and intuition] has gone" (BSWM 129). Whitman is that uniquely American "earth mystic." Fanon's citing of an unnamed or imaginary claimant to a Western mystical tradition reconjures the Prospero-Caliban metaphysics. This, or Mannoni's positing of it, takes Wright in search of origins. Where Mannoni's so-called Prospero and Caliban complex contributes to our understanding of the formation of the "colonial situation" and the attitudes evinced by that situation, Wright pursues the imaginary search for the initial contact between two alien personalities. His sketch of "When the World Was Red" for his mood trilogy depicts the dialectic of *socius* and *psyche* not as a creation of colonialism, but as itself the originary fertilization and formation of colonialism.[26]

Fanon acknowledged the merit of Mannoni's social psychology of colonialism to be its singling out of the importance of the "colonial situation" and the "attitudes" of the colonial antagonists. He was, at the same time, critical of Mannoni's Eurocentric essentialism and his moral relativism regarding degrees of racism. In claiming the existence of a so-called authentic African personality that demurs to authority and power, an essence which Mannoni believed even transcended the very dependency complex that he theorized had come about as a consequence of the creation of the "colonial situation," Mannoni not only undermined the significance of his own construction ("the colonial situation"), but he fell into a metaphysical racism that was by definition ahistorical.

Wright's strategy, by contrast, avoided such pitfalls. His approach was historical without being historicist by not reading the present into the past and making foundationalist assertions about the so-called non-European personality. Instead, Wright constructed an historical imaginary as a hermeneutical device for investigating the meaning of social dependency and power. After all, the formation of the new historico-racial schema of the New World, or modernity, functions in the service of power and its forms of domination.

Wright is wise enough, however, to situate his construct in a *literary*, rather than a social scientific, imaginary. The relations between the Aztecs and the Conquistadors were not only constitutive of colonialism, but of the modern Western world; the latter were not constitutive of the initial contact of the "new world" with the "old world." Wright, in other words, was careful not to make any essentialist claims about a so-called authentic Amerindian or meso-American personality.

The phenomenological nature of Wright's appropriation of Mannoni's original insight, in "When the World Was Red," was no less radical than Fanon's explicit critique of Mannoni. The discursive formation of the social psychology on which to hang essentialist claims about race, racial memory, and teleology is itself the product of what Aimé Césaire refers to in the words of his re-textualized Prospero as "the jungle . . . laying siege to the cane."[27] Wright took seriously Mannoni's speculations on the meaning of the "cult of the dead," as Mannoni analyzed it as the governing agency of the African personality. It seemed possible to escape racial essentialism through opening the anthropology of the African to Freudian social psychology. What this approach ignored was that the Enlightenment inheritance of the science of man originated in the mythology of race. Therein lies its extant positivism.

Freeing "race" of the essentialism of the old Enlightenment humanism required not so much a postmodernist abolition of humanism but the radical construction of a "new humanism." Wright and Fanon understood that we are obligated to rethink Mannoni's dependency complex to, as it were, decolonize it as an imaginary of Western humanism—that is, as a moment in the formation of the "new humanism" of black modernity.

Notes

I wish to thank Michael L. Flug, the archivist of the Vivian Harsh Collection of the Carter G. Woodson Library, Chicago Public Library, for making the Horace Cayton papers available to me, and for our many insightful discussions on Richard Wright and the "Chicago Renaissance." His service was invaluable in securing materials from the Richard Wright Papers, especially "When the World Was Red," at Yale University's Beinecke Library.

1. A minor exception to this is Michel Fabre, "Frantz Fanon et Richard Wright," in Elo Dacy, ed., *L'Actualité de Frantz Fanon* (Paris: Karthala, 1986), pp. 169–180.

2. D. Ray and R. M. Farnsworth, eds., *Richard Wright: Impressions and Perspectives* (Ann Arbor: University of Michigan Press, 1973), p. 150. In his letter to Wright, Fanon lists Wright's works with which he was then familiar, including those short pieces published in *Les Temps Modernes* and *Présence Africaine*. The availability of much of Wright's work in French by 1953 was impressive. See Charles T. Davis and Michel Fabre, *Richard Wright: A Primary Bibliography* (Boston: G. K. Hall, 1982), for a bibliography of Wright's work in French translation.

3. E. Fox-Genovese and E. D. Genovese, "Illusions of Liberation: The Psychology of Colonialism and Revolution in the Work of Octave Mannoni and Frantz Fanon," in S. Resnick and R. Wolff, eds., *Rethinking Marxism: Struggles in Marxist Theory—Essays for Harry Magdoff and Paul Sweezy* (New York: Autonomedia, 1985), p. 139.

4. "Black Orpheus" (*Orphée Noir*) was the famous preface that Sartre wrote to the 1948 anthology of Negritude poetry edited by Léopold Senghor. Some, such as the Martinican Marxist-Hegelian intellectual René Ménil and the Haitian Marxist writer René Depestre, have argued that Sartre is in fact the ideological progenitor of Negritude. See Michael Richardson, ed., *Refusal of the Shadow: Surrealism and the Caribbean*, trans. Krzysztof Fijalkowski and Michael Richardson (London: Verso, 1996), p. 9, and René Despestre, "Hello and Goodbye to Negritude," in Manuel Moreno Fraginals, ed., *Africa in Latin America: Essays on History, Culture, and Socialization*, trans. Leonor Blum (New York: Holmes & Meier, 1984), pp. 270–271. For a recent revised translation of Sartre's "Black Orpheus," see Robert Bernasconi, ed., *Race* (Oxford: Blackwell, 2001), pp. 115–142, especially p. 140 n. 1, for a brief bibliographic history of the essay.

5. This refers to Chester Himes's *If He Hollers Let Him Go* and to the World War II film *Home of the Brave*, works that Fanon discusses in conjunction with Sartre's *The Respectful Prostitute* and Wright's *Native Son* at the end of "The Fact of Blackness." For a new translation of this most-discussed essay of Fanon's *Black Skin, White Masks*, with Fanon's original title "The Lived Experience of the Black" restored, see Bernasconi, *Race*.

6. In his 1980 interview with Benny Levy, Sartre confessed that, while writing the preface to Fanon's *The Wretched of the Earth*, "I was seeing a lot of Fanon, who was deeply violent, and that certainly accounted for my mode of expression." See Jean-Paul Sartre and Benny Levy, *Hope Now: The 1980 Interviews*, trans. Adrian van den Hoven (Chicago: University of Chicago Press, 1996), p. 94.

7. Maurice Merleau-Ponty, *The Primacy of Perception, and Other Essays on Phenomenological Psychology: The Philosophy of Art, History and Politics*, ed. J. M. Edie (Evanston, Ill.: Northwestern University Press, 1964), p. 101. Henceforth PPOE.

8. See Lou Turner, "Demythologizing the Authoritarian Personality: Reconnoitering Adorno's Retreat from Marx," in Nigel Gibson and Andrew Rubin, eds., *Adorno: A Critical Reader* (London: Blackwell, 2002), pp. 150–171.

9. M. Fabre, *The Unfinished Quest of Richard Wright* (New York: William Morrow, 1973), p. 597 n. 30 (henceforth UQ); Fabre, *Richard Wright: Books and Writers* (Jackson: University Press of Mississippi, 1990), pp. 236–244 (henceforth RWBW).

10. In a review of Robert J. Butler's critical anthology *The Critical Response to Richard Wright* (1995), one reviewer, M. Lynn Weiss, argues, "If Wright scholars ignore most of his work in exile, we will fail to know the depth and breadth of his vision and talent. The non-fiction travel narratives document Wright's insatiable curiosity about the origins of modernity, of which the African Diaspora and slavery were pivotal events." Cf. M. Lynn Weiss, "The Critical Response to Richard Wright," *African-American Review* 31, no. 2 (Summer 1997): 337–339.

11. R. C. Holub, "Nietzsche's Colonialist Imagination: Nueva Germania, Good Europeanism, and Great Politics," in S. Friedrichsmeyer, S. Lennox, and S. Zantop,

eds., *The Imperialist Imagination: German Colonialism and Its Legacy* (Ann Arbor: University of Michigan Press, 1998), pp. 45–49.

12. The Marxist-humanist philosopher Raya Dunayevskaya wrote a critical synopsis of Sartre's play in 1953 in which she incorporated the reactions of a black worker, Charles Denby, the author of the working-class underground classic *Indignant Heart: A Black Worker's Journal* (1952) (Detroit: Wayne State University Press, 1989). Denby, a black Southern worker, viewed Sartre's play as a farce from a rather different vantage-point than did Wright, a black Southern intellectual. In Denby's view, Sartre's black character is "crazy": "Not that he became crazy first then when the lynch mob was outside, but that he was crazy, was born crazy," because "[a]ny normal Negro would put up a hell of a resistance." For Denby, Sartre "is a contradiction in himself." While he exposes the hypocrisy of the Southern white power structure, he has the guilt-ridden black character say just what the powers-that-be believe him to say. "Southern whites *wish* such a character existed but they *know* better" (emphasis in the original). Sartre makes the black character say what Southern whites want him to say, though they don't dare entertain such fantasies. In Denby's view Sartre's play is farcical because of the improbable characters and behaviors he creates, and which Wright's critical evaluation of the screenplay adaptation sought to correct. See R. Dunayevskaya, *The Raya Dunayevskaya Collection: Marxist-Humanism—A Half-Century of Its World Development* (Detroit: Wayne State University Archives of Labor and Urban Affairs, Walter P. Reuther Library, 1988–89). Henceforth RDC.

13. Frantz Fanon, *Black Skin, White Masks* (New York: Grove Press, 1967), p. 139. Henceforth BSWM.

14. What is so often overlooked is that Wright's own lived experience as a black man was caught up in his life as a writer in something more than autobiographical terms. Wright, for instance, wrote "The Man Who Lived Underground," only to have publishers and agents reject all but its last existentialist section, ignoring the first two sections on racism and police brutality. They also ignored the autobiographical experiences of racism and the police harassment that he met with in the Clinton Brewer case, involving a talented black prisoner who identified with Wright's Bigger Thomas, and on whose behalf Wright interceded to win his release from a New Jersey prison, only to learn later that the prisoner committed murder a second time, killing a woman he loved. Wright collaborated on the Brewer case with the psychiatrist Frederic Wertham, who found in it confirmation of the Freudian ideas he had developed in his book *Dark Legend*. The two also collaborated in trying to establish a psychiatric clinic in Harlem for juvenile delinquents and mental patients. Wright wrote an essay on the Lafargue Clinic, "Psychiatry Comes to Harlem," and a second piece using actual case files, "Juvenile Delinquency in Harlem." See the Horace Cayton Papers, Vivian Harsh Collection, Carter G. Woodson Library, Chicago Public Library.

15. Richard Wright, "Neuroses of Conquest," *The Nation*, no. 183 (20 Oct. 1956): 330–331.

16. One recent critical evaluation of Wright's views of Africa by Ngwarsungu Chiwengo is in an unbroken continuum of African scholarly criticisms of Wright's *Black Power*. "Entrapped by the very rhetorical and ideological structure he seeks to undermine, he [Wright] is incapable of constructing a self distinct from Western technology, individualism, democracy, literacy, and humanity. His inability to

trace a black subjectivity without Western paradigms is foreshadowed [in *Black Power*] by Justice Thomas of the Nigerian Supreme Court. The 'evolue' Justice Thomas, civilized and Westernized, ensures that his lengthy connection with Europe is recognized, and that he is differentiated from '[t]hose cannibal natives running naked in the bush.' Wright despises him and diagnoses Thomas as suffering from 'Frantz Fanonian alienation (dis)ease' because of Thomas's desire to emulate and measure his achievements by British demeanor and intellectualism." See Ngwarsungu Chiwengo, "Gazing through the Screen: Richard Wright's Africa," in Virginia Whatley Smith, ed., *Richard Wright's Travel Writings: New Reflections* (Jackson: University Press of Mississippi, 2001), p. 31. Chiwengo gives no page citation to *Black Power*, or to any other Wright work, for the reference to "Fanonian alienation." Moreover, the discussion is rather confused. On the one hand, Wright is criticized for placing Africa's salvation in the hands of its elites even as he is criticized for being critical of them. On the other hand, if using the concept of "Fanonian alienation" is a Western paradigm, then it is one which critically undermines the colonial elite as much as it does Western paradigms themselves.

17. O. Mannoni, *Prospero and Caliban: The Psychology of Colonization*, trans. P. Powesland (Ann Arbor: University of Michigan Press, 1990), p. 24. Henceforth PC.

18. Aimé Césaire, *Discourse on Colonialism* (New York: Monthly Review Press, 1972), p. 46.

19. J. McCulloch, *Black Soul, White Artifact: Fanon's Clinical Psychology and Social Theory* (Cambridge: Cambridge University Press, 1983), p. 220. Henceforth BSWA.

20. It seems to me that the very fate of Fanon's liberatory perspectives hinges on his critique of Mannoni. Any "new humanism" is made impossible so long as we fail on the level at which Fanon references Jaspers's culpability for feeling ourselves into the human experiences of others simply because we allow human attitudes to be separated from their objective situation. Mannoni's racial relativism and racial essentialism conspire against the very logic of his own original insight. This culpability or obligation "as the explicit human reality of feeling oneself responsible for one's fellow man" is a social ontology that exists in action; that is, "When I express a specific manner in which my being can rise above itself, I am affirming the worth of my action for others" (BSWM 89 n. 9).

21. J. M. Reilly, "Richard Wright and the Art of Non-Fiction: Stepping Out on the Stage of the World," in A. Rampersad, ed., *Richard Wright: A Collection of Critical Essays* (Engelwood Cliffs, N.J.: Prentice Hall, 1995), p. 182.

22. Eugene Miller proposes an early French connection in Wright's thinking on what would become his concept of mood in the mid-1950s. Citing Wright's "Blueprint for Negro Writing" and an unpublished circa 1935 "aesthetic manifesto" that Wright entitled "Personalism," Miller identifies Henry Barbusse and Jean Richard Bloch as undisclosed influences on Wright. Bloch's — *& Co.* showed Wright that "a novel [was] basically made of images—emotional perceptions of reality—but philosophically and emotionally united to such an extent that the unity itself becomes the 'ruling symbol' of the work. This all-controlling unity symbol carries any 'message' or 'judgment' the author makes." Miller concludes that "Wright was expressing here a concern about the problem of authorial intrusion into fiction, one he was still to be struggling with in the late 1950s."

Wright's 1950s mood concept seems connected to the "Personalism" essay in another sense, viz., its suggestion of "Whitman's Democratic Vistas, where Whitman, who had inspired a number of French writers associated with Bloch and Barbusse . . . romantically envisions a society developing best from the interiority of individual subjects." See Eugene Miller, "Richard Wright, Community and the French Connection," *Twentieth Century Literature: A Scholarly & Critical Journal* 41, no. 3 (Fall 1995): 265–280.

23. See the Horace Cayton Papers 83/03, Box 12, Ralph Ellison Folder. Taped interview with Ralph Ellison, Sept. 8, 1968. Transcribed by Carol Adams. Vivian G. Harsh Collection, Carter G. Woodson Library, Chicago Public Library. Fabre, who made liberal use of the Cayton Papers for his seminal biography of Wright (at times without attribution), dates the exchange between Wright and Ellison on Unamuno as 1940 instead of 1945.

24. G. W. F. Hegel, *Hegel's Logic of World and Idea, Being a Translation of the Second and Third Parts of the Subjective Logic,* trans. H. Macran (Oxford: Clarendon Press, 1929), p. 120.

25. Cf. Lou Turner, "On the Difference between the Hegelian and Fanonian Dialectic of Lordship and Bondage," in L. R. Gordon, T. D. Sharpley-Whiting, and R. White, eds., *Fanon: A Critical Reader* (London: Blackwell, 1996), pp. 134–151.

26. Beyond the spectacular facts of the New World Conquest, centered around the Montezuma-Cortes encounter, is the significance of the new historico-racial schema originating out of that encounter. While this is surely the phenomenological basis upon which Wright explores the historico-religious schema produced by the encounter, the two form a synthetic whole as the natural history of racial modernity. Historians as different as William Prescott and Hugh Thomas have been attracted, despite the dramaturgy of the Conquest, to its prophetic dimensions, and to the startling probabilities of the theistic war of the worlds. Though one-sidedly presented, this prophetic dimension, of course, is Mannoni's concern in his study of the Malagasy—or, rather, in his study of their conquest. The originary historico-racial schema of the New World contains discursive tensions that resonate more profoundly today. That, in fact, constitutes the reflexive identity of modernity. In other words, the discursive tensions that resonate in the historico-racial schema of the New World are a consequence of the inter-generational returns to its historic origins, which is also a return to the racial—that is, *mestizo*—origination of what Braulio Muñoz calls "The New Man," or the "Cosmic Race." Cited in Oleg Zinam and Ida Molina, "The Tyranny of the Myth: Doña Marina and the Chicano Search for Ethnic Identity," *The Mankind Quarterly* 32, no. 1–2 (Fall/Winter 1991): 3–18; 17. See Braulio Muñoz, "On the New Man," *Comparative Civilizations Review* 12 (Spring 1985): 69. Aside from Prescott's magisterial, though Eurocentric, history of the Conquest, which was what Wright relied on, see Bernal Diaz, *The Conquest of New Spain* (New York: Penguin, 1983), for an account of the internal social and political upheaval already undermining the Aztec empire long before Cortes's band of adventurers appeared on the Yucatan coast.

27. See Aimé Césaire, *A Tempest: Based on Shakespeare's The Tempest—Adaptation for a Black Theatre,* trans. Richard Miller (n.p.: Ubu Repertory Theatre Publications [1969] 1985), p. 75.

Ten

Alienation and Its Double; or, The Secretion of Race

Kelly Oliver

If "the black man is not a man," as Frantz Fanon claims at the beginning of *Black Skin, White Masks*, who is he?[1] Fanon answers that "the black is a black man" and he suggests that the rest of the book is his attempt to delineate the difference between a man and a black man (BSWM 8). Echoing Sartre, Fanon describes man's confrontation with "a zone of nonbeing, an extraordinarily sterile and arid region, an utterly naked declivity where an authentic upheaval can be born" (BSWM 8). But this echo rings false and becomes more and more ironic as the book progresses. In response to this idea that man is a confrontation with nothingness, that man is a return to himself from the alienation in front of the Other who provoked this confrontation, Fanon says that "the black man lacks the advantage of being able to accomplish this descent into a real hell" (BSWM 8); that is, that the black man lacks the advantage of a confrontation with his own freedom by asserting his subjectivity against his alienating otherness reflected in the white man. If a man goes through alienation to become a being who, as Sartre says, makes himself a lack of being so that there might be being, for Fanon a black man's alienation within a racist culture—what we should perhaps call a double alienation to distinguish it from the alienation of (white) man—prevents him from making himself a lack of being. Fanon says that the black man is "the result of a series of aberrations of affect, he is rooted at the core of a universe from which he must be extricated" (BSWM 8). And to extricate him from this core in which he is rooted Fanon proposes "nothing short of the liberation of the man of color from himself," which is to say the liberation of the man of color from the world of being in itself into the world of meaning (BSWM 8). Another way to put it is that Fanon proposes nothing short of giving the black man back his lack.

The separation between the world of being in itself and the world of meaning is variously described by Hegel as the difference between in itself and for itself, by Heidegger as beings in the world and *Dasein* whose being is meaning, by Lacan as the fundamental division of the subject or alienation itself, and by Sartre, echoing Hegel, as the difference between being in itself and being for itself. In the *Phenomenology of Spirit* Hegel says, "Self-consciousness exists in and for itself when, and by the fact that, it so exists for another; that is, it exists only in being acknowledged."[2] The process of acknowledgment or mutual recognition is motivated by what he calls desire, which is always the double movement of a return to the self of, or from, an alienating otherness inherent in self-consciousness. For Hegel the movement from in itself to being for itself, or self-consciousness, finally comes through activity or work. Work allows the negativity or alien objectivity inherent in consciousness to become explicit. This, in turn, allows one to make negativity or alien objectivity one's own and, in so doing, to make one's existence one's own: "In fashioning the thing, he [the bondsman] becomes aware that being-for-itself belongs to him, that he himself exists essentially and actually in his own right" (PS 118). Consciousness overcomes its negativity or alienation by making its own negativity an object for itself—that is, by turning back on itself through the movement of negativity or lack that is desire.

In *Black Skin, White Masks,* in a section entitled "The Negro and Hegel," Fanon summarizes Hegel's notion of man: "Man is human only to the extent to which he tries to impose his existence on another man in order to be recognized by him" (BSWM 216). But since Fanon insists that within racist culture the black man is rendered not a man, what Hegel says about man does not apply to the black man within colonial ideology. More specifically, Hegel's analysis of the master-slave dialectic that gives birth to self-consciousness does not apply to the white master and the black slave. After describing the conflict essential to the Hegelian dialectic of lord and bondsman, Fanon says, "There is not an open conflict between white and black. One day the White Master, *without conflict,* recognized the Negro slave" (BSWM 217). Fanon points out that for Hegel this type of recognition without conflict cannot yield independent self-consciousness (BSWM 219). Even when black slaves are freed and recognized as persons or *men*—or, as Fanon says, "the machine-animal-men" are promoted "to the supreme rank of men"—they still do not have independent self-conscious existence in Hegel's sense (BSWM 220) because they do not act. They do not gain their freedom through their own activity or work. Rather, Fanon says, "The upheaval reached the Negroes from without. The black man was acted upon. Values that had not been created by his actions, values that had not been born of the systolic tide of his blood, danced in a hued whirl round him" (BSWM 220). These values are still the "values secreted by his masters" (BSWM 221). In order to become independent, the slave needs to create his own values. Without doing so, he has not moved from the world of being into the world of meaning.

In a footnote, Fanon says,

I hope I have shown here the master differs basically from the master described by Hegel. For Hegel there is reciprocity; here the master laughs at the consciousness of the slave. What he wants from the slave is not recognition but work. In the same way, the slave here is in no way indentifiable with the slave who loses himself in the object and finds in his work the source of his liberation. The Negro wants to be like the master. Therefore he is less independent than the Hegelian slave. In Hegel the slave turns away from the master and turns toward the object. Here the slave turns toward the master and abandons the object. (BSWM 220–221)

I have argued elsewhere that Fanon is not merely opposing the Hegelian ideal of mutual recognition to the reality of black slavery and oppression but also that his work suggests that the ideal itself becomes corrupt and pathological in the colonial situation.[3] Insofar as the demand for recognition is created by the colonial situation in which the recognition of humanity is denied to the colonized, the demand for recognition itself becomes a symptom of the pathology of colonization. Fanon insists that "the former slave wants to *make himself recognized*" (BSWM 217) and that his sense of his own self-worth must come through his own action and meaning or values, which can come through violent resistance to dominance.[4]

The Colonization of Psychic Space

The need for recognition from the white colonizers is the result of the pathology of oppression. What Fanon calls the *inferiority complex* of the oppressed is created by the colonial situation. He says, "The feeling of inferiority of the colonized is the correlative to the European's feeling of superiority. Let us have the courage to say it outright: It is the racist who creates his inferior" (BSWM 93). "The black soul," says Fanon, "is a white man's artifact" (BSWM 13). And in *A Dying Colonialism*, he says that "it is the white man who creates the Negro."[5] In order to justify exploiting the colonized and taking their land, the colonizer must make them inferior. And, in order to make them inferior, the colonizer must racialize them, which is to say that the colonizer must, at first, make their inferiority natural rather than, or in addition to, social or cultural; only later can more subtle forms of racism maintain domination (DC 35, 37). As Fanon explains in *Toward the African Revolution*, "It is not possible to enslave men without logically making them inferior through and through. And racism is only the emotional, affective, sometimes intellectual explanation of this inferiorization. The racist in a culture with racism is therefore normal. He has achieved a perfect harmony of economic relations and ideology" (TAR 40). In other words, the colonist justifies economic exploitation using racist ideology. Racism is normal or natural only because race is naturalized. Fanon continues, "Every colonialist group is racist. . . . Race prejudice in fact obeys a flawless logic. A country that lives, draws its substance from the exploitation of other peoples, makes those people inferior. Race prejudice applied to those peoples is normal" (TAR 41).

Yet, Fanon maintains that colonization goes further than taking land or rendering the colonized inferior. While racism can provide the emotional and intellectual justification for colonization, the convolutions of guilt in the colonial identity formation and its production of values prepare the way for an even greater psychic justification. In *The Wretched of the Earth,* Fanon argues,

> It is not enough for the settler to delimit physically, that is to say with the help of the army and the police force, the place of the native. As if to show the totalitarian character of colonial exploitation the settler paints the native as a sort of quintessence of evil. Native society is not simply described as a society lacking in values. It is not enough for the colonist to affirm that those values have disappeared from, or still better never existed in, the colonial world. The native is declared insensible to ethics; he represents not only the absence of values, but also the negation of values. He is, let us dare to admit, the enemy of values, and in this sense he is the absolute evil. He is the corrosive element, destroying all that comes near him; he is the deforming element, disfiguring all that has to do with beauty or morality; he is the depository of maleficent powers, the unconscious and irretrievable instrument of blind forces. (WE 41)

This notion that the native represents the very negation of the colonists' values resonates with Fanon's analysis in chapter 6 of *Black Skin, White Masks,* in which he describes the process of colonialism and oppression as one through which the colonizer projects onto a racialized and inferior other all of the unwanted qualities in himself (BSWM 190). The very identity of the colonizers is dependent upon the oppression/repression of their projected fantasy of the colonized. Unlike contemporary theorists who suggest that this type of projection or abjection of the Other is necessary to fortify the boundaries of the proper self, Fanon insists that both the superiority complex of the colonizer and the inferiority complex of the colonized are pathological.[6] He says, "The Negro enslaved by his inferiority, the white man enslaved by his superiority alike behave in accordance with a neurotic orientation" (BSWM 60). For Fanon, this pathological relation between inferiority and superiority perverts humanity. It is not just the black man who is dehumanized in the colonial situation; the white man also loses his humanity. This is why Fanon insists on the need for a new humanity in order to put an end to colonization and oppression.[7]

The black man is forced to identity with the white superego that rules the colonial society, a sadistic superego that first projects evil and everything inhuman onto the colonized and then excludes it from proper civilization.[8] The white man's violent attempts to expel his own otherness, which he has projected onto the bodies of those whom he oppresses necessarily brings the return of the repressed both in the form of his own barbarism and in the form of guilt. Fanon's study of the effects of colonization on the colonizer suggests that it is the convolutions of guilt that initiate the move from making the colonized inferior in order to justify taking his land and enslaving him, to making him the repressed unconscious Other against whom the white man defines his very identity by attempting an absolute exclusion of the extreme of his own otherness projected on the bodies of those whom he oppresses.

In *Black Skin, White Masks*, Fanon describes what he calls the "internalization" of inferiority by the colonized (BSWM 11). The first stage in this process is primarily economic and the second stage is psychic, but there is an inherent connection between the two. For Fanon, the social and the psyche are intertwined and there is no separating one from the other. Indeed, his criticism of traditional psychoanalysis is that it focuses on the individual outside of the context of his social situation.[9] "The black man's alienation," he says, "is not an individual question" (BSWM 11). He adds, "In the *Weltanschauung* of a colonized people there is an impurity, a flaw that outlaws any ontological explanation. Someone may object that this is the case with every individual, but such an objection merely conceals a basic problem. Ontology—once it is finally admitted as leaving existence by the wayside—does not permit us to understand the being of the black man. For not only must the black man be black; he must be black in relation to the white man. . . . The black man has no ontological resistance in the eyes of the white man" (BSWM 109–110). It is impossible to answer the ontological question "what is the black man" since he exists only in relation to the white man. And while the same can be said of the white man, Fanon claims that in the colonial system of values the black man has no ontological resistance—that is, his being is determined in advance by the white man, which is not true of the white man. The alienation of oppression is not a universal phenomenon. It is not the alienation inherent in all subjectivity or in every individual.

Fanon continues to drive this point home in his discussion of the way that colonization forces black youth to choose between family and society. Discussing the family, he says, "But, it will be objected, you are merely describing a universal phenomenon, the criterion of maturity being in fact adaptation to society. My answer is that such criticism goes off in the wrong direction, for I have just shown that for the Negro there is a myth to be faced. A solidly established myth. The Negro is unaware of it as long as his existence is limited to his own environment; but the first encounter with a white man oppresses him with the whole weight of his blackness" (BSWM 149–150). Again, it is the fact that the colonized is oppressed by the preformed stereotypical image of himself propagated by the colonizer that makes his alienation unique. The colonization of psychic space presents us with a type of alienation unique to oppression, a type of double alienation that goes beyond the alienation inherent in the human condition and suffered by all individuals.

It is through economic oppression that the colonizer also levels psychic oppression, an oppression that cuts to the quick of the individual psyche to create the "mass attack against the ego." Fanon says, "If his psychic structure is weak, one observes a collapse of the ego. The black man stops behaving as an actional person. The goal of his behavior will be The Other (in the guise of the white man), for The Other alone can give him worth. That is on the ethical level: self-esteem" (BSWM 154). Conversely, psychic oppression is a crucial means through which the colonizers not only attempt to render the colonized docile but also justify their own violence. This dialectic of social and psychic phenomena creates the oppressive situation of colonization. The colonized internalize the racist stereotypes and value system created by their white oppressors. When the colonists take over the economy, in a significant sense they also colonize the means of production of value in society, not only economic value, but all values and meaning itself ("The Other alone can give him worth").[10] This double process of controlling both economic and psychic value is what makes colonization so deadly. Through economic subordination and the technological propagation of images of inferiority, colonization and racism create the aberrations of affect that Fanon describes in *Black Skin, White Masks.* One of the deadliest weapons of colonialism is its attempt to force the colonized to internalize its value system in which they are rendered subhuman, animals, incapable of rational thought or morality, and so on. The morality of colonialism reduces the colonized to their bodies, which become emblems for everything evil within that morality. This identification of the colonized with his body—and, more specifically within racist culture, with his skin—leads Fanon to call the process of internalization of inferiority a process of *epidermalization* (BSWM 11). The black man is reduced to nothing but his skin, black skin, which becomes the emblem for everything hateful in white racist society.

The logic of the internalization of colonial values, however, is a paradoxical logic and as such it is destined to fail. The colonized are forced to internalize an image of themselves as subhumans lacking a soul, mind, psyche, or ego as the seat of agency. In other words, the colonized are forced to internalize an image of themselves as lacking any internal life. Paradoxically, in order for the internalization of inferiority to be successful, they must internalize the lack of the ability to internalize. If they are merely bodies, subhuman animals unthinkingly reacting to stimulus, how can they internalize the racist colonial values? In spite of the fact that the logic of colonialism founders on its own paradox and ensures that colonization can never totally succeed—that even if you can colonize the land you can never completely colonize psychic space—still the material dominance of colonial values is bound to have adverse affects on the psychic life of the colonized. Throughout his work, Fanon describes the radically disabling effects of racism and colonization on the psyche of the oppressed that must be counterbalanced by equally radical resistance in order to liberate not only the physical space and the economy, but also the psychic space of the colonized.

Fanon's description of the psychic fallout of colonization is striking in *A Dying Colonialism* when he claims,

> It is not the soil that is occupied. It is not the ports or the airdromes. French colonialism has settled itself in the very center of the Algerian individual and has undertaken a sustained work of cleanup, of expulsion of self, of rationally pursued mutilation. There is not occupation of territory, on the one hand, and independence of persons on the other. It is the country as a whole, its history, its daily pulsation that are contested, disfigured, in the hope of a final destruction. Under these conditions, the individual's breathing is an observed, an occupied breathing. It is a combat breathing. (DC 65)

Colonialism affects the economy, the infrastructure, and the physical environment but it also affects the psyche, the sense of self, the bodies, and the very being of the colonized. Even their breathing is occupied breathing. Colonialism attacks the bodily schema of the colonized.[11]

The Bodily Schema and the Secretion of Race

In *Black Skin, White Masks*, Fanon says, "In the white world the man of color encounters difficulties in the development of his bodily schema [*schéma corporel*]" (BSWM 110).[12] He defines bodily schema as "a slow composition of my *self* as a body in the middle of a spatial and temporal world—such seems to be the schema. It does not impose itself on me; it is, rather, a definitive structuring of the self and of the world—definitive because it creates a real dialectic between my body and the world" (BSWM 111). The bodily schema, then, is the sense of self in the world; it is not imposed on the self but constitutes the very sense of embodied subjectivity. As Gail Weiss suggests in her recent book, body images are not what I experience but what I experience with; they are not objects of my perception or consciousness, but the agents of perception and consciousness.[13] But for the man of color, below the corporeal schema is "a historico-racial schema" that is sketched "not by 'residual sensations and perceptions primarily of a tactile, vestibular, kinesthetic, and visual character' [Jean Lhermitte's definition of bodily schema in *L'image de notre corps*] but by the other, the white man, who had woven me out of a thousand details, anecdotes, stories" (BSWM 111).

In his essay "Algeria Unveiled," Fanon vividly describes the effects of colonization on the bodily schema of Algerian women as the veil becomes overdetermined within both colonial domination and Algerian resistance (DC). There he says that "without the veil she has an impression of her body being cut up into bits, put adrift; the limbs seem to lengthen indefinitely. When the Algerian woman has to cross the street, for a long time she commits errors of judgment as to the exact distance to be negotiated. The unveiled body seems to escape, to dissolve. . . . The absence of the veil distorts the Algerian woman's corporeal pattern. She quickly has to invent new dimensions for her body, new means of muscular control; [she] relearns her body, re-establishes it in a totally revolutionary fashion" (DC 59). This dialectic between body and world, between body and psyche, creates what Fanon calls the revolutionary woman. Her body and her sense of herself are in a dialectical relationship with her world and the colonial situation. As resistance requires that she lose the veil and pass as a Western woman, she renegotiates both her physical and her psychic space. As resistance requires that she uses the veil to hide the new revolutionary woman whom she has become, she again renegotiates the relationship between her clothes, traditions, the artillery of resistance, and men, both colonizers and colonized. Fanon says, "The Algerian woman's body, which in an initial phase was pared down [without the veil], now swelled [with the veil full of armaments]" (DC 62).

In *Black Skin, White Masks*, full of the pain of his own experiences, Fanon describes the effects on the bodily schema of the man of color from the Antilles who sees himself as white until he is interpolated as black by Europeans. Consider two passages in particular. In the first passage Fanon says, "The Antillean does not think of himself as a black man; he thinks of himself as an Antillean. The Negro lives in Africa. Subjectively, intellectually, the Antillean conducts himself as a white man. But he is a Negro. That he will learn once he goes to Europe; and when he hears Negroes mentioned he will recognize that the word includes himself as well as the Senegalese" (BSWM 148). The second passage reads, "We have seen in fact that the Antillean who goes to France pictures this journey as the final stage of his personality. Quite literally I can say without any risk of error that the Antillean who goes to France in order to convince himself that he is white will find his real face there" (BSWM 153 n. 16).

Although Fanon's writings on the status of race have been interpreted in different ways, he consistently maintains that "white" and "black" are relative terms that refer more to social standing than to some natural skin color in itself; there is no skin color in itself. In the Antillean (and the European) whom Fanon describes, whiteness is primarily associated with an idea of civilization and culture and only secondarily attached to skin color. Whiteness and blackness are part of an ideology created to justify exploitation which becomes a psychological justification for one's own sense of oneself as superior. Fanon insists, "There is no white world, there is no white ethic, any more than there is a white intelligence" (BSWM 229). Skin color, or its significance, is created by a racist colonial logic. For the West to maintain that the ideals of democracy, freedom, and justice are its own creations is racist arrogance. Against those who would claim that Western civilization is the intellectual property of the white man, Fanon argues, "I am a man, and in this sense the Peloponesian War is as much mine as the invention of the compass" (BSWM 225).[14]

In connection with the Antillean's view of himself as white, I want to turn to a long footnote on Lacan's mirror stage. There Fanon claims that the Antillean mirror image is imagined as white or without color (BSWM 162) and that ultimately while the white man can turn the black man into his Other, his negative which assures his positive identity, the black man cannot do the same with the white man. The white man is not the black man's Other in the same way that the black man is the white man's Other. Indeed as Fanon describes it, blackness is also Other for the black man. In several places Fanon says that the Antillean considers the Senegalese black and associates them with violence (e.g., BSWM 161 n.).

Throughout *Black Skin, White Masks*, Fanon describes the double alienation by which the black man identifies with white values that make blackness bad, but then he realizes that he is black and has to choose between denying his own blackness and identifying himself with the abject of white culture (BSWM 197, 100). The onset of this double alienation begins with the black man's contact with racist white culture. Fanon maintains that while in white culture the superego, or the assimilation of authority, begins in early childhood for the white child, for the black there is another, more sadistic superego that he encounters only upon contact with the white world: "A normal Negro child, having grown up within a normal family, will become abnormal on the slightest contact with the white world" (BSWM 143).[15] Fanon describes the pathological effects of the internalization of the white sadistic superego as "the white man inject[ing] the black with extremely dangerous foreign bodies" (BSWM 36). The black child is injected with the white superego, which makes him abject himself. Fanon says that these dangerous white values are "secreted by his masters" (BSWM 221) and he suggests that Negritude, or the embrace of blackness, is a reaction against those white values through which the black man secretes race: "In the face of this affective ankylosis of the white man, it is understandable that I could have made up my mind to utter my Negro cry. Little by little, putting out pseudopodia here and there, I secreted a race" (BSWM 122). The white man secretes values that force the black man to secrete a race in self-defense. In a provocative passage, Fanon muses that maybe the bodily fluids of blacks change when they encounter white society in the same way that the hormones of the husband change when the wife becomes pregnant (BSWM 22). The white mirror image that brings with it the white superego is not just a visual perception but affects the bodily schema—that is, the very bodily being of the black man.

These effects are the opposite of those on the white man of the black as mirror Other. In the passage that I quoted above about black children assimilating the white superego and becoming abnormal, Fanon also maintains that this is the "opposite" effect from a white child assimilating the white superego through which he abjects the black body and thereby fortifies his own identity. At another point, engaging with Anna Freud's theory of ego-withdrawal as a defensive mechanism against failure, Fanon claims that while ego-withdrawal may be a means of defense for whites, it is impossible for blacks whose egos have been colonized by white values; withdrawing into the self is not a defense against failure when, within the white values, that black self is precisely the source of the failure. His analysis of the effects of colonization on the bodily schema of blacks has led Fanon to the conclusion "that there is a dialectical substitution when one goes from the psychology of the white man to that of the black" (BSWM 150). I would like to return once again to Fanon's engagement with Lacan's notion of the mirror stage in order to develop the idea that oppression leads to, and operates through, a colonization of psychic space.[16]

Fanon's explicit engagement with Lacan's mirror stage appears in the long footnote in the section in which Fanon diagnoses what he calls the "Negrophobia" that results from whites projecting their own unacceptable desires onto blacks. The footnote begins with Fanon asking what would happen if the mirror image the young white saw were black. He goes on to claim that blacks are the Other for whites, presumably in the sense of that which whites exclude as other from their own identities. In tandem, he argues that the mirror image for young blacks is neutral or ultimately white. In this way, taking Lacan's emphasis on the imaginary and fictional direction in the mirror stage, Fanon claims that the mirror image is not primarily a visual perception but imaginary. For "perception always occurs on the level of the imaginary," and this is how Antilleans *perceive* themselves and their fellows "in white terms" (BSWM 163).

Of particular importance in applying Fanon's analysis to Lacan's mirror stage is the relation between what Lacan calls the *specular I* and the *social I*. Lacan postulates that the specular I—the I of the mirror stage—sets up the social I. He suggests that the alienation inherent in the specular image becomes a central component of all relationships with others, which makes all relationships aggressive and hostile on some level. It is in the development of the relation between the psyche and the social that Fanon's theories provide their most powerful challenge to, and productive revision of, psychoanalytic theory. Whereas Lacan and other Freudian psychoanalysts attribute alienation to a split in the ego caused by discrepancies between the ideal-ego and reality, in the case of the colonized, Fanon identifies an alienation that is not inherent in the individual but social in nature. While neither Freud's nor Lacan's account of the ego or its development takes us outside of the social, Fanon's shift in focus from the individual to the social in diagnosing psychic formation presents us with a reversal of Lacan's mirror stage.

Lacan maintains that the function of the mirror stage is to "establish a relation between the organism and its reality—or, as they say, between the *Innenwelt* [inner-world] and the *Umwelt* [outer-world]."[17] Because of the "specific prematurity of birth in man [*sic*]," the imaginary or fictional direction of the mirror with its images compensates for the motor coordination and skills lacking in the "premature" infant. Through the mirror stage, the infant breaks "out of the circle of the *Innenwelt* into the *Umwelt*" by virtue of what Lacan calls the orthopedic image of itself as a totality with agency in the world (E 4; cf. E 2). In the beginning, the "jubilant assumption of his [*sic*] specular image by the child at the *infans* stage, still sunk in his [*sic*] motor incapacity and nursling dependence, would seem to exhibit in an exemplary situation the symbolic matrix in which the *I* is precipitated in a primordial form, before it is objectified in the dialectic identification with the other, and before language restores to it, in the universal, its function as a subject" (E 2). In this way, the mirror stage sets up and prefigures the subject's dependence upon the dialectic identification with the other. The specular gives birth to the social by presenting a mirror image through which the child can construct itself as whole and the seat of agency.

Lacan emphasizes that the specular image in the mirror stage sets up the fiction of agency prior to the social: "The important point is that this form situates the agency of the ego, before its social determination, in a fictional direction, which will always remain irreducible for the individual alone, or rather which will only rejoin the coming-into-being of the subject asymptotically, whatever the success of the dialectical syntheses by which he must resolve as *I* his discordance with his own reality" (E 2). This process is what Lacan calls the "deflection of the specular *I* into the social *I*" (E 5).

The mirror stage, then, has several constituent stages. Through it, the child goes from experiencing itself as a fragmented body-out-of-control to gaining a sense of itself as a totality with agency to act on the world. What Lacan calls this "temporal dialectic" soon gives way, however, to "the assumption of the armour of an alienating identity, which will mark with its rigid structure the subject's entire mental development" (E 4). This alienation is caused by the fact that the individual's sense of itself as an active agent or ego is produced through fiction, practically a hallucination or mirage, or what Lacan also calls a misrecognition of itself in the mirror (see E 2, 6). There is always a split between the inner world and the outer world, between the subject and its Ideal-I, or perfectly delightful mirror image. Experiencing the alienation from its ideal will become the essence of the social. "This moment in which the mirror-stage comes to an end [the moment of the deflection of the specular *I* into the social *I*] inaugurates, by the identification with the imago of the counterpart and the drama of primordial jealousy . . . the dialectic that will henceforth link the *I* to socially elaborated situations" (E 5). The alienation inherent in subjectivity brings with it aggression and hostility in relation to others, with whom the drama of the mirror stage is necessarily repeated.

Fanon maintains that until the black child becomes aware of its blackness in relation to whiteness as defined by white culture, its psychological development is "normal." But, when the black child sees itself for the first time reflected in the mirror of white culture, it undergoes the effects of a reversed mirror stage. Whereas Lacan describes the orthopedic function of the Ideal-I encountered in the mirror image which gives the child the empowering fiction of its own agency and unity, Fanon describes the pathological function of the white Ideal-I encountered by blacks in the white mirror of identity. Rather than give blacks the empowering fiction of agency and unity, the white ideal reflects back powerlessness and fragmentation.

As if describing the experience of the reversed mirror stage of the oppression, Fanon says, "[m]y body was given back to me sprawled out, distorted, recolored, clad in mourning in that white winter day" (BSWM 113). In the mirror of white domination, the black body is not reflected as whole or an active agent but as "animal," "bad," "mean," "ugly," and not human (BSWM 113). In the reversed mirror stage, racism, through epidermalization, reduces the ego to skin, not even a fragmented body. Rather than create or maintain the illusion of agency and wholeness that supports the ego, the subject is deflated to a sense of self as nothing but skin.

While Lacan's mirror stage begins with the solidification of the ego and ends with a defensive alienation that the ego uses against others to protect itself, Fanon's reversed mirror stage begins with a challenge to the ego and ends with debilitating double alienation that leaves the ego susceptible to being othered within the dominant culture. Whereas within the Lacanian scenario the gap between the inner world and the outer world that results in alienation makes a virtue of necessity when it gives rise to the fiction of the active agency of the ego, for Fanon the gap between the ego as active agency and cultural fiction of the inferiority and powerlessness of colonized people makes vice necessary.

Rather than set up the fiction of the ego and its agency, the reversal of the mirror stage caused by oppression becomes a "mass attack against the ego" (TAR 252) that undermines the sense of agency (BSWM 154). This reversal of the mirror stage is akin to Freud's, and later Lacan's, stage of secondary narcissism. But, rather than work to form the ego through an identification with another person as in Freudian or Lacanian secondary narcissism, racism makes an identification with the white oppressor both necessary and impossible for people of color. More than this, Fanon suggests that rather than solidify the ego, racist identifications undermine the ego. So, unlike the identifications with the other formative to the ego in secondary narcissism, the identification with the oppressive other in the reversed mirror stage works to compromise the ego and its agency.

While Lacan's later formulation of the gaze in relation to subject formation may be more akin to Fanon's thoroughly social I, still he does not distinguish between the alienation inherent in all subject formation and the alienation unique to oppression or colonization in particular.[18] In his seminar XI, "The Four Fundamental Concepts of Psychoanalysis," Lacan maintains that alienation is fundamental to the subject (FFC 235). As he describes it, this is because man is born into a world that he did not create, a pre-existing world, the world of the Other: "We depend on the field of the Other, which was there long before we came into the world, and whose circulating structure determines us as subjects" (FFC 246). À la Heidegger, for Lacan, we are thrown into a world that we did not make.

The subject appears at the division between the world of being and the world of meaning, which is to the world of the Other. It is this fundamental division between being and meaning inherent in subjectivity that Lacan calls alienation (FFC 210). As Lacan describes it, alienation is the either/or choice between being and meaning. The subject cannot have both at once. Lacan explains, "If we choose being, the subject disappears, it eludes us, it falls into non-meaning. If we choose meaning, the meaning survives only deprived of that part of non-meaning that is, strictly speaking, that which constitutes in the realization of the subject, the unconscious. In other words, it is of the nature of this meaning, as it emerges in the field of the Other, to be in a large part of its field, eclipsed by the disappearance of being, induced by the very function of the signifier" (FFC 211). The signifier is dependent upon this division between being and meaning for its functioning. It operates only as a stand-in for an absent being. The word is not the thing and functions only by virtue of its separation from the thing. So, too, the subject is not being, but to return to Sartre, the subject is a being who makes itself a lack of being. If the subject is reduced to being, then there is no subject, only some thing-in-itself. On the other hand, if the subject is placed solely in the realm of meaning, then it is just as much in jeopardy of disappearing as it is if it is placed solely in the realm of being. The subject must in some sense be a being first and foremost. For Lacan, this means that the subject must have an un-conscious; its being is what he calls the real that resides within the uncon-scious. The split between being and meaning makes alienation the essence of the subject. It is neither and both at the same time. Yet, it doesn't belong to either.

For Lacan, whether it is the alienation of the gap between the mirror image and the body, that between the ego ideal and the fragmented body in the mir-ror stage, or the split between being and meaning of seminar XI, alienation is inherent in the subject. Several contemporary critics use Lacanian psycho-analytic theory to suggest that racist oppression is another version of this alienation at the heart of human subjectivity. For example, Homi Bhabha says that "For Fanon, like Lacan, the primary moments of such a repetition of self [in the Other] lie in the desire of the look and the limits of language."[19] Bhabha's reading of Fanon with Lacan suggests that there is no alienation specific to oppression or colonization but, rather, that the alienation described by Fanon is the same as the alienation described by Lacan as inherent in all subjectivity. I argue, on the contrary, that the alienation of colonization and oppression is different from the alienation inherent in becoming a subject de-scribed in various ways by philosophers from Hegel, Heidegger, Sartre, and Lacan to Butler, Žižek, and Bhabha.[20] For Fanon, the alienation inherent in the subject, or what he calls man, does not capture the alienation of oppres-sion because within the colonial situation the black man is a black man and not a man.

When Fanon discusses the effect of social forces on the psyche, he is not merely referring to the fact that language or the symbolic order precedes any individual's ascension to it. He does not simply mean that because meaning is created prior to the individual, alienation is inevitable. Rather, particular kinds of degrading or dehumanizing meanings and the social forces of domination and oppression prevent the individual from participating in meaning-making and tie subjectivity to some body part, thereby producing a double-alienation and a double-misrecognition that are not inherent in all subject formation but are peculiar to the pathology of oppression. The alienation of oppression described by Fanon is the result of the dominant culture's denial of individuality and humanity to members of the oppressed group; more specifically, it is the result of the dominant racist culture's denial of the oppressed peoples' access to the world of meaning as meaning-makers.

Fanon argues that the black man does not get the chance to face the alienation inherent in becoming a man, an individual against society, because a black man is not distinguished from his group; he is not an individual. He describes the way that the colonial values dehumanize and deindividuate the colonized:

> I begin to suffer from not being white to the degree that the white man imposes discrimination on me, makes me a colonized native, robs me of all worth, all individuality, tells me that I am a parasite on the world, that I must bring myself as quickly as possible into step with the white world, 'that I am a brute beast, that my people and I are like walking dung-heap that disgustingly fertilizes sweet sugar cane and silky cotton, that I have no use in the world'. Then I will quite simply try to make myself white: that is I will compel the white man to *acknowledge* that I am human. (BSWM 98; my emphasis).

Fanon's analysis suggests that whereas white culture values individuality and the merits associated with this individualism, oppression works through denying individuality to the oppressed by stereotyping them. The racialized other is seen as always and only a representative of a group, while the race "neutral" or "normal" dominant white is seen as an individual whose merit is self-determined. Insofar as the black man is deindividuated, he is not the man who struggles for his individuality against the social. Or, more precisely, he has to engage in a double struggle against the social in order to gain the privilege of struggling for his individuality.

Furthermore, as Fanon describes the separation between a man and a black man, it becomes clear that what the black man lacks is the very lack or alienation that makes subjectivity possible. Within the colonial values it is not just that the black man is denied individuality but he is also denied humanity. He is not considered fully rational or capable of subjectivity and agency. He is denied the transcendence that Sartre attributes to man. He is not allowed to make himself a lack of being in order to become self-conscious. Rather, he is chained to his being, to his body, more particularly to his skin, by colonial values. In his critical engagement with Sartre's *Black Orpheus*, Fanon responds, "In terms of consciousness, the black consciousness is held out as an absolute density, as filled with itself, a stage preceding any invasion, any abolition of the ego by desire" (BSWM 134–135). Contra man, within the colonial world-view a black man represents a stage prior to desire, prior to the lack that initiates the desire and negativity necessary for self-consciousness, for being-for-itself. Fanon continues, "Still in terms of consciousness, black consciousness is immanent in its own eyes. I am not a potentiality of something, I am wholly what I am. I do not have to look for the universal. No probability has any place inside me. My Negro consciousness does not hold itself out as a lack" (BSWM 135). Colonization makes the black man a lack of a lack and through the process of disalienation Fanon attempts to give the black man his lack back.

Fanon criticizes Sartre's claim that Negro poetry, and Negritude itself, is a minor stage in history, which like all others will pass, that Negritude is pre-determined by the dialectic of history. Fanon objects to this pre-existing meaning already determined in advance. In response to Sartre, he says, "And so it is not I who make a meaning for myself, but it is the meaning that was already there, pre-existing, waiting for me" (BSWM 134). He rejects Sartre's suggestion that black poetry and black meaning do not come from their own suffering but have been waiting for a particular turn of history. Indeed, this view of the black man's meaning as predetermined is the heart of the colonial logic, which maintains that the black man is determined in advance by history as subhuman and ripe for subservience. He is subject to manifest destiny, which is to say white destiny or, as Fanon says, "For the black man there is only one destiny and it is white" (BSWM 10). The meaning of the black man is assigned by the white other; Fanon argues that even Sartre engages in naming the black man's meaning: "At the very moment when I was trying to grasp my own being, Sartre, who remained The Other, gave me a name and thus shattered my last illusion" (BSWM 137). The struggle to liberate psychic space from colonization hinges on the black man's ability to make meaning for himself. He doesn't want recognition from the white colonists, an impossible recognition; rather he wants to *recognize himself*. It is precisely the sense of arriving too late to create one's own meaning that makes the colonization of psychic space so effective.

Fanon describes going to films and waiting to see himself, his meaning already predetermined by racist stereotypes: "I wait for me" (BSWM 140). He laments, "You come too late, much too late. There will always be a world—a white world—between you and us" (BSWM 122). This sense of arriving too late is different from Lacan's, Heidegger's, or Sartre's sense of being thrown into a world that is not of your making.[21] The alienation of being thrown into the world differs dramatically from the double alienation of being thrown there as one who is incapable of meaning-making. For Heidegger the connection between human beings and meaning is definitive. And, for Sartre, while we are thrown into a pre-existing world of meaning, we are responsible for meaning-making and for the meaning of the world. We become part of, and responsible for, that world of meaning. This is what makes us human beings, beings who mean. What Fanon describes is not simply arriving into a world of meaning that pre-exists us—that is true of everyone—but arriving too late into a white world in which you are defined as a brute being who does not mean and therefore is not a fully human being. Your responsibility for meaning, and more particularly for the meaning of your own body and self, has been usurped by the White Other. This is why Fanon says, "I came into the world with the will to find meaning but then I found that I was an object. Sealed into that crushing objecthood" (BSWM 109); or, "All I wanted was to be a man among other men. I wanted to come lithe and young into a world that was ours and to help to build it together" (BSWM 112–113); but "without responsibility, straddling Nothingness and Infinity, I began to weep" (BSWM 140). Double alienation is the result of being thrown into a world that is not of your making, a world of pre-existing meanings, but *as one who is incapable of meaning-making.* And the greatest pain of this alienation comes from the fact that the meaning of your own body has been already defined for you.

Fanon's most striking example of the alienation from his own body caused by coming too late into the white world of meaning is in *Black Skin, White Masks*, in which he describes the experience on the train when he is interpolated as Negro by a white child who says "Look, a Negro. . . . Mama, see the Negro! I'm frightened!"

> In the train it was no longer a question of being aware of my body in the third person but in a triple person. In the train I was given not one but two, three places. . . . It was not that I was finding febrile coordinates in the world. I existed triply: I occupied space. I moved toward the other . . . and the evanescent other, hostile but not opaque, transparent, not there, disappeared. Nausea. I was responsible at the same time for my body, for my race, for my ancestors. . . . I discovered my blackness, my ethnic characteristics; and I was battered down by tom-toms, cannibalism, intellectual deficiency, fetishism, racial defects, slave-ships, and above all else, above all: "Sho' good eaten." . . . What else could it be for me but an amputation, an excision, a hemorrhage that spattered my whole body with black blood? . . . My body was given back to me sprawled out, distorted, recolored, clad in mourning in that white winter day. (BSWM 112–113)

Racist values reduce his very being to his body, his skin, and then determine the meaning of that body and skin. Within the colonial economy, he is not free to actively participate in the creation of the meaning of his own body. This is why he must violently and by all means resist the colonial economy: not just to regain his land or resources, or his culture and traditions, but to reclaim his body and its psychic space.

The experience of alienation, of seeing oneself in triplicate that Fanon describes, echoes W. E. B. Du Bois's notion of double consciousness proposed fifty years earlier. Du Bois poignantly describes the double-consciousness forced on those marked by race in a racist culture. In *The Souls of Black Folk* he says, "This double-consciousness, this sense of always looking at one's self through the eyes of others, of measuring one's soul by the tape of a world that looks on in amused contempt and pity. One ever feels his twoness,—an American, a Negro; two souls, two thoughts, two unreconciled strivings; two warring ideals in one dark body, whose dogged strength alone keeps it from being torn asunder."[22] Forty-five years after Fanon, and almost a full century after Du Bois, in *Seeing a Color-Blind Future* Patricia Williams again describes the double-consciousness endemic to the fragmented subject of racism: "For black people, the systematic, often nonsensical denial of racial experiences engenders a sense of split identity attending that which is obviously inexpressible; an assimilative tyranny of neutrality as self-erasure. It creates an environment in which one cannot escape the clanging of symbolism of oneself. This is heightened by contrast to all the silent, shifty discomfort of suffering condescension. There's that clunky social box, larger than your body, taking up all that space. You need two chairs at the table, one for you, one for your blackness."[23] Williams's "clunky social box" resonates with Fanon's descriptions of the social body or socially inscribed bodily schema of the black man. The double alienation of racism is a bodily alienation. For Fanon, meaning and body, social and body, psyche and soma cannot be separated. The body and psyche are social, and vice versa: the social is embodied.

Fanon's writings are full of metaphors for meaning or social values that evoke their bodily origins and effects. In *Black Skin, White Masks*, he speaks of the *injection* of white values into native culture as *dangerous foreign bodies*, the *epidermalization* of racist values, the effect of colonization on *bodily fluids*, alienation as an *amputation* or *hemorrhage*, the skin as a *uniform*, putting out *pseudopodia* and *secreting* a race, and values born of the *systolic tide of blood*. In *The Wretched of the Earth*, he says, "In the colonial world, the emotional sensitivity of the native is kept on the surface of the skin like an *open sore* which flinches from the caustic agent; and *the psyche shrinks back*, obliterates itself and finds outlet in *muscular* demonstrations which have caused certain very wise men to say that the native is a hysterical type" (WE 56; my emphasis). And, in both books he talks about the effects of colonialism on and in the muscles.

The colonization of psychic space cannot be separated from the colonization of the body. We live the body as a social body, as a bodily schema, which for the black man in a racist culture becomes "assailed at various points, the corporeal schema crumbled, its place taken by a racial epidermal schema" (BSWM 112). If body and mind are both part of the corporeal schema through which we experience ourselves and the world, then there is no fundamental split between being and meaning. For Fanon, alienation is not inherent in the human condition. As he says at the beginning of *Black Skin, White Masks*, man's consciousness may be a process of transcendence, but it is also haunted by love and understanding (BSWM 8); it is not just transcendence. Indeed, by the end of *Black Skin, White Masks*, it seems as if transcendence comes only through the body and the liberation of its psychic space. Fanon concludes *Black Skin, White Masks* with his provocative "final prayer" that suggests that it is the body, or more precisely his body, even his black body, that makes transcendence possible: "O my body, make of me always a man who questions!" (BSWM 232).

Notes

1. Frantz Fanon, *Black Skin, White Masks* (1952), trans. C. L. Markmann (New York: Grove Press, 1967), p. 8. Henceforth BSWM.

2. G. W. F. Hegel, *Phenomenology of Spirit*, trans. A. V. Miller (Oxford: Clarendon Press, 1977), p. 111. Henceforth PS.

3. See my *Witnessing: Beyond Recognition* (Minneapolis: Minnesota University Press, 2001), chapter 1.

4. Unlike Hegel's scenario, this resistance may indeed require killing white others, we might say, in order to create whiteness as Other. As Fanon says, "From the moment that you and your like are liquidated like so many dogs, you have no other resource but to use all and every means to regain your importance as a man. You must therefore weigh as heavily as you can upon the body of your torturer in order that his soul, lost in some byway, may finally find once more its universal dimension" (*The Wretched of the Earth*, trans. Constance Farrington [New York: Grove Press, 1968 (1961)], p. 295; henceforth WE). Violent resistance restores the sense of agency or action lost through oppression. Fanon says, "At the level of individuals, violence is a cleansing force. It frees the native from his inferiority complex and from his despair and inaction; it makes him fearless and restores his self-respect" (WE 94, cf. 293). Cf. Frantz Fanon, *Toward the African Revolution: Political Essays*, trans. Haakon Chevalier (New York: Grove Press, 1967 [1964]), p. 121; henceforth TAR.

5. Frantz Fanon, *A Dying Colonialism*, trans. Haakon Chevalier (New York: Grove, 1965 [1959]), p. 47. Henceforth DC.

6. In *Witnessing: Beyond Recognition*, I suggest that theorists such as Jean Paul Sartre, Julia Kristeva, and Judith Butler, among others, in various ways propose that subjectivity is dependent upon excluding or abjecting the Other.

7. See Robert Bernasconi's discussion of Fanon's vision of a new humanity in his essay "Casting the Slough: Fanon's New Humanism for a New Humanity," in Lewis Gordon et al., eds., *Fanon: A Critical Reader* (Malden, Mass.: Blackwell Publishers, 1996), pp. 113–121; henceforth CS/FCR. There, Bernasconi delineates some of the differences between European humanism and Fanon's vision of a new humanism: "Whereas European humanism is differential and survives only so long as the non-European is defined as subhuman, the new humanism liberates both colonized and colonizer" (CS/FCR 116). He also points out that for Fanon it is through the colonized's struggle against their oppression that this new humanity will be born. He emphasizes both the important function played by violence in nation building and collective history and the necessity of leaving the resulting new humanity an open question, or "unforeseen" (CS/FCR 118–121). Although I won't get into the debates over the usefulness of Fanon's notion of a

new humanism for a new humanity, I am interested not only in the sense of collectivity that Fanon attributes to violence by the oppressed but also in the sense of agency that he suggests is restored through violent acts. If the colonizer attempts to render the colonized a subhuman object incapable of rational thought and subjective agency, then active resistance serves to restore a sense of agency to the oppressed. Fanon says, "At the level of individuals, violence is a cleansing force. It frees the native from his inferiority complex and from his despair and inaction; it makes him fearless and restores his self-respect" (WE 94, cf. 293; cf. TAR 121). For Fanon, violence is one effective means (along with love and understanding) to address what he calls the "mass attack against the ego" leveled against the colonized by the colonialism (WE 252).

8. In an intriguing essay entitled "The Postcolonial Unconscious; or, The White Man's Thing," reading Fanon, Juliet Flower MacCannell argues that colonization infects the colonized with "the white man's thing," or the white man's primal trauma, which is inappropriate to the black native. She also expands on some of Fanon's suggestions about the sadistic white superego (in *The Hysteric's Guide to the Future Female Subject* [Minneapolis: University of Minnesota Press, 2000], pp. 57–92).

9. In particular, see his criticisms of Adler in chapter 7 (BSWM 213–215).

10. Fanon describes the complex relationship between economic and technological control and the production of values and meaning in his essay "This is the Voice of Algeria," which is on the role of radio in both the colonization and liberation of Algeria (DC 69–98).

11. Fanon takes his notion of bodily or corporeal schema from Jean Lhermitte's *L'Image de notre corps* (Paris: Nouvelle Revue Critique, 1939). Lhermitte's book also influenced Merleau-Ponty's use of the notion of what he calls a postural or corporeal schema in his 1960 lecture "The Child's Relations with Others," in which he attributes the first use of this notion to British neurologist Henry Head. Head first used the idea of body image in an article with Gordon Holmes, "Sensory Disturbances from Cerebral Lesions," that appeared in the journal *Brain* in 1911, in which he says, "Anything which participates in the conscious movement of our bodies is added to the model of ourselves and becomes part of these schemata; a woman's power of localization may extend to the feather in her hat" (*Brain* 34 [1911]: 188). He followed up this research in volume 2 of his *Studies in Neurology* (London: Oxford University Press, 1920). Merleau-Ponty maintains, "The consciousness I have of my body is not the consciousness of an isolated mass; it is a postural schema. It is the perception of my body's position in relation to the vertical, the horizontal, and certain other axes of important coordinates of its environment" ("The Child's Relations with Others," trans. William Cobb, in Maurice Merleau-Ponty, *The Primacy of Perception*, ed. James Edie [Evanston, Ill.: Northwestern University Press, 1964 (1960)], p. 117; henceforth PP). Merleau-Ponty also concludes that "this entire placement of the corporeal schema is at the same time a placing of the perception of others" (PP 123). Even more than Merleau-Ponty, Fanon makes the corporeal schema social. Others have made a distinction between body image and bodily schema. See especially Gallagher and Cole's "Body Image and Body Schema" in Donn Welton, ed., *Body and Flesh* (Malden, Mass.: Blackwell, 1998), pp. 131–148.

12. See Frantz Fanon, *Peau noire, masques blancs* (Paris: Éditions du Seuil, 1952), p. 89.

13. Gail Weiss, *Body Images* (New York: Routledge, 1999), p. 66.

14. Fanon's remarks suggest that a new humanity must think outside of this economy of ownership that renders concepts, as well as bodies and skin, property. Patricia Williams's body of work fastens onto the problem of property and ownership in relation to race in ways that promise to open up new possibilities for thinking through and beyond the economy of property, which is to say the economy that makes slavery possible.

15. Fanon's claim that there might be a "normal" childhood within the colonial situation before the child encounters white society is problematic. If he is suggesting that childhood or family life is at some point a safe haven from the effects of colonialism, then I would disagree. On the other hand, if he is suggesting that within the colonized imaginary there is a space before or beyond racism and colonization, then I find this suggestion provocative. At this point, I merely cite Fanon's problematic claim even though it demands further analysis.

16. Some of the paragraphs on Lacan that follow are taken from my *Witnessing: Beyond Recognition*, chapter 1.

17. Jacques Lacan, *Ecrits*, trans. Alan Sheridan (New York: Norton, 1977), p. 4. Henceforth E.

18. Cf. Jacques Lacan, *The Four Fundamental Concepts of Psycho-Analysis*, trans. Alan Sheridan (New York: Norton, 1981 [1973]), pp. 67–78. Henceforth FFC.

19. Homi Bhabha, "Interrogating Identity: Frantz Fanon and the Postcolonial Prerogative," in Bhabha's *The Location of Culture* (New York: Routledge, 1994), p. 45.

20. I develop this argument in my forthcoming book *The Colonization of Psychic Space*.

21. In this essay I have not analyzed Heidegger's and Sartre's notions of alienation in relation to Fanon's, but I have explicitly engaged Fanon only with Lacan to suggest the significant differences between their notions of alienation, I develop my claims about Heidegger and Sartre in my forthcoming book *The Colonization of Psychic Space*.

22. W. E. B. Du Bois, *The Souls of Black Folk* (New York: New American Library, 1969 [1903]), p. 45. In *The Colonization of Psychic Space*, I distinguish double alienation from double consciousness.

23. Patricia Williams, *Seeing a Color-Blind Future* (New York: Farrar Straus, 1998), p. 27.

Eleven

(Anti-Semitic) Subject, Liberal In/Tolerance, Universal Politics

Sartre Re-petitioned

Erik Vogt

Einen einzigen Satz haltbar zu machen,
auszuhalten in dem Bimbam von Worten.

Es schreibt diesen Satz keiner,
der nicht unterschreibt.

— Ingeborg Bachmann

Why is it that the drift into post-history and post-politics in the face of and "after" Auschwitz has been marked by violent intrusions of traditional as well as postmodern styles of racism? How can one account for the upsurges in Europe of a primarily differential racism not only in the territory of former Yugoslavia but, in an uncanny correspondence, also in the very hearts of certain Western and Central European countries (for example, Austria, Germany, France, and Switzerland)?[1] And is this "racism without races" operative in those consensual communities not to be grasped by a ghost genealogy in terms of the specter of universalized anti-Semitism[2]—the perception of each ethnic and/or cultural "alterity" as an uncanny, threatening double? A specter kept alive by the disavowed relationship between a concealed, encrypted Holocaust in their nationalist narratives and the insistent vacancy of the "Jewish Question?"[3] In other words, does today's emergence of a universalized anti-Semitism not engender the figure of a resurgence of the publicly repressed anti-Semitic milieu of European modernism in contemporary thought and politics?

Sartre's *Anti-Semite and Jew* was certainly one of the first texts to frame *la question juive*. But one could ask in general, Is there anything in Sartre's writings, in his philosophical and political inheritance, that has not already been sufficiently gathered together? Has it not already become one with itself in a presumed unity, the legibility of a legacy as given, natural, transparent, and univocal, thus effacable? And since the political force in Sartre's texts supposedly has been historically neutralized and rendered ineffective (by the very politics that they announced), is one not restricted to mere academic exercises in enervating his homogenized corpus, provided that the revolt which initially may have inspired insurrection remains silenced? Clearly, the silence that has been maintained about Sartre's injunction to translate strategies of writing/reading into a transformational political practice has foreclosed any endeavor to reclaim for Sartrean politics "a taste of timeliness"[4] and a responsibility for today.

Recalling the canonized interpretations of Sartre's *Anti-Semite and Jew,* one will not fail to notice that their relative stability (and monosemy) is due to a certain procedure of framing, enabling them to "fix" the monstrous truth and identity of that text. To be more precise, this procedure of framing decides about the borders as well as the signatures of this text by operating in two stages. First, the Sartrean text is seen as being fully subsumable under the Hegelian and Marxist tradition of dissolving Jews and the "Jewish Question." Thus framed, Sartre not only seems to repeat the Hegelian and Marxist exclusion of the Jews from history by claiming that the Jews lack substantial reality and historicity, but he is also read as regarding anti-Semitism as merely an inevitable result of class conflict under fascism and capitalism. In short, he reduces the Jews and the specificity of the Jewish question to a mere socioeconomic category.[5] Thus, this seems to be a case of underwriting/writing-under Sartre's texts, surreptitiously turning the stereotypes that he denounced into the animating forces of his writing.[6] In short, three signatures, those of Hegel, Marx, and anti-Semitism—or, to put it more concisely, three quotations that fully determine the texture of *Anti-Semite and Jew*—exhaust its possible interpretation.[7]

Let me remark briefly on this reading, according to which the signature of Sartre's *Anti-Semite and Jew* can be translated without any reserve—that is, dissolved into an already existing philosophical corpus marked by a subcutaneous anti-Semitism. One recent variation suggests that although Sartre himself is not an anti-Semite, he becomes one temporarily "in the space of his text," insofar as the latter produces an "anti-Semitic effect" testified to already by the very evocation of the "Jewish question."[8] But is then Sartre, *the* philosopher of responsibility, ultimately responsible for his writing? Or is he only quoting from the already existing tradition of anti-Semitic writing: repeating, re-citing fragments of the discursive tradition characterizing French prewar society? Consequently, Sartre, who is perceived as the author of his anti-Semitic text, is therefore only the effect, the result of the very citations making up the "space of his text." But does this interpretation, claiming Sartre's unacknowledged complicity with anti-Semitism, not fail to decipher Sartre's highly coded, more often than not ironic re-inscription of anti-Semitic discourse, and thus its requirements for certain shifts in perspective? Moreover, would one not have to extend the aforementioned criticism even to "Jewish publications" reiterating exactly the same language and vocabulary in their attempt to formulate the "Jewish question?"[9] And since it is history—that is, the pre-existing social and linguistic community—that speaks through the subject, would one not have to claim that ultimately the subject of anti-Semitic speech has to be exempted from responsibility?[10] However, is the very denial of responsibility not exactly one of those distinctive features that, according to Sartre, constitute the very ideological field of anti-Semitism?

One certainly always enters history (and the history of a text) *in medias res* without being able to justify the purely narrative assumption that there be a nonreversible chronological sequence. Both texts and practices elude such simplistic genealogies by remaining responsive to transformations and reinscriptions even beyond their particular moment in a chronological sequence and by being reinterpreted and combined and contaminated by other texts and practices. Texts and practices and their represented positions persist at sites or re-emerge, even after they have been "sublated" into others, thus exceeding the simple logic of linear development. And is it not unsublated remainders that keep texts in certain heterogeneity with themselves—remainders that, in the particular case of Sartre's *Anti-Semite and Jew*, might have received their status as effaced figures or ciphers by a double repression, disavowal, or foreclosure that continues to be acted out?[11]

Let me then return to the crypt created by the very abjection of Sartre's text in contemporary discourses on anti-Semitism by rereading Sartre's ideological-critical de-totalization of (French) anti-Semitism with some elements of Slavoj Žižek's essentially philosophical and political reflection on certain Lacanian concepts.[12] Traversing anew *Anti-Semite and Jew* with the politically charged concepts of fantasy and enjoyment will not only bring into relief Sartre's critique of liberal democracy in terms of a disavowed form of anti-Semitism, it will also imply a suspension of the abstract humanism framing liberal democracy (and its necessary supplements, nationalism and racism) by means of an elementary gesture of politicization consisting in reasserting the paradox of a *singulier universel*.

The relationship between the Sartrean and the Lacanian subject could be described as that of a mutual, though unacknowledged, mortgage. In order not to open up again too many texts that are, after all, available and in principle legible, let me recall that Sartre's subject is included in a chain of other names: presence-with-itself, non-self-identity, non-coincidence-with-itself, and so on. What is more, one can justifiably establish a family resemblance between the subject of enunciation and the For-itself as that which is not what it is, and is what it is not. For both Lacan's subject of the unconscious and Sartre's For-itself are devoid of any essentiality—that is, both are characterized as lack of being. Therefore, it is also possible to claim a coincidence between Sartre's ego (*moi*) and Lacan's subject of the enunciated.[13] Finally, do not both describe the subject in inter-subjective terms as hysterical in its ceaseless questioning of its own existence: "Am I really that, and what does the Other want from me?"

Almost all of Sartre's philosophical and literary texts stage this split structure of the subject. The ego as mirror image, its imaginary status and identity, rests upon a series of (always failed) identifications. And it is on this very background that Sartre's concept of the subject as lack emerges due to the failure of identification. The infrastructure rendering any identity resulting from identification as unstable identity, split identity, or even non-identity, is also operative in his first "Portrait of an Anti-Semite." Consider these passages from "Childhood of a Leader" (1938) depicting a young man, Lucien Fleurier, attempting to cover over the constitutive lack in the level of representation through continuous identification acts:

> My name is Lucien Fleurier but that's only a name. I'm stuck-up. I'm not stuck-up. I don't know, but it doesn't make sense. . . . Who am I? . . . "What am I, *I*?" There was this fog rolling back on itself, indefinite. "I!" He looked into the distance; the word rang in his head and then perhaps it was possible to make out something, like the top of a pyramid whose side vanished, far off, into the fog. Lucien shuddered and his hands trembled. "Now I have it!" he thought, "now I have it! I was sure of it: *I don't exist!*"[14]

This passage exhibits the imaginary fixity of the I, an imaginary formation that is actually caught in a movement of identification that reproduces this lack within subjective structure. By splitting the I, the dialectic of *desire* (for consistency and unity) is restored. That is, the subject meets lack where it seeks fullness and identity. Consequently, this mirror image dramatizes the desire for self-identity as an inherently unrealizable desire; it bears witness to the fact that the I is originally de-centered, part of an opaque network whose meaning and logic elude its control.

And it is after identificatory detours through surrealism and psychoanalysis, the encounter with members of the Action Française, and the reading of Barrès's *Déracinés* that Fleurier discovers what, by eliminating the lack, sustains the identity of his name: "Lucien Fleurier," he thought, "a peasant name, a real French name" (W 130). He is finally interpellated and recognized by the Other that assigns him a place in the social-symbolic structure and provides him with the scenario of (national) self-identity:

> And how much he preferred the unconscious, reeking of the soil, which Barrès gave him, to the filthy, lascivious images of Freud. To grasp it, Lucien had only to turn himself away from a sterile and dangerous contemplation of self: he must study the soil and subsoil of Férolles, he must decipher the sense of the rolling hills which descended as far as the Sernette, he must apply himself to human geography and history. Or, simply return to Férolles and live there: he would find it harmless and fertile at his feet, stretched across the countryside, mixed in the woods, the springs, and the grass like nourishing humus from which Lucien could at least draw the strength to become a leader. (W 131–132)

Thus, Fleurier constantly seems to search for the point in the symbolic universe that will reflect back to him a likeable self-image. In anti-Semitism he finds this symbolic identification:

But Lucien's anti-Semitism was of a different sort: unrelenting and pure, it stuck out of him like a steel blade menacing other breasts. . . . Lucien felt self-respect for the second time. But this time he no longer needed the eyes of Guigard: he appeared respectable in his own eyes. . . . The real Lucien—he knew now—had to be sought in the eyes of others, in the frightened obedience of Pierrette and Guigard. (W 142)

Consequently, Lucien's image of authority clearly emanates from the anti-Semitic community that grants him the desired ontological consistency: "They were *waiting* for him long before his father's marriage: if he had come into the world it was to occupy that place: 'I exist,' he thought, 'because I have the right to exist.'" (W 143)

In *Anti-Semite and Jew*, Sartre continues to rely on psychoanalytical concepts to configure anti-Semitism, establishing a psychic dyad between the anti-Semitic subject and the Jew, thus revealing the radically inter-subjective character of anti-Semitic fantasy. Sartre's criticism of (anti-Semitic) ideology, however, will not go through French anti-Semitism in order to unearth some true Jewish reality. Rather, it is through the reiteration of anti-Semitism's imaginary "reasoning" about the "Jew" that his discursive procedure endeavors to demonstrate how the anti-Semitic field has to be conceptualized as an effect produced by the totalization of heterogeneous properties through the construction of the figure of the "Jew." Let me gather some quotes that announce Sartre's shift in perspective:

A man may be a good father and a good husband, a conscientious citizen, highly cultivated, philanthropic, *and* in addition an anti-Semite. He may like fishing and the pleasures of love, may be tolerant in matters of religion, full of generous notions on the condition of the natives in Central Africa, *and* in addition detest the Jews. If he does not like them, we say, it is because his experience has shown him that they are bad, because statistics have taught him that they are dangerous, because certain historical factors have influenced his judgment. Thus this opinion seems to be the result of external causes.[15]

Far from experience producing his idea of the Jew, it was the latter which explained his experience. If the Jew did not exist, the anti-Semite would invent him. (ASJ 13)

It is therefore the *idea* of the Jew that one forms for himself which would seem to determine history, not the "historical fact" that produces the idea. (ASJ 16)

It has become evident that no external factor can induce anti-Semitism in the anti-Semite. Anti-Semitism is . . . at one and the same time a passion and a conception of the world. . . . It is this syncretic totality which we must now attempt to describe. (ASJ 17)

From the very outset, Sartre rejects any "extra-ideological" approach intent on examining whether the anti-Semitic charges against the Jews might contain some experiential or historical truth, for that would perpetuate the epistemologically untenable (non)position of a *pensée de survol* simply re-inscribing "reality" as the support for a traditional critique of ideology. And his dialectical reversal bars even the recourse to some undistorted, pre-ideological level of everyday experience not yet in the service of anti-Semitism. For it is this very distance which is maintained by the "good father and good husband, the conscientious citizen," who in addition is an anti-Semite, that allows anti-Semitism to seize hold of its subject. Žižek points to the gap that supposedly separates and maintains a distance between the "non-ideological" experience and the ideological mask of anti-Semitism as that which obfuscates the efficacy of anti-Semitic ideology. "The gap itself can be turned into an argument for anti-Semitism: an ideology succeeds when even the facts which at first sight contradict it, start to function as arguments in its favor."[16]

The anti-Semitic discourse constructs not only the idea of the Jew as a phantom-like entity that exists at a distance from Jewish reality, but it turns this very distance as the ultimate argument against the Jews. For this reason, Sartre begins to re-mark the subjective position of the anti-Semite. The anti-Semitic subject is constituted by a desire for closure, "for impenetrability"; he is "attracted by the durability of a stone" (ASJ 18).

"We have here a basic fear of oneself and truth. What frightens them is not the content of truth, of which they have no conception but the form itself of truth, that thing of indefinite approximation. It is as if their own existence were in a continual suspension. But they wish to exist all at once and right away" (ASJ 18–19). Here one begins to see how anti-Semitism has constructed the figure of the Jew to escape, that is, to suture its own fissures and structural inconsistency. It is then easy to articulate the network of symbolic "over-determination" (ASJ 79) produced by anti-Semitism:

> On the one hand, Jews are seen as uncivilized: dirty, uncultured, philistine, backward, superstitious, carnally driven, and bestial in sexuality. But on the other hand, they are also overcivilized: overly cultured, cosmopolitan, decadent, degenerate, too progressive, too successful, too modern, too urban, deviant and diseased in sexuality.[17]

This series of heterogeneous antagonisms—economic, political, moral-religious, sexual—which is condensed into the "Jew" is, however, not merely a projection and an externalization of the inner conflict pertaining to the anti-Semitic subject: one also has to recognize the inversion at work in the self-enclosed strategy of anti-Semitism. For only then does it become apparent that anti-Semitism revolves around the "Jew" as that "unattainable X," as that what is "in Jew more than Jew:"[18]

> The Jew, he says, is completely bad, completely a Jew. His virtues, if he has any, turn to vices reason of the fact that they are his; work coming from his hands necessarily bears this stigma. If he builds a bridge, that bridge, being Jewish, is bad from the first to the last span. The same action carried out by a Jew and by a

Christian does not have the same meaning in the two cases, for the Jew contami-
nates all that he touches with an I-know-not-what execrable quality. (ASJ 33–34)

Moreover, this condensation of the "Jew" functions as support of a displacement that enables anti-Semitism to transpose social antagonisms inherent
in capitalism onto the antagonism between the totalized, organic unity of
French society and the Jews as its corrupting force. Thus it is not French society itself that is marked by antagonisms—the source of corruption is located, rather, in a particular entity, the Jew (associated with capital: "money
is Jewish," and so on). The spectral presence of the "Jew" becomes now legible
as a symptom, a disfigured and displaced representation, the repressed real,
of the social antagonisms inherent in French society.

Sartre not only determines the function of the "Jew" in French anti-
Semitism by dismantling the work of displacement and condensation that is
operative here; he also attempts to explain how this unrepresentable X, the
"Jew," has captured the desire of French anti-Semitism. In Žižek's words, he
accounts "for the way the 'Jew' enters the framework structuring French enjoyment." And this framework is to be conceptualized as "fantasy that is basically a scenario filling out the empty space of a fundamental impossibility,
a screen masking a void" (SOI 126).

Now, how does anti-Semitism organize its sense of enjoyment? Jacques-
Alain Miller's formula of the "theft of enjoyment" sheds further light on Sartre's claim that hatred of the Jew is a constitutive feature of anti-Semitism.
The "Jew" wants to steal the anti-Semite's enjoyment, the kernel of his existence that cannot be symbolized. The fundamental paradox brought to light
by Sartre is then that the anti-Semite claims to be in possession of "the *thing,*
given to him once and for all," which is, however, simultaneously presented as
something unattainable for and threatened by the "Jew," his "money," his "intelligence."[19]

The true Frenchman, rooted in his province, in his country, borne along by a
tradition twenty centuries old, benefiting from ancestral wisdom, guided by
tried customs, does not *need* intelligence. His virtue depends upon the assimilation of the qualities which the work of a hundred generations has lent to the
objects which surround him; it depends on property. . . . The anti-Semite can
conceive only of a type of primitive ownership of land based on a veritable magical rapport, in which the thing possessed and its possessor are united by a bond
of mystical participation; he is the poet of real property. . . . To put it another
way, the principle underlying anti-Semitism is that the concrete possession of a
particular object gives as if by magic the meaning of that object. Maurras said
the same thing when he declared a Jew to be forever incapable of understanding
. . . Racine. . . . Why? Because I possess Racine—Racine and my country and
my soil. Perhaps the Jew speaks a purer French than I do, perhaps he knows
syntax and grammar better, perhaps he is even a writer. No matter; he has spoken this language for only twenty years, and I for thousand years. The correct-

ness of his style is abstract, acquired; my faults of French are in conformity with
the genius of the language. (ASJ 23–24)

And:

It is in opposing themselves to the Jew that they become suddenly conscious of
being proprietors: in representing the Jew as robber, they put themselves in
the enviable position of people who could be robbed. Since the Jew wishes to
take France from them, it follows that France must belong to them. Thus they
have chosen anti-Semitism as a means of establishing their status as possessors.
(ASJ 25)

Moreover, Sartre's traversing of the anti-Semitic fantasy suggests that
French society's hatred of the Jews is its hatred of the excess belonging to
capitalism itself. In other words, the hatred in French anti-Semitism is the
hatred of its own internal social antagonisms sutured by the dream of a capitalism without excess ("Jew"). Let me therefore examine in more detail the
fundamental ideological fantasy forming the support for the French anti-
Semite's sense of nation(-alism). The vision of a French society not being split by an antagonistic division is constructed on the basis of this social-
ideological fantasy.

Sartre refers in particular to Barrès's and Maurras's nationalist vision of a
lost France that must be reappropriated by means of an emphasis on the role
of nation, soil, tradition, and heritage in the constitution of the true French
individual. David Carroll has convincingly demonstrated that

tradition in Barrès' discourse performs the same function as race in race theories, enabling the French to be preformed and providing cultural rather than
racist typologies of what is to be French. Tradition enables modern Frenchmen
to have roots in a past origin . . . an origin that all the French supposedly carry
within themselves as their cultural endowment—in their spirit, their unconscious, or their soul, rather than in their blood.[20]

The fundamental ideological fantasy invoked by French anti-Semitism reveals
itself to be the French nation as a pure and steadfast community animated by
a national-aesthetic energetics. This organic solidarity has always already in-
tegrated individual utterances into and subsumed under a unified cultural
norm that subsequently figures as the site of political totalization. That is, it
becomes the ultimate foundation for a certain imagined national space in
which, in the name of a particular *ethnos*, both the individual and the collective are substantially embodied. "The anti-Semites would be horrified at set-
ting themselves up as a certain fraction of French opinion. . . . They prefer to
represent themselves as expressing in all purity, in all passivity, the sentiments of the *real* country in its indivisible state" (ASJ 32). Furthermore, the
gap between this ontopology of the French nation, this "axiomatics linking
indissociably the ontological value of present-being to its situation, to the
stable and presentable determination of a locality, the topos of territory, native

soil, city, body in general,"[21] on the one hand, and the capitalist society split by antagonistic struggles on the other hand, is filled up by the "Jew." In other words, the "Jew" as the foreign intruder contaminating the French body functions as "a fetish which simultaneously denies and embodies the structural impossibility of society: it is as if in the figure of the Jew this impossibility had acquired a positive, palpable existence—and that is why it marks the eruption of enjoyment in the social field."[22]

The "Jew" is that spectral appearance supposed to fill up the hole in French society so that the latter can constitute itself as harmonious *Volksgemeinschaft*. Thus, it is this organic French nation, this "third person," that the anti-Semite hopes to win over to his side. It is this Other that is supposed to assign to him his proper place, to essentialize his being in terms of a definition of a privileged, distinctive, and unified *ethnos*. And this self-referential interpellation of the anti-Semite is conditional upon the hetero-referential interpellation of the "Jew": "The anti-Semite is not afraid of himself, but he sees in the eyes of the others a disquieting image—his own—and he makes his words and gestures conform to it" (ASJ 21) The anti-Semite makes himself an instrument of this fictive *ethnos* that interpellates concrete individuals as members of a nation. When he attacks Jews, he does so from the position of this Other: he speaks as the representative for the Other speaking through him. The ontological consistency of the anti-Semitic subject, that supplement inherent to French nationalism, is thus dependent upon two conditions: that the existence of the French nation is ontologically consistent, and that he is its tool (SNE 154):

> Only, the anti-Semite has his conscience on his side: he is a criminal in a good cause. It is not his fault, surely, if his mission is to extirpate Evil by doing Evil. The *real* France has delegated to him the powers of her High Court of Justice. . . . He feels in himself the lightness of heart and peace of mind which a good conscience and the satisfaction of a duty well done bring. (ASJ 49–50)

One can agree with the claim that the French anti-Semite always already finds himself enveloped by a specific historical and nationalist tradition of anti-Semitism and its discursive variations; he never simply invents anti-Semitic speech. But does the anti-Semitic subject not also re-invent the symbolic space of the French nation with every anti-Semitic utterance? If so, the ontological consistency of the French nation is always radically dependent on the subject: "Anti-Semitism is a free and total choice of oneself, a comprehensive attitude one adopts not only toward Jews but toward men in general, toward history and society" (ASJ 17). And: "These principles enable him to enjoy a strange sort of independence, which I shall call an inverted liberty" (ASJ 32). And it is here that the question of the anti-Semite's responsibility is brought into relief regarding his vital attachment to an intensive perverse (sadistic) pleasure—or enjoyment:[23]

What the anti-Semite contemplates without intermission, that for which he has an intuition and almost a taste, is Evil. He can thus glut himself to the point of obsession with the recital of obscene or criminal actions which excite and satisfy his perverse leanings; but since at the same time he attributes them to those infamous Jews on whom he heaps his scorn, he satisfies himself without being compromised.

. . .

A destroyer in function, a sadist with a pure heart, the anti-Semite is, in the very depths of his heart, a criminal. What he wishes, what he prepares, is the death of the Jew. (ASJ 49)

The anti-Semite experiences his speech and actions as a kind of transgression that accounts for the surplus enjoyment that he derives from assaulting the Jews. The anti-Semite is therefore responsible insofar as he enjoys the "inverted liberty" generating this additional enjoyment (consisting in being part of a larger, trans-individual body: the *real* France).[24]

A simple belief in the danger of the non-symbolizable kernel located in the "Jew" would, however, be insufficient to sustain the dread that constitutes anti-Semitism; thus, it is necessary that anti-Semitism produce its own community of belief. The egalitarianism that, according to Sartre, is inherent to anti-Semitism, constitutes a "mechanical solidarity" (ASJ 29) in which each member believes in the belief of others. And the "temperature of this community-in-fusion" (ASJ 29) is created exactly by the "imaginary Jew" of anti-Semitism: "The collectivity has no other goal than to exercise over certain individuals a diffused repressive sanction" (ASJ 30). The anti-Semite "wants his personality to melt suddenly into the group and be carried away by the collective torrent. He has this atmosphere of the pogrom in mind when he asserts 'the union of all Frenchmen'" (ASJ 31).

But do the Jews not have "one friend: the democrat? . . . No doubt he proclaims all men have equal rights; no doubt he has founded the League for the Rights of Man" (ASJ 55). But why is Sartre nonetheless critical of this humanitarian figure, of his extensive benevolence, his civilizing mission, and his desire to dispense charity and humanity to all forms of ethnic identity? Why does he interpret the liberal democrat's attempt to panoptically house the Jews under the same French roof as a strategy of assimilation that conceals a disavowed form of reflective anti-Semitism?

What underlies and gives body to the liberal democrat's position is the functionalist fantasy that renders the subject equal to its traces. In other words, according to its analytic "spirit," the subject can be fully grasped in its use or function. To the liberal democrat, "a physical body is a collection of molecules; a social body, a collection of individuals. And by individual he means the incarnation in a single example of the universal traits which make up human nature" (ASJ 55). This definition of the subject in terms of the "ensemble of the traits which make up an individual" (ASJ 56) eliminates, however, not only the interiority of the subject, but also its interior lack. And, as Sartre shows, this functionalist fantasy seems to be sustained by the structural suspicion that in the Jew this principle has defaulted. To put it more concisely, included in this fantasy of a perfect reciprocity of social relations is the Jew as the negation of the principle that produces this fantasy. Once again, the Jew has become a symptom—this time, of functionalism. Thus, Sartre writes,

> For a Jew, conscious and proud of being Jewish, asserting his claim to be a member of the Jewish community without ignoring the bonds which unite him to the national community, there may not be so much difference between the anti-Semite and the democrat. The former wishes to destroy him as a man and leave nothing in him but the Jew, the pariah, the untouchable; the latter wishes to destroy him as a Jew and leave nothing in him but the man, the abstract and universal subject of the rights of man and the rights of the citizen. (ASJ 57)

Liberal democratic tolerance displays an attitude that, from a kind of empty global position, involves a patronizing respect for the "Jew." As such, however, this has to be deciphered as an inverted, self-referential form of anti-Semitism, since it maintains a distance to the Jew made possible by its own privileged universal position. And it is from this privileged empty point of universality that the liberal democrat is able to depreciate the particular Jewish culture in terms of unconditional excess and a specific cultural enjoyment that has to be sacrificed for the sake of a homogenized social space:[25] "Thus there may be detected in the most liberal democrat a tinge of anti-Semitism; he is hostile to the Jew to the extent that the latter thinks of himself as a Jew" (ASJ 57). The liberal democratic image of society as a whole that can be reduced functionally to the sum of its parts with no remainders requires simultaneously the inclusion of the Jew qua "man" and the exclusion of the Jew qua "Jew." What this structured social body in which each part has its place cannot tolerate is the symptomatic, displaced, and excessive element which belongs to the whole without being properly its part.[26] For it is the latter that destabilizes the natural functional order of relations in a society that rests on the identity of the whole with the all. And it is this very identity that Sartre constantly de-totalizes and denounces as humanity always and necessarily marked by the exclusion and rejection of those whose ethnicity and culture cannot be borne, of those who are deprived of a capacity for enunciation not already identifiable within liberal democratic society.

Where, however, does the inscription of Sartre's singular signature become visible in *Anti-Semite and Jew*? Of course, he does not sign the ideology of anti-Semitism. He is certainly not a signatory to the liberal democratic cause, with its claim of neutrality and impartiality, since its supposed tolerance conceals the fact that anti-Semite and liberal democrat have to be grasped in terms of their speculative identity. Nor does he simply underwrite an explicitly philo-Semitic discourse of the strange and uncanny "Other," the "unrepresentable" Jew.[27] For the latter remains caught in the historical horizon of anti-Semitism precisely in its attempt to imagine a radical Otherness. That is, the philo-Semitic discourse ultimately fails to examine the way that the identity of this "Other" is already mediated by anti-Semitism. Is one then left with the conclusion that Sartre simply performs the standard critico-ideological procedure that recognizes a particular content behind some abstract universal notion, that is, with the denunciation of a false, neutral universality?

Denis Hollier[28] convincingly argues that *Anti-Semite and Jew* puts into play a complex stratification of (breaking) silences. As he shows, Sartre not only intends with this text to break the silence of the Jews themselves, their "policy of self-effacement," but also and primarily that of the French public: "In the *Lettres françaises,* without thinking about it particularly, and simply for the sake of completeness, I wrote something or other about the sufferings of the prisoners of war, the deportees, the political prisoners, and the Jews. Several Jews thanked me in a most touching manner. How completely must they have felt themselves abandoned, to think of thanking an author for merely having written the word "Jew" in an article!" (ASJ 72). Sartre also seems to make clear that his breaking the silence, his intervention, carries within itself the promise of fusing the joy of the Jews (at being liberated) with the joy of the French nation (ASJ 87). Thus, this imaginary of the "group-in-fusion" which is supposed to make the Jews (and their enjoyment) part of the French society becomes Sartre's cipher for the only possible political struggle against French anti-Semitism: "Anti-Semitism can exist only in a society where a rather loose solidarity unites strongly structured pluralities; it is a phenomenon of social pluralism. In a society whose members feel mutual bonds of solidarity, because they are all engaged in the same enterprise, there would be no place for it" (ASJ 181). However, does this not simply exhibit the ethno- or Francocentrism of Sartre's view of the Jew's situation? Is his celebration of cosmopolitanism and universalism not distinctly French? That is, does he not espouse an alternative model of synthesis (the Jewish synthetic identity) that, although juxtaposed to that of anti-Semitism, relies nonetheless upon the complicity between universalism and nationalism, thus ultimately forcing the Jews into assimilation?[29] If so, what emerges here is the specter of totalitarianism that, according to the standard reading of Sartre, haunts his concept of totalization that erases all differences and pluralities for the sake of a final synthesis. The Jews would lose their *Gestaltlosigkeit* and their existence in diaspora in a collective subjectivity identical to its own context without any void. One would then have to claim that Sartre's "We" assimilates all heterogeneity and appropriates it with no concern for its particular historical context. Deprived of all antagonisms and differences, this collective subject remains without any relation to something other than itself. That is how the philosophical common sense usually arrives at its verdict on Sartre's totalitarian project.

But does Sartre not also assert that any attempt at synthesis finally gives way to the disseminating forces that are always already at work in it, a de-totalized totality? And that it is totality which has to be grasped as an instrument of terror, whereas totalization implies the very opposite, that is, the impossibility of ever attaining such a position of totality?[30]

Sartre is not involved in a quasi-communitarian operation invoking France as a synthetically structured homogeneous and substantial social space that functions as the positive universality to which the particular content of the Jews has to assimilate (see SW 210–212). Rather, he demonstrates that antagonisms are inherent to "French universality" itself and that these actual antagonisms legitimize the existing divisions of the whole into functional parts. And this also forms the basis for the following claim: "Anti-Semitism is a passionate effort to realize a national union *against* the division of society into classes" (ASJ 149). Sartre's political gesture is not simply one of protesting the wrong that the Jews suffered and of opening up a public space in which their voices can be heard and recognized; it presents the Jews, the excluded, as the stand-ins for the whole of society. This particular demand of breaking the silence on behalf of the Jews is not simply to be incorporated into the smooth circulation of negotiable French interests, but starts to function as the metaphoric condensation for the restructuring of the entire French edifice, of the reinvention of political space.[31] "In the same way, we must say that anti-Semitism is not a Jewish problem: it is *our* problem" (ASJ 152). And: "Not one Frenchman will be free so long as the Jews do not enjoy the fullness of their rights. Not one Frenchman will be secure so long as a single Jew—in France or *in the world at large*—can fear for his life" (ASJ 153). Sartre's political subjectivization, identifying the point of inherent exclusion with the whole of French society, generates a kind of short-circuit between the universal and the singular, the paradox of the *singulier universel* in which the singular incarnates the universal. Subjectivity and universality are therefore not mutually exclusive, but essentially belong together. That is, the authentic community that Sartre envisions in terms of the solidarity of a common struggle for true universality-to-come is produced by the discovery that the impasse of the Jew is one's own impasse. This "identification with the symptom" undermines the framework of fantasy defining the ideological self-understanding of French society—that is, the anti-Semitic framework in which the symptom appears as a foreign intrusion and not as the site at which the concealed truth of the existing social order erupts. This identification with the Jew simultaneously implies a disidentification (see D 139) of the French subject so that the gap within the self-identity of "I am French" rendered invisible by the anti-Semitic figure of the "Jew" becomes visible again.

> It is our words and our gestures—*all* our words and *all* our gestures—our anti-Semitism, but equally our condescending liberalism—that have poisoned him. . . . In this situation there is not one of us who is not totally guilty and even criminal; the Jewish blood that the Nazis shed falls on all our heads. (ASJ 135–136)

Perhaps we shall begin to understand that we must fight for the Jew, no more and no less than for ourselves. (ASJ 151)

This, then, is the kernel of Sartre's *engagement:* to accept the necessity of taking sides as the only way to be effectively universal. If there is no neutral position or a return to some neutral universal and substantial content (the notion of man, of humanism), if any semblance of neutrality has always already sided with anti-Semitism, then, on the one hand, the militant, divisive struggle against anti-Semitism remains constitutive:[32] "The Jewish problem is born of anti-Semitism; thus it is anti-Semitism that we must suppress in order to resolve the problem" (ASJ 147). And on the other hand, this struggle for the Jewish subject as unique and irreducible to the particular concrete totality into which he is inserted promotes a universality-in-becoming negating the symbolic confines of both anti-Semitism and philo-Semitism. Indeed, in a gesture similar to that of the "expropriation of the expropriators," *Anti-Semite and Jew* declares war against anti-Semitism by re-inscribing as the site of the universal the performative contradiction par excellence, the "authentic French Jew who is in full war."[33] "The Jew can choose to be authentic by asserting his place as Jew in the French community, with all that goes with it of rights . . . he may feel that for him the best way to be French is to declare himself a *French Jew*" (ASJ 139)[34]

It is apropos of the authentic French Jew, this singular universality as the power of negativity undermining the fixity of the particular context of French society, that the sole maxim of Sartre's politics of authenticity becomes tangible. That is, not to surrender one's internal conflict, one's division, not to reconcile the split in terms of either bad faith or sincerity, but rather to prolong the conflict with oneself, to reconcile with the split.

Notes

I would like to thank Jim Watson, Tom Flynn, and Mary Anne Franks for their helpful and critical reflections, which, I hope, found their way into this text.

1. On the continuity of anti-Semitism in those countries, see Alex Bein, *The Jewish Question: Biography of a World Problem,* trans. H. Zohn (New York: Herzl Press, 1990); H. Kurthen, W. Bergmann, and Rainer Erb, eds., *Anti-Semitism and Xenophobia in Germany after Unification* (New York and Oxford: Oxford University Press, 1997); Pierre Birnbaum, *Anti-Semitism in France: A Political History from Léon Blum to the Present,* trans. M. Kochan (Cambridge: Basil Blackwell, 1992); Michel Wincock, *Nationalism, Anti-Semitism, and Fascism in France,* trans. Jane Marie Todd (Stanford, Calif.: Stanford University Press, 1998); Bruce F. Pauley, *From Prejudice to Persecution: A History of Austrian Anti-Semitism* (Chapel Hill and London: University of North Carolina Press, 1992). For the persistence of a disavowed and displaced anti-Semitism in Austria see my "What Are Poets For—in Austria—'After' Auschwitz?" in H. Schweitzer, ed., *History and Memory* (Lewisburg, Pa.: Bucknell Press, 1998), pp. 91–114, and "Austria's Heading," in

J. Watson, ed., *Contemporary Portrayals of Auschwitz* (Amherst, N.Y.: Humanity Press, 2000), pp. 327–340.

2. Slavoj Žižek explains the universalization of anti-Semitism in contemporary racism in terms of a displacement of the classic relation between nationalism and racism within the field of racism. See his *Metastases of Enjoyment: Six Essays on Woman and Causality* (London: Verso, 1994), p. 79.

3. This is the connection that is brilliantly established in Elizabeth J. Bellamy, *Affective Genealogies: Psychoanalysis, Postmodernism, and the "Jewish Question" after Auschwitz* (Lincoln and London: University of Nebraska Press, 1997).

4. That seems to be the explicit task in Denis Hollier, ed., *Jean-Paul Sartre's Anti-Semite and Jew: A Special Issue*, *October* 87 (special issue; MIT Press, 1999). Henceforth SASJ.

5. See "Aus den Arsenalen: Eine Debatte über Jean-Paul Sartres Réflexions sur la question juive," in *Babylon. Beiträge zur jüdischen Gegenwart* (Frankfurt am Main: Verlag Neue Kritik, vol. 2, July 1987); for texts on Marx and the Jewish question see Paul L. Rose, *Revolutionary Anti-Semitism in Germany: From Kant to Wagner* (Princeton, N.J.: Princeton University Press, 1990), and Robert S. Wistrich, *Between Redemption and Perdition: Modern Anti-Semitism and Jewish Identity* (London: Routledge, 1990).

6. See Lawrence D. Kritzman, *Auschwitz and After: Race, Culture, and the "Jewish Question" in France* (New York: Routledge, 1995), pp. 98–118.

7. William Connolly's *Identity / Difference: Democratic Negotiations of Political Paradox* (Ithaca and London: Cornell University Press, 1991), pp. 99–106, presents one of the few sympathetic readings that sees Sartre's text as a viable account not only for anti-Semitism, but also for racism, sexism, and nationalism.

8. See Susan Suleiman, "The Jew in Sartre's *Réflexions sur la question juive:* An Exercise in Historical Reading," in L. Nochlin and T. Garb, eds., *The Jew in the Text* (London: Thames and Hudson, 1995), pp. 202–208.

9. See Sandy Petrey, "Reflections of the *Goyishe* Question," in SASJ 117–128.

10. See Renata Salecl, "See No Evil, Speak No Evil: Hate Speech and Human Rights," in Joan Copjec, ed., *Radical Evil* (London and New York: Routledge, 1996), pp. 150–168. Henceforth SNE.

11. This double repression not only refers to the absence of *Anti-Semite and Jew*, but also, and more generally, to the absence of Sartre's thought in contemporary discussions. For an attempt to bring back Sartre into recent debates see my *Sartres Wieder-holung* (Vienna: Passagen Verlag, 1994). Henceforth SW.

12. Both Bellamy's *Affective Genealogies* and Yannis Stavrakakis's *Lacan and the Political* (London and New York: Routledge, 1999), pp. 104–108, allude to a certain parallelism between Sartre's *Anti-Semite and Jew* and Žižek's ideologico-critical reading of anti-Semitism. However, neither text traces their deeper affinities.

13. See P. de Haute, "Psychanalyse et existentialisme: A propos de la théorie lacanienne de la subjectivité," *Man and World* 23 (1990): 453–472, and his article "Lacan's Philosophical Reference: Heidegger or Kojève," *International Philosophical Quarterly* 32, no. 2, issue no. 126 (June 1992): 225–238. See also Mikkel

Borch-Jacobson, *Lacan: The Absolute Master*, trans. D. Brick (Stanford, Calif.: Stanford University Press, 1991).

14. Jean-Paul Sartre, *The Wall and Other Stories*, trans. Lloyd Alexander (New York: New Directions Paperbook, 1948), p. 99. Henceforth W.

15. Jean-Paul Sartre, *Anti-Semite and Jew*, trans. George J. Becker (New York: Schocken Books, 1970), p. 8. Henceforth ASJ.

16. Slavoj Žižek, *The Sublime Object of Ideology* (London and New York: Verso, 1989), p. 49; henceforth SOI. The line of my argument is heavily indebted to Žižek's crucial insights.

17. Stuart Zane Charmé, *Vulgarity and Authenticity: Dimensions of Otherness in the World of Jean-Paul Sartre* (Amherst: University of Massachusetts Press, 1991), p. 127.

18. Following Lacan's formula from *The Four Fundamental Concepts of Psychoanalysis*, ed. Jacques-Alain Miller, trans. Alan Sheridan (New York: Norton, 1998).

19. For the "theft of enjoyment," see Jacques-Alain Miller, *Extimité*, unpublished seminar, and Slavoj Žižek, *Mehr-Geniessen. Lacan in der Populärkultur* (Vienna: Turia+Kant, 1992), pp. 88–94; for "Jewish intelligence," see Sander Gilman, *Smart Jews* (Lincoln: University of Nebraska Press, 1996).

20. David Carroll, *French Literary Fascism: Nationalism, Anti-Semitism and the Ideology of Culture* (Princeton, N.J.: Princeton University Press, 1995), p. 30.

21. Jacques Derrida, *Specters of Marx: The State of the Debt, the Work of Mourning, and the New International*, trans. P. Kamuf (New York: Routledge, 1994), p. 82.

22. Slavoj Žižek, *The Plague of Fantasies* (London and New York: Verso, 1997), p. 76.

23. See Etienne Balibar, *Masses, Classes, Ideas: Studies on Politics and Philosophy Before and After Marx*, trans. J. Swenson (New York and London: Routledge, 1994), who shows that the racist perception of the world is always sexually overdetermined.

24. It would be interesting, although beyond the scope of this text, to pursue the relationship between speech/writing, transgression, responsibility, and enjoyment in Sartre's texts, in particular in his *What Is Literature?* written around the same time as *Anti-Semite and Jew*. For an excellent discussion of Sartre's theory of writing as performative that should no longer be framed in terms of a theory of representation, see Suzanne Guerlac, *Literary Polemics: Bataille, Sartre, Valéry, Breton* (Stanford, Calif.: Stanford University Press, 1997), pp. 57–94.

25. Would it not be possible to extend Sartre's critique of the liberal democrat also to fashionable multiculturalism? Moreover, is the simple affirmation of difference enough to prevent anti-Semitism? In his *The Future of a Negation: Reflections on the Question of Genocide*, trans. M. B. Kelly (Lincoln and London: University of Nebraska Press, 1998), p. 117, Alain Finkielkraut writes, "Instead of playing the assimilation game and excusing themselves for being different, they are now ready to defend and 'assume' their difference. But perhaps they (we) are only following in the enemy's footsteps. In fact it is likely that in abandoning the language of sameness, future anti-Semitism *will rely on difference* in order to spew its diatribes and will tap the untainted prestige of alterity for its energy and its new innocence."

26. This formulation is taken from Jacques Rancière, *Dis-agreement / Politics and Philosophy*, trans. Julie Rose (Minneapolis and London: University of Minnesota Press, 1999), p. 125. Henceforth D.

27. Elizabeth J. Bellamy shows convincingly in *Affective Genealogies* how anti-Semitic discourse and the philo-Semitic discourse (of the French Heideggerians) share some surprising structural similarities. I do not think, however, that her criticism can also be applied to the case of Sartre, as my discussion of Sartre's strategic universality will attempt to show. For an interpretation of the complex relationship between Sartre's thought and Jewish messianism see Steven S. Schwartz-schild, "Jean-Paul Sartre as Jew," *Modern Judaism* 3, no. 1 (Feb. 1983): 39–73.

28. Denis Hollier, "Mosaic: Terminable and Interminable," in SASJ 139–160.

29. This is the claim of Harold Rosenberg, "Does the Jew Exist? Sartre's Morality Play about Anti-Semitism," in his *Discovering the Present: Three Decades in Art, Culture, and Politics* (Chicago: University of Chicago Press, 1973), pp. 281–283; see also Naomi Schor, "Anti-Semitism, Jews, and the Universal," in SASJ 107–116. My reading of Sartre's conception of the universal radically differs from that developed by Schor.

30. See F. Jameson, *Postmodernism, or the Cultural Logic of Late Capitalism* (Durham, N.C.: Duke University Press, 1991), p. 331.

31. A reinvention that can be found in texts by Balibar and Rancière with their insistence on the (split) universal; see also the discussion by Žižek in his *The Ticklish Subject: The Absent Centre of Political Ontology* (London and New York: Verso, 1999), pp. 125–244; henceforth TS.

32. And is there not a structural similarity between Sartre's plea for intolerance concerning anti-Semitism and Žižek's plea for a renewal of a leftist politics and its suspension of the Law? In the face of the present re-emergence of anti-Semitism, one should be "dogmatic" and prevent anti-Semitic utterances, since those are not to be a matter for "open, rational, democratic discussion." See also TS 221–228.

33. Richard J. Bernstein marks the similarities between Arendt's "conscious pariah/parvenu" and Sartre's "authentic/inauthentic Jew" in his *Hannah Arendt and the Jewish Question* (Cambridge, Mass.: MIT Press, 1996), pp. 195–197. It seems that, among other things, this established parallelism might also call into question the commonly assumed demarcation separating Jewish from non-Jewish, that is, potentially "anti-Semitic," accounts of the "historicity/non-historicity" of Jewish memory. See Hollier, SASJ 157. And once again, one is here close to Sartre's sense of authenticity. To assume fully the consequences of one's choice, the impossible situation of ultimate responsibility, will leave one with "dirty hands."

34. Sartre's suggestion that the authentic Jew freely assume his imposed destiny marks clearly the gap separating his notion of authentic choice from the vulgar liberal freedom of choice. For *Anti-Semite and Jew*, written at a time of the territorialization of Israel on the geopolitical map, should be read as a textual interpellation that addresses the authentic Jew and his free identification with the task of inscribing Jewish difference into the very history that had forced him into exile. Only then does he recognize himself as being chosen by history to accom-

plish this task. And it is exactly this point that the inauthentic Jew misses: although he understands that each of his decisions is contextualized, he perceives that very context as "objective," not as one retroactively constituted by a decision. In short, he fails to see himself as agent engaged in a present situation. Strictly speaking, the inauthentic Jew deprives himself of any choice, insofar as the conditionality of free choice on making the proper/authentic choice seems to elude him.

Twelve

Sartre and the Social Construction of Race

Donna-Dale Marcano

That race is a social construct is, by now, old news, at least in philosophical circles. But what does it mean to say that a group that is, for instance, racially defined is a social construct? How we understand the process of constitution and related identities is important beyond the conceptual reality or non-reality that defines the group. The goal of this paper, then, is to provide intelligibility to this process of constitution. What is at stake in providing intelligibility to the process of group constitution is whether or not the group has agency or freedom in its own constitution, whether one can provide historical intelligibility of the group and its relationship to the larger social field, and whether or not one can account for the existence of groups.

In this essay, I explore two models of group constitution employed by Sartre, the first from *Anti-Semite and Jew*,[1] which bases group constitution and identity on the gaze of the dominant Others, and the second from his later work *Critique of Dialectical Reason*, volume 1,[2] which places the group as a prominent facilitator of history that *produces* itself in the domain of the Other. For the later Sartre, the genesis of groups is found in the events, the materiality, and the group members' work and antagonisms, set against a background of need and an effort at concerted praxis. I will argue that the more nuanced conception of the social construction of the group found in *Critique* envisages a complex and dynamic account of group formation and identification, an account that acknowledges the need for group identities particularly among those who have been historically oppressed as members of that group. This account better serves a politics of difference as an account of the social production of groups while simultaneously recognizing a certain necessity to group formation. In other words, we must have a more dialectical reading of group constitution, one that traverses the nominalism/realism dichotomy and attempts to go beyond it.

A general argument against maintaining group identities is the tendency, by a group's members as well as others outside the group, to codify its attributes and limit the individual's possibilities for transcendence by terrorizing its members. This is the dilemma: one is forced, by others within the group, to be "this" type of person or one is looked upon by others outside the group as only as "this" type of person. So, maintaining something like a racialized group identity appears to maintain racism. Understanding that a racial identity is constructed challenges the tendency to codify or essentialize the nature of group identities. If we know that characteristics, behavior, and tendencies of a group and individuals in a group are constructed through social, though normalizing, concepts, then we can dissolve the dilemma by disengaging individual identity from notions of an essential nature ascribed to whole segments of a population.

Social constructionism generally argues against inevitability and, most importantly, points to a "fact" of contingency, so to speak, of which we are not aware. According to Ian Hacking, in *The Social Construction of What*,[3] social constructionism maintains a primary thesis: "X need not have existed, or need not be at all as it is. X, or X as it is at present, is not determined by the nature of things; it is not inevitable" (SCW 6). Having established this premise, theorists may go on to argue that to the extent that it is true then X should be changed or abandoned. Since, in general, the social construction thesis is a critical project that challenges the order of things, a move to radically change or abandon that order can seem to be a logical next step. However, this latter move may not be required because one can determine that a particular experience or object is socially constructed but give no suggestion that it should be changed or abandoned. Race is a good example of how one can arrive at different conclusions; for instance, once accepting that race is socially constructed one can argue for terminating the use of the concept to identify individuals or groups, or one can argue that despite the fact that race is not a biological or natural given, it is still plausible to maintain it.

Hacking reminds us that social construction can sometimes seem trivial if we are not clear about exactly what is being constructed. Most certainly, we can say that much of what we take for granted occurs within social reality, things such as property, money, banks, contracts, marriage, and so on. Yet, we can recognize that there are events that occur in a social matrix and still discuss an aspect of an event or experience as being socially constructed. Hacking uses the example of the social construction of women refugees (SCW 9–11). A discussion of women refugees as a social construction admits that individual women fleeing from persecution, famine, or warfare are obviously situated in relation to a particular social context determined by particular social events. But the point of discussing women refugees is to understand that such a classification is socially constructed and how it becomes so.

This particular classification was brought about by institutions, material infrastructures, policy, lawyers, and so on, thereby creating a kind of person, a species that is the woman refugee. That the idea of a woman refugee occurs within a social matrix seems trivially obvious, but Hacking reminds us that being so classified has implications regarding the behavior, experience, and course of action, which determine an individual as part of this group. Importantly, then, when an individual is so classified, her experiences are changed, and equally salient is that the classification of "woman refugee" affects how others comprehend the life of a particular woman. We may even say that to the extent that the classification changes the lives of these women and alters the way they view themselves in the larger social matrix, the individuals themselves are socially constructed, at least indirectly. So, for instance, though the *idea* of "woman refugee" is created via institutions, lawyers, social workers, activists, and immigrant groups to address women fleeing from persecution, famine, or war, the life of any individual woman who might be classified as such will be affected. Whether a woman can stay, must hide, or must find alternative ways to stay in the host country will be affected by being labeled as such. One can imagine that there are women who are fleeing who have not thought to themselves, "I am a woman refugee, which means that I am entitled to or prohibited from . . . " something or another. One can also imagine that once she is identified as a woman refugee, this identification will play an important part in how the woman comes to see herself and recounts the narrative of her fleeing, in addition to determining her future options in light of this identity. Hacking stresses that we must understand what is being constructed in social construction talk: ideas (or concepts), or objects under these concepts. Furthermore, it is necessary that within such a discussion one attend to the interaction between the concept, the object, and practices.

I bring Hacking's work to the forefront in order to give the reader a sense of the problem of social construction for any undertaking that intends to examine a politics of difference or cultural pluralism. It suggests to me that as we consider a plurality of identities, whether ethnic, racial, sexual, or other, and recognize that such identities are constructed and therefore susceptible to transgression and/or rejection, we need to develop a model of social construction that recognizes that while such identities are not inevitable, they are not trivially social. To put this another way, it seems that social construction talk implies a lack of foundation to identities, as if necessity is tied only to the biological or metaphysical, that can easily denigrate identities as illusory or made up. To this extent, understanding the role of social construction in the formation of group identities can suggest that those identities are negatively and predominantly determined from the outside and are, as such, unstable and worth dissolving.

In my work, I am particularly concerned with racial identity and difference. Today, we have come to understand that race, contrary to its nineteenth-century scientific pretensions of categorizing humans into biological kinds called races, is a socially constructed concept (which we now too easily dismiss as pseudo-science).[4] Still, eighty years after Du Bois proclaimed that science had little foundation for the categorization of humans into races but that race was nonetheless real, race remains a lived experience for many people. Whether experienced as positive or negative, or, as is usually the case, both, race continues to be a socially important aspect of American culture, even as we are in the midst of a call to get rid of it. How we understand the contextual realities of groups and their relation to lived experience is important. To address this, I think it necessary that we understand the ways in which group identities can be viewed.

The First Model: The Anti-Semite Creates the Jew

In *Anti-Semite and Jew*, Sartre provides an analysis of French anti-Semitism in postwar France. Proclaiming that the anti-Semite creates the Jew, Sartre attempts to characterize the anti-Semite and his relationship to the Jew, as well as the Jew's response to an imposed group identity. It is worth noting that Sartre was both praised and criticized by the Jewish community, with many of the criticisms centered upon his ignorance of Judaism—the religion and its history—and the Jewish community. Nevertheless, this work continues to resonate for the task of understanding the dilemma of group identity—a dilemma in which the experience of being a Jew, the experience through which one is conscious or reflective of such an identity, an experience which one may attempt to accept or reject, is in fact, created by the anti-Semite.

What the anti-Semite of 1944 has is an *idea* of the Jew that was created by the anti-Semite's forefathers and subsequently inherited by later generations. The idea of the Jew which the anti-Semite has formed for himself, Sartre states, "would seem to determine history, not the 'historical fact' that produces the idea. . . . Thus, wherever we turn it is the *idea of the Jew* that seems to be the essential thing" (ASJ 16–17, RQ J 18). In fact, Sartre argues that the Jew could have been assimilated into the nation, but because of the political and social efforts of Christian communities that limited his function, the Jew remained in limited social roles. Thus, the habits, functions, and traits derived from those limited social roles, including the roles themselves, came to be considered inherited characteristics of the Jew. Yet this is exactly what unifies the Jewish community. It is the "situation" that forms Jewish identity. Sartre writes, "It is neither their past, their religion, nor their soil that unites the sons of Israel. If they have a common bond, if all of them deserve the name of Jew, it is because they have in common the situation of a Jew, that is, they live in a community which takes them for Jews" (ASJ 67, RQ J 81). Sartre identifies the idea of the Jew as that which creates the situation of being taken for a Jew by the French. It is not "race," understood by Sartre as an arbitrary mixture of somatic characteristics and intellectual and moral traits, but the idea and the situation created through the idea, that determines Jewish identity.[5]

What we have, then, is a socially constructed idea of a group called the

Jews, and the construction of the idea of the Jew occurs through the efforts and gaze of a community, the French community, which sees these "others" as outside its bonds of history and nationality. The anti-Semite, of course, considers himself the one who is really French, the one connected to the soil. The Jew, on the other hand, remains the stranger, an unassimilable intruder at the heart of society. Sartre also understood the diasporic condition of Jews as constituting a historical loss of the bonds of a national identity that inhibited the conditions for group identity. As a result, Jews lacked a community of interests or beliefs; ultimately, having no homeland meant that they had no history.

Through the eyes of the anti-Semite, the Jew exists as Jew and is tied to other Jews. It is the gaze, the situation, which forces upon the Jew the responsibility for all other Jews: "It is to be responsible in and through one's own person for the destiny and the very nature of the Jewish people. For, whatever the Jew says or does, and whether he has a clear or vague conception of his responsibilities, it is as if all his acts were subject to a Kantian imperative, as if he had to ask himself before each act: 'If all Jews acted as I am going to do, what would happen to Jewish life?'" (ASJ 89, RQ J 108–109). Being a Jew is being abandoned to the situation. The situation provides the foundation for "race" such that denying the Jewish race is to deny the situation (ASJ 89, RQ J 108–109). Sartre's account tells of the strange demand issued forth from the *idea:* One cannot choose to not be a Jew. The Jew is trapped in an experience of humiliation, alienated radically, with no recourse but to confront and accept the situation.

Consequently, the idea of the Jew creates a dilemma for the Jew. On the one hand, the anti-Semite reifies Jewish identity. On the other hand, the Jew must face the democrat, his one friend, the champion of equal rights, rights of man, and a universal human nature. The democrat rejects the idea of the Jew and recognizes only "man" with universal traits, rebuking any assertion of identity that may persist beyond the individual, or, as Sartre remarks, "beyond individuals who exist in an isolated state" (ASJ 89, RQ J 108–109). For the democrat, the Jew does not exist; there is no Jewish consciousness, no class consciousness, no Negro consciousness. There is no particular consciousness contextualized in a "situation"; thus the particular is dismissed in favor of the universal. This attitude harbors what Sartre considers to be an ironic tinge of anti-Semitism; the democrat is hostile to the Jew because he thinks himself a Jew. The Jew, then, can be too Jewish. In the eyes of the anti-Semite, the Jew is reproached for *being* a Jew while, in the eyes of the democrat, the Jew is reproached for willfully considering himself a Jew (ASJ 58, RQ J 69). The notion of *being* here, in the case of the anti-Semite, signifies the object-ness, the essence, which is Jewish nature; one *is* a Jew, like a rock is a rock and nothing else. The democrat rejects any such particularized essence but at the same time rejects the willful assumption of a particularized identity. Ultimately the democrat leaves us with the notion that there are no Jews, and there is thus no Jewish question (ASJ 57, RQ J 67). The Jew, then, is denounced as

a Jew in the eyes of both the democrat and the anti-Semite. He faces a difficult situation, caught between friend and enemy, wherein "the former wishes
to destroy him as a man and leave nothing in him but the Jew . . . the latter
wishes to destroy him as a Jew and leaving nothing in him but the man, the
abstract and universal subject of the rights of man and the rights of the citizen" (ASJ 57, RQ J 68).

Sartre understood his discussion of the "situation" as a middle term between the essentialization of the Jew through the notion of race, as biological
and fixed, and an abstract human nature that forecloses concrete specificity.
The notion of "situation" uncovers the contingency of race while at the same
time providing a foundation for the construction of the Jew and Jewish identity. Recognizing the situation as the foundation for Jewish group identity,
Sartre asks, "Does the Jew exist? And if he exists, what is he? Is he first a Jew
or first a man?" (ASJ 59, RQ J 69). The answer is yes: the Jew does exist, his
existence as a Jew is determined by the situation.

W. E. B. Du Bois, in the "The Conservation of Races," had already posed
this dilemma and question some fifty years earlier. Arguing against minimizing race distinctions and the proclamation of human brotherhood "as though
it were the possibility of an already dawning tomorrow" in response to the
deprecation of the intellectual, moral, and political abilities of blacks in
the race discourse of the time, Du Bois called to conserve a notion of race. He
explicitly states the dilemma:

> What, after all, am I? Am I an American or am I a Negro? Can I be both? Or is
> it my duty to cease to be a Negro as soon as possible and be an American? If I
> strive as a Negro, am I not perpetuating the very cleft that threatens and sepa-
> rates black and white America? Is not my only possible practical aim the sub-
> duction of all that is Negro in me to the American?[6]

To be American, in this case, is to be white, to be man, the universal—just as
to be French, Christian, is to be man, the universal. Du Bois finds that this
dilemma causes a tremendous amount of self-questioning—something that
Sartre noticed as a part of the Jewish condition. Should I deny? Should I accept? These questions are forceful in that their foundation is that "one is not
free not to be a Jew." Should one deny the existence of Jews, or blacks, it is
precisely this denial that shows the force of the "situation"; precisely because
one is a Jew or a black one must deny being a Jew or a black. Sartre notes,
regarding the difference between himself and the Jew who denies, "I who am
not a Jew, I have nothing to deny, nothing to prove; but if the Jew has decided
that his race does not exist; it is up to him to prove it" (ASJ 89, RQ J 108).

Sartre's conception of the Jew is one in which the identity of the Jewish
community is found within a situation that disallows both the freedom to be
a Jew and the freedom to not be a Jew. The Jew is so situated not because of
race, religion, ethnicity, or simply politics, but from the outside, in the idea
created by the anti-Semite and within a concrete situation resulting from this

idea. Additionally, the Jewish community is a quasi-historical community. Since they have lost all historical bonds, historical self-knowledge is confined to their being grouped and identified as such in an already existent system of social division.

We can see how Sartre's model of group constitution and identification coincides with the first premise of the social construction thesis: Jewish identity, created through the idea, is taken for granted and appears inevitable but is in fact not determined by the nature of things. Thus, the idea of the Jew as a social construct is attributable primarily to the anti-Semite, and to this extent, Jewish identity is determined from the outside and negatively so. And so it goes with how we understand race in America today: race is merely a concept created by the racist and given the face of scientific fact. But this model neglects the ways that groups play a part in the formation of their own identities as well as their agency, in some part, in constituting the group. It neglects what history has shown, that groups, in fact, engage in internal dialogues and actions regarding their existence or nonexistence—a dialogue that takes place within and, at the same time, against the "situation" created by the racist. Furthermore, Sartre seems to make a fatal flaw, a flaw that the anti-Semite makes, and that is the assumption of a "real" history (of the French) versus a quasi-history of the Jews, as if national identity is born out of itself.

The Second Model: Critique of Dialectical Reason

In volume 1 of *Critique of Dialectical Reason*, Sartre retains an antagonistic conception of group constitution. However, he attempts to go beyond a conception of the construction of the group as constituted primarily by a dominant Other or Others. What distinguishes Sartre's work in the *Critique* from his earlier work is his increased attention to the social and political sphere. *Anti-Semite and Jew* is an example of his nascent concern with the political, which, for him, meant discussing freedom and consciousness within the situation of individuals and groups, particularly the oppressed. I mention the oppressed because Sartre believed, as early as *Being and Nothingness* (1943), and maintained to some extent through his later writings, that the dominant class did not possess a class or group consciousness equal to that of the oppressed.[7]

Sartre's increased awareness of materiality led him, by the time of the *Critique*, to add other prominent concepts: dialectical history, praxis, need, the practico-inert, totalization, and negation. The goal of the *Critique* is to provide intelligibility to the nature of reality—that is, to provide intelligibility to socio-historical and political existence; in order to understand the relationship between men and history, one must understand the "permanent and dialectical unity of freedom and necessity" (CDR 35, CRD 154). History, as a dialectical movement, proceeds from the individual; it is not a blind law, an external force, but a result of "totalization of concrete totalizations effected by a multiplicity of totalizing individualities" (CDR 37, CRD 155).[8] Despite beginning with the individual, Sartre is arguing against the notion that "everyone simply follows his inclinations and that these molecular collisions produce large scale effects," insisting that this notion cannot provide any intelligibility to historical development (CDR 35, CRD 154). Nevertheless, beginning with the individual means that there is no hyper-organism determined by some external law.

For Sartre, the individual is always the locus of a free constituting praxis while the group is always constituted. A society may be separated into classes, but this by itself is not enough to constitute the group. In such stratifications, individuals may be situated in a common material structure or engaged in a common enterprise without a felt recognition of unity. For instance, I might be a laborer and recognize my neighbors as laborers as well, but this fact by itself does not constitute us a group with a common interest. The individual in this type of loose organization retains a sense of her praxis as her own. The collective is dominated by the seriality of individuals and therefore the alterity of the Other, what can be considered a serial isolation of each individual. As McBride puts it, "'Serial' collectives are agglomerations of human beings engaged in some enterprise to which a common name can be given but which far from unifying them, reinforces their isolation."[9] Thus, class divisions may exist de facto without class consciousness. But these stratifications may be threatened, and efforts to maintain the social system lead to the imposition of laws and institutions designed to maintain the status quo. In order to do so, an exploiting class works in concert as what Sartre describes as a "unity of individuals in solidarity" (CDR 346, CRD 450). Individuals in an exploiting class act in individual interest but with the consequence of creating institutions that serve to protect that interest. The result is that the exploited class becomes aware of its condition of impotence as well as of its common interest and its "material being as a collective and as a point of departure for a constant effort to establish lived bonds of solidarity between its members" (CDR 346, CRD 450). We should assume here that many instances of such efforts could, over time, determine the constitution of a group. For instance, in the United States, multiple institutional measures played part in developing an African American group. One such effort was the requirement for black slaves to wear a particular type of cloth. In the early nineteenth century, Northern textile mills made cheaper fabrics in order to compete with British mills. These cheaper fabrics made from Southern cotton were used to clothe slaves. The slave's manual labor demanded a cheap but durable fabric. Yet, no such requirement, in the way of a law, demanded that slaves had to wear such fabrics. In 1822, in response to slaves wearing ordinary clothing, a South Carolina grand jury required that slaves wear only coarse clothing, arguing "that every distinction should be created between whites and the Negroes, calculated to make the latter feel the superiority of the former."[10] Within an already established class division, the earlier utilitarian demand for work clothes gave way to establishing the demand, beyond utility, to maintain stratification and the awareness by the slaves of their common material conditions.

Constitution of the group occurs when the collective recognizes a common need or common danger manifested by the efforts of another group and consequently identifies a common objective from which a common praxis is determined. The group thus defines itself by this common objective (CDR 350, CRD 454). What is important here, however, is that the members of the group discover themselves and their impotence to the extent that an already existent group determines them through the unity of its praxis. It is due to an original tension of need (*le besoin*), Sartre argues, that the possibility for change and common praxis exist. Sartre's notion of need cannot be developed here but, in sum, it is best defined as "the organism living itself in the future through present disorders as its own possibility and consequently as the possibility of its own impossibility" (CDR 83, CRD 197). Group consciousness occurs on all levels of materiality and need. As such, Sartre cautions that "the origin of any restructuration of a collective into a group is a complex event which takes place simultaneously at every level of materiality" (CDR 349, CRD 453). Oppressed classes move from being mere collectivities to revolutionary group praxis when the limits of realities prove the impossibility of change and thus the impossibility of life (CDR 349–350, CRD 453–454).[11] Hence, the impossibility of change is the object needing to be transcended so that there is life (CDR 350, CRD 454).

As much as the group is constituted in relation to the unified efforts of another group, it is not merely constituted from the outside but is constituted by its members, through the free praxis of individuals: "Neither common need, nor common praxis, nor common objectives can define a community unless it makes itself into a community by feeling individual need as common need, and by projecting itself, in the internal unification of a common integration toward objectives which it produces as common" (CDR 350, CRD 454). Thus, groups constitute themselves in relation to a felt common danger or common need, but this common need fulfills an individual need, which in turn determines common objectives. Individual impotence, felt as a constraint on free praxis and therefore freedom to satisfy needs, is negated and transformed through common objectives as free relations among individuals constituting the group. A community is established, then, within a greater aim for individual self-determination, an aim instituted as a defense against a threat that aims at annihilation. Insofar as this is true, the process of constitution is conditioned by the transcendent action of one or more already constituted groups—that is, in the domain of the Other (CDR 362, CRD 467). However, unity of self-determination comes to the collective fusing as a group as a structure of alterity and "as needing to be realized by self-determination" (CDR 362, CRD 467). This statement reflects Sartre's understanding that while the group is conditioned by an external action of another individual or group, and it was not the intention of either to constitute the group, formation of the group is its own product insofar as it is a *need* that arises from individual free choices. The group is not constituted intentionally by the praxis of the Other, but the Other conditions it as a negation of its own unity while, in response to the other-praxis, the group produces itself.

> Thus, the developing group is not constituted intentionally by the praxis of the Other and it is led to self-determination, and through reorganization of the environment by the Other, in so far as the unity of the other praxis conditions it as the negation of its own unity (or as totalization through systematic destruction). In this sense, though the unity of the group is its own product and is always here, wherever its members act (at least abstractly and in theory), it is also characterized by a structure of flight, since the induction proceeds from the outside inward without being either necessarily or generally desired by other groups. (CDR 362, CRD 467)

Groups constitute themselves as determination and negations of the collective from which they sprang as well as the negation of the rest of the social field (CDR 664, CRD 747). This means that the group's praxis is always in a relation to the collective that it dissolved as well as to other groups, individuals, or worked matter (materialized praxis) (CDR 664, CRD 747). The consequence is that the group's praxis changes the social field as it practically produces new and unifying realities in the social field and material structures. This process, in turn, structures the social field so that in other groups, whether hostile or friendly, it effects modification. Second, the result of group praxis is necessarily alienated. Alienation here means that the concrete objective of the group as it is realized in the practical field is subject to manipulation by other groups and the practico-inert in the common field. The other thus necessarily appropriates the object produced through a group's praxis, and this appropriation endows the object "with real polyvalence which deprives the object of any univocal, uncontested signification" (CDR 665, CRD 748). The object becomes multi-dimensional and carries within it the possibility of contradictory significations that return to the group as unrealizable significations, related to *elsewhere* (CDR 665, CRD 748). The outcome of this dialectical circularity is that the common field serves as mediation between the object and the group that modifies the group to the extent that the group has modified other communities. Lastly, despite efforts to retain the original unity of the group, its praxis can never result in a hyper-organism. The group is always susceptible to degeneration or reversion into the series whereby relations with the other is determined by alterity:

> Such, ultimately, are the limits of its praxis: born to dissolve the series in the living synthesis of a community, it is blocked in its spatio-temporal development by the untranscendable statute of organic individuality and finds its being, outside itself, in the passive determinations of inorganic exteriority which it had wished to repress in itself. It is formed in opposition to alienation . . . but it

cannot escape alienation any more than the individual can, and it thereby relapses into serial passivity. (CDR 668, CRD 748)

For Sartre, the group constitutes itself out of need and from its foundation in passive seriality. To this extent, it creates a unity that is always and already undermined by a return to seriality. The group and identification of the group by its members can never remain static but is always susceptible to change. However, we can maintain that groups are necessary in determining new social realities, new common fields, that allow freedom from individual impotence through common action. Furthermore, though the group is constituted in the domain of the Other, it finds its unity not merely in the gaze of the Other that signifies alterity but through free praxis asserted in response to a constituting praxis. Sartre's concern is to go beyond the abstract notions of both the individual as isolated and the community as hyper-organism. In providing for an intelligibility of class that does not oversimplify class-being as either demobilized or always united, Sartre argues that class manifests itself as an institutionalized apparatus, as an ensemble of direct-action groups, and as a collective: "All three statutes are in practical and dialectical connection with one another through a process which is itself conditioned by the historical conjuncture as a whole" (CDR 685–686, CRD 767). To this end, group identities are produced, sustained, dissolved, or allowed to lapse on different levels.

According to the social constructionist, race as a category has no foundation in necessity precisely because it is entirely constructed. The only necessity that could be involved in racialized identities would derive from some presumably natural or biological reality; once that necessity is denied, then race as a category is rejected, and racialized individuals no longer exist, whatever their lived experience might tell them. By contrast, in the *Critique*, Sartre claims that the relationship between necessity and freedom is dialectical rather than oppositional, as is the relationship between the natural and social: "[M]an is mediated by things to the same extent that things are mediated by man" (CDR 79, CRD 193). In consequence, there is a necessity for group formation and identification, the foundation of which is the basic need of the individual to interact with the environment and with others; yet this necessity entails freedom—the freedom to act, to form bonds with others. So, although groups and group praxis are constituted in the field of the Other, their constitution is developed dynamically in relation to a multiplicity of praxes in the practical field, including the individuals' own projects.

Conclusion

Both of Sartre's models show that groups are not fixed, natural, essential entities but are constituted. Yet, the first model provides only a limited account of the historical conditions that underlie formation of the group. This model speaks little to how a group, recognized as the "outside," determines the meaning and values of its identity. By starting with the idea, which structures the social distinctions, the oppressed group's identity remains determined by the idea and the situation. In a sense one could argue that the group is contingent and given its necessity from the outside. Very little can be said, on the basis of this model, about the group's own agency, how it is constituted, or the process of its continual and dialectical history of reorganization and destabilization as these take place in response to the idea and material conditions. Sartre's second model enables us to explain how and why members of an oppressed group positively assume and create an identity for themselves, even in the face of an antagonistic group or social field. In light of this, we understand why individuals qua individuals work to create a unity or identify with a category that in most cases would be detrimental to assume in the first place. Because the group is always constituted through the praxis of its members and in the domain of the Other, this model enables us to view group identity as historical and dialectical so that one can account for the internalized discussions of the meaning and manifestations of the identity. In other words, we can account for the continual discussions that groups have concerning what it means to exist or not, changes in how the group names itself, renewed calls for unity, and acknowledgment that no such unity exists. The reading of group identities as static neglects the various levels on which individuals live their group identity concretely.

In conclusion, I have presented two ways of looking at how racialized identities are constructed. I have argued that the second model from the *Critique* provides a more nuanced view regarding the process of construction. This model avoids the trap of thinking that the idea or term comes first and then constitutes the existence of individuals within that group. To this extent it offers a comprehensive analysis from which to discuss group identities that rejects either a wholly nominalist or an essentialist account of the existence of groups. But most importantly, I have shown that there is necessity to the formation of group identities, particularly for the oppressed.

Notes

1. Jean-Paul Sartre, *Anti-Semite and Jew* (New York: Schocken Books, 1995 [1948]), pp. 16–17; henceforth ASJ. *Réflexions sur la question juive* (Paris: Editions Morihien, 1946; Paris: Editions Gallimard, 1954), p. 18; henceforth RQ J.

2. Jean-Paul Sartre, *Critique of Dialectical Reason* (London: Verso Books, 1982); henceforth CDR. *Critique de la Raison Dialectique* (Paris: Editions Gallimard, 1985 [1960]); henceforth CRD.

3. Ian Hacking, *The Social Construction of What* (Cambridge, Mass.: Harvard University Press, 1999), pp. 5–7. Henceforth SCW.

4. See Robert Young, *Colonial Desire: Hybridity in Theory, Culture, and Race* (Lon-

don: Routledge, 1995), pp. 27–28. Young argues that cultural and racial identities may be retrospectively constructed as more fixed and essentializing than they were. He notes that the term "pseudo-scientific racial theory" is used by present-day commentators "as if the term 'pseudo' is enough to dismiss it with ease: but what the term implies is that racial theory was never simply scientific or biologistic, just as its categories were never wholly essentializing . . . the racial has always been cultural, the essential never unequivocal."

5. Sartre does not deny that there is a Jewish race—or, rather, Jewish races—but he insists that race as a configuration of physiognomy and intellectual and moral traits is no more believable than the Ouija board. Here he is arguing against the modern notion of race. He also recognizes what traits, especially physical traits, are used to discern the Jew differ in different places. Additionally, it is not only that one cannot determine a Jew, and thus a Jewish race, through assigned characteristics, but also that any religious bonds or national community that Jews may have had which could distinguish them as a race have long been lost. Thus, what determines Jews as a race is the idea or, more importantly, the situation. See ASJ 60–67, RQ J 73–81.

6. W. E. B Du Bois, "The Conservation of Races," in *The Souls of Black Folk*, ed. David Blight and Robert Gooding-Williams (Boston: Bedford Books, 1997), p. 233.

7. See the section on "We-Subjects," in *Being and Nothingness,* trans. and ed. Hazel Barnes (New York: Washington Square Press, 1956), pp. 547–556.

8. Sartre refers to this understanding of the dialectic as dialectical nominalism, a term that acknowledges that human beings create the dialectic History. In a footnote (CDR 37 n. 18; CRD 133 n.), Sartre also states that dialectical nominalism is also a dialectical realism. This refers to his understanding that the dialectic cannot be valid unless it reveals necessity and, therefore, intelligibility.

9. William McBride, *Sartre's Political Theory* (Bloomington: Indiana University Press, 1991), p. 136.

10. See *USA Today,* Feb. 21, 2002, vol. 20, no. 115. "WestPoint Stevens: Textile firm linked to rough 'Negro cloth' slaves had to wear." This article was one of a series discussing current legal attempts for reparations via U.S. companies that profited from slavery.

11. The transformation of the collective to group praxis includes the recognition that the real which defines itself by the impossibility becomes the impossibility of life. "Indeed what is called the *meaning of realities* is precisely the meaning of that which, in principle, is forbidden. The transformation therefore occurs when the impossibility itself becomes impossible, or when the event reveals that the impossibility of change is an impossibility of life" (CDR 349–350; CRD 453–454).

Thirteen

The Interventions of Culture
Claude Lévi-Strauss, Race, and the Critique of Historical Time

Kamala Visweswaran

The View from Afar,[1] the title of one of the later collections of essays by Claude Lévi-Strauss, draws its inspiration, the author tells us, from the idea in Japanese Noh theater that in order to be a good actor it is necessary to know how to look at oneself the way the audience does—as "seen from afar." For Lévi-Strauss, this "summed up the anthropologist's attitude, looking at his own society, not as a member inside it, but as other observers would see it, looking at it from far off in either time or space."[2] Those familiar with Lévi-Strauss's work will understand this statement as consistent with his self-reflexive attitude toward the "science of man." The "view from afar" was a recurring theme for Lévi-Strauss, most famously mobilized in his reply to Jean-Paul Sartre in the last chapter of the *Savage Mind* and expressed through a quotation from Jean Jacques Rousseau: "One needs to look near at hand if one wants to study men; but to study man, one must look from afar; one must first observe differences in order to discover attributes."[3] This essay explores, through an examination of Lévi-Strauss's less studied writings, how Rousseau's view came to summarize succinctly the core of Lévi-Strauss's philosophical anthropology and his somewhat paradoxical writings on race.

I will not be arguing, however, that Lévi-Strauss had a structuralist position on race of the kind proposed by his contemporary Louis Dumont, but rather that a fuller understanding of his writings on race helps us to understand the essence of his humanist philosophy.[4] Lévi-Strauss first thought to give *The View from Afar* the title *Structural Anthropology, Volume 3*, and it opens, somewhat surprisingly, with an essay called "Race and Culture," which has received relatively little attention. Significantly, his first essay on the subject, "Race and History," is to be found as the last essay of *Structural Anthropology, Volume 2*. Though not usually read as such, "Race and History" can be seen as one of his earliest statements of the philosophical humanism underlying his form of structural analysis. But between the last chapter of *Structural Anthropology, Volume 2*, and the first essay of *The View from Afar*, he enacted an analytic shift from "Race and History" to "Race and Culture," and I also seek to understand that shift in this essay.

For those familiar with Lévi-Strauss's work, the oddity is not so much that his first essay on race was historical in nature, but that he took up the subject of race itself—one apparently at odds with the rest of his structuralist project. For the more discerning student, however, the question is not why Lévi-Strauss wrote on race at all, but why he didn't write *more* on race. His work on the subject was limited to two essays, both commissioned by UNESCO, he has explained more than once, apparently to indicate that left to his own devices he would not have written about race at all.[5] The irony is that one of the most trenchant critics of the effects of modern racism upon so-called primitive peoples, and one who had suffered its effects during World War II,[6] himself never developed an analysis of racism that went beyond the nineteenth-century salvage anthropology of Franz Boas.

Race and History

Any discussion of Lévi-Strauss's essay "Race and History" must first explore his understanding of history. His emphasis on the historical character of "race" is unsurprising once we remember his indebtedness not only to Boas's views on the subject, but also to the Annales school of historiography.[7] In thus seeking to unify the field of historical investigation by making "primitive societies" the object of history, Lucien Febvre and Marc Bloch, founders of the Annales d'Histoire Economique, made it clear that the distinction posed by evolutionist thought between civilized societies with history and "primitive" societies possessed only of culture, was invalid—a point that Lévi-Strauss would elaborate on in response to Sartre,[8] but which he first indexed in "Race and History." Moreover, it was the intellectual interaction between these heretofore separate branches of history ("civilized" and "primitive") that would provide genuine "insights into culture." Since Lévi-Strauss never saw the study of history and culture as separate endeavors, it is understandable that the first volume of *Structural Anthropology* actually opens with the essay "History and Anthropology." It affirmed the importance of structural history to his project with a nod toward Lucien Febvre's understanding of "psychological attitudes and logical structures," which could be grasped only indirectly,[9] even as the historical particularism of Boas provided the empirical framework for his views on historical time.

First published as a pamphlet for UNESCO in 1952, "Race et Histoire"[10] provoked violent reactions, according to one of Lévi-Strauss's biographers. Essayist Roger Callois rejected the esteem in which Lévi-Strauss held primitive society, arguing instead for the proven superiority of the West. Lévi-Strauss responded with an article published in *Les Temps Modernes*.[11] The controversy may have been unique to the French intellectual sphere: in the United States, certainly, much of the fire on the subject had already been drawn by Franz Boas, whom Lévi-Strauss considered to be a "master-builder," if not a "founder" of anthropology (RH 4). In later interviews, Lévi-Strauss acknowledged Boas's considerable influence upon his work and credited Boas with originating the modern critique of racism: "For example, [Boas] is the one who proved, in his work on physical anthropology, that the cephalic index, considered by anthropologists as an invariable trait that could be utilized to define the races, was a function of environmental influences. . . . The criticism of racism begins with Boas" (CLS 38).

"Race and History" is not an easy essay to summarize, though of all the UNESCO essays published during the 1950s, it is arguably the only one still read today. One of Lévi-Strauss's interviewers has called it a "classic antiracist document," and Lévi-Strauss himself testified to its staying power by noting wryly that "not a year goes by without Lycee students coming to see me [about the essay] or telephoning and saying, We have a report to do and we don't understand a thing!" (CLS 148, 150).

In ways that are quite striking, Lévi-Strauss's essay is a profoundly postwar document, shaped by the 1950 and 1951 UNESCO *Statements on Race* as well as the 1948 *Déclaration des Droits de L'homme*. In its tone and sweep, however, "Race and History" seems more turn-of-the-century than mid-century in its attempt to harness the evolutionary, archaeological, linguistic, and mythological data of a Boasian four-field anthropology to a critique of modern racism. Its dense and imbedded argumentation, too, seems heavily indebted to Boas's 1894 essay "Human Faculty as Determined by Race," the work that would form the backbone of his classic *The Mind of Primitive Man* (and which is prominently cited in Lévi-Strauss's own bibliography to "Race and History").

Boas and Lévi-Strauss could be said to share a belief in "the psychic unity of mankind"; thus both held that chance was behind the advance of some civilizations and not others. Yet Lévi-Strauss would depart from Boasian historicism by offering a quintessentially philosophical account of the time of societies, producing a critique of humanism itself as an adequate philosophy of history. While both Boas and Lévi-Strauss sought to reconcile cultural relativism with a theory of progress (CLS 147), and thus, in a sense, posed the same questions of race and history, they would provide radically different answers to those questions.

"Race and History," like much social science of the time, did not dispute the biological reality of race. Though Ashley Montagu's 1941 paper "The Meaninglessness of the Anthropological Conception of Race" had sparked debate at the time that Lévi-Strauss was writing, the prevailing consensus of the scientific community formulating the UNESCO *Statements on Race* was that race was a biological entity amenable to scientific study.[12] Like Boas, whose central argument was that "achievement and the aptitude for achievement had been confounded," Lévi-Strauss held that race in the "purely biological sense" should not be confused with the social and psychological products of civilization (RH 220). But in asserting that there were many more human cultures than human races, Lévi-Strauss held that the nature of cultural diversity must be investigated "even at the risk of allowing the racial prejudices whose biological foundation has so lately been destroyed to develop again on new grounds" (RH 221). Rephrasing Boas's question in "Human Faculty As Determined by Race," Lévi-Strauss asked, "If there are no innate racial aptitudes, how can we explain the fact that the white man's civilization has made the tremendous advances with which we are familiar while the civilizations of the coloured peoples have lagged behind, some of them having come only half way down the road, and others being still thousands or tens of thousands of years behind the times?" (RH 221) While Boas would argue that the main difference between the civilizations of the Old and New worlds was purely a matter of time, and that "historical events appear to have been much more potent in leading races to civilization than their faculty,"[13] Lévi-Strauss would emphasize the importance of the neolithic and industrial revolutions for human society and note that if humanity had remained stationary for nine-tenths or more of its history, "the reason was not that paleolithic man was less intelligent or less gifted than his neolithic successor but simply that, in human history, the combination took a long time to come about; it might have occurred much earlier or much later. There is no more significance in this than there is in the number of spins a gambler has to wait before a given combination is produced; it might happen at the first spin, the thousandth, the millionth, or never" (RH 251). Moreover,

> If we were to treat certain societies as "stages" in the development of certain others, we should be forced to admit that, while something was happening in the latter, nothing—or very little—was going on in the former. In fact, we are inclined to talk of "peoples with no history" (sometimes implying that they are the happiest). This ellipsis means that their history is and will always be unknown to us, not that they actually have no history. . . . In actual fact, there are no peoples still in their childhood; all are adult, even those who have not kept a diary of their childhood and adolescence. (RH 230–231)

Lévi-Strauss would insist that human societies made varying use of their past time—"that some were dashing on while others were loitering along the road," suggesting two types of history: "a progressive acquisitive type" and another "equally active and calling for the utilization of much talent, but lacking the gift of synthesis which is the hallmark of the first" (RH 230–231). One can recognize here the basis of Lévi-Strauss's later distinction between "cold" and "hot" societies: what he termed in "Race and History" "static" and "moving cultures."[14] But in his view, such societies existed not in an evolutionary continuum, which would imply an increasing rank of mental or moral progress, but in stratigraphic discontinuity. "Static societies" were not so much resistant to change as in possession of a different structure to absorb it. "All innovations, instead of being added to previous innovations tending in the same direction, would be absorbed into a sort of undulating tide which, once in motion, could never be canalized in a permanent direction" (RH 231).

Yet the distinction between static cultures and moving cultures could also be seen as arising from a difference in position. Here we see Lévi-Strauss's figure of the traveler first emerge: "It is possible to accumulate far more information about a train moving parallel to our own at approximately the same speed (by looking at the faces of the travelers, counting them, etc.) than about a train which we are passing or which is passing us at a high speed, or which is gone in a flash because it is traveling in a different direction" (RH 237). Likewise with cultures, "they appear to us to be in more active development when moving in the same direction as our own, and stationary when they are following another line" (RH 237). Lévi-Strauss concluded,

> Whenever we are inclined to describe a human culture as stagnant or stationary, we should therefore ask ourselves whether its apparent immobility may not result from our ignorance of its true interests, whether conscious or unconscious, and whether, as its criteria are different from our own, the culture in question may not suffer the same illusion with respect to us. In other words, we may well seem to one another to be quite uninteresting, simply because we are dissimilar. (RH 237)

For Lévi-Strauss, the division of societies according to different time-scales posed a challenge to understanding their very essence. For this reason, perhaps, he held that it was diversity itself that constituted inequality: "One could not claim to have formulated a convincing denial of the inequality of the human *races*, so long as we fail to consider the problem of the inequality—or diversity—of human *cultures*, which is in fact—however unjustifiably—closely associated with it in the public mind" (RH 237).

Lévi-Strauss's introduction of the "problem of diversity" can be seen as a product of the tension between the "human condition" in his work and the need to understand cultural specificity.[15] But the "problem of diversity" can also be read as an ingenious refiguring of Rousseauian natural man in a postwar era that saw the scientific project of the UNESCO *Statements on Race* as part of the same philosophical and humanist project as the "Declaration of the Rights of Man." As Lévi-Strauss put it,

> The preamble to UNESCO's second Statement on the race problem very rightly observes that the thing which convinces the man in the street that there are separate races is "the immediate evidence of his senses when he sees an African, a European, an Asiatic and an American Indian together." Likewise, the strength and the weakness of the great declarations of human rights has always been that, in proclaiming an ideal, they too often forget that man grows

to man's estate surrounded, not by humanity in the abstract, but by a traditional culture, where even the most revolutionary changes leave whole sectors quite unaltered. (RH 226)

Though Lévi-Strauss asserted, "Such declarations can themselves be accounted for by the situation existing at a particular moment in time, and in a particular space" (RH 226), an oblique reference, perhaps, to the all-too-recent Nazi past that instigated the declaration of human rights, his concern here is not with historical context. Indeed, Lévi-Strauss himself suggests that the problem of diversity is a timeless one: one intrinsic to human nature. Thus "modern man has launched out on countless lines of philosophical and sociological speculation in a vain attempt to achieve a compromise between these contradictory poles, and to account for the diversity of cultures, while seeking, at the same time, to eradicate what still shocks and offends him in that diversity" (RH 226). The problem of diversity, in other words, is that humanity cannot really comprehend it and, in its attempt to universalize itself, it seeks to turn unlike into like, thus homogenizing and eventually eliminating other cultures.

This suspicion of other cultures is what Lévi-Strauss termed the "Ethnocentric Attitude," found among primitives who imagined themselves the "true people," in Antiquity when everything not Greco-Roman was held to be "barbarian," or in modernity when everything not "Western" was deemed "savage." For Lévi-Strauss, "This attitude of mind which excludes savages from human kind is precisely the attitude most strikingly characteristic of those savages. We know in fact, that the very concept of humanity as covering all forms of the human species, irrespective of race or civilization came into being very late in history, and is by no means widespread" (RH 225). This double movement to a historical moment which marks the exclusion of certain types of thought as characteristic of its universalizing impulse in many ways anticipates Lévi-Strauss's reply to Sartre's misapprehension of historical knowledge:

> The diversity of social forms, which the anthropologist grasps as deployed in space, present the appearance of a discontinuous system. So, thanks to the temporal dimension, history seems to restore to us, not separate states, but the passage from one state to another in a continuous form. And as we believe that we apprehend the trend of our personal history as a continuous change, historical knowledge seems to do more than describe beings to us from the outside, or at best give us intermittent flashes of insight into internalities, each of which are so on their own account while remaining external to each other: it appears to re-establish our connection, outside ourselves with the very essence of change. (SM 256)

Lévi-Strauss's description of cultural change also contained the seeds to the solution of the "problem of diversity." For those cultures that had achieved cumulative forms of history, an alliance or coalition was both necessary and desirable. Yet no society was intrinsically cumulative in nature: "Cumulative history is not the prerogative of certain races or cultures, marking them off from the rest. It is the result of their *conduct* rather than their *nature*" (RH 252). Thus, "A culture's chance of uniting the complex body of interventions of all sorts which we describe as a civilization depends upon the number and diversity of the other cultures with which it is working out, generally involuntarily, a common strategy" (RH 251). For Lévi-Strauss, "world civilization" could represent no more than "a world-wide coalition of cultures, each of which would preserve its own originality" (RH 254).

It is easy to see how many of Lévi-Strauss's readers could read into the idea of a "world coalition of cultures" an optimism that was not quite consonant with his own attitude. For Lévi-Strauss himself held that while "the greater the diversity between the cultures . . . the more fruitful the coalition," the inevitable result would be uniformity, bringing about the death of cultural diversity (RH 255). The remedy existed in broadening the coalition either by increasing internal diversity (capitalism being an instance of increasing internal differentiation) or by admitting new partners (as through colonialism and imperialism). Thus, "Exploitation is possible only within a coalition; there is contact and interchange between the major and the minor parties" (RH 256). This is the closest that Lévi-Strauss comes to analyzing the relationship of inequality to race, but in the end he reduces the source of conflict to a human universal, the principle of identity and difference: "Humanity is forever involved in two conflicting currents, the one tending toward unification, and the other towards the maintenance or restoration of diversity" (RH 257).

Indeed, the close of Lévi-Strauss's essay appears to represent a compromise with the contradiction that he described as fundamental both to human nature and to changing human society. He calls upon international institutions to preserve diversity:

> It is not enough to nurture local traditions and to save the past for a short while longer. It is diversity itself which must be saved, not the outward and visible form in which each period has clothed that diversity, and which can never be preserved beyond the period which gave it birth. . . . We can see the diversity of human cultures behind us, around us, and before us. The only demand that we can justly make [. . .] is that all the forms this diversity may take may be so many contributions to the fullness of all the others. (RH 258)

It is Lévi-Strauss's turn toward a humanist celebration of diversity that exposes his inability to yoke an analysis of the principle of identity and difference to an understanding of modern racism and that prompts his turn toward biology in "Race and Culture." Yet, in holding that "no culture is capable of a true judgment of any other, since no culture can lay aside its own limitations" (RH 240), Lévi-Strauss suggested that Western valuations of other cultures were relative and that its humanism was open to critique. In further cautioning that "acceptance of the Western way of life, or certain aspects of it, is by no means as spontaneous as westerners would like to believe," and that "Western culture's claim to superiority is not founded upon free acceptance" but upon "inequality of force" (RH 241, 242), he seemed to be working the same groove of argument as that established by Boas. It is my contention that "Race and History" engages the question of temporality by questioning the West's understanding of its own historicity. Where Boas's historical particularism sought an empirical basis for adjudicating the claims of cultural progress, Lévi-Strauss's critique of the construction of historical time would lead to a critique of humanism itself. It is this theoretical project that Lévi-Strauss's second essay on race develops. But to understand fully the ways in which "Race and Culture" both breaks from and extends the philosophical critique of humanism that "Race and History" inaugurates, some attention to Lévi-Strauss's writings during the twenty-year period between the two essays on race is necessary. The next section details the arguments of "Race and Culture" in relation to "Race and History," while the final two sections discuss his critique of humanism in a series of works written between 1955 and 1971.

Race and Culture: A Philosophical Reprise?

The English translation of "Le Regard Éloigné," *The View from Afar,* originally published in 1985, opens with "Race and Culture," a lecture delivered in 1971 at the behest of UNESCO on the occasion of the International Year of Action to Combat Racism and Racial Discrimination. Lévi-Strauss himself would admit that the lecture "caused an uproar" and a "lively scandal," leading other observers to wonder whether he hadn't completely reversed his position on race (CLS 148–149). On March 25, 1971, *Le Monde* called the lecture "heretical," judging that *"le public ne laissa pas d'être un peu surpris,"* while the *Chicago Daily News* ran a Paris-datelined story with the header "Hippies feel 'race' bias, says scholar."[16] Lévi-Strauss himself would attribute his invitation to the UNESCO conference to the success of "Race and History" and the expectation that he would serve up the same "basic truths." In his view, the contrariness of "Race and Culture" was the result of his having overstated the conclusion to "Race and History" twenty years earlier "in order to serve the international institutions," while his own "disgust" at his former obligingness convinced him that in order to be useful to UNESCO, he would have to speak in "complete frankness" (VA xiii).

In some ways, it is easy to sympathize with critics of Lévi-Strauss's second essay; its conclusion is pessimistic, and in place of the celebratory coalition of cultures is a warning couched in the guise of cultural counsel:

> Humanity . . . if not resigned to becoming the sterile consumer of the values that it managed to create in the past, is capable of giving birth to bastard works, to gross and puerile inventions, and must learn once again that all true creation

implies a certain deafness to the appeal of other values, even going so far as to reject them if not denying them altogether. For one cannot fully enjoy the other, identify with him, and yet at the same time remain different. (VA 24)

If we can see how Lévi-Strauss's words might have upset those who had come to expect optimistic conclusions, the preface to *The View from Afar* actually contains an extended attempt to summarize the five "sins" that "Race and Culture" committed in the eyes of the international community. First, his attempt to reconcile the data of population genetics with campaigns against racism drew the charge of "putting the fox in the sheepfold." Second, he attempted to distinguish "racism [as] a doctrine that claims to see the mental and moral characteristics of a group of individuals . . . [and] as the necessary effect of a common genetic heritage" from "attitudes that are normal, even legitimate, and . . . unavoidable" (VA xiv). Third, he warned against the celebration of cultures "such that each would lose any attraction it could have for the others and its own reason for existing." Fourth, he cautioned UNESCO against reveling in "high-flown" words and received arguments if it wanted to change humanity.[17] Fifth, he cautioned the organization against hiding behind "contradictory assertions" (VA 19). The first two issues are what lie at the heart of "Race and Culture"; let me treat them in reverse order.

When Lévi-Strauss attempted to distinguish racism as a doctrine from "normal, even legitimate attitudes," he actually opened up a critique of his first essay. As he was to argue in the preface to "Race and Culture,"

> Nothing so much compromises the struggle against racism, or weakens it from the inside . . . as the undiscriminating use of the word racism, by confusing a false, but explicit theory with common inclinations and attitudes from which it would be illusory to imagine that humanity can one day free itself or even that it will care to do so. This verbal bombast is comparable to the one that, at the time of the Falklands conflict, led many politicians and journalists to speak in terms of a struggle against a vestige of colonialism, about what was, in fact, simply a squabble like those which occur about the regrouping of land among peasants. (VA xv)

Here we can clearly see the difficulties of Lévi-Strauss's philosophical understanding of race for comprehending contemporary political events, though it is perhaps in attempting to distinguish it from an explicit, politicized use of doctrine to legitimize social inequality that he comes closest to recognizing his own theory's limits. In other words, if his philosophical understanding of race could account for modern racism, why would he feel obliged to define racism as a "false but explicit theory" from "common inclinations and attitudes"? This, in turn, makes it all but impossible for him to comprehend how racist beliefs do not always depend on negative ideology, but often lie embedded in common inclinations and attitudes.

If "Race and History" substituted a set of dispositions (the "ethnocentric attitude") for a definition of race and, by extension, racism, "Race and Culture" offered a definition of racism without a corresponding analysis of it. Lévi-Strauss himself seemed conscious of this problem, which he attempted to address by offering ever more specific definitions of racism. In an interview with Didier Eribon on his views on race published in 1991, for example, he pontificated,

> [W]hat is racism? A specific doctrine, which can be summed up in four points. One, there is a correlation between genetic heritage on the one hand and intel-lectual aptitudes and moral inclinations on the other. Two, this heritage, on which these aptitudes and moral inclinations depend, is shared by all members of certain human groups. Three, these groups, called "races," can be evaluated as a function of the quality of their genetic heritage. Four, these differences authorize so-called superior "races" to command and exploit the others, and to eventually destroy them. (CLS 150)

When Eribon asked Lévi-Strauss to clarify whether the hostility of one cul-ture toward another was racism, he responded,

> Active hostility, yes. Nothing gives one culture the right to destroy or even op-press another. This negation of the other inevitably takes its support from tran-scendent reasons: either racism or its equivalent. But that cultures, all the while respecting each other, can feel greater or less affinity with certain others is a factual situation that has always existed. It is the normal course of human con-duct. By condemning it as racist, one runs the risk of playing into the enemy hand, for many naïve people will say, if that's racism, then I'm racist. (CLS 150)

We can see here the problem with reducing racism to set of attitudes rather than emphasizing material practices or institutions. Yet, in Lévi-Strauss's at-tempts to clarify his understanding of what constitutes racism, he seems to understand the difficulty with his analysis of how racial distinctions emerge. If racial distinctions are constituted by human nature—by humanity's need to differentiate itself from others, he can neither explain why cultures should co-exist peacefully nor what leads them to conflict or violence. Thus,

> By itself, the diversity of cultures would pose no problem beyond the objective fact of its existence. Nothing really prevents different cultures from co-existing and maintaining comparatively peaceful relations, which, as proved by historical experience, can have different foundations. Sometimes each culture calls itself the only genuine and worthwhile culture; it ignores the others and even denies that they are cultures. Most of the peoples that we term "primitive" give them-selves a name that signifies "the True Ones," "The Good Ones," "The Excel-lent Ones," or even quite simply, "The Human Beings," and apply to other peoples a name that denies their humanity—for example, "earth monkeys" or "louse eggs." Hostility and sometimes even warfare may have prevailed between cultures, but the aims were chiefly to avenge wrongs, to capture victims for sacrifices, and to steal women or property—customs that may be morally repug-nant to us, but that seldom or never went so far as to wipe out or subjugate a whole culture as such because one did not accept the other's existence. (VA 6)

We can see here how the distinction between negative cultural beliefs toward others and racism is the result of the tension in Lévi-Strauss's work between what is unique and culturally specific in "primitive" societies and what they seem to illustrate about universal human nature. Yet it is clearly the failure of his extension of how "primitive" societies constitute cultural difference to explain fascist final solutions that leads him to define racism as a negative ideology based upon biological or genetic difference. It is precisely because he reaches the limit of his own philosophical argument—its inability to define racism and the violence and destruction unleashed by it—that he has sought out biology. Since he had no political understanding of racism, he turned to the prevailing definition of the times: one that portrayed racism as false, negative valuation attributed to biological difference.

"Race and Culture" thus did not advance Lévi-Strauss's understanding of racism, while it did shift the grounds of his relativist commitments to rather unsteady biological terrain—the same terrain paradoxically mapped by the UNESCO Statements on Race.[18] Where Lévi-Strauss's first essay produced an ingenious, if inadequate, philosophy of race, his second essay attempts the same resolution that Boas and his students made: to see culture as socially constructed and race as a biological entity (see RCA). Thus Lévi-Strauss asks, "Does anthropology feel that it can on its own explain the diversity of cultures? Can it succeed in doing so without citing factors that elude its own rationality—without, moreover, making too hasty a judgment about their ultimate nature, which is beyond anthropology's province to declare biological?" (VA 6) While he in some sense wants to bracket the notion of race—"We know what a culture is, but not what a race is; and we probably do not need to know in order to attempt to answer the question raised by the title of this chapter" (VA 6)—he also wants to preserve its potential utility. His main intervention in this regard is to pose what he terms a reversal between the relationship of race and culture:

> Throughout the nineteenth and in the first half of the twentieth century, scholars wondered whether and in what way race influences culture. After establishing that the problem stated in this way cannot be solved, we now realize that the reverse situation exists: the cultural forms adopted in various places by human beings, their ways of life in the past or in the present, determine to a very great extent the rhythm of their biological evolution and its direction. Far from having to ask whether culture is or is not a function of race, we are discovering that race—or what is generally meant by this term—is one function among others of culture. (VA 13–14)

In "Race and Culture," Lévi-Strauss addresses the genetic studies done on isolated populations in Africa and South America and explains, "So long as we replace the point of view of 'cultural macro-evolution,' with that of 'genetic micro-evolution,' collaboration becomes possible once again between the study of races and the collaboration of cultures" (VA 16). Yet the collaboration between the study of races and that of cultures also reproduced a troubling analogy between cultural and biological evolution,[19] whereby "cultural barriers are almost of the same nature as biological barriers," "genetic recombination plays a part comparable to that of cultural recombination," and "organic evolution and cultural evolution are not only analogous but complementary" (VA 16–18). Lévi-Strauss insisted that once the "old demons of racist ideology" were driven out and proven to have no scientific basis, the road was clear for a "positive collaboration between geneticists and anthropologists to investigate how and in what way the distribution maps of biological and cultural phenomena shed light on one another" (VA 19).

Though Lévi-Strauss spends the bulk of the essay arguing for a correct interpretation of the relationship of organic to cultural evolution, toward the end of the essay he suggests an argument for racism based upon the lifeboat analogy of Malthusian economics:

> Are we so sure that the racist form of intolerance results chiefly from the wrong ideas of this or that group of people about the dependence of cultural evolution upon an organic evolution? Might not these ideas be simply ideological camouflage for more concrete oppositions based on a desire to subjugate other groups and maintain a position of power? Such was certainly the case in the past. But even granting that these relationships of force are diminishing, might not racial differences continue to serve as a pretext for the increasing difficulty of living together, as unconsciously felt by Humanity in the grips of population explosion? . . . Racial prejudices have reached their greatest intensity when directed toward human groups that have been limited by other groups to inadequate territory and to an insufficient allowance of natural goods so as to reduce their dignity in their own eyes and in those of their powerful neighbors. (VA 19–20)

Here it is difficult to disentangle what part is human biology (the group or population) that is adapting to limited environmental circumstances, and what part is human nature—all groups faced with a similar set of circumstances will respond similarly. And when Lévi-Strauss announced, "What not long ago was called the problem of the races eludes the domain of philosophical speculation and moral homilies with which we were too frequently satisfied" (VA 19–20), he seemed to discount his own arguments in "Race and History" by privileging population genetics. In truth, he seems to be saying that the problem lies not with the use of the model of organic evolution to understand race but with human nature, "the desire to subjugate other groups and maintain a position of power." Thus, the passage above, while using the language of population ecology, actually reprises the terms of argument found in "Race and History."

In Lévi-Strauss's own view, "Race and Culture" was only an elaboration of the themes initially laid out in "Race and History."[20] And sure enough, "Race and Culture" again revisits the problem of diversity, reintroduces the metaphor of the train traveler to understand differences in historical time, and raises the question of differing notions of humanity. As if to underscore the philosophical position of that earlier essay, in "Race and Culture" Lévi-Strauss gestured even more strongly to his understanding of the historical constitutedness of Western civilization and humanism as an unacknowledged reflection of its own historical and cultural specificity by suggesting that different forms of humanism exist, some grounded in indigenous cultures and some in Buddhist philosophy. Thus,

> Indigenous philosophy may even contain the idea that human beings, animals, and plants share a common stock of life, so that any human abuse of any species is tantamount to lowering the life expectancies of human beings themselves. All these beliefs may be naïve, yet they are highly effective testimonies to a wisely conceived humanism, which does not center on man, but gives him a reasonable place within nature, rather than letting him make himself its master and plunderer, without regard for even the most obvious needs and interests of later generations. (VA 13)

"Race and Culture" thus extends the critique of Western civilization that Lévi-Strauss began in *Tristes Tropiques:*

> By isolating man from the rest of creation and defining too narrowly, the boundaries separating him from other living beings, the Western humanism inherited from Antiquity and the Renaissance has deprived him of a bulwark; and, as the experiences of the 19th and 20th centuries have proved, has allowed him to be exposed and defenseless to attacks stirred up within the stronghold itself. This humanism has allowed ever closer segments of humanity to be cast outside arbitrary frontiers to which it was all the easier to deny the same dignity as the rest of humanity, since man had forgotten that he is worthy of respect more as a living being than as lord and master of creation—a primary insight that should have induced him to show his respect for all living beings. (VA 23)

While one might argue that Lévi-Strauss attempts to resolve the tension between universality and cultural specificity in "Race and History" by shifting the terrain of argument to population genetics in "Race and Culture," it is an uneasy resolution at best, and one that is at odds with the philosophical humanism that resonates throughout his work. Indeed, it is Lévi-Strauss's elaboration of philosophical alternatives to the Western humanistic tradition that becomes the thread tying "Race and Culture" to "Race and History." His attempt to link the emphasis upon harmony between man and nature to a critique of Western humanism can be seen more clearly by turning to his writing on Rousseau and his 1956 essay "The Three Humanisms."

Jean Jacques Rousseau and the Three Humanisms

In Lévi-Strauss's writing on race, we can see the seeds of an irresolvable tension or contradiction between universalism and specificity for which hope or optimism, and later a kind of biological realism, is the only antidote. Yet his thinking on race is heavily indebted to Rousseau's *Discourse on the Origins and*

Foundations of Inequality.[21] In an essay written for the 225th anniversary of Rousseau's birth in 1962, "Jean Jacques Rousseau, Founder of the Sciences of Man," published at the same time as *The Savage Mind*, Lévi-Strauss explored again Rousseau's notion of the "View from Afar." Proclaiming that Rousseau did not just anticipate ethnology but founded it by posing man in his relation to nature and culture as the subject of ethnology, Lévi-Strauss again echoed the philosopher's famous words, "When one wants to study men one must look around oneself; but to study man, one must first learn to look into the distance; one must first see differences in order to discover characteristics" (SA 35).

With perhaps a hint of self-irony, Lévi-Strauss held that these two contradictions had to be resolved in every ethnological career. In fact, "The methodological rule which Rousseau assigns to ethnology and which marks its advent also makes it possible to overcome what, at first glance, one would take for a double paradox: that Rousseau could have simultaneously advocated the study of the most remote men, while mostly given himself to the study of that particular man who seems the closest—himself; and secondly that, throughout his work, the systematic will to identify with the other goes hand in hand with an obstinate refusal to identify with the self" (SA 35).

Lévi-Strauss credits Rousseau with having been the first to develop an alternate self-reflexive philosophy to the *cogito's* "I think therefore I am," anticipating the relationship between self and other in the famous maxim "I is another":

> This faculty—Rousseau did not neglect to repeat—is compassion, deriving from the identification with another who is not only a parent, a relative, a compatriot, but any man whatsoever, seeing only that he is a man, and much more: any living being, seeing that it is living. Thus man begins by experiencing himself as identical to all his fellows. And he will never forget this primitive experience, despite demographic expansion. . . . This demographic expansion will have forced him to diversify his ways of life. . . . It will also have forced him to know how to differentiate himself. . . . The total apprehension of men and animals as sensitive beings (in which identification consists) precedes the awareness of oppositions—oppositions first between common characteristics, and only later between human and non-human. (SA 38)

Lévi-Strauss claims that Rousseau's discoveries in the *Confessions* are first, the identification with others, and second, the refusal to identify with oneself. Thus, "These two attitudes complement each other, and the latter even forms the basis of the former: in truth, I am not 'me' but the weakest, the most humble of 'others'" (SA 39).

In reading Rousseau's *Confessions*, Lévi-Strauss anticipates the work of his own memoirs, *Tristes Tropiques*, and asks, "What does the ethnologist write but confessions?" Lévi-Strauss's ingenious intervention in this essay is to read Rousseau against the grain of the egoism of the Cartesian legacy:

Never better than after the last four centuries could a Western man understand that, while assuming the right to impose a radical separation of humanity and animality, while granting to one all that he denied the other, he initiated a vicious circle. The one boundary, constantly pushed back, would be used to separate men from other men and to claim—to the profit of ever smaller minorities —the privilege of a humanism, corrupted at birth by taking self-interest as its principle and its notion. (SA 41)

The notion of a corrupt, self-interested humanism is central to Lévi-Strauss's thinking on racism and is a point to which I will return. Here I want to underscore Lévi-Strauss's understanding that Rousseau's notion of identification not only constituted "the real principle of the human sciences and the only possible basis for ethics" but that the principle of identification is the only thing "uniting beings whom the interests of politicians and philosophers are everywhere else bent on rendering incompatible: me and the other, my societies and other societies, nature and culture, the sensitive and the rational, humanity and life" (SA 43).

The closing words of the essay on Rousseau reveal the core of Lévi-Strauss's philosophical anthropology, and indeed the key to his version of structuralism: one less informed by the principle of binary oppositions than by an understanding of the philosophical principle of identity and difference, upon which are founded the most fundamental, but not mutually incompatible, oppositions between self and other; one's own society and those of others. Lévi-Strauss's tone was hopeful in 1962, as it had been in 1952, and in a way that is not reflected in the closing words of "Race and Culture."

Lévi-Strauss's reliance upon a humanistic understanding of the relationship between identity and difference certainly prevented him from developing an analysis of racism as a structured and structuring principle of inequality. And yet he was not naive about the history of humanistic thought and developed a critique of humanism which, while not as far-ranging as Michel Foucault's, may well have preceded it.[22] Indeed, in an earlier article, "The Three Humanisms," published for the French magazine *Demain* in 1956,[23] Lévi-Strauss would marshal a reading of Rousseau to articulate his contribution to a distinctly democratic humanism.

In this complex and compact essay, several uses of the term "humanism" emerge. Lévi-Strauss begins by asserting that ethnology is not a new science, but the most ancient, the general form of what we designate as humanism. And yet the emergence of classical antiquity as a distant past of Renaissance Europe also led to the simultaneous emergence of two forms of humanism in the recognition that "no civilization can define itself if it does not have at its disposal some other civilization for comparison. The Renaissance rediscovered in ancient literature forgotten notions and methods. But more important still, it realized the means of putting its own culture in perspective— by confronting contemporary concepts with those of other times and places" (SA 272). Interestingly, Lévi-Strauss would identify the study of classics and of other societies as sharing a common intellectual method: the technique of *dépaysement* or estrangement. Thus, "The only difference between classical culture and ethnographic culture resides in the dimensions of the known world in their respective epochs. At the beginning of the Renaissance, to Western man, the human universe was circumscribed by the limits of the Mediterranean basin . . . but it was already known that no fraction of humanity could aspire to understand itself without reference to all other human beings" (SA 273). He argues that the conception of humanism broadened with the onset of geographical exploration in the eighteenth and nineteenth centuries and that the incorporation of the study of the civilizations of India and China into universities as "nonclassical philology" showed the inability to recognize that "it was the same humanistic movement, only encroaching on new territory." To the classical humanism of the early Renaissance and the "non-classical" humanistic study of Asian civilizations, he added the study of "disregarded or so-called primitive civilizations," which represented "humanism traveling through its third stage" (SA 273). Yet while the "classical" and "non-classical" humanisms kept the languages and literatures of these civilizations as their object, the "new civilizations" of ethnology posed a challenge to humanism in its third movement; "Hence the need of ethnology to provide humanism with new tools of investigation" (SA 273). For Lévi-Strauss, ethnology surpassed traditional forms of humanism by bringing together "procedures characteristic of all spheres of knowledge: including both the human sciences and natural sciences" (SA 273).

Lévi-Strauss's deft handling of temporality is worth noting: he does not accord historical primacy to classical humanism, except as it emerges as the first phase in the West's own historical consciousness. Indeed, the most ancient form of humanism is to be found in the ethnological study of the so-called new civilizations—their newness, clearly being seen as a function of their recognition by the West. Moreover, he reserved his strongest criticisms for classical humanism, which was limited not only by its object but by its beneficiaries, the privileged classes, while the "exotic humanism" (one might say "Orientalism") found itself tied to the industrial and commercial interests that supported it. The aristocratic humanism of the former and the bourgeois humanism of the latter were "created from privileged civilizations for the privileged classes" and would be superseded by a "democratic humanism," according to Lévi-Strauss. This humanism would seek "its inspiration in the midst of the most humble and despised societies," proclaiming that "nothing human can be strange to man," and calling for "the reconciliation of man and nature in a generalized humanism" (SA 274).

It was in the attempt to elucidate and draw upon a humanism located within the Rousseauian tradition that Lévi-Strauss found his clearest reply to his critics for generating an objectivist science, one that did not take into account the words and feelings of its subjects by reducing them to abstract principles of thought. "How was it possible," Sartre would ask contemptuously of Lévi-Strauss, "to study men like ants?" Certainly, Lévi-Strauss's tendency to romanticize "the reconciliation of man and nature" also led him at times to articulate a dispassionate, even antiseptic, view of other societies as laboratories, or "experiments." This is clear in his inaugural address to the Collège de France in 1960, as he accepted a chair in social anthropology on the heels of his success with *Tristes Tropiques*:

> It happens in anthropology experimentation precedes both observation and hypothesis. One of the peculiarities of the small societies we study is that each constitutes a ready-made experiment because of its relative simplicity and the limited number of variables required to explain its functioning. On the other hand, these societies are alive and we have neither the time nor the means to do something about them. By comparison with the natural sciences, we enjoy an advantage and suffer from a handicap: We find our experiments already set up but we cannot control them. (SA 15)

Yet the anthropologist's "experiment," as it was constituted by field research, was also, according to Lévi-Strauss, the nurse and mother of doubt, "the philosophical attitude par excellence." And anthropological doubt did not consist only of knowing that one knew nothing, "but of resolutely exposing what one thought one knew . . . to buffetings and denials directed at one's most cherished ideas and habits best able to rebut them. Contrary to appearances . . . it is by its more strictly philosophical method that ethnology is distinguished from philosophy" (SA 26). In further distinguishing sociology from ethnology, Lévi-Strauss noted, "The sociologist objectifies for fear of being misled. The ethnologist does not experience this fear since the distant society he studies is nothing to him, and since he is not compelled in advance to extract all its nuances, all its details, and even its values; in a word, all that in which the observer of his own society risks being implicated" (SA 26). In the end, the overriding paradox of Lévi-Strauss's work is that his dispassionate view of society was also nurtured by an intensely passionate humanism.

Lévi-Strauss devoted the final words of his inaugural speech to the Collège de France to those "savages whose obscure tenacity still offers us a means of assigning to human facts their true dimensions":

> Men and women who, as I speak, thousands of miles from here, on some savannah ravaged by brush fire or in some forest dripping with rain, are returning to camp to share a meager pittance and evoke their gods together. These Indians of the tropics, and others like them throughout the world who have taught me their humble knowledge . . . soon, alas, destined to extinction through the impact of the illnesses and—to them more horrible still—the modes of life we have brought them. To them I have incurred a debt which I can never repay even if, in the place in which you have put me, I could justify the tenderness I feel for them, and the gratitude I owe them, by continuing to be as I was among them, and as, among you, I would never want to cease from being; their pupil, and their witness. (SA 32)

But alongside the moving words of homage to dying peoples came an equally passionate defense of anthropology from the charge of colonialism:

"Our investigations are sometimes said to be sequels of colonialism. The two are certainly linked, but nothing could be more false than to hold anthropology as the last manifestation of the colonial frame of mind, a shameful ideology which would offer colonialism a chance of survival" (SA 31). Though in "Three Humanisms" Lévi-Strauss did not explicitly make the linkage between Renaissance humanism and colonialism, his inaugural address seeks implicitly to affirm Rousseau's tradition of renaissance humanism, seemingly "atoning" for the aristocratic and bourgeois corruptions of Renaissance thought:

> What we call the Renaissance truly marked the birth of colonialism and anthropology. Between the two, confronting each other from the time of their common origin, an equivocal dialogue has been pursued for four centuries. If colonialism had not existed, the rise of anthropology might have been less delayed. But anthropology might not have been moved to implicate all mankind (and it has now become its role to do so) in each of its particular case studies. Our science reached its maturity the day that Western man began to understand that he would never understand himself as long as there would be on the surface of the earth a single race or a single people whom he would treat as an object. Only then was anthropology able to affirm itself as an enterprise renewing the Renaissance and atoning for it, in order to extend humanism to the measure of humanity. (SA 32)

Confessions: "A World on the Wane"

When *Tristes Tropiques* appeared in French in 1955, it was an instant sensation and catapulted Lévi-Strauss to international fame. The English translation of *Tristes Tropiques* did not appear until 1961, but it was clearly produced as part of the same analytic project as *The Savage Mind* and the essays on Rousseau and the "Three Humanisms." Indeed, the self-reflexive and philosophical themes that mark these works were first introduced in "Race and History." Part elegy, part disquisition, *Tristes Tropiques* hovers between witnessing a "primitive" world on the wane[24] and acknowledging membership in a civilization that has led to its demise.

The signs of Lévi-Strauss's engagement with Rousseau first emerged in the pages of *Tristes Tropiques,* in which he tells of going to the "ends of the earth in search of what Rousseau called 'the barely perceptible advances of the earliest times' . . . in search of a state which . . . 'no longer exists, perhaps may never have existed, and probably will never exist'" (TT 316). And it was in those sad tropics that Lévi-Strauss found Rousseau's "noble savage." For generations of political theorists, Rousseau's "state of nature" was a myth or political fiction—it never existed. Yet, in a contradictory way, it channels Lévi-Strauss's concern with "primitive" cultures such that he studies them as an experiment or exemplar of human nature, all the while pronouncing that they do not represent the childhood of the West.[25]

Tristes Tropiques extends Rousseau's philosophical journey to a practice of reflection about travel, time, and cultural difference. The figure of the philosopher is accompanied by his companion, the traveler, and while the figure of the traveler first makes its appearance in Lévi-Strauss's writing in "Race and History," the theory of travel and the theme of cultural diversity and communication are expanded upon in *Tristes Tropiques.* As a witness to the ravages of racism and colonialism, Lévi-Strauss finds himself subject to an infirmity of vision:

> [W]hile I complain of being able to glimpse more than the shadow of the past, I may be insensitive to reality as it is taking shape at this very moment, since I have not reached the stage of development at which I would be capable of perceiving it. A few hundred years hence, in this same place, another traveler, as despairing as myself, will mourn the disappearance of what I might have seen, but failed to see. I am subject to a double infirmity: all that I perceive offends me, and I constantly reproach myself for not seeing as much as I should. (TT 43)

Yet it is the memory and forgetting of the passage of time between worlds that establishes the seductive temporality of *Tristes Tropiques.* And we can see at work in *Tristes Tropiques* Lévi-Strauss's peculiarly stratiographic view of history that first finds its expression in "Race and History."

Tristes Tropiques is, after all, written as a memoir, and we can perhaps forgive Lévi-Strauss's tendency to romanticize the figure of the traveler who brought in his wake colonialism and economic exploitation. Yet the traces of mourning which continued to wend their way through Lévi-Strauss's writing also left it vulnerable as a philosophy of race and racism. One is tempted to suggest that Lévi-Strauss's own experience of racism was displaced onto a philosophical journey, the figure of the old-world traveler mediating new worlds of difference and *dépaysement.* Lévi-Strauss surely understood that the irony of his own *dépaysement* at the hands of the Vichy regime would mark his "confessions" in the same way Rousseau's *Confessions* demarcated for him a new method for humanism. Yet even as Lévi-Strauss recorded the effects of racism upon primitive peoples, he was never able to push his own understanding of racism beyond a generalized theory of human nature. His analysis of race essentially left all of the difficult questions about racism—how it worked and why it emerged as one of the major forces of modern history—unasked.

Notes

I thank Robert Bernasconi, Jeff Lustig, Bettina Bergo, and Max and Nicolas Prat for their help with this essay.

1.   Claude Levi-Strauss, *The View from Afar,* trans. Joachim Neugroschel and Phoebe Hoss (New York: Basic Books, 1985 [1971]). Henceforth VA.

2. Claude Lévi-Strauss and Didier Eribon, *Conversations with Claude Lévi-Strauss* (Chicago: University of Chicago Press, 1991), p. 181. Henceforth CLS.

3. Quoted in Claude Lévi-Strauss, *The Savage Mind* (Chicago: University of Chicago Press, 1966), p. 247; henceforth SM. See also "Jean Jacques Rousseau, Founder of the Sciences of Man," in *Structural Anthropology*, trans. Monique Layton (London: Allen Lane, 1973), vol. 2, p. 35; henceforth SA.

4. See Christopher Johnson, "Structuralism, Biology and the Linguistic Model," in Julian Wofreys et al., eds., *The French Connections of Jacques Derrida* (New York: SUNY Press, 1999)—henceforth FC—that considers the influence of structuralism and biology upon Lévi-Strauss's essay "Race and History." I thank Robert Bernasconi for this reference. See also Kamala Visweswaran, "An Idea of Race, a Philosophy of Hierarchy: Louis Dumont's *Homo Hierarchicus*," in Robert Bernasconi, ed., *Race: Blackwell Readings in Continental Philosophy* (London: Blackwell's, 2001), pp. 205–217.

5. Author's interview with Claude Lévi-Strauss, December 9, 1997; Paris. See also CLS 61, 148–150.

6. Lévi-Strauss was characteristically oblique in referring to the racism of World War II in later interviews (see CLS 155–157 and Annie Cohen-Solal, "'Claude L. Strauss' in the United States," *Partisan Review* 2 [Spring 2000]: 252–260). In *Tristes Tropiques*, Lévi-Strauss spoke matter-of-factly about the "race laws" that prevented him from teaching in the Lycée and disdainfully of an "over-rated" philosophy teacher named Gustave Rodrigues, "who committed suicide in 1940 when the Germans entered Paris" (trans. John and Doreen Weightman [London: Jonathan Cape, 1973], p. 51; henceforth TT). His most moving pronouncements on his experiences with the Vichy regime are found in the opening pages of *Tristes Tropiques*. When he sought passage from France to New York in 1941, the official in charge was reluctant to take on board a former first-class passenger, whom he still regarded as an ambassador of French culture. Lévi-Strauss observed dryly that the official's scruples might have been misplaced, as he had spent the previous two years traveling in cattle trucks and sleeping in sheep folds; in short, "potential fodder for the concentration camp" (TT 24). Of the war itself, and the politics of the Vichy regime, Lévi-Strauss would say (as did many of his compatriots) that France had experienced a *"drôle de guerre,"* but that "no superlative could do justice to the war as it had been experienced by the officers stationed in Martinique" (TT 27). He concluded, "It was rather as if the Vichy Authorities, in allowing us to leave for Martinique, had sent them a cargo of scapegoats on whom these gentlemen could relieve their feelings" (TT 28).

7. For a slightly different assessment of Lévi-Strauss's relationship to the Annales school, see H. Stuart Hughes, "Structure and Society," in E. Nelson Hayes and Tanya Hayes, eds., *Claude Lévi-Strauss: The Anthropologist as Hero* (Cambridge, Mass.: MIT Press, 1970), pp. 41–42. Lévi-Strauss also fell in and out with various members of the Annales school at different points in time. See CLS 62–64, 120–123.

8. In the final chapter of *The Savage Mind,* "History and Dialectic," Lévi-Strauss argues, "I regard Anthropology as the principle of all research, while for Sartre it raises a problem in the shape of a constraint to overcome or a resistance to reduce.

And indeed, what can one make of people 'without history' when one has defined man in terms of dialectic, and dialectic in terms of history? Sometimes Sartre seems tempted to distinguish two dialectics: the true one which is supposed to be that of historical societies, and a repetitive, short-term dialectic which he grants the so-called primitive societies whist at the same time placing it very near biology" (SM 248).

9. See "History and Anthropology," SA 23. See also Lévi-Strauss's remarks in "The Scope of Anthropology": "The History of historians does not need defending, but it is no attack on it either to say (as Braudel admits) that next to a short-scale time span there exists a long-scale time-span; that some facts arise from a statistical and irreversible time and others from a mechanical and reversible one; and that the idea of a structural history contains nothing which could shock the historian" (SA 16).

10. The essay was reprinted in English as part of a UNESCO collection called *Race and Science* (New York: Columbia University Press, 1961). Henceforth RH.

11. See Marcel Henaff, *Claude Lévi-Strauss and the Making of Structural Anthropology* (Minneapolis: University of Minnesota Press, 1998), p. 254.

12. See Kamala Visweswaran, "Race and the Culture of Anthropology," *American Anthropologist* 100, no. 1 (1995): 70–83. Henceforth RCA.

13. " . . . no great weight can be attributed to the earlier rise of civilization in the Old World, which is satisfactorily explained as a chance. In short, historical events appear to have been much more potent in leading races to civilization than their faculty, and it follows that achievements of races do not warrant us to assume that one race is more highly gifted than another." In George Stocking, ed., *A Franz Boas Reader* (Chicago: University of Chicago Press, 1974), pp. 226–227.

14. See G. Charbonnier, "Clocks and Steam-Engines," in *Conversations with Claude Lévi-Strauss* (London: Jonathan Cape, 1969 [1961]), p. 33: "I would say that in comparison with our own great society, with all the great modern societies, the societies studied by the anthropologist are in a sense 'cold' societies rather than 'hot' societies, or like clocks in relation to steam engines. They are societies which create the minimum of that disorder which the physicists call 'entropy,' and they tend to remain indefinitely in their initial state, and this explains why they appear to us as static societies with no history."

15. His essay "The Anthropologist and the Human Condition," in VA, explicitly develops this theme.

16. See UNESCO May Press Reviews, 1971. COM/OPI/PD.5-page 6, Item 30, "Colloquium on Race at UNESCO." I thank Jens Boel, chief of the UNESCO Archives for help in locating this reference.

17. "The inadequacy of the traditional answers may explain why the ideological struggle against racism has proved ineffective in practice. Nothing indicates that racial prejudices are declining; and after brief periods of local calm, everything points to their resurfacing elsewhere with greater intensity. Hence the need felt by UNESCO periodically to resume a struggle whose outcome appears uncertain at best" (VA 19).

18. Johnson (FC 137, 139, 147) argues that "Race and History" articulates an implicitly biological model. I think that this is only clear in "Race and Culture" and is

consistent with the public appearances that Lévi-Strauss made with structuralist-minded biologists like François Jacob in 1968 and 1972. On the UNESCO *Statements on Race,* see RCA.

19. Lévi-Strauss himself saw the analogy between the study of race and the study of culture to be purely a formal one. Author's interview Sept. 12, 1997.

20. Author's interview with Lévi-Strauss Sept. 12, 1997.

21. For a somewhat divergent reading of Rousseau's influence upon Lévi-Strauss, see Thomas Shalvey, "Rousseau and Lévi-Strauss," in *Claude Lévi-Strauss, Social Psychotherapy and the Collective Unconscious* (Chicago: University of Chicago Press, 1966), pp. 58–81.

22. Foucault's critique of humanism seems to have been most fully elaborated in his *Les Mots et Les Choses* (1966), published in English as *The Order of Things* in 1973. However, the seeds of his critique of humanism are arguably also found in his published dissertation of 1954, "Maladie Mentale et Psychologie," the basis of what would become "Histoire de la Folie" or *Madness and Civilization: A History of Insanity in an Age of Reason,* published in 1961. I thank Bettina Bergo for these references.

23. Reprinted as the first section to the essay, "Answers to Some Investigations" (SA 271–274).

24. The first English translation by John Russell for Criterion Press (1961) was actually titled *A World on the Wane.*

25. I thank Jeff Lustig for this point.

Fourteen

All Power to the People!

Hannah Arendt's Theory of
Communicative Power in a
Racialized Democracy

Joy James

Introduction: The (Color-)Blind Search for Power

Hannah Arendt's innovative, liberal political thought provides insights into the complexities and contradictions of the world's premier democracy, its racialized practices and policies, and its mythologized status. Derived from personal experience as well as political practice and theory, Arendt's theory of power posits that it is neither force, domination, nor oppression; power is collective action for a common ideal rooted in freedom. A German Jew who survived Nazi genocidal campaigns during World War II, Arendt fought in the French Resistance and saw her mentors and friends Karl Jaspers and Martin Heidegger come to their own realizations about power, community, and violence: Jaspers was persecuted by the Nazis; Heidegger became one. Her adopted country, the United States, offered Arendt the space and platform to advocate for the return of a mythologized democracy, the Athenian *polis*, in order to valorize and solidify American democracy (a bourgeois democracy, one which functions as empire). Yet, this revival reifying rigidly distinct spheres of governance/domination fails to include a sustained critique of institutional racism and racialized exclusion and domination in her host nation.

Arendt's theory of power as communication rather than domination is based on the division of space into the non- or pre-political private realm and the political public realm.[1] Such a division engenders power as communication, according to Arendt, for the private realm "frees" inhabitants of the public realm from labor and work, biological and material necessity. She appears not to see that her idealized political state, the Aristotelian *polis*, subverted and undermined power and politics by oppressing the household. With the *polis* of ancient Greece as her model for democratic power, Arendt ignores

249

the fact that enslavement and economic exploitation and forced relegation to the "powerless" private realm enabled an Athenian elite (of propertied males) to practice democracy. Subjugation constructed a restrictive public space dedicated to the ideal of power as communication, reason, and persuasion, a site advocating freedom but built on oppression. The practice of power as communication by an elite citizenry predicated on the enslavement and exploitation of the majority (women, children, men) is the historical reality of the United States. This historical legacy (of genocide, slavery, and imperialism) has profound implications for political power, freedom, and community. Although Arendt shares with the Black Panther Party, a black anti-racist Marxist militant organization created in 1966, a populist mandate—all power should reside with the people—she is much more restrictive about who constitutes "the people."[2]

Binary opposition to designate superiority/inferiority and normalcy/deviancy as biologically inscribed is common in a racialized democracy; political speech routinely attributes criminality, deviancy, corruption, and pathology to "the nonwhite" or non-European. The ultimate political binary is that of the civilized/savage. In binary opposition, anti-black racism has played a critical historical role in rationalizing economic, social, and political hierarchies. Arendt's binary divisions, adopted from the *polis*, mask racism (which was not the foundation of slavery in ancient Greece) by concealing the private realm of domestic service, field labor, and child-rearing as the designated work for racialized peoples (and women). Reproducing the split between the public and private realms as necessary for the manifestation of true power, her uncritical embrace of polarities and hierarchies promotes elitism based on subordination. With racism as such a persistent and pervasive feature of American democracy, polarities and hierarchies become "naturalized." The dualism to which she subscribes dismisses the political significance of the "private realm" and the bodies contained and policed there, allowing the personified public body to appear as both representative and universal (with little mention of the homogeneity of its appearance—propertied males racialized as white). The political person—naturalized and universalized as affluent, masculine European (or some approximation thereof)—shapes Arendt's color- and gender-blind analyses. Her model is premised on an inequality marked by assumptions of biologically determined superiority/inferiority; this model impedes critiques of white supremacy, patriarchy, (gender and) racial domination, and state violence.[3]

Over centuries, dominance, violence, and terror have become institutionalized in the United States within households, slave quarters, and labor fields and camps, and are manifested most extremely within prisons. Thus, legislation as well as domestic and foreign policies and practices have created political spheres (both public and private) in which generalized racial attitudes and beliefs signify who is worthy of self-rule and who is subject to be ruled—that is, who has the right to economic and political determination and who is less than truly "human."

State violence (through the laws, the police, the military) practiced in the "private" realm shapes the practice and sites of power in the public realm but also incites communicative power and democratic action among those resisting oppression and exclusion from governing. The practice of voting disenfranchisement of African Americans through bureaucracy (poll tax), violence (imprisonment), and terror (lynching and/or police brutality) also suggests that the private realm was never truly understood in the United States as a site void of the practice of politics. Hence, political and state interventions in the private realm (really realms, given the multiple sites of political exile—household, factory, field, prison—which overlap and reside within each other) by governing elites to quell rebellions, from Nat Turner to the Black Panther Party, were not merely law-enforcement responses to criminality. Although the state represented them as such to claim that it has/had no political trials, political prisoners, or political executions,[4] these were political maneuvers to reinforce and segregate political space and governance. Native and African Americans have historically been immersed in distinctions between domination and democratic power for freedom and community (see the slave narratives of abolitionist Frederick Douglass, or the memoirs of anti-lynching crusader Ida B. Wells). Collective responses to enslavement, segregation, and imprisonment were infused by discussions and practices concerning violence, power, and liberation during the time of Arendt's writings on civil disobedience, violence, and revolution in the 1960s. The Deacons for Defense and Justice, based in North Carolina, won their battles with the Ku Klux Klan but lost to the U.S. government and so were dispersed and exiled; the Black Panther Party, initially organized as the Black Panther Party for Self-Defense in Oakland, California, had to confront police brutality against and police executions of blacks, only to be decimated within four years by an FBI counterintelligence program and its own internal contradictions. Add to this the writings of prison intellectual and former Black Panther field marshal George Jackson, author of *Soledad Brother* and *Blood in My Eye*,[5] whose killing by California prison guards in 1971 sparked New York's Attica Prison uprising weeks later (Attica became the site of one of the bloodiest state repressions to destroy the exercise of communicative power, initiated by force but elevated to negotiations for better food, health care, and less guard brutality against men in captivity). Any of these events, seriously studied for the exercise and contradictions of power and violence, could have profoundly altered Arendt's allegiance to the state and her belief in its rehabilitation. None of these events merited much attention or consideration from her, perhaps because these political agents had already been delegated pre-political roles, and their places of power and communicative interaction—rural Southern black communities, impoverished urban black neighborhoods, and prisons whose populations would become increasingly racially determined—had been designated as non-political sites.

Action within the private realm to challenge expressions of public power and domination exercised (by law and police) in the public realm to manage or control the private realm and its dissent are, in the United States, phenomena heavily shaped by race and repression. Ignoring the historical and contemporary specificities of this democracy and its racialized state violence and dominance allows Arendt to construct a theory of power that floats freely above a foundation mired in racially fashioned domination. A clearer vision requires that one review what Arendt's political thought omits: major trajectories shaping the understanding and practice of power in the United States.

During the Civil War, which initially was not fought to abolish slavery, the Thirteenth Amendment to the U.S. Constitution (the Emancipation Proclamation) codified rather than ended slavery, proclaiming it legal for those duly convicted of a crime. Following the Civil War, when private ownership of humans was banned, the Thirteenth Amendment's legalization of slavery for those convicted of crimes fueled the convict lease system—that is, the state owned humans. Under this joint venture between the state and private industry, African Americans were criminalized (crimes included economic competition with whites and exercising political power, along with theft or harm to people) and worked to death at faster rates than they had been under slavery.[6] The prison replaced the plantation, and public ownership of racialized humans meant a renewal supply of labor through police sweeps. Over the decades, Slave Codes became Black Codes and, later, the basis for Jim Crow segregation, refining binary divisions and the dichotomy between dominance and power embedded in a racial state. Government policies/legislation and social practices worked to politically and economically disenfranchise a racialized domestic realm (populated by Native, African, and Latin Americans) and a racialized foreign realm qua domestic realm populated by indigenous peoples, Africans, Latin Americans, and Asians (hence the appearance of a metaparadigm in which U.S. foreign and domestic policies seem to mirror each other in terms of the treatment of the non-European as colonized/dependent Other).

Diminished power became naturalized as part of the American political landscape because of the foundation upon which the (Athenian *polis*) American democracy was built: self-governance predicated on the rule of other humans (constructed as inherently inferior). Democratic power, which extended to collective control of the state, was never intended for all of the people. Responding to the trajectory of racism that stems from slavery through the convict prison lease system through Jim Crow back into the prison industrial complex, despite desegregation legislation and integrationist policies, suggests that the militant assertion "All Power to the People!"—for the Panthers, governing power to the racialized mass, the "lumpen," workers, laborers, the unemployed, and the criminally employed—sought to destroy that trajectory.

Arendt's liberalism, which appears not to have considered that the Athenian *polis* and its progeny might in fact be Trojan horses, rejected such anti-racist radicalism. Challenging the fundamental flaw of democracy, as we know it, anti-racist radicals (among whom the Panthers of the late 1960s and early 1970s came to epitomize the uncompromised defiance of the racially determined "household" or private realm) demanded liberation through revolutionary change in U.S. domestic and foreign policies.

This struggle to expand and realize communicative power and construct a nonracial democracy is as old as the nation-state. Arendt's personal observations of racism in the United States during the 1950s and 1960s, the decades of the Southern civil-rights movement and the rise of black power movements, centered on Jim Crow segregation and racist terror. The civil-rights movements of the 1950s and 1960s transformed American politics and inspired mobilization among and between various sectors of the politically and socially disenfranchised; women, gays and lesbians, people with disabilities, Chicanos/Latinos, Native Americans formed movements, and the poor, immigrants, and the criminalized organized. Arendt's pronouncements about the civil-rights movement were "ambivalent" at best. Criticizing desegregation activism in the battles for school integration in Little Rock, Arkansas, while condemning racism in general, she failed to discern a racial phenomenon other than social racism, which she decried. However, disenfranchisement on a continuum, hidden behind "private" sentiments of racial ideology and preference, creates a facade of universal democracy. This facade obscures racial dominance and state violence as political acts against the political power of the private realm. Racism is political, not merely social; as a political phenomenon in the United States, it was never fully analyzed by Arendt.

Arendt's lack of attention to the phenomenon of racial ruling within the United States reflects her relegation of the racialized and criminalized to the outer realms. Understanding the limitations to the manifestation of power valorized by Arendt requires an understanding of the racial dominance and violence embedded within U.S. democracy. It is critical to examine the political implications of the racist nature of policing and incarceration. Arendt warned about the military-industrial complex of her time,[7] but given her insufficient attention to racial dominance, she could not anticipate the continuance of slavery through the prison-industrial complex. Prison, the most excluded realm within the private sphere, is also a space where power and domination appear in their most extreme forms.

In 2000, at the turn of the new century, two million people, some 70 percent of them African, Latino/Chicano, Native American, or Asian American, lived behind bars in U.S. prisons, jails, and detention centers, three times the number documented twenty years earlier. Although some might argue that this nether realm is populated by those who "chose" it by demonstrating their incapacity for "human togetherness" (Arendt's term discussed below), surely we must note the "coincidence" that the construction of a population unfit for self-governance and communicative power remains racially determined. Although they comprise only 12.5 percent of the U.S. general population, African Americans comprise 50 percent of the U S. prison population. In a democracy in which nearly one in every twenty-five adults goes to jail each year, one in three black males is tied to the criminal-justice system (and, in states which strip the franchise from felons, they potentially cannot vote). What would it mean for a democracy to *create* a private realm of bodies to be ruled, and to racially mark them? Consider the following: One is eight times more likely to be sentenced to prison if one is black than if one is white for a similar offense. Defendants receive multiple times the sentencing for use or sale of crack—considered a black urban drug—as opposed to powder cocaine—considered a white suburban indulgence. Although the majority of drug (cocaine) offenders are whites, most defendants sentenced to prison for drug use and sale are African Americans and Latinos; although the proceeds from the "drug war" are mostly concentrated in European and European American banks and finance, the wars against drugs, both domestic and foreign, target the non-European (American). Logically, one might deduct that such wars function not merely on the level of criminal justice or law enforcement but on the level of political inclusion or exclusion.[8] By racially fashioning the "criminal" or "public enemy," one determines the parameters of political community and communicative power and who is capable or worthy of it. Racial profiling and policing ranges from the infraction "DWB" (driving while black or brown) and "voting while black or brown" in the 2000 presidential election to xenophobia and anti–Muslim/Arab racist assaults following the September 11, 2001, attacks on the World Trade Center and the Pentagon. The idealized *polis* or democratic state is the ultimate gated community as the sequestered space of democratic power.

The final exclusion from political community is, of course, through death. State executions are racially determined in part (50 percent of those now on death row are people of color, from minority groups representing only 20 percent of the U.S. population).[9] From 1977 to 1986, 90 percent of prisoners executed were convicted of killing whites, although the number of black victims was approximately equal; in fact, one is four times more likely to be sentenced to death for being convicted of killing a white person than of killing a black person.[10] (Ironically, there appears to be a diminishment of the "3/5 human being" status which the U.S. Constitution granted to enslaved blacks.)

It is not that Arendt ignored racism. While condemning it, she tended either to generalize or to selectively examine it. Her examinations, which include torture and economic profiteering from racism, exempt the United States, as in her discussion of imperialism and totalitarian terror. For example, she sees totalitarian terror as a twentieth-century phenomenon and as relatively new in political history. Her assertion that totalitarian terror is a relatively new form of government oppression is ill-informed. Genocide is not unique to the twentieth century, assuming that one would agree that genocide is a byproduct of totalitarian terror. As a form of state racial terror, it is a relatively stable feature in history through European and American imperialism. Arendt notes in "Imperialism," in *The Origins of Totalitarianism,* the late-nineteenth-century genocide of twenty million Congolese by the Belgian government. The genocide of the Native populations of the Americas by Europeans and Americans also predates the twentieth century and reflects the roots of twentieth-century totalitarianism and terror in eighteenth- and nineteenth-century imperialism and genocide.[11] In "On Violence," Arendt suggests that the legacy of Europe's imperial, racial wars and conquests offers a cautionary tale: "The much-feared boomerang effect of the 'government of subject races'. . . on the home government during the imperialist era meant that rule by violence in faraway lands would end by affecting the government of England, that the last 'subject race' would be the English themselves" (OV 153).[12] What transpires when the new "race" (as socially constructed) is a hybrid construction of and for the propertied "American"—an American whose racially influenced notions of dominance are masked in the guise of economic or national(ist) superiority or "law-abiding" conformity and citizenry?

Arendt's discussions of anti-Semitism create a somewhat abstract totalitarian terror as she fails to explore fully how Nazi terrorism was based upon racist ideology (reportedly, both Nazis and Afrikaners, creators of apartheid in southern Africa, cited U.S. development of reservations to imprison, impoverish, and starve Native Americans as a model to emulate). Racism transforms subjects into either rulers or the ruled. Racism is a fundamental component of terror, and so of violence. Hence, colonized peoples, Native Americans and African-Americans, have disproportionately been the targets of excessive violence and terror emanating from the state and its racialized (white) majority. With racial violence and exclusion, the reduction of (human) subjects to (animal) objects transforms repression into "work" much like politics is transformed into making and work.[13]

Arendt viewed the risks we take in neglecting communicative power. We can appreciate her arguments for power and against domination, while noting that being "color-blind" or closed to an analysis of U.S. racial ruling renders aspects of her thought overly abstract and indifferent to racial control.

Communicative Power

Arendt argues that power is communal rather than coercive. It cannot be exercised over someone, it can only be practiced with others. Dependent upon community, it is a collective enterprise, one rooted in non-coercive relationships for the common good. Power as community and relationship becomes the goal or end rather than the means for some other objective. Arendt does not discount the role that specific goals or objectives play in inspiring political associations; rather, she maintains that transcending all specific or limited ends is the ideal.

Arendt's theory of political power directly contrasts with the prevailing notion of power as control posited by Max Weber.[14] For her, the contemporary "human condition" is one of disappearing political power, person, and space; it is one of disappearing humanity as words and deeds become characterized by violence and domination rather than by reason and persuasion. Confusion about the "nature" of power stems from "a firm conviction that the most crucial political issue is, and always has been, the question of who rules whom?" She continues, "It is only after one ceases to reduce public affairs to the business of dominion that the original data concerning human affairs appear, or, rather, reappear, in their authentic diversity."[15] The current confusion, argues Arendt, stems from Western political philosophers who have historically misunderstood their enterprise by adhering too rigidly to the "Platonic approach." That is, they overemphasized the search for ideal forms and eternal truths, confused politics with ruling (perhaps opportunistically to ensure the "peace" needed for contemplation), and located contemplation apart from the world of action and experience. What many have failed to comprehend, she argues, is that political community exists where "the revelatory quality of speech and action comes to the fore where people are with others and neither for nor against them—that is, in sheer human togetherness."[16]

In place of the ancient Greek vocabulary of ruling, European nation-state sovereignty, the Hebrew-Christian patriarchal tradition of obedience to law, and John Stuart Mill's psychology of the will to dominate,[17] Arendt offers another interpretation of politics and power: "The Athenian city-state . . . had in mind a concept of power and law whose essence did not rely on the command-obedience relationship and which did not identify power and rule or law and command. It was to these examples that the men of the eighteenth-century revolutions turned when they ransacked the archives of antiquity and constituted a form of government, a republic, where the rule of law, resting on the power of the people, would put an end to the rule of man over man, which they thought was a 'government fit for slaves'" (OV 139). Yet, the eighteenth-century American revolution worked to consolidate the economic power of the ruling elite landowners; the Founders' intent was to restrict possibilities for economic democracy and for increasing the size of the political electorate. For Arendt, power is found in citizens' non-coerced consent. In a representative government the people are supposed to rule those who govern them. Without consent there is neither power nor legitimate government.

Plurality expressed in the need and desire for communication and collective action characterizes both a democratic nation and the human condition, according to Arendt. Plurality, like friendship, exists only between peers; without equality, commands replace communication; then there is neither common ground for communication nor anything (i.e., diversity and uniqueness) to communicate. Plurality embodies both commonality and diversity; for Arendt, political equality is contingent upon admittance into the political peerage or community. Those excluded are prevented from practicing this power. The basis for racially determined exclusion logically should be a central issue in this theory of politics and power in which arbitrary exclusion based only upon the ability to exclude contradicts power as communication; in addition, exclusion based on a "universal truth" of inferiority and inclusion based on "superiority" contradicts *Existenz* philosophy.

Arendt cites a number of obstacles (which, given the construction of the public realm, preclude any mention of racism, sexism, or impoverishment) that diminish human togetherness and power. This diminution occurs when politics is misperceived as either making (instrumentality) or being similar to warfare; when tyranny curtails power; when the "myth of the strong man" distorts power's communal nature; and when violence supercedes communicative action: "Whenever human togetherness is lost, as for instance in modern warfare, where men go into action and use means of violence in order to achieve certain objectives for their own side and against the enemy. . . . In these instances . . . speech becomes indeed 'mere talk,' simply one more means toward the end, whether it serves to deceive the enemy or to dazzle everybody with propaganda. . . . In these instances action has lost the quality through which it transcends mere productive activity" (HC 180).

Tyranny and Violence

Tyranny is the antithesis of democracy. The tyranny of a racialized democracy resides in its ability to use violence and domination much more freely against marginalized sectors, whether Native Americans on reservations or Palestinians in occupied territories. It is not fully clear how Arendt would distinguish between state violence and state terror in connection to U.S. destabilization of democratic movements within its borders and of "Third World" governments.[18] Yet, U.S. politics revolve around coeval manifestations of democracy and tyranny, of collective power expressed in its electoral bodies and dominance through violence or terror. For instance, tyranny within American democracy allowed the use of police terror to destabilize anti-racist dissent. Before his execution by the Chicago police department and the FBI in December 1969 in a COINTELPRO (counterintelligence program) operation,[19] twenty-one-year-old Black Panther leader Fred Hampton, in call and response, rallied organizers with the familiar Panther chant: "All Power to the People! Brown Power to Brown People, Red Power to Red People, White Power to White People, Black Power to Black People."[20]

Arendt ignored the promise and pitfalls of radical antiracist organizations such as the Black Panthers, the American Indian Movement, the Young Lords, the Brown Berets, and the Independentistas (all groups argued for the right of self-defense from racial and state violence, and some of their members bore arms). She preferred to lump them generically into a category of rebellious minorities, unsuited and perhaps, at least temporarily, unqualified for the burden of full citizenship in this democratic state. The rebels who truly interested her were the white, middle-class, disaffected university and college students protesting the Vietnam War (her students at the New School in New York City, the heirs apparent to her romanticized *polis*). In "On Revolution," Arendt endorses physical resistance to oppression in the form of revolution. Yet, that resistance is never extended to radical antiracist formations, so when antiracists withdrew their consent because the government lost its legitimacy, she possessed no framework to analyze the ensuing battle between the state and its subject racialized minorities. She argues that people choose violence over action because they idealize violence: the "implications of violence inherent in all interpretations of the realm of human affairs as a sphere of making" produced a glorification of violence as the only means for "making" political change. Criticizing middle-class white students for romanticizing violence, Arendt denounces the "strong Marxist rhetoric of the New Left [which] coincides with the steady growth of the entirely non-Marxian conviction, proclaimed by Mao Tse-tung, that 'Power grows out of the barrel of a gun'" (OV 113). (The Panthers sold Mao's "Little Red Book" to finance the purchase of guns for their patrols to monitor racist and brutal police in Oakland; in fact, working-class Black Panthers sold the book, at a considerable mark-up, to middle-class white students at UC Berkeley.)

The outcome of all political action, because it embodies freedom, is never completely predictable; consequently, it is unlike violence as a tool or technique. Politics is characterized by freedom rather than control; so, too, is violence, with its unpredictability. There is no certainty of the intended outcome, writes Arendt, although violence is generally employed to ensure intended results, it remains arbitrary and uncontrollable.

There are instances when violence or war is the only logical or rational choice; yet it is illogical and irrational to romanticize violence, using it indiscriminately, and to institutionalize it within the political community by confusing or equating it with power. (This, of course, was one of the failings of the Panthers—their tragic and destructive responses to violent state repression by the FBI's COINTELPRO.) Arendt elaborates:

> Violence, being instrumental by nature, is rational to the extent that it is effective in reaching the end that must justify it. And since when we act we never know with any certainty the eventual consequences of what we are doing, violence can remain rational only if it pursues short-term goals. Violence does not promote causes, neither history, nor revolution, neither progress nor reaction; but it can serve to dramatize grievances and bring them to public attention. As Conor Cruise O'Brien (in a debate on the legitimacy of violence in the Theatre of Ideas) once remarked, quoting William O'Brien, the nineteenth-century Irish agrarian and nationalist agitator: Sometimes "violence is the only way of ensuring a hearing for moderation." To ask the impossible in order to obtain the

possible is not always counterproductive. And indeed, violence, contrary to what its prophets try to tell us, is more the weapon of reform than of revolution. (OV 176)

Arendt notes that if "goals are not achieved rapidly, the result will be not merely defeat but the introduction of the practice of violence into the whole body politic. Action is irreversible, and a return to the *status quo* in case of defeat is always unlikely" (OV 177). According to Arendt, student radicals did not recognize that the practice of violence engenders a more violent world. She writes that student rebels' idealization of violence as the cornerstone of change is derived from a faulty interpretation that views history as "a continuous chronological process, whose progress, moreover, is inevitable, violence in the shape of war and revolution may appear to constitute the only possible interruption" (OV 132). Presenting an intellectualized abstraction of why people resort to violence for change, she contradicts her quotation of O'Brien that "sometimes violence is the only way of ensuring a hearing for moderation." Of course, what must follow to ensure not just a more violent world is action: "It is the function, however, of all action, as distinguished from mere behavior, to interrupt what otherwise would have proceeded automatically and therefore predictably" (OV 132–133). But if one does not consider the Other to be human or civilized, there can be no negotiations, only domination, and the prospect of more violence and terror erupting in response to violence and terror (both past and potential, both real and imagined).

Tyrants who aspire to power as control and politics as ruling may or may not use force; non-violent tyrants "if they know their business may well be 'kindly and mild' in everything" (HC 221). Whether violent or nonviolent, tyranny encourages citizens to preoccupy themselves with manufacturing and the acquisition of property, positions, or titles: All tyrants "have in common the banishment of the citizens from the public realm and the insistence that they mind their private business while only 'the ruler should attend to public affairs'" (HC 221).[21] Part of what is to be acquired and maintained is the existential wealth of racial superiority.

Addressing material needs or desires, as well as fears, tyranny "buys" one out of political freedom, power, and political community. (If corporate capitalism's and consumer culture's obsession with material wealth creates a citizenry more interested in status and money than in developing identity and realizing humanity through power, arguably capitalism undermines communicative power and political community and would be the focus of an extensive critique by Arendt.) States can combine violent and nonviolent methods to deter the development of democratic power, mingling persuasion and coercion.[22] For Arendt, the great danger of tyranny that combines power and violence (two distinct phenomena that can appear together) is not so much the brutal, physical oppression of the people as it is the loss of community and political efficacy of both citizenry and tyrant. Tyranny "prevents the development of power, not only in a particular segment of the public realm but in its entirety; it generates, in other words, impotence . . . " (HC 202). In addition to tyranny, Arendt was concerned with a greater evil—terror. Terror is the extreme manifestation of violence. Contrasting violence with terror, she states that she would not characterize violence as "evil" and so implicitly characterizes terror as such. For her, political terror is found only within totalitarianism—specifically, Nazism and Stalinism as described in *The Origins of Totalitarianism*. Terror magnifies all the destructive elements of violence and emerges when violence has destroyed every form of political action, power, and resistance. Its effectiveness depends upon the destruction of all community, upon the "social atomization" or alienation of the individual citizens who fear to speak or act collectively (OV 154–155).[23]

War technology accelerated the chain reaction or "snowball effect" of violence, according to Arendt. Violence, once initiated, is uncontrollable; nothing exemplifies this more than the image of nuclear war, which points not only to the uncontrollable nature of violence but to the finality of its destruction. Few have analyzed the phenomenon of violence, though many have concentrated on war and warfare, according to Arendt, and the neglect of the study of violence has much to do with the perception of violence as so ingrained in human affairs that violence itself became a "marginal phenomenon." "Anybody looking for some kind of sense in the records of the past was almost bound to see violence as a marginal phenomenon. Whether it is Clausewitz calling war 'the continuation of politics by other means' or Engels defining violence as the accelerator of economic development, the emphasis is on political or economic continuity, on the continuity of a process that remains determined by what preceded violent action" (OV 110–111). Arendt quotes Russian physicist Andrei Sakharov: "A thermonuclear war cannot be considered a continuation of politics by other means" for it entails universal suicide (OV 111).[24]

One World

For Arendt, international affairs provided the initial stage (she argues this because she discounts [domestic] violence in the private realm) for the appearance of violence and provided the space for its final appearance: "The chief reason warfare is still with us is neither a secret death wish of the human species, nor an irrepressible instinct of aggression, nor, finally and more plausibly, the serious economic and social dangers inherent in disarmament, but the simple fact that no substitute for this final arbiter in the international affairs has yet appeared on the political scene" (OV 107). She argues that Hobbes's statement that "Covenants, without the sword, are but words" is likely to remain true "so long as national independence, namely, freedom from foreign rule, and the sovereignty of the state, namely, the claim to unchecked and unlimited power in foreign affairs, are identified [as synonymous]" (OV 107). A nation may remain independent of any other nation without retaining its sovereignty, which Arendt defines as the refusal to defer to a higher authority (e.g., world community). Sovereignty and independence are not synonyms; the former fosters resistance to recognized arbiters.

Maintaining that the construction of power stems from communal practice rather than dominance, and that community signifies plurality, diversity, the many, her critique of nation-states' refusal to limit expansionism allows her to write that "sovereignty, the ideal of uncompromising self-sufficiency and mastership, is contradictory to the very condition of plurality . . . [no one] can be sovereign because not one . . . [but many] inhabit the earth" (HC 234). This plurality and power in fact manifest in activism to counter the state's refusal to allow it to be disciplined by international law and human rights conventions.

Since the United Nations and the World Court lack the "sword" to enforce their decisions, violence remains a "natural element" of international politics. The reduction of violence inherent in international affairs is possible, writes Arendt, only if individual nation-states acknowledge a higher authority than their own sovereignty. Echoing Karl Jaspers, she maintains that "nations must renounce sovereignty for the sake of a world federation." The fear of global destruction, she writes, produces an "intolerable position of global responsibility," one which Jaspers attempts to address with a concept of world citizenship that bases the solidarity of humanity on "mutual understanding and self-clarification on a global level."[25]

Arendt's appreciation of Immanuel Kant and Jaspers led her to advocate strongly world community and world citizenry: Humanity and power find their fullest expression in world community based on diversity, acceptance, and communication. Through its foreign policy, the United States extends the private realm, of the less than civilized, the subordinate, the politically unworthy, the non-peer, to the so-called Third World—the peoples of Africa, Asia, Latin America, and the Middle East. Not only to governments (many of which are not democratic or are democracies in name only) but to the disenfranchised confined to the private realms—the poor, women, imprisoned radicals are deemed politically unworthy for world citizenship.

Can democratic theorists afford to ignore the fact that the United States undermines institutions that sustain world community? Although the International Court of Justice and the United Nations were created in response to World War II, the United States declares itself to be bound by neither the International Court of Justice nor by proclamations of the United Nations such as the Universal Declaration of Human Rights.[26] In theory, human-rights protections exist for everyone in the United States under the International Covenant on Civil and Political Rights and the international convention's ban on racial discrimination, abuse, and torture. The United States continues to exempt itself from international human-rights obligations and place itself above the law; the government can weaken treaties it ratifies with reservations. The United States' withdrawal from the International Tribunal on War Crimes in May 2002, and from the earlier (September 2001) United Nations World Conference Against Racism and Xenophobia in South Africa, heralded its aloof position toward antiracist initiatives. It failed to sign on, as the European Union did, to a statement designating the slave trade as a "crime against humanity." Yet within days, the United States would condemn the September 11, 2001, terrorist attacks as "a crime against humanity," call upon Americans to relinquish voluntarily their political rights, and demand global solidarity in a world community united to isolate and "destroy"—a word of finality and eschatology—terrorism. War is pursued with diminishing democratic input in a military campaign initially named "Infinite Justice" and overseen by the Pentagon, the White House, and its new Cabinet-level post for the "Defense of Homeland Security."

The challenge of extending all power to all of the people requires a willingness to shoulder and share democratic responsibilities while rejecting promises of protection, comfort, and supremacy: "It is the obvious short-range advantages of tyranny, the advantages of stability, security, and productivity, that one should beware, if only because they pave the way to an inevitable loss of power, even though the actual disaster may occur in a relatively distant future" (HC 222). Finally, the very possibility of realizing "All Power to the People!"—not the police or ruling elites determining domestic and foreign policies but the mass resisting institutionalized force and violence from others and themselves—relies upon a democracy where the permeable boundaries between public and private, self-governance and subjugation, are neither reified nor romanticized. How, then, in a bourgeois democracy might "We the People" seeking to "form a more perfect union" share ideals and communicative power with the masses and the impoverished in whatever national and international realms we encounter each other?

Notes

1. See Robert Bernasconi, "The Invisibility of Racial Minorities in the Public Realm of Appearances," in K. Thompson and L. Embree, eds., *Phenomenology of the Political* (Dordrecht, Netherlands: Kluwer Academic Publishers, 2000), and "The Double Face of the Political and the Social: Hannah Arendt and America's Racial Divisions," *Research in Phenomenology* 26 (1996): 3–24.

2. See Charles Jones, ed., *The Black Panther Party [Reconsidered]* (Baltimore: Black Classic Press, 1998) for analyses of the Black Panthers.

3. For a discussion of "state violence," see Joy James, *Resisting State Violence: Radicalism, Gender and Race in U.S. Culture* (Minneapolis: University of Minnesota Press, 1996).

4. Amnesty International documents that approximately one hundred individuals are being held as political prisoners in the United States. The longest held, those

associated with the Black Panther Party, were incarcerated during Arendt's life-time. She appears to not have made mention of political prisoners and likely failed to study U.S. repression against anti-racism. See Kenneth O'Reilly, *Racial Matters: The FBI's Secret File on Black America, 1960–1972* (New York: Free Press, 1989). J. Edgar Hoover, long-time director of the FBI, initiated surveillance against Martin Luther King Jr. (and FBI agents sent King messages suggesting that he commit suicide before it was revealed that he was a "moral fraud" given his extramarital affairs) and designated the Black Panther Party the number-one threat to the internal security of the United States.

5. George Jackson, *Soledad Brother: The Prison Letters of George Jackson* (New York: Random House, 1970), and *Blood in My Eye* (Baltimore: Black Classic Press, 1970).

6. See Matthew Mancini, *One Dies, Get Another: Convict Leasing in the American South, 1866–1928* (Columbia: University of South Carolina Press, 1996); and Angela Y. Davis, "From the Convict Lease System to the Super-Max Prison," in Joy James, ed., *States of Confinement: Policing, Detention and Prisons* (New York: St. Martin's Press, 2002), pp. 60–74.

7. Arendt cites the rhetoric from the military, the government and the Pentagon, jargon which arose, she writes, when World War II was followed not by peace but by the "Military-Industrial-Labor Complex." Such jargon states, "The priority of war-making potential as the principal structuring force in society"; "economic systems, [as well as] political philosophies and corpora juris serve and extend the war system, not vice versa"; "war itself is the basic social system, within which other secondary modes of social organization conflict or conspire" (Hannah Arendt, "On Violence," in *Crises of the Republic* [New York: Harcourt, Brace, Jovanovich, 1969 (1972)], p. 111; henceforth OV).

8. Arendt rejects any analysis of gender domination and gender violence. However, it is important to note the status of women in the private realms. The last group of the private realm to be legally granted the vote in the United States, women, while a small percentage of the imprisoned, have seen their incarceration rates dramatically increase. The patriarchal punishments of the private realm, within the family, have been relocated to bureaucracy, where the state acts as surrogate father seeking paternal control. Most of the women incarcerated in the United States are nonviolent offenders convicted of economic crimes or drug use. The majority are mothers, poor, and women of color (black women receive longer jail time and higher fines than white women do for the same crimes). Within the concentric realms of the private realm, caged women find themselves subject to new forms of physical and sexual abuse, which in the international arena is defined as "torture."

9. Over 65 percent of juvenile offenders sentenced to death since the 1976 reinstitution of the death penalty have been either black or Latino; one of the few democratic nations to execute minors, the United States has executed more youths than has any other industrialized nation.

10. When the United States did not submit a 1995 report on its compliance with the Convention Against Torture, non-governmental organizations issued a report.

Morton Sklar, ed., *Torture in the United States: The Status of Compliance by the U.S. Government with the International Convention against Torture and Other Cruel, Inhuman or Degrading Treatment or Punishment* (Washington, D.C.: World Organization Against Torture, 1998).

The report notes the major areas of noncompliance in the United States: the death penalty, prison conditions and the treatment of refugee detainees; physical and sexual abuse of women in prisons; the return of refugees to situations of torture and persecution and their long-term detention under abusive conditions. Other violations include U.S. shelter for torturers who worked with the Central Intelligence Agency or were trained at the School of the Americas in Ft. Benning, Georgia; and arms sales that support torture in foreign countries.

11. Implications for this legacy in the twenty-first century require sustained and serious study. In an interview with B92, Belgrade radio, in September 2001, Noam Chomsky observed, "The horrendous terrorist attacks on Tuesday are something quite new in world affairs, not in their scale and character, but in the target. For the US, this is the first time since the War of 1812 that its national territory has been under attack, even threat. Its colonies have been attacked, but not the national territory itself. During these years the US virtually exterminated the indigenous population, conquered half of Mexico, intervened violently in the surrounding region, conquered Hawaii and the Philippines (killing hundreds of thousands of Filipinos), and in the past half century particularly, extended its resort to force throughout much of the world. The number of victims is colossal.

"For the first time, the guns have been directed the other way. The same is true, even more dramatically, of Europe. Europe has suffered murderous destruction, but from internal wars, meanwhile conquering much of the world with extreme brutality. It has not been under attack by its victims outside, with rare exceptions (the IRA [Irish Republican Army] in England, for example). It is therefore natural that NATO [North Atlantic Treaty Organization] should rally to the support of the US; hundreds of years of imperial violence have an enormous impact on the intellectual and moral culture."

12. OV 153. Arendt quotes Commager from "Can We Limit Presidential Power?" *The New Republic,* April 6, 1968.

13. For studies of the genocide of colonized people in the United States, see Peter Matthiessen, *In the Spirit of Crazy Horse* (New York: Viking, 1983), and Manning Marable, *How Capitalism Underdeveloped Black America* (Boston: South End Press, 1983).

14. Jurgen Habermas writes, "Max Weber defined power (Macht) as the possibility of forcing one's own will on the behavior of others. Arendt, on the contrary, understands power as the ability to agree upon a common course of action in unconstrained communication. Both represent power as a potency that is actualized in actions, but each takes a different model of action as a basis." Jurgen Habermas, "Hannah Arendt's Communication Concept of Power," *Journal of Social Research* 44, no. 1 (Spring 1977): 4.

Habermas maintains that *The Origins of Totalitarianism* and *On Revolution* are the basis for Arendt's theory of power; yet, he asserts, because both totalitarianism and revolution are aberrations in Western mass democracies they are insufficient bases for the construction of a theory which is to have broad application; therefore Arendt provides a weak foundation for a comprehensive theory of power as communication. Her theory of power, however, is found and developed in *The Human Condition* (1956), *The Life of the Mind* (1978), and *Lectures on Kant's Political Philosophy* (1983). Within these works she explicates her theory of power as community and relationship and community as the ultimate goal and precondition for all non-violent human interaction and loss of the true meaning and practice of power as communal.

15. OV 142–143. See also Hannah Arendt, "Reflections on Violence," *New York Review of Books,* Feb. 27, 1969.

16. Hannah Arendt, *The Human Condition* (Chicago: University of Chicago Press, 1958), p. 180; henceforth HC.

17. For John Stuart Mill, according to Arendt, obedience is the first lesson of civilization; this coexists with two contradictory desires or inclinations: one, to exercise power over others; two, to not have power exercised over oneself. Quoting from Mill's *Considerations on Representative Government* (1861, pp. 59, 65 [Arendt's citation]), Arendt counters, "If we could trust our own experiences in these matters, we should know that the instinct of submission, an ardent desire to obey and be ruled by some strong man, is at least as prominent in human psychology as the will to power, and, politically, perhaps more relevant. . . . Conversely, a strong disinclination to obey is often accompanied by an equally strong disinclination to dominate and command. Historically speaking, ancient institution of slave economy would be inexplicable on the grounds of Mill's psychology. Its express purpose was to liberate citizens from the burden of household affairs and to permit them to enter the public life of the community, where all were equals; if it were true that nothing is sweeter than to give commands and to rule others, the master would never have left his household" (OV 138–139).

18. See the writings of Noam Chomsky and Ward Churchill for descriptions of violence and terror in U.S. domestic and foreign policies.

19. The FBI's counterintelligence program (COINTELPRO) was initiated by then FBI director J. Edgar Hoover. Consisting of illegal actions ranging from break-ins to assassinations, it served to disrupt and destroy antiracist and anti-war movements inside the United States in the 1960s and early 1970s, exemplifying the government's opposition to human rights. In 1975, the Senate Select Committee to Study Governmental Operations with Respect to Intelligence Activities (the "Church Committee," named after Senator Frank Church [D–Idaho]) investigated COINTELPRO and publicly exposed the FBI's clandestine program. See Kenneth O'Reilly, *Racial Matters,* and Ward Churchill and Jim Vander Wall, *Agents of Repression: The FBI's Secret Wars against the Black Panther Party and the American Indian Movement* (Boston: South End Press, 1992). In the aftermath of September 11, political pundits have blamed the Church committee and its prohibitions of state malfeasance (assassination of heads of state) for the U.S. "weakness" that enabled terrorist attacks.

20. See the documentary *Eyes on the Prize: A Nation of Laws?* (Boston: Blackside, 1993), pp. 68–71 for a record of Hampton's electrifying persona and the FBI

counterintelligence program that led to the deaths of Hampton and Mark Clark, and eventually the deaths or imprisonment of other antiracist militants and revolutionaries. See also Philip Foner, ed., *The Black Panther Speaks* (New York: Da Capo Press, 1995).

21. Arendt quotes "Aristotle, *Athenian Constitution* XV.5" (Arendt's citation).

22. For discussions of the concepts of "conspicuous consumption" and "false needs," see, respectively, Thorstein Veblen, *Theory of the Leisure Class* (Boston: Houghton Mifflin, 1899), and Herbert Marcuse, *One Dimensional Man* (Boston: Beacon Press, 1964).

23. Atomization "is maintained and intensified through the ubiquity of the informer, who can be literally omnipresent because he no longer is merely a professional agent in the pay of the police but potentially every person one comes into contact with." Arendt maintains that the "decisive difference between totalitarian domination, based on terror, and tyrannies and dictatorships, established by violence, is that the former turns not only against its enemies but against its friends and supporters as well, being afraid of all power, even the power of its friends" (OV 154).

24. Prior to the disintegration of the Soviet Union, bipartisan authors of a 1988 Heritage Foundation report, *Discriminate Deterrence*, argued that a "winnable" nuclear war was an unmarketable concept. Although then-President Ronald Reagan marketed the image of an "evil empire," *Discriminate Deterrence* maintained that the "East/West" conflict must be de-emphasized to allow U.S. conflicts with the "Third World" to shape policy into the twenty-first century. The U.S. had intervened militarily in the "Third World" over thirty times since the end of World War II ("interventions" included invasions; funding of military juntas and coups, counterrevolutionaries, and death squads; and carpet bombings). Waged without formal declarations of war, post–World War II conflicts usually reflected U.S. counterrevolutionary ideology and government conflicts with (often Soviet-backed) liberation movements in Africa, Asia, Latin America, and the Caribbean. Such wars often targeted civilians as the United States reserved most of its funding for terror in "Third World" countries. *Discriminate Deterrence* states that to protect U.S. interests and allies in the Third World requires greater national consensus on both means and ends and fewer legislative restrictions. U.S. economic military assistance flowed to "Third World allies" routinely condemned in the international community for human-rights atrocities (such as death squads in El Salvador, genocide in Guatemala, occupations and dictatorships in the Middle East, contra terrorists in Nicaragua and Angola). "U.S. interests" funded combatants whose terror campaigns most often victimized women, children, and noncombatants in so-called soft targets—farming cooperatives, schools, daycare centers, and hospitals. That is, the private realm was the space for the implementation of foreign policy and the ruling of subjugated peoples/nations racialized by the West. See Joy James, *Resisting State Violence*.

25. Hannah Arendt, *Men in Dark Times* (New York: Harcourt, Brace & World, 1968), p. 83.

26. On December 10, 1948, the General Assembly of the United Nations adopted the Universal Declaration of Human Rights. Its thirty articles outline the major pre-

cepts for human rights and civil society while the preamble asserts that the inherent dignity, equality, and the "inalienable rights of all members of the human family are the foundation of freedom, justice and peace in the world. Drafted in response to the atrocities of a world war, the Declaration describes "the advent of a world in which human beings shall enjoy freedom of speech and belief and freedom from fear and want has been proclaimed as the highest aspiration of the common people." Democratic tyrannies can ostensibly promote "freedom from fear" by removing from society segments of its population (deviants, criminals, poor, blacks) deemed to be dangerous and destabilizing to individuals and the social collective.

Fifteen

Beyond *Black Orpheus*
Preliminary Thoughts on the Good of African Philosophy

Jason M. Wirth

Truth depends not only on who listens but on who speaks.
—Birago Diop

Colonial administrators are not paid to read Hegel.
—Jean-Paul Sartre

I

In 1981, Peter O. Bodunrin (of the University of Ibadan, Nigeria) argued, "Philosophy in Africa has for more than a decade now been dominated by the discussion of one compound question: Is there an African philosophy, and if there is, what is it? The first part of the question has generally been unhesitatingly answered in the affirmative. Dispute has been primarily over the second part of the question, as various specimens of African philosophy presented do not seem to pass muster."[1] If we accept Bodunrin's chronology, African philosophy's identity crisis is now over a quarter century old. Before then, perhaps many discourses vied for wisdom and some were eradicated or at least critically enervated by the colonizing force of certain specimens of purported Western wisdom (Christianity, the "White Man's Burden," "Science," "Progress," the "History of Spirit," "Corporate Profits," etc.). If there is perceived a need to philosophize such that there is some kind of contribution to philosophy that can be designated African philosophy, then there must be some sense, so the argument goes, of what constitutes the domain of philosophy such that the adjective "African" may or may not to some extent be appended to it. If specimens of African thinking are to be brought to the tribunal of philosophy, then what is needed is the most fundamental of critiques—that is, an articulation of the domain proper to the activity of philosophy itself. If one does not know what philosophy per se is, then how can one pass judgment on Africa's past and future contributions to it? The question as to the identity of an African philosophy has recently revealed itself to be more fundamentally an interrogation of philosophy's inaugural question: its evaluative demarcation of its own activity. In this paper, I will explore both

268

the centrality of this question to contemporary African philosophy and why this question emerged in this way. In doing so, I will insist that the question of the nature, or even the possibility, of an African philosophy emerges with reference to its inheritance of European modes of philosophical activity. I will attempt to explore the nature of this reference by situating African philosophy's quest for a sense of its own activity in relationship to Sartre's celebrated essay on Negritude, *Black Orpheus*.

Given the above problematic, it is not surprising that the opening words of Abiola Irele's introduction to the second edition of the classic by Paulin J. Hountondji (of the National University of Benin), *African Philosophy: Myth and Reality*, reflect on philosophy's unmatched capacity for self-interrogation. "Philosophy can be regarded as the most self-conscious of disciplines. It is the one discipline that involves by its very nature a constant process of reflection upon itself."[2] In the same vein, Henry Odera Oruka (of the University of Nairobi, Kenya), in a 1982 paper, "Sagacity in African Philosophy," claimed that "current African professional philosophy is predominantly a metaphilosophy. Its central theme is the question 'What is philosophy?' And a corollary of this question is 'What is African philosophy?' In actual practice this philosophy is a discussion of the claim to the effect that some given thoughts or beliefs qualify or do not qualify as philosophy. And so it becomes a philosophical analysis and interpretation of the general concept, 'philosophy.'"[3]

Testimony to the centrality of the question of philosophy's identity crisis at the heart of African philosophy's self-quest is provided in anthologies such as Tsenay Serequeberhan's *African Philosophy: The Essential Readings* (1991) and Emmanuel Chukwudi Eze's *Postcolonial African Philosophy: A Critical Reader* (1997). Many of the articles in these books struggle with this question, offering arguments running the gamut from a universal sense of philosophy replete with a subset of African philosophy to a disruption of the centrality of a shared notion of philosophy. One of the most noted defenders of a universal sense of philosophy is Hountondji. In *African Philosophy: Myth and Reality*, among other works, he quite persuasively enervates the ethnophilosophic and ethnographic myth that assumes that one can derive the philosophy of a people by recording their shared cultural practices and thoughts, because this assumes that they were ever, at any time, uniformly shared. It has to "account for an imaginary unanimity" (MR 62) and must assume "the fiction of a collective system of thought" (MR 56)[4] or what he called "the dogma of unanimism" (MR 62). On this point, Hountondji is in agreement with V. Y. Mudimbe when he distinguishes the "practice of philosophy" from the tacit operation of a *Weltanschauung*.[5] The latter may be of interest to a philosopher and it may reflect the vestiges of a philosophy, but it is different from the "intellectual practice of philosophy" which "works on" *Weltanschauungen* (IA 156). I would furthermore add that in many, if not all, philosophical traditions it would be difficult to argue that philosophers have always reflected their times rather than assumed a heretical relation to them. It is difficult to imagine a culture in which every citizen was a sage, or Brahmin, or enlightened in the ways of wisdom. Philosophical practice is an exceptional activity, engaged in the critical evaluation of a culture's perceived wisdoms.

After this critique of unanimism, however, Hountondji argues for African contributions to philosophy which, despite possible differences in content, would "refer back to the essential unity of a single discipline, of a single style of inquiry" (ER 112). Might not the very heresy of philosophy draw one to question the possibility of an essential disciplinary unity to philosophical inquiry? Or, perhaps more worrisome, does this not run the risk, as E. Wamba-Dia-Wamba (of the University of Dar Es Salaam) asks, that "African philosophy gives grounding to and systematizes the fundamental ideological insights of the political actors of neocolonial states" (ER 240)? After all, "the theory of resistance against imperialism is often expressed as antiphilosophy, a permanent critique of philosophy by the masses of African people who view philosophy as the theory justifying the oppressive hierarchization of the colonial state power" (ER 243).

Innocent Onyewuenyi offers another variation of the universality of philosophy in "Is there an African Philosophy?" He answers in the affirmative, claiming, "Philosophy is a universal experience. Every culture has its own worldview. . . . What is generally agreed about philosophy is that it seeks to establish order among the various phenomena of the surrounding world, and it traces their unity by reducing them to their simplest elements" (ER 37). That there have been many philosophers who have done this is no doubt the case, although it is certainly debatable that all philosophers would even consider this to be a valuable task, even though, as Onyewuenyi later claims, "No culture has *the* order or *the* last word" (ER 38). Bodunrin, for his part, concludes that a "department of philosophy in a university is one among many other academic departments in the university, but in order that the foundations of the discipline be well laid it is necessary that that the boundaries of it be clearly delimited" (ER 84). Clearly? Were this possible, might one not ask, more fundamentally, whether this would be desirable or valuable?

Following Serequeberhan's anthology, D. A. Masolo published *African Philosophy in Search of Identity* (1994),[6] a magisterial summary of the question that, once thought through, emerges as not just the question of an African philosophy in search of identity but of philosophy per se under such an analysis.[7] In what follows, I hope again to take up this perhaps most fundamental of all questions as it comes into focus under the lens of African philosophy's self-quest by asking about the *value* of a certain way of answering such a question. Whence emerges the demand that philosophy, indeed, thinking itself, orient itself to its own activity, and how valuable—that is, how *good*—is such a claim? As the Owl of Minerva takes stock of its travels, will it be able, when all is said and done, to recognize itself? If so, might this be at the expense of the *Good*?

II

Masolo began his text with the claim that the "birth of the debate on African philosophy is historically associated with two related happenings: Western discourse on Africa, and the African response to it" (AP 1). The first moment of the contest, the Western discourse on Africa—that is, the implicit and explicit colonization of Africa, its organization and formation within the European *episteme*—is already a fact. Despite the inevitability of slippage and distortion, the transparency within which one might be authorized to speak in the name of the truth of the cultural elements that comprise the good life has already been established. In *The Invention of Africa,* Mudimbe argued that "the explorer, the soldier, and the missionary," the three expansionist modalities of Westernization, "all implied the same purpose: the conversion of African minds and space" (IA 48). Equipped with the "authority the truth," colonization absorbed most of Africa, its other, into its discursive formation, a "fulfillment of the power of Western discourses on human varieties" (IA 16). Even thinkers of the order of Hegel (following a Eurocentric and racist tradition that includes Hume and Kant) claimed that Africa "is no historical part of the world; it has no movement or development to exhibit. Historical movements in it—that is in its northern part—belong to the Asiatic or European world."[8] With such a profound obstruction to the recognition of its cultural history, the question of an African philosophy cannot ignore the catastrophe of its new history: the lingering, sometimes traumatic memory of colonization. Even the very idea of an African philosophy already implies the idea of an Africa—of something held together by an idea that we designate Africa—and this, as Mudimbe, as well as Kwame Anthony Appiah, has argued, was a colonial idea.[9]

Hence, the second moment of the debate, "the African response to it," already assumes a decolonizing imperative and the milieu of the colonial memory. Given that the stage had already been set by a colonizing machinery that shaped the colonized into an Other (a non-European), Kipling's "half devil, half child" to be reformed, converted (Christianized), or more straightforwardly exploited, the question of an African philosophy assumes—one could even say, inherits—a relationship between these two contesting moments.

How might one best characterize the contact between these two contesting moments?

1. Does one assume that philosophy is the exemplary guise of rationality and thank the colonizers for having discharged their burden to the half devils and half children? This would assume that philosophy already understands its activity as essentially logical and hence can divide cultures into mature (logical) and immature (illogical). Furthermore, and more importantly, is logic, the obstinacy of the Same, necessarily the precondition of the Good, of what is properly philosophical in a philosophical discourse?

2. Does one attempt to show that Africa always was rational or at least capable of rationality? Does one say then, as C. A. Diop (of Senegal) forcefully argues in *The African Origin of Civilization*,[10] that Egypt, and hence Africa, was the real cradle of the West? This may historically be the case, and it is no doubt a rather stark reminder of racist ideological commitments that such things are ignored, but again does that mean that those cultures, albeit certainly capable of logic, that did not value logic did not consequently value the good of philosophy? Does one have conferences on one of Kant's teachers, the Ghanaian rationalist Anton-Wilhelm Amo, who studied in Holland and who later, following Leibniz, defended in 1734 a treatise on the extra-cognitive status of perception?[11] While this is exciting work, and while it may at last bring back into focus the critical importance of Africa in general and Egypt in particular,[12] is there not some real danger of reducing the possibility of African philosophy to the value of rational analysis? Wamba–Dia–Wamba argued that such a prop "to prove that black Africa also had her philosophers, is meaningful only from the perspective of the European ethnocentric (and racist) problematic" (ER 235). That there would be other concerns and that such concerns could qualify as the good of philosophy does not exclude logic, but it does not center philosophy's emphasis exclusively on logic. An extra-logical emphasis is not necessarily a contradiction of logic—not to mention that this contradiction relies on logic for its force—but a difference in focus.[13]

3. Does one simply refuse the terms of the colonizer? Would such an option be possible? Even if one were seduced by the nostalgia for a return, is a pre-colonial beginning per se at all accessible? Although Aimé Césaire, for example, strongly identified with the figure of Africa and the cataclysmic presence of a lost Africa is everywhere in his writings, he nonetheless did not advocate a naive return to an Africa that would somehow have survived untouched by its catastrophic contact with Europe. An unsullied, pre-colonial Africa no longer exists. Nor did Césaire argue, despite the catastrophe of the slave trade and colonialism, that contact with Europe was in each and every way a loss. The problem was not contact per se. "The truth is that I have said something very different: to wit, that the great historical tragedy of Africa has been not so much that it was too late in making contact with the rest of the world, as the matter in which that contact was brought about."[14] Césaire insisted that Negritude's dream of Africa was not a nostalgic sentimentality for an irretrievable past. Furthermore, were one simply to yearn for a lost past, perhaps for a past that existed only in feverish fantasies, does this not exoticize African tradition by assigning it an excess of alterity, as if Africa did not welcome some measure of cultural exchange, as if it wanted to refuse all things non-African in favor of some mythic past? Jean-Marie Makang rejects this ethnographic exaggeration of traditional Africa's cultural remoteness, claiming that "by reducing African traditions to a fixed past and to a nostalgia for an original state, the ethnological discourse strips African people of their historicity, and the universe on which tradition rests is mythical: that is, one

which continues under the mode of its absence or its being passed over. But a mythical and nostalgic universe does not affect the ordering of things in the present; it is, therefore, incapable of helping present generations of Africans in their striving for control over their own destiny."[15]

4. Does one simply accept anything in Africa that is uncommon to Euro-trained eyes as automatically good and worthy of respect? In "Is There an African Philosophy?" E. A. Ruch wondered if such paternalism were not "similar to the attitude of a parent feigning rapture and ecstasy before a painting produced by his child at kindergarten: the painting is really awful, but one must not discourage these little ones!"[16] Is this the toothless relativism of a night when all philosophies must be black?

Hountondji is especially strong on this point. If one simply valorizes the good of all things African as automatically good, indeed, as good per se just because they are African, one assumes the a priori power of the colonizing gaze. The need to be African, the need to valorize oneself as such, automatically assumes the gaze of the colonizer before whom one must justify oneself. It is to reduce the good of African philosophy to the struggle for recognition that characterized the master/slave dialectic in Hegel's *Phenomenology of Spirit*. For the slave to refuse slavery, the slave needs to be recognized as no longer slavish by the master. The slave has something to prove to the master, for it was the very eyes of the master that constituted the slave as such and it is these very same eyes that must be contested. Look! I never was a slave! I was just like you! Purely African philosophy is not philosophy for Africans. It has "been built up essentially *for a European public*" (MR 45). The quest for an African past probably never was reactionary, and it not only enervates the reality of African philosophical activity by reducing African thought to an imaginary and unconscious unity allegedly shared by all Africans, it denies Africans the possibility of developing a critical posture regarding their own traditions.

> The quest for originality is always bound up with a desire to show off. It has meaning only in relation to the Other, from whom one wants to distinguish oneself at all costs. This is an ambiguous relationship, inasmuch as the assertion of one's difference goes hand in hand with a passionate urge to have it recognized by the Other. As this recognition is usually long in coming, the desire of the subject, caught in his own trap, grows increasingly hollow until it is completely alienated in a restless craving for the slightest gesture, the most cursory glance from the Other. (MR 44)

5. Or have we not begun to think this collision, this contact and exchange, this intrusion between worlds, between *Sprachgeister*, carefully enough? If so, might not reconsideration also force us to reconsider the sense of philosophy that we bring to our study? Is the struggle for recognition between subalternating and subalternated worlds a good model for the good of philosophy?

As Césaire argued in his *Discourse on Colonialism*, "I admit that it is a good thing to place different civilizations in contact with each other; that it is an excellent thing to blend different worlds; that whatever its particular genius may be, a civilization that withdraws into itself atrophies; that for civilizations, exchange is oxygen." The question is not one of exposure to the foreign, but the manner of that exposure. Césaire continued, "But then I ask the following question: has colonization really *placed civilizations in contact*? Or, if you prefer, of all the ways of *establishing contact*, was it the best? I answer *no*" (DC 11).

III

Our question at this point, then, seems to be something like, What manner of exchange allows us to think philosophically at all, let alone in the more restrictive sense of the possibility of an African philosophy? Already this question seems to be admitting a supplementary question: is it anything other than an ideological posit to assume that there is any essential "idea" of either Africa or philosophy, let alone a way of conjoining these two putatively "essential" ideas?

At this point I would like to turn briefly to one of the most influential and hotly contested models of contact, Jean-Paul Sartre's *Orphée Noir*, his 1948 introduction to Leopold Senghor's anthology of Negritude poetry.[17] Sartre, the then recent author of *Being and Nothingness*, was certainly not going to locate the object of Negritude in an a priori African or Third World or racialist[18] essence. Clearly, for Sartre, there is no question of retrieving an a priori human essence. In fact, for Sartre, Negritude was a forceful response to the fact that in *le regard* of the white European, dark skins were constructed as essentially toxic. Following the force of Hegel's master/slave dialectic in which, for Hegel, "in so far as it is the action of the *other*, each seeks the death of the other,"[19] there can be no master without the mastered. There can be no slavery without the construction of enslavement. Dark skin acquires its toxicity in the eye of the colonizers who, in order to see themselves as masters and colonizers, must construct what is other, in this case, dark skin, different languages, different cultural values, and so on, as toxic and hence appropriate for enslavement (for their own enrichment, of course. Here enrichment would mean assimilation into the inaugural posit). "Each," according to Hegel, "is for the other the middle term, through which each mediates itself with itself and unites with itself. . . . They *recognize* themselves as *mutually recognizing* one another" (PS 112). In the ensuing struggle for recognition, the master can retain his or her identity only insofar as the slave either capitulates to the master's toxic status or until the master relinquishes his or her difference.

For Sartre, Negritude initially occupies the placeholder of the negative moment, the "no" that negates the inaugural posit of the master. For Sartre, the Negritude poet "wishes to be at the same time a beacon and a mirror."[20] The Negritude poets are a mirror because their negation, their racism, reflects the co-dependence and impotence of the inaugural racist posit. The master needs the slave, just as the day needs the night, to recognize himself as the daylight of mastery. The master is white, with all of the normative advantages that that entails, precisely because the master sees that he is not black, with all of its imputed normative disadvantages. The slave, however, negates the colonizing and denigrating force of the master's gaze, no longer recognizing himself within the master's construction and thereby showing the master that it is he who is enslaved by the racism of his inaugural posit. However, this negation is not the positing of a new identity. In saying no to both slavery and the master's self-enslavement, the poet beacons toward a future in which there is neither master nor slave but freedom (the realm of the emancipated "proletariat"). Hence Negritude is "no more a *state*, nor an existential attitude; it is a Becoming" (BO 57).

The third moment in the dialectic of racism and "anti-racist racism" is freedom. In saying that black is beautiful, the person of color is not saying that this is true per se. The person of color is saying, I am not the toxin that I would be in your eyes! The poets' freedom, their soul, so to speak, is Eurydice, rescued from the hell of racism and colonial exploitation.[21] But if Eurydice is seized, if she is captured by Orpheus's gaze, the black soul is lost in the constitutive gaze. "Black is not color, it is the destruction of this borrowed sheen which falls from the white sun" (BO 30). Hence the task of Negritude is not the foundation of a new essence, for that would be to lose Eurydice by regarding her, but the task of negativity, of an "antiracist racism" (BO 15). "Thus Negritude is dedicated to its own destruction, it is passage and not objective, means and not the ultimate goal. At the moment the black Orpheus most directly embraces this Eurydice, he feels her vanish from between his arms" (BO 60). The Negritude poem, then, is a revolutionary negation, a bullet the tip of which reflects the racist humanism of the white imperial subject back into the whites of its *regard* and the firing of which beacons liberation from the colonial *regard*. The dialectical reality of the colonizing eye could also be seen, for example, in the initial dynamic of W. E. B. Du Bois's location of the veil by which the double consciousness of the color line emerges. As Shamoon Zamir has argued, "The gaze of the other is in Du Bois, as in Sartre, the '*original fall*' that fixes the freedom of activity into passivity."[22]

Eurydice, the reclaimed African soul, is the beacon of a "future universalism which will be the twilight of his Negritude" (BO 62). However, the reduction of Negritude—indeed, of Africa and her diaspora—as well as the status of this new, dialectically derived, albeit non-essentialist, universalism, was met by many with great suspicion. Frantz Fanon protested that the reduction of African experience to mere negative relationality "has destroyed Black enthusiasm."[23] The negative moment was only its inaugural moment of disalienation or, as Wole Soyinka later described it, "The first stage of African liberation has been externally directed; it was the phase of liberation *from*. The conversionary use of the colonial language was logically related to this phase."[24] Without reverting to an a priori essentialism, must one think of the second moment only in its negative character? Is its positive character to be located only in the "universalism" of the third moment? Whose universalism would this be? Despite the power of many of Sartre's insights, is there not some danger in eclipsing the positive content of the second moment in the universalism (even if that is freedom) of the third moment? Whose freedom is this universal freedom?

Chinua Achebe indirectly addressed this question by taking up the relationship between African expression and the universal. Responding to a critic who found an African novel that was universal enough to transcend its location in Africa, Achebe asked, "Does it ever occur to these universities to try out their game of changing names of characters and places in an American novel, say, a Philip Roth or an Updike, and slotting in African names just to see how it works?" Of course not. "It would never occur to them to doubt the universality of their own literature. In the nature of things the work of a Western writer is automatically informed by universality. It is only others who strain to achieve it. So-and-so's work is universal; he has truly arrived!"[25] The universal, the location of the *pan* in either Africa or the West, is not the location of a taxonomically delineated center. For Achebe, the *pan* is the heterogeneity of world cultural expression without a single culture having the claim to be its referee: "Let every people bring their gifts to the great festival of the world's cultural harvest and mankind will be all the richer for the variety and distinctiveness of the offerings" (PCSR 61). A feast, I might here say, that expresses the heterogeneity of the Good which does not arrive to referee the diversity of its harvests. The Kenyan Ngũgĩ wa Thiong'o insisted upon a similar model of heterogeneity when he claimed that the "wealth of a common global culture will then be expressed in the particularities of our different languages and cultures very much like a universal garden of many-colored flowers. The 'flowerness' of the different flowers is expressed in their very diversity."[26] Both Achebe and Ngũgĩ argue for a kind of Leibnizian normative cultural monadology. Each monad, opaque with reference to itself, indirectly mirrors the Good in its own, irreducibly singular way.

One can also see this concern operating in the later thinking of Aimé Césaire. In his interview with René Depestre, for instance, Césaire claimed that *Négritude* was a process of "disalienation" and "detoxification" (DC 68), not merely one that negated *le regard* of the Eurocentric self-posit by having "asserted that our Negro heritage was worthy of respect . . . and that its values were values that could still make an important contribution to the world" (DC 76), but one that did so in such a way that it affirmed not merely dialectical difference, but the heterogeneity of and within Africa. No doubt, Negritude is the bullet that says that Africa partakes uniquely and diversely in the Good, but it did not necessarily need the degradation of the colonial regard to clarify this goodness. Its goodness is not merely a dialectical response; it is the affirmation of a heterogeneous expression of the Good. It says, This Good never was your Good! It does not need to say this by locating the Good in the properties of blood or other strategies of essence. Speaking of his indebtedness to the surrealists, Césaire claimed that "if I apply the surrealist approach to my situation, I can summon up these unconscious forces. This, for me, was a call to Africa" (DC 68). Africa—not an intelligible quiddity, nor merely a dialectical negation, but "a plunge into the depths" (DC 68). Hence Césaire, following Senghor, could not hold to a universal surrealist poetry or a universal communism. "In other words, their poems were colorless" (DC 69).

These comments do not destroy the power of the negative moment. Without its violence, we hear only ourselves and want to see only ourselves, we recognize only ourselves—either our accomplishments or those who remind us of our superiority by means of their imputed inferiority. No doubt, the condition for the possibility of an African philosophy involves the deconstruction of the self-constitution of the superior subject. However, does not the other say more than "no," and does not the annihilation of all subjectivity to the silence of its origin also ensure that no one, not even the colonizing subject, will be heard? If all saying is reduced to saying nothing, then the Good loses its capacity to surprise and, as Appiah phrased it, one has the institutionalization of a "mode of reading that seems to share its motto with the Holiday Inn: the best surprise is, apparently, no surprise" (FH 65). If one only hears silence in the wake of "the evacuation of specificity" (FH 72), then silence becomes not only a subject, but a subject whose silent din renders all heterogeneity inaudible.[27]

Silence speaks, but not just English, or French or Portuguese for that matter. And hence, as Ngũgĩ contended, "Thus the peoples of the Third World had refused to surrender their souls to English, French, or Portuguese" (MC 35).

IV

There are two modes in which the silence of the Good irrupts into language: the hybridity of language and the trembling of languages before each other. Both modes register the inability of the good of a language ever to fully orient itself to the silence of its origin. Silence at the heart—nay, as the subject—of a language continues to intrude normatively upon language.

As we have already seen, Negritude was not only the revolutionary bullet, the whirlwind that the colonizer had sown, the "shadows from whence a new dawn will break,"[28] but it was the hybrid refashioning of language, the disrupting intrusion of an African unconscious. Negritude was the jazz of language, not only, like the jazz solo, producing something new out of rigid motifs, much like Du Bois claimed that the Sorrow Songs transformed tired Anglican hymns, but doing so out of formerly discarded instruments. As Achebe phrased it,

But, in any case, did not the black people in America, deprived of their own musical instruments, take the trumpet and the trombone and blow them as they had never been blown before, as indeed they were not designed to be blown? And the result, was it not jazz? Is anyone going to say that this was a loss to the world or that those first Negro slaves who began to play around with the discarded instruments of their masters should have played waltzes and fox-trots?[29]

Despite the power of hybridity, a power that exceeds even post-colonial interventions, there remains the question of irreconcilable linguistic practices. Although he is most famous for locating Negritude in sub-Saharan Africa's alleged dialectical inversion of European rationality (*L'émotion est nègre comme la raison hellène*[30]) and hence remaining open to Kwame Anthony Appiah's critique of "racialism" (i.e., "The truth is that there are no races: there is nothing in the world that can do all we ask race to do for us" [FH 45]), Léopold Senghor, in an address on the idea of *Africanité* given in 1967 at the University of Cairo, added another degree of complexity to his argument.[31] Speaking as a "grammarian" (FA 81) and working not from deep convictions, but from "what I modestly call a 'working hypothesis'" (FA 39), Senghor located Negritude in a grammatical ethnotype, that of the "fluctuent": one who is "buffeted about by his emotions that are aroused by external causes. Hence the predominance, in Negro-African languages, of the imperfective aspect— of the unaccomplished action—and the predominance of the *present* tense over the perfective aspect and the past tense" (FA 40). Hence, for Senghor, Negro-African languages proceed by "polymorphic dialectics" (FA 80). The universe is a "network of different but complementary forces which are . . . the expression of powers contained in God, the only true being" (FA 79–80). Hence, Negro-African languages are "polypartite, or more exactly, *polyvalent*" (FA 81). Although Senghor may, in a kind of linguistic racialism, be asking the immense complex of African languages to do too much, and although some of his analysis still seems not to have extricated itself from the spell of Father Tempels, he is still making a striking suggestion: Sub-Saharan African languages, unlike bipartite Arabic languages or logical European languages, grammatically value a divine subject which expresses itself as difference. Such languages, even if they did not typify all of Africa south of the Sahara, would intrude violently on European languages.

In his final prose work in English before he went "Gikuyu and Kiswahili all the way," Ngũgĩ argued that "language was the most important vehicle through which that power [the colonial phase of imperialism] fascinated and held the soul prisoner. The bullet was the means of physical subjugation. Language was the means of spiritual subjugation."[32] He gives a vivid example of the losses incurred when he was forced to abandon Gikuyu, the language of his childhood, for English. Gikuyu was not only the language of childhood stories about hares outwitting hyenas, but also the language whose beauty transfixed the ear beyond content-oriented speaking.

> We therefore learnt to value words for their meaning and nuances. Language
> was not a mere string of words. It had a suggestive power well beyond the im-
> mediate and lexical meaning. Our appreciation of the suggestive magical power
> of language was reinforced by the games we played with words through riddles,
> proverbs, transpositions of syllables, or through nonsensical but musically ar-
> ranged words. . . . The language, through images and symbols, gave us a view
> of the world, but it had a beauty of its own. (LAL 11)

Not only do languages not say the same things in commensurate ways, but the
very nature of the relationship to things themselves is already evaluative.
Ngũgĩ argued, "Language carries culture, and culture carries, particularly
through orature and literature, the entire body of values by which we come to
perceive ourselves and our place in the world . . . Language is thus inseparable
from ourselves as a community of human beings with a specific form and
character, a specific history, a specific relationship to the world" (LAL 16).

Languages, as vehicles not merely of communicative transactions (for who
is authorized to speak and what can be heard are a priori evaluative questions),
are not interchangeable. In this respect, Masolo realized the importance of
the "rationality debate" for African philosophy's identity crisis. When Peter
Winch in *The Idea of a Social Science* argued, following Wittgenstein's *Logische
Untersuchungen,* for the incommensurability of language games and its revolutionary impact on the very idea of a social science, Anglo–American ration-
alists angrily retorted that rationality, a *logos* that transcended the accidents
of particular *logoi,* held or could hold force in all languages. Rather than address this claim directly, one need only claim not that some languages admit
of rational exchange and others do not, but that the claim that logic is the
paramount value of language assumes, prior to logic, the value of logic. Not
that logic is devoid of value but that since it assumes value, the primacy of this
value cannot be assumed in all languages. Even if one does not accept the full
extent of Senghor's generalizations about sub-Saharan linguistic polyvalence,
those languages still speak of languages irreducible to our own, to a claim of
the Good that exceeds the demand that one think it as the intelligible substra-
tum of thinking. Ngũgĩ's rabbits dashed among hyenas, sometimes giving
way to words that said nothing but said it beautifully, albeit not in the way that
other languages would say it. It is, after all, as Ngũgĩ claimed, "the final triumph of a system of domination when the dominated start singing its virtues" (LAL 20). In a time when Newt Gingrich concludes from the strife in
Canada between English and Québécois that it is important that America remain monolingual, silence is not heard, let alone its polylinguistic thunder.
Meanwhile, as Ngũgĩ lamented, "The Christian bible is available in unlimited
quantities in even the tiniest African language" (LAL 26).

Perhaps at this point we might attempt to think the Good of language in an
analogous fashion to the debate between the Anglican missionary Mr. Brown
and Akunna in Achebe's 1958 novel *Things Fall Apart.* Speaking through an
interpreter, itself not an insignificant detail, Mr. Brown and Akunna "spent

long hours" in Akunna's *obi* discussing religion without ever coming to any agreement. Mr. Brown, sent to the Igbo by his God, replete with the clarity of purpose requisite for proselytizing zeal, argued against Akunna's defense of the Igbo belief in numerous minor deities, although they, like the world, were created by a supreme god, Chukwu. "'There are no other gods,' said Mr. Brown. 'Chukwu is the only God and all the others are false.'" Akunna responded that Chukwu created messengers "so that we could approach Him through them." Mr. Brown, claiming that the notion of a God needing helpers or messengers was, in effect, anthropomorphic, and he worried that one serves the minor deities at the expense of the supreme God. "'That is not so. We make sacrifices to the little gods, but when they fail and there is no one else to turn to we go to Chukwu.'" Chukwu was a last resort and the minor deities were a first resort, because "we are afraid to worry their master." At this Mr. Brown contrasted the fear that the Igbo feel before Chukwu with the kindness of the Anglican God: "'In my religion Chukwu is a loving father and need not be feared by those who do His will.'" For Mr. Brown, confidence in the love of God and the clarity of its imperatives both justifies and fosters the Christian mission to usurp African sensibilities. It no longer knows fear and trembling before its imperative. Akunna, on the other hand, responded that "we must fear Him when we are not doing His will . . . And who is to tell its will? It is too great to be known."[33] As Achebe later remarked in an interview: "I can't imagine Igbos traveling four thousand miles to tell anybody their worship was wrong!"[34]

English, like all "master" languages, forgets the sublimity of its anterior silence and hence remains oblivious to its status as a minor divinity among minor divinities. Perhaps, Kant, apropos of Akunna and the sublimity of Chukwu, has something to say here when he claims in the third *Kritik* that the "virtuous person fears God without being afraid of God."[35]

V

Contact, then, is the recognition that all languages intrude upon each other. They interrupt each other when foreign tongues no longer say merely "bar bar bar bar" and hence can no longer be dismissed as the indiscernible discourse of the *barbaros*. No doubt the hybridity of the master languages results from minor literatures renegotiating what can be syntactically accommodated. But if the colonial language is the only language that prevails, even though the condition for the possibility of its perseverance is its hybridity, a single language becomes the continuing center, which, despite the frequent decenterings by minor literatures, always manages to recoup itself, reorient itself with regard to its activity, even if this now means continuing to re-identify itself because its center is shifting—shifting, realigning, but never altogether disintegrating. The colonial language is akin to Edward Said's "Orientalism," which "depends for its strategy on the flexible *positional* superiority, which puts the Westerner in a whole series of possible relationships with the Orient without ever losing him the upper hand" (PCSR 90). In the same way that no language can recoup its own center or exhaust saying with what has been said, no particular language can claim to be the center. Saying is the non-centerable expressivity of the heterogeneity of the Good.

In this sense one might say of the Cartesian and post-Cartesian demand for the location and appropriation of a centralized subjectivity, the very dynamic that inaugurated Sartre's colonial dialectic, is the demand that one speak only one's own language and sew the mouths shut of all those who would still speak barbarian languages. I first am because I am already within a language game, and hence the *cogito ergo sum* presupposes the *I speak therefore I am*. In this sense, Heidegger in *Sein und Zeit* (1927) reversed the Cartesian *cogito ergo sum* to the *sum ergo cogito*, such that the "'*sum*' is then asserted first, and indeed in the sense that 'I am in the world.'" [36] I "am," that is, I can be only inasmuch as I am already in a world and that I already find myself participating in its lines of equivalence. I think because I can speak, or, more radically, thinking can reflect upon itself as an "I" only insofar as this is granted as a possibility within a world of speaking. Or, as Senghor phrased it in his *Africanité* address, "[I]n the beginning was the Word, *in the beginning was Grammar*" (FA 78).

This is not to say that I am arguing for the toothless relativism of an uncritical piety before all acts of speech that are not of the provenance of my world. I am, rather, speaking of the heterogeneity of the Good in its inexhaustibly fluid but not merely random lines of orature and literature. I want to insist that African philosophy cannot avoid the question of the language within which it argues and writes and that this is one of the most fruitful sites in which it can negotiate its relationship to a Eurocentric world.

I would like to conclude with a moment in thinking that I am adapting from Henry Odera Oruka's "Sagacity in African Philosophy." Oruka distinguishes between "philosophic sagacity" and "culture philosophy," the latter being a species of an ethnophilosophical embrace of the equation that a community's culture is the same as its philosophy. Citing both Marcel Griaule's 1965 interview with a sage in *Conversations with Ogotemmeli* and Prof. Sodipo and Dr. Hallen's interviews with the sages among the Yoruba, Oruka faults them with conflating mere sagacity with philosophic sagacity. In order to be a sage, one need only know, albeit in some exemplary fashion, the Yoruba traditions. "In other words, they are the spokesmen of their people, but they speak what after all is known to almost every average person within the culture" (ER 51). Again, a *Weltanschauung* may be a tacit philosophy, but it is not the practice of philosophy itself in its normatively and linguistically specific localities. This conflation of an uncritical relationship with one's culture and the critical practice of philosophy, however, does not apply to all of the sages. "As sages they are versed in the beliefs and wisdoms of their people. But as thinkers, they are rationally critical and they opt for or recommend only those aspects of the beliefs and wisdoms which satisfy their rational scrutiny" (ER 51). "Philosophic sagacity," then, "is often a product and a reflective reevaluation of the culture philosophy" (ER 52). Although I am obviously objecting to Oruka's reduction of the force of the good's intrusion to the techniques of "rational scrutiny," I would like to suggest that philosophic sagacity could be read as something like the irruption of minor literatures within a "culture philosophy" and that by "minor literatures" I mean the irruption into syntax of hybrid forces within a language as well as the intrusion of different languages into the alleged centrality of dominant languages.[37] Language, like the Good of philosophy, does not come to recognize itself because it is continually interrupted by the Good.

The question is no longer, What does Africa—not the Africa drawn up by the colonial powers in Berlin toward the end of the nineteenth century, but that vast complex of languages and cultures, intruding on each other, reflexively intruding on themselves, intruding on the very idea that one could identify Africa as a set of properties, intruding on the pretense of either an "us" or a "them"—have to add to our canons of properly oriented thinking? The question is, In what ways does it intrude upon them? What are its valences, its lines of force, and its lines of escape? What philosophic sagacities intrude upon the worlds of Western languages, including upon our own sagacious self-intrusions—provided that "we" do not constitute ourselves in such a way that we only hear ourselves? Contact is the possibility of intrusion, an obsession with the unconscious in all of its languages, a philosophical sagacity that roams the Babel—not the "bar bar"—of discursive formations.

It is with this idea of the Good, then, that one can revisit the controversial definition of African philosophy provided by Hountondji. "By 'African philosophy' I mean a set of texts, specifically the set of texts written by Africans and described as philosophical by the authors themselves" (MR 33). "African philosophy equals African philosophical literature. That is, the whole of philosophical texts produced by Africans" (MR ix). What is striking in this definition is its refusal to link philosophical activity to a purported continent-wide way of thinking. Philosophy, with its restless questioning, moves among the extraordinary heterogeneity of culture within Africa as well as among the many Africas within Africa as they interact with the many other centers outside of Africa. The "African" in African philosophy is a difference that really makes a difference. But it is not a difference that marks a fixed or mummified context (a tacit and unanimous consensus within or without Africa as to what, in the end, "African" denotes). Rather, it marks the internal dynamism of a cultural context that struggles with both itself and the rest of the world as it continuously seeks new sources of oxygen, of spirit. It is in this sense that African philosophy is not an ethnophilosophical creation of Africa. It is a philosophy of Africa that insists that African philosophy is the critical activity of Africans.

Notes

1. Peter O. Bodunrin, "The Question of African Philosophy," in Tsenay Serequeber-han, ed., *African Philosophy: The Essential Readings* (New York: Paragon House, 1991; henceforth ER), p. 63.

2. Paulin J. Hountondji, *African Philosophy: Myth and Reality,* 2nd ed., trans. Henri Evans with Jonathan Rée (Bloomington: Indiana University Press, 1996). Hence-forth MR.

3. In ER 48.

4. "Ethnophilosophy is a pre-philosophy mistaking itself for a metaphilosophy, a philosophy which, instead of presenting its own rational justification, shelters lazily behind the authority of a tradition and projects its own theses and beliefs on to that tradition" (MR 63).

5. V. Y. Mudimbe, *The Invention of Africa: Gnosis, Philosophy, and the Order of Knowledge* (Bloomington: Indiana University Press, 1988), p. 156. Henceforth IA.

6. D. A. Masolo, *African Philosophy in Search of Identity* (Bloomington: Indiana University Press, 1994). Henceforth AP.

7. Masolo concludes, "There is no justifiable reason, therefore, why one individual or group should try to tailor-make African philosophy by prescribing what ought to be its content, method of reasoning, and standards of truth" (AP 251).

8. G. W. F. Hegel, *The Philosophy of History,* trans. J. Sibree (New York: Dover, 1956), p. 99. For Hume, Kant, and Hegel, among others, on Africa in all of its disturbing detail, see Emmanuel Chukwudi Eze's anthology *Race and the Enlightenment: A Reader* (Cambridge, Mass.: Blackwell Publishers, 1997). Kant, for example, argued, "The Negroes of Africa have no feeling that rises above the trifling" (55). Hume infamously was "apt to suspect the negroes and in general all other species of men . . . to be naturally inferior to whites. There never was a civilized nation of any other complexion than white" (33).

9. Appiah argues, "[T]he notion of a specifically African identity began as the product of a European gaze." In Anthony Appiah, *In My Father's House: Africa in the Philosophy of Culture* (Oxford: Oxford University Press, 1992), p. 81. Hence-forth FH.

10. Cheikh Anta Diop, *The African Origins of Civilization,* trans. Mercer Cook (Chicago: Lawrence Hill Books, 1974).

11. For a discussion of Amo, see Hountondji, MR 111–130.

12. As Appiah puts it, "If Diop and his followers—a group we might call the 'Egyptianists'—are right, then ancient Egypt deserves a more central place than it currently has in the study of ancient thought: and if they are right then it should be studied intensely in Africa and Europe and Australasia, wherever there is an interest in the ancient world. If European or American or Australasian intellectuals are too blinkered or too deeply chauvinistic to accept this, then maybe these matters will only be studied in Africa. But that would be a matter for regret" (FH 102).

13. Quoting Garth Hallet's critique of Benjamin Lee Whorf, Masolo made this point this way: "Their focus is different, that is all. One attends to one aspect, the other to another" (AP 58).

14. Aimé Césaire, *Discourse on Colonialism* (1955), trans. Joan Pinkham (New York: Monthly Review Press, 1972), p. 24. Henceforth DC.

15. Jean-Marie Makang, "Of the Good Use of Tradition: Keeping the Critical Perspective in African Philosophy," in Emmanuel Chukwudi Eze, ed., *Postcolonial African Philosophy: A Critical Reader* (Cambridge, Mass.: Blackwell Publishers, 1997), p. 327.

16. E. A. Ruch, "Is There an African Philosophy?" *Second Order* 3, no. 2 (July 1974): 4.

17. Léopold Senghor, *Anthologie de la nouvelle poésie nègre et malgache de langue française* (Paris: Presses Universitaires de France, 1948).

18. I am borrowing this term from Appiah: "*Racialism*—that there are heritable characteristics, possessed by members of our species, which allows us to divide them into a small set of races, in such a way that all members of these races share certain traits and tendencies with each other that they do not share with any other race" (FH 13).

19. G. W. F. Hegel, *The Phenomenology of Spirit* [1807], trans. A. V. Miller (Oxford: Oxford University Press, 1977), p. 113. Henceforth PS.

20. Jean-Paul Sartre, *Black Orpheus* (Paris: Présence Africaine, 1976), p. 17. Henceforth BO. Sartre makes this point again in his 1961 preface to Frantz Fanon's *The Wretched of the Earth:* "Of course; first, the only violence is the settler's; but soon they will make it their own; that is to say, the same violence is thrown back upon us as when our reflection comes forward to meet us when we go towards a mirror." Trans. Constance Farrington (London: Penguin Books, 1967), p. 15.

21. "And I shall name this poetry 'orphic' because this untiring descent of the Negro into himself causes me to think of Orpheus, going to reclaim Eurydice from Pluto" (BO 21).

22. Zamir is, of course, analyzing Du Bois's 1903 *The Souls of Black Folk*. Zamir goes on to claim, apropos of Hegel and later Sartre, that "Du Bois is caught here between a transcendence of and a simultaneous entrapment in concrete existence. He holds the world that fixes his freedom into an object state in 'common contempt,' choosing to live 'above it in a region of blue sky'" (141). *Dark Voices: W. E. B. Du Bois and American Thought, 1888–1903* (Chicago: University of Chicago Press, 1995), p. 139.

23. Quoted in AP 31. For a good general discussion of Sartre's essay and its adherents and discontents, see AP 24–37.

24. Wole Soyinka, "Language as Boundary," in his *Art, Dialogue, and Outrage: Essays on Literature and Culture* (New York: Pantheon, 1994), p. 91.

25. Chinua Achebe, "Colonialist Criticism," in Bill Ashcroft, Gareth Griffiths, and Helen Tiffin, eds., *Post-Colonial Studies Reader* (New York: Routledge, 1995), p. 59. Henceforth PCSR.

26. Ngũgĩ wa Thiong'o, "Creating Space for a Hundred Flowers to Bloom: The

Wealth of a Common Global Culture," in his *Moving the Centre* (Portsmouth, N.H.: Heinemann, 1993), p. 24. Henceforth MC.

27. Asking if the subaltern can speak, Gayatri Spivak argued that the wholesale deconstruction of the Subject has amounted to the concealment of the subject because, by reducing subjectivity to silence, it has reduced its capacity to speak at all, let alone heterogeneously. "The much publicized critique of the sovereign subject thus actually inaugurates a Subject" (PCSR 24). "But one must nevertheless insist that the colonized subaltern *subject* is irretrievably heterogeneous" (PCSR 26).

28. Sartre, preface to *The Wretched of the Earth*, 12.

29. Achebe, PCSR 61. Or, as the Indian philosopher Raja Rao claimed, attempting to write in the more universal language of English, "One has to convey in a language that is not one's own the spirit that is one's own" (PCSR 296).

30. Quoted in Masolo, AP 26.

31. Léopold Sedar Senghor, *The Foundations of "Africanité" or "Negritude" and "Arabité,"* trans. Mercer Cook (Paris: Présence Africaine, 1971). Henceforth FA.

32. Ngũgĩ wa Thiong'o, "The Language of African Literature," in his *Decolonising the Mind: The Politics of Language in African Culture* (Portsmouth, N.H.: Heinemann, 1986), p. 9. Henceforth LAL.

33. Chinua Achebe, *Things Fall Apart* (New York: Fawcett Crest,), pp. 164–65.

34. Quoted in FH 114.

35. Immanuel Kant, *Kritik der Urteilskraft* (Berlin: Walter de Gruyter, 1968), section 28. "So fürchtet der Tugendhafte Gott, ohne sich vor ihm zu fürchten . . . "

36. Martin Heidegger, *Being and Time,* trans. John Macquarie and Edward Robinson (New York: Harper and Row, 1962), p. 254 [§ 43 at I/6(b)].

37. I am borrowing the term "minor literature" from Deleuze and Guattari's *Kafka: Toward a Minor Literature.* "[M]inor no longer designates specific literatures but the revolutionary conditions for every literature within the heart of what is called great (or established) literature." Gilles Deleuze and Félix Guattari, *Kafka: Toward a Minor Literature,* trans. Dana Polan (Minneapolis: University of Minnesota Press, 1986), p. 18.

Appendix: What the Black Man Contributes

Léopold Sédar Senghor

TRANSLATED BY MARY BETH MADER

Wisdom lies not in reason but in love.[1]
—André Gide, *Later Fruits of the Earth*

They (Negroes) shatter the mechanical rhythm of America, and one must be grateful to them for this; people had forgotten that men can live without bank accounts and bathtubs.[2]

—Paul Morand, *New York*

That the Negro is already present in the development of the New World is not established by the presence of African troops in Europe; they would prove only that he is participating in the demolition of the former order, the old order. It is in a number of singular works by contemporary writers and artists that the Negro reveals his current presence, as well as in several other works—perhaps less perfected, but moving nonetheless—created by black men. It is not about this presence alone that I wish to speak here; beyond this, I especially wish to speak of all the potential presences that the study of the Negro permits us to glimpse.

I adopt the word [Negro] following other authors; it is convenient. Are there Negroes, pure Negroes, black Negroes? Science says no. I know that there is and has been a Negro culture, whose sphere included the countries of the Sudan, Guinea, and the Congo, in the classic senses of the words. In the words of the German ethnologist, "The Sudan thus itself also possesses an indigenous and vibrant civilization. It is a fact that exploration in Equatorial Africa has encountered only vigorous and fresh ancient civilizations everywhere that the preponderance of Arabs, Hamite blood, or European civilization has not removed the powder from the wings of the black moths that once were so beautiful. Everywhere!"[3] A culture that is one and united. "I know no northern people that can compare to these primitives for the unity of their civilization."[4] I specify: civilization. A culture that is born of the reciprocal action of race, tradition, and milieu, and that, having emigrated to America, remains intact in style, if not in ergological elements. The civilization has disappeared, is forgotten; the culture has not been extinguished.[5] And slavery, as a matter of fact, compensated for the milieu and for the disintegrating effect of cross-breeding (*métissage*).

It is of this culture that I would like to speak, not exactly as an ethnologist. I will devote myself to its human flowering—more particularly, to the new boughs grafted onto the old human trunk. With partiality, of course. The faults of Blacks are known enough for me not to return to them—among other unpardonable ones is that of not assimilating at the deepest reaches of their personality. I do not say "of not letting their style assimilate." All that interests me here, all that is interesting, are the fertile elements that their culture brings, the elements of the Negro style. And Negro style endures as long as the lively—should I say eternal?—Negro soul endures.

We will first briefly study the Negro soul, and then its conception of the world, from which religious and social life follow; finally, we will examine the arts, which are a function of these last two. All that will then remain will be for me to bind into one sheaf the riches that we will have gathered in the course of this study, in a humanist spirit.

A good number of works have been published on the Negro soul. It remains a mysterious forest below the flight of airplanes. Fr. Libermann used to say to his missionaries, "Be Negroes with the Negroes so as to win them to Jesus Christ." That is, rationalist thought, mechanico-materialist explanations, explain nothing. Here less than elsewhere. How many were devoured by the Minotaur, who would not have strayed with the help of Ariadne, of Emotion-Femininity? It is precisely a thoroughly rationalist deliberate confusion to explain the Negro by his utilitarianism when he is practical, and by his materialism when he is sensual.

Does one wish to understand his soul? Let's make ourselves a sensibility like his. With no literature between subject and object, with no imagination in the usual sense of the word, with neither subject nor object. Let colors lose none of their simple intensity, forms none of their weight or volume, and sounds none of their carnal singularity . . . The Negro body, the Negro soul, is permeable to apparently imperceptible rhythms, to all the solicitations of the world—and not solely to those of the cosmos. This sensibility is moral as well. It is a frequently noted fact that the Negro is sensitive to spoken words and ideas, and, further, that he is singularly sensitive to the sensible—dare I say sensual?—qualities of speech, to the spiritual, non-intellectual qualities of ideas. Fine speaking seduces him, as do the communist theorist, the hero, and the saint. "His voice stirred men," it was said of Fr. Dahin.[6] Which gives the impression that the Negro is easily assimilable, when it is above all he who assimilates. Whence the enthusiasm of Latins in general, and of missionaries in particular, for the ease with which they believe themselves to "convert" or to "civilize" Negroes. Whence, often, their sudden despondency in the face of some irrational and typically Negro revelation: "We do not know them . . . we cannot know them," admits this same Fr. Dahin on his deathbed, after more than fifty years in Africa.[7]

An emotive sensibility. Emotion is Negro, as reason is Hellenic. Water wrinkled by every breath of air? "Soul of open air"[8] battered by winds, whose fruit often falls before ripening? Yes, in one sense. The Negro today is richer in gifts than in works. But the tree plunges its roots far into the earth, the river runs deep, carrying along precious grains of gold dust. And the Afro-American poet sings

I've known rivers
Ancient, dusky rivers
My soul has grown deep like the rivers[9]

Let's close the parentheses. The very nature of the Negro's emotion—of his sensibility, moreover—explains his attitude before the object that is perceived with such an essential intensity. It is a state of abandon that becomes need, an active attitude of communion—indeed, identification—no matter how strong the action—I was going to say the personality—of the object. A rhythmic attitude. Remember this phrase.

But, since the Negro is emotive, the object is perceived in its morphological characteristics and in its essence at the same time. One speaks of the realism of passionate people, and of their lack of imagination. Negro realism, in inhuman situations, will react with the humanness that leads to humor. For the moment, I will say that the Negro cannot imagine the object as different from him in its imperceptible essence. He lends to it a sensibility, a will, and a soul of a man, but those of a black man. It has been pointed out that this is not exactly crude anthropomorphism. The spirits, for example, do not always take a human form. One speaks of the animism of the Negroes; I will say their anthropopsychism. Which is not necessarily—which is not—Negro-centrism; we will see this further on.

Thus, all of nature is animated by a human presence. Nature is humanized, in the etymological and current sense of the word. Not only animals and the phenomena of nature—rain, wind, thunder, mountain, river—but also trees and stones are made men—men who retain some original physical features, as instruments and signs of their personal soul. This is the most profound trait, the eternal trait, of the Negro soul, the one that, in America, has been able to resist all the efforts at economic slavery and "moral liberation." "It is surely in order to raise taxes, grumbles Mme. Vache,[10] who, having hastily put on a heavy layer of white face powder, donned her canary-yellow satin shoes, and slipped on her sky-blue chiffon dress with the wide embroidered flounces, and, sweating, breathless, but thrilled about this occasion to sport her *créoles* and her French gold necklace, sets out for the village, mounted atop a mule."[11] Like a Negro woman—and like a cow. Even the flowers in *The Green Pastures*[12] possess, with a Negro accent, an altogether Negro submission to the will of the Lord: "O.K., Lord."

Such is the Negro soul, if it is such as to be defined. That it is the daughter of the milieu, and that Africa is the "Dark Continent," I grant. For here the effect of the milieu is particularly perceptible. Due to the light, so primitively pure, on the savanna and at the edges of the forest, where civilizations were born: bare light that lays bare, that reveals the essential, the essence of things, as it were. Due to this climate, whose violence both exalts and crushes. I grant this, if it explains things better. In any case, religion and society are explained in turn by this soul.

It is said, and repeated even more, that the Negro contributes nothing new to religion—neither a doctrine, nor a morality, only a certain religiosity. But, upon reflection, isn't the important thing here this contemptuous claim or, rather, the reality of the contempt? I nevertheless wish to examine this doctrine and morality without being duped.

First of all, these distinctions have no currency. They say, "Be Negroes with the Negroes," but they know neither how to classify, nor how to count, not even how to make distinctions.

"I believe in God, the Father Almighty, maker of heaven and earth." The beginning of the Creed has never astonished any Negro. In fact, the Negro is a monotheist for as far back as one goes in his history, and everywhere. There is but a single God, who created all, who is all power and all will; all the powers and all the wills of the spirits and ancestors are but emanations from Him. But this God, say the well-informed, has vague attributes, and is uninterested in men. Proof of this is that he is not worshipped, and sacrifices are not offered to him. Indeed. He is love: one does not have to protect oneself against his wrath. He is powerful and happy: he does not eat, nor does he need libations. But this is not a God of wood, a sort of "nonentity."[13] My Serer[14] grandmothers, I recall, turned to Him in times of great distress. They dressed as men, with all the gear, fired shots, and launched arrows at the sky. They even went so far as to issue vulgarities . . . in French. And God, beginning to beam, hearkened.

Worship concerns the spirits and the ancestors. It is fitting to note, with Maurice Delafosse, the greatest—I mean the most attentive—of the French Africanizers, that ancestor worship seems to be of early origin, therefore more Negro. Besides, it is generalized throughout all of Black Africa. A sacrifice is not the clause of a contract— "quid pro quo," any more than is a magical practice with a strictly utilitarian aim, as in the secret societies. These societies are of relatively late origin, and I would see in them, for my part, a too-human superstitious distortion. Proof of this is the way that these magical practices develop in the degenerate Negro societies of America. I see three purposes for sacrifices: to participate in the power of the superior spirits, among which are the ancestors; to commune with them emotively to the point of a sort of identification; finally, to be charitable to the ancestors. For the dead, all-powerful though they are, do not have "life," and they cannot obtain for themselves these "earthly foods" that give living its intense sweetness.

No, neither fear nor material cares dominate the religion of Negroes, though they are not absent from it, though the Negro likewise feels human anguish. But love—and charity, which is love—makes the action. "What the laborer looks at from afar when he stands up," a Toucouleur[15] saying has it, "is the village. It is not the desire to eat that causes this, it is the entire past that draws him in that direction." A similar feeling moves the son who works for his father, and the man who labors for the community. The feeling of familial and community communion is projected backward in time and into the transcendent world, to the ancestors, to the spirits, and unconsciously to God. The logic of love.

Consequently, what does morality matter, and what does it matter if there are no sanctions? But there is a morality, which is enforced here-below, morally, through the reprobation of community members and through the conscience of the community. The sense of dignity of Blacks is well known. Morality consists in not breaking the communion in God of living beings, the dead, and the spirits, and in maintaining this communion through charity. And he who ruptures this mystic bond is properly punished by isolation.

Let's consider the word "religiosity" again. What the Negro contributes is the faculty to perceive the supernatural in the natural, the sense of the transcendent, and the active state of abandon that accompanies it—love's abandon. It is an element of his ethnic personality as deeply rooted as is animism. The study of the American Negro provides proof of this. With the "radical" poets themselves—that is, the communizing poets—the religious feeling springs up suddenly, very high, from the depths of their negritude. "Father Divine," who *Paris-Soir* has so often mocked, would not have won over the Negro masses if he had not promised and given to his "angels," besides feasts, the more intoxicating joys of the soul. Negro hysteria? "Postulation of the nerves,"[16] as Baudelaire said, which prevents the New World from peacefully adoring its Golden Calf.

Here we've reached the heart of the humanist problem. It's a matter of knowing: "What is the goal of man?" Is it in himself alone that he should find his answer, as Guéhenno, following Michelet and Gorki, holds?[17] Or is man truly man only when he surpasses himself to find his consummation outside of the self, and even outside of man? It is indeed, as Maritain says, following Scheler, a matter of "concentrating the world in man" and "expanding man into the world." The Negro achieves this by negrifying God and by making man—whom he does not deify—participate in the supernatural world.

> Lord, I fashion dark gods, too,
> Daring even to give You
> Dark despairing features . . . [18]

The Afro-American poets prefer to address themselves to Christ, to the Man-God.

We will now consider the natural side of the unitary order of the world: Negro society.

Not only is the family the social unit, among Negroes, as elsewhere, but, further, the society is composed of concentric circles of greater and greater breadth, tiered on top of each other, imbricated over each other, so to speak, and formed on the very model of the family. Several families that speak the same dialect and feel that they share a common origin form a tribe; several tribes that speak the same language and live in the same land can establish a kingdom; and several kingdoms enter in their turn into a confederation or an empire. Whence the importance of the study of the family. I will simply point out the elements of it that must continue to make the Negro family fruitful, and permit it to square with a new humanism, by enriching it. For, as Westermann writes, "If the Africans succeed in preserving it [the family] intact during the transition period, in purifying it from unhealthy elements, and in saving it from degeneracy, there need be no anxiety about their future."[19]

What is the unity of the small family, the family in the narrow sense? It has economic unity, since the good of the family is common and undivided. It has moral unity, since the ultimate goal of the family is to procreate children who continue to live out the tradition, to maintain and multiply the spark of life in their bodies and in their souls, piously.

But this unity is not unaware of individuals, subordinated though they are to the unity of the group. In addition to the common good, the wife and children have their own personal goods, which they can augment and freely make use of. The children receive a liberal education, although at the age of initiation it is harsh. They are not beaten, and in their age groups they carry out their apprenticeship to manhood on their own. And contrary to popular opinion, the woman is man's equal. The fiancé is not consulted any more than is the fiancée, but they accept their betrothal and live out their acceptance, which is more important than the feeling of choosing.[20] The woman is not purchased; one merely compensates her family. The proof of this is that when she has suffered some offense from her husband, she retreats to her parents; and he must come to humble himself and offer reparation. At least, this is the custom among the Serer. For the woman is the mother, the trustee of life, and the guardian of tradition. Superficial minds have compared her to a beast of burden. Indeed, in the division of labor—because there is a division, not a hierarchization—her task is often heavier, but so increases her responsibility, her dignity. As paradoxical as it may seem, the black woman who becomes a French citizen loses some of her liberty, her dignity.

The family, in the narrow sense, is not an autonomous group: it lives in the clan family "square." This clan family, in the sense of gens, is the true Negro-African family. It includes all the descendants of a single ancestor, a man or a woman. It is here that the unified aspect of the family, the foundation and prefiguration of Black society, best appears. The clan ancestor, himself a spirit and a sort of demi-god, is the link that joins the divine element to the human element. As such, he caused a spark of life to shoot forth and he continues to preserve it, to animate it as an eternal flame. It is he who obtained from the local spirit of the Earth the usufruct of a portion of the land for his descendants, as an inalienable, common good. The head of the family, the first-born of the living, is in his turn the link that joins the living to the dead ancestors. Closer to them, sharing in their knowledge and power, speaking to them familiarly, he is, more than being the family head, the priest, the mediator. He is the priest; for in this community, no one—especially not anyone who has some power—can act for himself alone. All give each other charity, and each life is deepened and multiplied in this familial communion of the living and the dead.

It is at the level of the tribe, rather than the kingdom, that one can most clearly grasp the solution that the Negro has provided for social and political problems. It is a solution that has matched, in advance, the "pluralist unity" that remains the ideal of humanists today—at least, of those for whom humanism is not a sort of vain amusement for the cultivated man.

The linked questions of property and work are at the base of the whole social problem. For each man, it is indeed a matter of living from his work, which is considered the essential source of property; above all, it is a matter of actually being liberated by one's work and liberated from one's work, of finding in it a source of joy and dignity. Far from alienating us from ourselves, work must make us discover our spiritual riches and make them flourish.

The vice of capitalist society is not to be found in the existence of property, which is the necessary condition for the development of the person; it is found in the fact that property does not essentially repose on work. But in Negro society, "work, or perhaps more precisely productive activity, is considered the sole source of property, though it can confer the right to property only for the object it has produced."[21] However—and critiques of capitalism have often stressed this—if natural resources and the means of production remain in the hands of a few individuals, property can be only theoretical. Here, again, the Negro had solved the problem in a humanist way. The land, as well as all it bears—rivers, streams, forests, animals, fish, and so on—is a common good apportioned among the families, and even sometimes among family members, who have temporary, usufructuary ownership of it. Moreover, the means of production in general, and the tools for work in particular, are the common property of the family group or the guild.

As a result, ownership of agricultural and artisan products is collective, since the labor itself is collective. Whence the supreme advantage that each man is materially guaranteed a "living minimum," according to his needs. "When the harvest is ripe," says the Wolof, "it belongs to everyone." Add to this another advantage, no less important from the point of view of personal life: acquiring the superfluous, the necessary luxury, is made possible by work, since individual property, regulated and limited, is not eliminated.

For Negroes, if they neglected the individual, did not subjugate the person, as some readily believe. The person seems to me to pertain less to the need for singularity that torments our modern individualists; it pertains less to the fact of distinguishing oneself than to the depth and intensity of spiritual life. Negroes have not debated the subject of the person—we know that they chat, and scarcely debate—they have helped the life of the person, even with the collective form of property.

"In order for a collective form of ownership to be an efficacious aid to personality," writes Maritain, "it is necessary that it not have for goal a depersonalized possession."[22] Among Negroes, man is bound to the collectively owned object by the juridical tie of custom and tradition—still more, and above all, by a mystical bond. Let's pause at this bond. The group—family, guild, age group, and so on—has a personality of its own that is felt as such by each member. The family is of the same blood; as we saw, it is the same shared flame. The guild is simply a clan family that has ownership of an "art." Thus, man feels himself to be a person—a communal one, I grant—when faced with the owned object. But the object itself, very frequently, is felt to be like a person. This is the case for natural phenomena: plain, river, forest. As I've said, in inhabiting the land, the ancestor is bound to it in the name of his family. And the Earth is a feminine spirit; the mystical marriage of the group and the Earth-Mother is "solemnly" celebrated.

Hence, ownership of the means of production, in the general sense of the term, is no longer something theoretical, transitory, illusory. The worker feels that he is someone, not a mere cogwheel in a machine. He knows that his intelligence and his arms freely work something that is definitely his. Even the man of the guild, whose trade is inferior to the peasant's labor, knows that he is irreplaceable. Thus, the primordially human needs for true liberty, for responsibility and dignity—the needs of the person—are satisfied.

And work is not drudgery but a source of joy, because it permits the being's realization and flourishing. It is notable that in Negro society, working the earth is the noblest form of labor. The Negro soul remains stubbornly that of the peasant. Just think of the United States. The Negro laborers in the North, the active voters, are nostalgic for the Southern plantations where their brothers live as serfs. And their poets sing:

Of fruit-laden trees by low-singing rills
And dewy dawns, and mystical blue skies
In benediction over nun-like hills . . . [23]

For working the earth permits the concord of man and "creation" that is at the heart of the humanist problem. For it is done to the rhythm of the world: a rhythm that is not mechanical, that is free and alive, the rhythm of day and night, of the seasons, which number two in Africa, of the plant that grows and dies. And the Negro, feeling himself in unison with the universe, rhythmically orders his work through song and the tom-tom. Negro work, Negro rhythm, Negro joy that is freed through work and that is freed from work.

Politics, it goes without saying, is closely related to the social. The latter is to the former as the artist's hand is to his mind. It is a matter of organizing, maintaining, and perfecting the City, a matter of governing and legislating. To govern requires authority; to legislate requires wisdom. Both must return to their sources: to strive for the good of the communities, the people, and the City. But in Western democracies today, these requirements go unrecognized. The legislator is elected, in the best of cases, by a party that is a jumble of material interests, and he legislates according to the dictates of a financial oligarchy, and for that oligarchy. The legislation is doubly inhuman, because it is doubly vitiated. As for the government, despite the police forces, which only increase in size, it has no authority; for authority rests on a spiritual pre-eminence, while the government is in the hands of cunning men and puppets, of politicians instead of statesmen.

It is otherwise in a typical Negro kingdom, as was the case in the Serer kingdom of Sine.[24] The legislative assembly is composed of high dignitaries and notables, heads of clan families—whence the wisdom derived from the knowledge of tradition, from experience of life, and from the feeling of one's responsibilities. It's a question of reconciling tradition and progress—the resistance to progress that is frequently denounced is less a matter of the Negro spirit than of geographical conditions.

And what of the authority of the king, who is an ancestor of a spiritual kind?[25] He symbolizes the unity of the kingdom. Originally, he is the descendant of the people's guide; and he represents the guide at the same time as he represents the people. The authority of the king: because the people "honors itself and its own past" in the person of the king.[26] Because the king is elected by the people through the intermediary of the principal family heads. Because the voters can suspend or depose him. It is an efficient power, since it rests on authority and is exercised through the intermediary of many ministers, whom the sovereign cannot choose or fire.

It's a long way from this community that fits a stock image[27] of harmony to the "Negro petty tyrant." A "pluralist unity": a city that is unified, founded on the image of natural communities and based on them. Even the guilds and the numerous associations are not without influence.

"And the individual?" I will be asked again. Again, I reply: the individual is neglected insofar as it is founded on a false liberty and on a differentiation of interests. It is entirely otherwise in the case of the person. I admit that Negro society has not been much concerned to develop human reason; and this is a gap. The person did not for this have any less chance to develop and to assert himself at the heart of associations, guilds, and deliberative, palavering assemblies. The importance of the palaver has not been sufficiently discussed. Equality and the feeling of one's dignity as a man prevailed there. This same feeling inspired all, including the servant and the captive. I knew some of them who committed suicide—the act of a free man—because they had been accused of lying or theft.

What the modern world has forgotten, and this is one of the causes of the current crisis in civilization, is that the flourishing of the person requires an extra-individualist orientation. It takes place only on the ground of the dead, in the climate of the family and the group. This need for fraternal communion is more profoundly human than is the need for withdrawal into oneself, as much as is the need for the supernatural. It has been said that pity is foreign to the Negro soul. Pity, perhaps, but not charity, not hospitality. For the "square," or the congregating of strangers, was found everywhere. It is a custom to invite the passerby to share the family meal. The first Whites to land were themselves considered to be heavenly guests. Among the

Wolofs, the highest praise one can bestow is *"Bega m'bok, bega nit"*: whoever loves his parents, loves people. To those who destroyed his civilization, to the slaver, to the lyncher, the Afro-American poets reply with words of peace alone:

> I return it loveliness,
> Having made it so;
> For I wore the bitterness
> From it long ago.[28]

This is no hollow fiction. This "humanity" of the Negro soul, this inability to hate lastingly, has helped to resolve the racial problem in Latin America, and even in North America. I believe that Negro contributions in the social and political domain will not end there. This would be the point to discuss the humanist role of ethnology. In the construction of a more human world, ethnology must make it possible to ask the best of each people. And the Black peoples will not arrive empty-handed at the meeting of the political and the social, in a world split between democratic individualism and totalitarian gregariousness.

In the meantime, Negro contributions to the world of the twentieth century have been conveyed especially in literature, and in art in general. The study of African literature and of the young Afro-American literature, interesting as it is, would take us too far. I wish to consider only the plastic arts and music. Only for practical reasons should they be separated; one finds the same elements in both, as one does in the African and the Afro-American, no matter what the specialists say about it. The value of the American ordeal will have been to make all that was not permanent and human vanish.

But these contributions will have been fertile only among rare artists. In general, fragmentary borrowings—empty of all vigor, because empty of all spirit—have been made. I fear that the surrealists themselves have not had an ever-delicate—that is, enlightened—sympathy for the Negro. How could it have been otherwise in a world subjected to matter and to reason, and where one denounces reason only to proclaim the primacy of matter? For this is certainly the cause of the decadence of nineteenth-century art; the manifestos "for French Art" published by the journal *Les Beaux-Arts* are telling. Realism and impressionism are but two sides of one same error. It is the adoration of the real that leads to photographic art. At most, the mind is content to analyze and combine the elements of the real, for a subtle game, a variation on the real. A natural consequence of Théophile Gautier's attitude: "My rebellious body will not recognize the supremacy of the soul, and my flesh does not admit that it should be mortified. . . . Three things please me: gold, marble and purple: splendor, solidity, color."[29] The preferences may vary, but not the spirit—the absence of spirit, I mean. Whence the attacks by Baudelaire against the "École païenne"; whence, later, those of a Cézanne and a Gauguin, whose disciples were to proceed in the direction of Negro art, to the point of meeting with it.

For the value of Negro art is to be neither game nor pure aesthetic enjoyment; it is to signify.

From among the plastic arts, I select the art that is most typical—sculpture. Even the decoration of the simplest pieces of popular furnishings, far from diverting them from their purposes and being useless ornament, stresses these purposes. Practical art, not utilitarian, and classic in this original sense. Art that is above all spiritual—it has wrongly been called idealist or intellectual—because it is religious. The essential function of sculptors is to represent the dead ancestors and spirits, in statues that are at once symbol and dwelling. It's a matter of making their personal soul, an efficacious will, be grasped and felt, a matter of making one accede to the surreal.

This is done by means of a human representation, and singularly through the representation of the human figure, the most faithful reflection of the soul. It is a striking fact that anthropomorphic statues, and among these, masks, predominate. Constant concern for the man-intermediary.

This spirituality is expressed in the most concrete elements of the real. The Negro artist is less a painter than a sculptor, less a designer than a model-maker, working solid matter in three dimensions with his hands, like the Creator. He chooses the most concrete matter: preferably bronze, ivory, gold, and wood, which is common and lends itself to the rawest effects as to the most delicate nuances. He uses colors little, and he always uses them in a form pure to the point of saturation: white, black, red— the colors of Africa. Above all, he uses lines, surfaces, volumes—the most material properties.

But since this art strives for the essential expression of the object, it is the opposite of subjective realism. The artist submits the details to a spiritual, therefore technical, hierarchy. Where many have wished to see only a lack of manual skill or an inability to observe the real, there is in fact will, at least consciousness of ordering (*ordination*)—or better, consciousness of ranking (*subordination*). I have already mentioned the prominence granted by the artist to the human face.

This ordering force that constitutes Negro style is rhythm.[30] It is the most sensible and least material thing. It is the vital element par excellence. It is the primary condition for, and sign of, art, as respiration is of life—respiration that rushes or slows, becomes regular or spasmodic, depending on the being's tension, the degree and quality of the emotion. Such is rhythm, originally, in its purity, such is it in the masterpieces of Negro art, particularly in sculpture. It is composed of one theme— sculptural form—that is opposed to a brother theme, like inhalation is opposed to exhalation, and that is reprised. It is not a symmetry that engenders monotony; rhythm is alive, it is free. For reprise is not redundancy, or repetition. The theme is reprised at another place, on another level, in another combination, in a variation. And it produces something like another tone, another timbre, another accent. And the general effect is intensified by this, not without nuances. This is how rhythm acts, despotically, on what is least intellectual in us, to make us enter into the spirituality of the object; and this attitude of abandon that we have is itself rhythmic.

It is classical art in the most human sense of the word, for it is "controlled romanticism," since the artist, controlling his emotive resources, arouses and leads our emotions to the idea, using the simplest, most direct, most definitive means. Everything converges on the goal. Here there is no anecdote, no embellishment, no flower. Nothing that distracts. In refusing to seduce us, the artist conquers us. Classical art as defined by Maritain: "Such a subordination of the matter to the light of form . . . that no material element issuing from things or from the subject is admitted into the work that is not strictly required as support for or vehicle of this light, and that would dull or 'debauch' the eye, ear, or mind."[31]

What was missing in the music of the waning nineteenth century was neither ideas nor an authentic spirituality. For France, it would suffice to mention César Franck and Gabriel Fauré. But young energy and fresh means were lacking. God, like the mind, is invisible to scientists. Men such as Claude Debussy, Darius Milhaud, and Igor Stravinsky felt the need to liberate themselves from conventional rules that had become sterile. And they went in search of unknown alluvium and "invisible seeds."

It is to these needs that Negro music, which in Europe is only beginning to be studied seriously, responds. For though people are sensitive to its effects, they have not yet advanced far into its technique. In Negro-African society, music does not constitute a self-sufficient art, any more than does sculpture. It originally accompanied ritual dances and songs. Secularized, it has not become independent: it finds its natural place in the collective expressions of the theater, agricultural work, and athletic contests. Even in the daily evening tom-tom sessions, it is not a pure aesthetic expression, but permits its faithful participants to commune more intimately with the rhythm of the dancing community, of the dancing World. Much of this has remained in Westernized, Americanized Negroes. Instinctively, they dance their music, they dance their life.

This is to say that Negro music, like sculpture, like dance, is rooted in the nourishing ground, that it is full of rhythms, sounds, and noises of the Earth. This is not to say that it is descriptive or impressionist; it likewise conveys feelings, though it is not sentimental. It brings the necessary energy to Western music, which is impoverished for being based on and developed according to arbitrary rules that are, above all, too restrictive.

I will not speak of the melodic contributions. They go without saying. That plot has been most thoroughly cleared. It is not the same for the modal realm. Its riches are still unknown. In part, this is because "specialists" have denied that there is a Negro harmony. Knowledgeable musicians such as Ballanta dispute this.[32] Negroes, they point out, sing in chorus; unlike most of the popular songs of other peoples, which are sung in unison, choruses among Negro peoples (*Négritie*) are composed of multiple parts. I myself recall how much trouble the good Father who directed our black children's choir had in getting us to sing in unison, without parts, or variations. Speaking of Negro choirs, Delafosse notes that their harmony is impeccable.[33] "Their rhythmical and melodic invention is prodigious (and apparently naïve)," writes Gide, "but what shall I say of their harmonics? For that is what I find especially surprising. I thought that all the songs here would be monophonic. This is the reputation that has been made for them, for there are no 'songs in thirds or sixths.' But this polyphony, in its widening and crushing of the sound is so disorienting to our northern ears that I doubt whether it be possible to take it down with our means of notation."[34] This polyphony disconcerts and is impossible to notate—the intervals as well as the melodic line—since the melodic and rhythmic forms are extremely subtle. Gide had said earlier, "Our popular songs, compared with these, seem poor, foolishly simple, rudimentary."[35] Alluvial lands, that only await bold and persevering pioneers.

The Negro contribution has been the most important and the most uncontested in the area of rhythm. We have seen throughout this study that the Negro is a rhythmic being. He is rhythm incarnate. The music is revealing in this regard. One will notice the importance granted to percussion instruments. Often the only accompaniment to the singing is the tom-tom or hand clapping. Sometimes the percussion instruments indicate the basic chords, from which the melody freely springs. What I said above about rhythm in sculpture must be reprised now. I would add that rhythm also drives the melody and the lyrics. It's what Americans call "swing." Essentially characterized by syncopation, it is far from being mechanical. It is composed of constancy and variety, of tyranny and imagination, of waiting and surprise; which explains how the Negro can delight in the same musical phrase for hours, for the phrase is not exactly the same.

Besides properly musical elements, the Negro has demonstrated the resources that one could draw from certain instruments that were ignored until now or arbitrarily scorned and confined in a subaltern role. Such was the case with percussive rhythm instruments, such as the xylophone. And likewise for the saxophone, the brass instruments, the trumpet and trombone. Thanks to the clarity, vigor, and nobility of their sounds, these instruments were just right for rendering the Negro style. Thanks, also, to all the delicately sweet and mysterious effects that the best jazzmen ("*hotistes*") have since drawn from them.

It is not only in musical composition that the Negro influence has been perceptible, nor is it only there that it promises to be fruitful; it will be further influential in interpretation. It is perhaps in this way that Afro-Americans have remained closest to the ancestral wellsprings. It's above all a matter of style, of soul.

Hugh Panassié has fully illuminated the Negro contributions to "*le jazz hot,*" the fundamental feature of which is interpretation. But this influence must still be extended to classical music, and perhaps more to singers than to orchestras. In a general sense, the value of the interpretation is found in the tone, which Panassié defines as "not only the manner in which the note is attacked, but even more the way in which it is held and the way in which it is terminated; in short, the way the note is given whatever expressiveness that it may have."[36] "It is the expression," he adds, "the accent which the performer imparts to each note, into which he throws the full force of his personality."[37] As "faithful" as are the interpretations by great artists such as Roland Hayes and Marian Anderson, there always remains something of a Negro interpretation. It is this particular way of surrounding the note, the sound, with a halo of flesh and blood that makes it appear so turbid and so troubling; this "naive" way of conveying in the most casual voice the most hidden spirituality. "The soloist," writes Gide, "has an admirable voice, with a quality completely different than what we require at the Conservatoire; a voice that seems sometimes to be choked by tears—and at times closer to sobs than to song—with sudden harsh tones, as if out of tune. Then, suddenly, there follow several very soft, disconcertingly sweet, notes."[38]

Limited though they may be, these Negro contributions have rather profoundly influenced contemporary music. Contemporary music has benefited from these contributions: it is richer, more spare, more muscled and more supple, more dynamic, more generous, and more human, because more natural. The old myth of Antaeus has not lost its truth.

It is with this Greek myth that I wish to end. It is not strange, this meeting of the Negro and the Greek. I fear that many who today invoke the Greeks betray Greece. A betrayal of the modern world that has mutilated man by making him the "rational animal," or, rather, by anointing him the "God of reason." The Negro service will have been to contribute, with other peoples, to remaking the unity of man and World:

to binding the flesh to the spirit, man to his fellow, stone to God. In other words, to binding the real to the spiritual surreal—through man not as the center, but as the pivot, the navel, of the World.

Notes

Léopold Sédar Senghor, *Liberté I: Négritude et humanisme*, © *Editions du Seuil*, 1964. Originally published as "Ce que l'homme noir apporte," in *L'Homme de couleur* (Paris: Librairie Plon, 1939), pp. 292–314.

All translations are Mary Beth Mader's, unless otherwise indicated.

1. André Gide, *Les nouvelles nourritures* (Paris: Gallimard, 1935), p. 22; trans. Dorothy Bussy, *The Fruits of the Earth* (Harmondsworth: Penguin, 1970), p. 149.

2. Paul Morand, *New York* (Paris: Flammarion, 1930), pp. 234–236; trans. Hamish Miles, *New York* (New York: Henry Holt, 1930), p. 270. Translation adapted.

3. Leo Frobenius, *Kulturgeschichte Afrikas* (Zurich: Phaidon, 1933), p. 15.

4. Ibid.

5. By "culture," I mean the spirit of the civilization; by "civilization," I mean the works and achievements of the culture. I thus understand these two terms in rather different senses than Henri Petiot Daniel-Rops does in *Ce qui meurt et ce qui naît* (Paris: Plon, 1937). But fundamentally this is just a terminological difference.

6. Marcel Sauvage, *Les Secrets de l'Afrique noire: sous le feu de l'équateur* (Paris: B. Grasset, 1981).

7. Ibid., p. 111.

8. Georges Hardy, *L'Art nègre: l'art animiste des noirs d'Afrique* (Paris: Henri Laurens, 1927), p. 80.

9. Langston Hughes, "Rivers," in *The Collected Poems of Langston Hughes*, ed. Arnold Rampersad (New York: Alfred A. Knopf, 1994), p. 23.

10. ["Mme Vache" means "Mrs. Cow." Trans.]

11. Lydia Cabrera, *Contes nègres de Cuba* (Paris: Gallimard, 1936), p. 87. With a very interesting preface by Francis de Miomandre. [Francis de Miomandre was the translator of the French edition. For the original see *Cuentos Negros de Cuba* (Havana: La Verónica, 1940), p. 93. Trans.]

12. [*The Green Pastures* is a controversial Pulitzer Prize–winning 1929 musical play by Marc Connelly, and a 1936 Warner Brothers film. It featured centrally music from the African-American spirituals tradition, arranged by Hall Johnson and performed by his choir. Trans.]

13. [The French word *soliveau* has a literal sense of "small joist," and a figurative sense of "nonentity." Trans.]

14. [The Serer are a Black West African people living principally in Senegal. Trans.]

15. [The Toucouleur are a Black West African people living chiefly in northern Senegal and southern Mauritania. Trans.]

16. [See Charles Baudelaire, "Notes nouvelles sur Edgar Poe," in *Nouvelles Histoires Extraordinaires par Edgar Poe* (Paris: Garnier-Flammarion, 1965), p. 44; trans.

Francis E. Hyslop, Jr., *Baudelaire on Poe* (State College, Pa.: Bald Eagle Press, 1952), p. 140. Translation adapted. Trans.]

17. Cf. Jean Guéhenno, *Jeunesse de la France* (Paris: Bernard Grasset, 1936), pp. 139–142 and passim.

18. Countee Cullen, "Heritage," in *Color* (New York: Harper & Brothers, 1925), p. 40.

19. Diedrich Westermann, *The African Today* (London: Oxford University Press, 1934), p. 133. Senghor cites the French translation, *Noirs et Blancs en Afrique* (Paris: Payot, 1937), p. 114.

20. Cf. Denis de Rougemont, *L'Amour et l'Occident* (Paris: Plon, 1939), pp. 302–305; trans. Montgomery Belgion, *Passion and Society* (London: Faber and Faber, 1956), pp. 303–305.

21. Maurice Delafosse, *Les Nègres* (Paris: Éditions Rieder, 1927), p. 44.

22. Jacques Maritain, *Humanisme Intégral* (Paris: Fernand Aubier, 1936), p. 202; trans. Joseph W. Evans, *Integral Humanism* (Notre Dame, Ind.: University of Notre Dame Press, 1973), p. 188.

23. Claude McKay, "The Tropics in New York," *Liberator* 3 (May 1920): 48. Reprinted in *Selected Poems of Claude McKay* (New York: Bookman Associates, 1952), p. 31. Cf. the poetic work by Jean Toomer, *Cane* (New York: Boni and Liverlight, 1923). Hence, Aimé Césaire, an Antillean student at the E.N.S. (École Normale Supérieure), was able to present a thesis on "the theme of the South in Negro-American literature" at the Sorbonne.

24. [Sine is a Senegalese delta region between the Sine and Saloum rivers. Trans.]

25. Cf. Daniel-Rops, *Ce qui meurt et ce qui naît*, pp. 37ff.

26. [D. Westermann, *The African Today*, p. 163; trans. *Noirs et Blancs en Afrique*, p. 136. Trans.]

27. ["Images d'Épinal" were popular prints depicting stock scenes of French life and culture. Beginning in the seventeenth century, they were manufactured in Épinal, a French city in the Vosges department that is also the birthplace of author Henri Petiot Daniel-Rops. Trans.]

28. Lewis Alexander, "Transformation," in *The Poetry of the Negro 1746–1949*, ed. Langston Hughes and Arna Bontemps (New York: Doubleday, 1949), p. 85.

29. Théophile Gautier, *Mademoiselle de Maupin* (Paris: Charpentier, 1866), p. 193; trans. Claude Kendall, *Mademoiselle de Maupin* (New York: Rosset and Dunlap, 1930), p. 185.

30. Cf. Paul Guillaume and Thomas Munro, *La sculpture nègre primitive* (Paris: Les éditions G. Cres, 1929), pp. 84–87; trans. *Primitive Negro Sculpture* (New York: Harcourt, Brace and Company, 1926), pp. 58–59.

31. Jacques Maritain, *Art et Scolastique* (Paris: L. Rouart et fils, 1927), p. 97; trans. Joseph W. Evans, *Art and Scholasticism and The Frontiers of Poetry* (New York: Charles Scribner's Sons, 1962), p. 57. Translation adapted.

32. Cf. N. G. J. Ballanta, preface to *St. Helena Spirituals*, cited by Alain Locke in *The Negro and His Music* (Washington, D.C.: Associates in Negro Folk Education, 1936), pp. 137–138. [The original is to be found in Nicholas George Julius Ballanta [-Taylor], *Saint Helena Island Spirituals: Recorded and Transcribed at Penn*

Normal, Industrial and Agricultural School, St. Helena Island, Beaufort County, South Carolina (New York: Stirmer, 1925), p. vi. Trans.]

33. Delafosse, *Les Nègres*, p. 64.

34. André Gide, *Retour du Tchad, suite du voyage au Congo, carnets de route* (Paris: Gallimard, 1928), p. 41; trans. Dorothy Bussy, *Travels in the Congo* (Berkeley: University of California Press, 1962), p. 234. Translation adapted.

35. André Gide, *Retour du Tchad*, p. 40; trans. *Travels in the Congo*, p. 233. Translation adapted.

36. Cf. Hugh Panassié, *Le Jazz hot* (Paris: Éditions R.-A. Corrêa, 1934), p. 79; trans. Lyle Dowling and Eleanor Dowling, *Hot Jazz: The Guide to Swing Music* (New York: M Witmark and Sons, 1936), p. 46. Translation adapted.

37. Ibid.

38. André Gide, *Retour du Tchad*, p. 41. [My translation. Cf. trans. *Travels in the Congo*, pp. 233–234. Trans.]

Contributors

Robert Bernasconi is Moss Professor of Philosophy at the University of Memphis. He is the author of two books on Heidegger and numerous articles on Continental philosophy, political philosophy, and race theory. He is the editor of *Race; The Idea of Race,* with Tommy Lott; and a reprint series, with Thoemmes Press, of eighteenth- and nineteenth-century books on race.

Sybol Cook is a Provost's Distinguished Pre-Doctoral Fellow at the University of Memphis, where her area of specialization is early modern and nineteenth-century moral and political philosophy. She is co-editing, with Ellen Feder and Karmen MacKendrick, *Philosophy: A Passion for Wisdom.*

Alain David is a professor of philosophy at Dijon and director of the program at the Collège International de Philosophie. He is the author of *Racisme et Antisémitisme* and editor, with Jean Greisch, of *Michel Henry, l'épreuve de la vie.*

Nigel Gibson teaches philosophy and postcolonial studies at Emerson College, Boston. He is a research associate in the departments of Africana studies at Brown University and of Afro-American studies at Harvard University. He is the editor of *Rethinking Fanon: The Continuing Dialogue* and *Adorno: A Critical Reader.*

Joy James is a professor of Africana studies at Brown University, where she teaches political and feminist theory. She is the author of *Resisting State Violence, Transcending the Talented Tenth,* and *Shadowboxing.* Her edited works include *The Black Feminist Reader, The Angela Y. Davis Reader, States of Confinement,* and *Imprisoned Intellectuals.*

David J. Levy is visiting professor of social theory at Middlesex University. He is the author of *Hans Jonas: The Integrity of Thinking*, *The Measure of Man: Incursions in Political and Philosophical Anthropology*, *Political Order: Philosophical Anthropology*, *Modernity and The Challenge of Ideology*, and *Realism: An Essay in Interpretation and Social Reality*. He is currently completing a book on Voegelin, Heidegger, and the German tradition and a work on animal origins and human distinctions considered in the light of philosophical anthropology.

Donna-Dale Marcano is originally from Trinidad. She is an assistant professor of philosophy at LeMoyne College, Syracuse, New York. Her doctoral dissertation at the University of Memphis examined the construction of racial identities.

Kevin Thomas Miles received his Ph.D. from DePaul University in Chicago and is presently an assistant professor of philosophy at Villanova University. He has published essays on Du Bois and race theory. Currently he is teaching and researching some of the ethical and political dimensions of ancient Greek philosophy that have influenced contemporary discussions of race.

Kelly Oliver is a professor of philosophy and women's studies at Stony Brook University. She is the author of several books, including *Family Values: Subjects between Nature and Culture*, *Subjectivity without Subjects: Desiring Mothers and Abject Fathers*, *Witnessing: Beyond Recognition*, and *Noir Anxiety: Race, Sex and Maternity in Film Noir*. She currently is finishing a book entitled *The Colonization of Psychic Space*.

Jacqueline Scott is an assistant professor of philosophy at Loyola University, Chicago. She has published several articles on Nietzsche and critical race theory, and she is currently working on a manuscript entitled *Nietzsche's Worthy Opponents: Socrates, Wagner, the Ascetic Priest, and Women*.

Léopold Sédar Senghor, poet, philosopher, and statesman, was one of the originators of the concept of Negritude. He founded the Senegalese Democratic Bloc and was the first president of the Republic of Senegal (1960–80). Senghor's many writings, translated into several languages, include *Chants d'ombre*, *Nocturnes*, *Langage et poésie négro-africaine*, *Liberté* (five volumes), and *Ce que je crois*. He died in 2001 at the age of ninety-five.

T. Denean Sharpley-Whiting is a professor of Africana studies and romance languages (French) and chair of Africana Studies at Hamilton College. Her latest book is *Negritude Women: Race Women, Race Consciousness, Race Literature*.

Sonia Sikka is an associate professor of philosophy at the University of Ottawa. She has written numerous articles on Heidegger, Lévinas and Nietzsche, including "Heidegger and Jaspers: Being, Language, Technicity" (*International Studies in Philosophy*, 2001); "How Not to Read the Other: 'All the Rest Can Be Translated'" (*Philosophy Today*, 1999), and "Heidegger's Concept of *Volk*" (*Philosophical Forum*, 1994). She currently works on the idea of cultural identity in the German philosophical tradition.

Ronald R. Sundstrom is an assistant professor of philosophy at the University of Memphis. He was awarded a Ford Foundation Fellowship in 1996. His research involves the intersections of race theory and African-American philosophy with issues in the philosophy of social science and political and social philosophy. He has published several articles on race, African-American philosophy, and the metaphysics of social categories.

Lou Turner is an assistant professor of sociology at North Central College, Naperville, Illinois. He is co-author of *Frantz Fanon, Soweto, and American Black Thought* and is research and public policy coordinator for the Developing Communities Project on Chicago's South Side. He has written extensively on Fanon, Marx, and Hegel; his forthcoming work is *Fetishism: A Marxist-Humanist Critique of the Natural History of Race.*

Jason M. Wirth is an associate professor of philosophy and chair of the Humanities Division at Oglethorpe University. He publishes in the areas of Continental philosophy, Africana philosophy, aesthetics, and comparative philosophy. His new book is *The Conspiracy of Life: Meditations on Schelling and His Time.*

Kamala Visweswaran is an associate professor of anthropology at the University of Texas, Austin, and is the author of *Family Subjects: Women, Feminism, Indian Nationalism* (forthcoming). She writes on law and critical race theory.

Erik Vogt is currently teaching at Wadham College, Oxford. He is the author of *Sartres Wieder-Holung* and *Zugänge zur politischen Ästhetik.* He has written numerous essays on German, French, and Italian philosophy and is editor of the series *Neue Amerikanische Philosophie.*

Index

Index